MODERNISM EDITED

Edinburgh Critical Studies in Modernist Culture
Series Editors: Tim Armstrong and Rebecca Beasley

Available

Modernism and Magic: Experiments with Spiritualism, Theosophy and the Occult
Leigh Wilson
Sonic Modernity: Representing Sound in Literature, Culture and the Arts
Sam Halliday
Modernism and the Frankfurt School
Tyrus Miller
Lesbian Modernism: Censorship, Sexuality and Genre Fiction
Elizabeth English
Modern Print Artefacts: Textual Materiality and Literary Value in British Print Culture, 1890–1930s
Patrick Collier
Cheap Modernism: Expanding Markets, Publishers' Series and the Avant-Garde
Lise Jaillant
Portable Modernisms: The Art of Travelling Light
Emily Ridge
Hieroglyphic Modernisms: Writing and New Media in the Twentieth Century
Jesse Schotter
Modernism, Fiction and Mathematics
Nina Engelhardt
Modernist Life Histories: Biological Theory and the Experimental Bildungsroman
Daniel Aureliano Newman
Modernism, Space and the City
Andrew Thacker
Modernism Edited: Marianne Moore and the Dial *Magazine*
Victoria Bazin
Modernism and Time Machines
Charles Tung

Forthcoming

Slow Modernism
Laura Salisbury
Primordial Modernism: Animals, Ideas, Transition (1927–1938)
Cathryn Setz
Modernism and the Idea of Everyday Life
Leena Kore-Schröder

www.edinburghuniversitypress.com/series/ecsmc

MODERNISM EDITED

Marianne Moore and the *Dial* Magazine

Victoria Bazin

EDINBURGH
University Press

Edinburgh University Press is one of the leading university presses in the UK. We publish academic books and journals in our selected subject areas across the humanities and social sciences, combining cutting-edge scholarship with high editorial and production values to produce academic works of lasting importance. For more information visit our website: edinburghuniversitypress.com

Edinburgh University Press Ltd
The Tun – Holyrood Road, 12(2f) Jackson's Entry, Edinburgh EH8 8PJ

First published in hardback by Edinburgh University Press 2019

Typeset in 10/12.5 Sabon by
Servis Filmsetting Ltd, Stockport, Cheshire.

A CIP record for this book is available from the British Library

ISBN 978 1 4744 1730 3 (hardback)
ISBN 978 1 4744 6390 4 (paperback)
ISBN 978 1 4744 1731 0 (webready PDF)
ISBN 978 1 4744 1732 7 (epub)

CONTENTS

LIST OF ILLUSTRATIONS

ACKNOWLEDGEMENTS

I have benefited from the support of a number of people while writing this book. In the initial phase, when I was beginning to think about Moore's editorial role at the *Dial*, I learnt a great deal from Jason Harding whose ground-breaking work on T. S. Eliot and the *Criterion* offered an exemplary model of how to write about the poet as editor of the modernist magazine. Jason's expertise and encouragement were invaluable at a time when the prospect of writing on the *Dial* seemed quite overwhelming.

Several Moore scholars have seen or heard parts of this book and I am grateful for their insights. In particular, I would like to thank Cristanne Miller who has been so generous with her time and so supportive throughout my career. Her detailed comments in her reader's report were invaluable and I kept them close as I wrote the book. Stacy Carson Hubbard and Fiona Green heard me talk on Moore and the *Dial* at the MSA in Sussex in 2013, reminding when I was immersed in periodical studies, that Moore was a poet as well as an editor. Elizabeth Gregory and Stacy Carson Hubbard practised a Mooreish edit on my essay for the edited collection, *Twenty-First Century Marianne Moore*. I learnt a lot about writing from their advice. In addition, there are several scholars who have undertaken ground-breaking editorial work that I am indebted to. Patricia Willis's *The Complete Prose of Marianne Moore* and Robin Schulze's *Becoming Marianne Moore: The Early Poems, 1907–1924* made Moore's work available and opened up the field to new and exciting research. Robin's recent critical discussion of Moore in *Degenerate Muse* has been immensely important to this project and I have drawn on it extensively here. I have also relied heavily on Linda Leavell's terrific biography of Moore, *Holding On Upside Down*. More generally, I wish to thank the community of Moore scholars, who continue to produce exciting, readable and provocative work on this extraordinary poet.

I have a community of scholars closer to home who I also wish to thank for reading chapters and offering advice. David Stewart, Julie Taylor, Melanie Waters and Rosie White at Northumbria University all read sections of the book for me and I thank them for their critical comments. Projects such as this one are difficult to complete without the understanding of those who manage teaching and research so I would like to thank David Walker as my head of department. In addition, Rebecca Beasley and Tim Armstrong at Edinburgh University Press have been patient, encouraging and critically astute editors and Ersev Ersoy has steered me through the final stages of publication. More generally, the Gendered Research Subjects group and its new iteration, the Gender and Society Research Hub have both been important scholarly support groups.

The expanding field of periodical studies has been another important community that has opened up to me through working on the *Dial*. Sue Currell read parts of the book and provided some thoughtful and extremely helpful advice. Working with Sue on establishing the Network of American Periodical Studies in 2015 has been one of the real pleasures of the past few years and through the symposia, I have learnt a great deal from other scholars working on magazines.

This research was supported in part by a British Academy small research grant which funded essential trips to the *Dial* archives at the Beinecke Library, Yale University and the Berg Collection at the New York Public Library. In addition, Northumbria University helped to fund a visit to the Rosenbach Museum and Library in Philadelphia. The research sabbatical scheme at Northumbria has allowed me the time and space to write this book and I am enormously grateful for that. Thanks also to Elizabeth Fuller, librarian and archivist at the Rosenbach Museum and Library, James Dempsey, Thayer's biographer, as well as to Joshua McKeon at the Berg at the New York Public Library and the librarians at the Beinecke at Yale, who have all helped me in various ways to complete this project.

Finally, I have friends and family who know all about this book, its trials and tribulations. Thank you to my dear but sadly departed Aunt Penny who talked with me about the book as we drove from New Jersey to the Catskills. Thank you to my mother, Susan Bazin, who has proof read several versions and who made crucial grammatical and stylistic interventions. Thanks to Liz White who never tired of asking, 'and how's the book?' Thanks to Migs, John, Beth, Noah and Uncle John for providing much needed respite from academic life. Thank you to Ben for reminding me how much books matter and finally, thank you to Andy for just about everything.

Permission for citations from unpublished material by Marianne Moore is granted by the Literary Estate of Marianne C. Moore, David M. Moore, Successor Executor for the Literary Estate of Marianne Moore. All rights reserved. E-book and world rights for these poems are granted by the Literary Estate of Marianne Moore. All rights reserved.

Grateful acknowledgment is made to the following.

The Rosenbach Museum and Library, The Henry W. and Albert A. Berg Collection of English and American Literature, The New York Public Library, Astor, Lenox and Tilden Foundations; The Beinecke Rare Book and Manuscript Library, Yale University Library.

'The Wine Menagerie', by Hart Crane from *Complete Poems of Hart Crane*, edited by Marx Simon. Copyright © 1933, 1958, 1966 by Liveright Publishing Corporation. Copyright ©1986 by Marx Simon. Used by permission of Liveright Publishing Corporation.

'Struggle of Wings', by William Carlos Williams from *William Carlos Williams: Collected Poems I, 1909–1939*, edited by A. Walton Litz and Christopher MacGowan © 1986 by Carnanet. Copyright © 1986 by A. Walton Litz and Christopher MacGowan. Used by permission of Carcanet and also used by permission of New Directions Publishing Corp.

I would like to also acknowledge and thank Dale Davis, the literary executor for the Estate of Dr Sibley Watson Jr and Tony Burke, literary executor for the estate of Kenneth Burke.

Grateful acknowledgement is made for permission to reprint the copyrighted images herein. They include: Two images by Georgia O'Keeffe, *Flagpole, First Painting* and *Flagpole, Second Painting* © Georgia O'Keeffe Museum / DACS 2018, an image by Marie Laurencin, *Young Girl* © Marie Laurencin/ DACS 2018 and Vanessa Bell's *The Party* © Estate of Vanessa Bell, courtesy Henrietta Garnett.

Though every reasonable effort has been made to seek permission to use unpublished material in this book, in some instances this has proved impossible. I would be glad to receive information leading to more complete acknowledgements in any subsequent printings.

SERIES EDITORS' PREFACE

This series of monographs on selected topics in modernism is designed to reflect and extend the range of new work in modernist studies. The studies in the series aim for a breadth of scope and for an expanded sense of the canon of modernism, rather than focusing on individual authors. Literary texts will be considered in terms of contexts including recent cultural histories (modernism and magic; sonic modernity; media studies) and topics of theoretical interest (the everyday; postmodernism; the Frankfurt School); but the series will also re-consider more familiar routes into modernism (modernism and gender; sexuality; politics). The works published will be attentive to the various cultural, intellectual and historical contexts of British, American and European modernisms, and to inter-disciplinary possibilities within modernism, including performance and the visual and plastic arts.

Tim Armstrong and Rebecca Beasley

In loving memory of Chris Houlton

INTRODUCTION

When recalling her experience of editing the *Dial* magazine between 1925 and 1929, Marianne Moore begins with a characteristically detailed description of the *Dial* offices in Greenwich Village:

> I think of the compacted pleasantness of those days at 152 West Thirteenth Street; of the three-story brick building with carpeted stairs, fireplace and white-mantelpiece rooms, business office in the first story front parlor, and in gold-leaf block letters, THE DIAL, on the windows to the right of the brownstone steps leading to the front door. There was the flower-crier in summer, with his slowly moving wagon of pansies, petunias, ageratum; of a man with straw-*ber*-ies for sale; or a certain fishman with pushcart-scales, and staccato refrain so unvaryingly imperative, summer or winter, that Kenneth Burke's parenthetic remark comes back to me – 'I think if he stopped to sell a fish my heart would skip a beat.'[1]

Moore's emphasis on the physical building that housed the magazine, her attention to the details of its interior and exterior, the sounds of the street and the camaraderie of working with others locates and connects the editorial role to a particular kind of social and cultural space, to the 'unvarying' routines of periodical production. The magazine's address and the understated elegance of the brownstone, its comfortable furnishings, its well-known signature, signify its cultural capital. Outside, street vendors are advertising and selling their wares, while inside, Moore and her colleagues are engaged in a comparable activity: the business of marketing and publishing modernism. Moore's retrospective account locates the publication and her editorial activities not only in terms of place, its geographical location but also within the social and economic spaces of modernity. Editorial labour and the production of the magazine are caught up in the pulsating rhythms of an expanding consumer culture: the 'refrain' of the salesman, the economic 'imperative[s]' of the market.

Locating Moore as editor of the *Dial* makes visible her contribution even as it complicates the notion of editorial agency. I argue that Moore's editorial agency was an effect of the magazine's discursive signature, its place in the market, its style as well as its content. The cultural authority that 'Miss Moore' accrued was generated by the *Dial*'s image of distinction, its reputation as a cultural tastemaker and its powers of cultural consecration. This is not to diminish Moore's significance as an editor; on the contrary, it reveals the extent to which Moore occupied a position of extraordinary power and authority in the late 1920s. Thus while this book seeks to reinsert Moore into the cultural history of modernism, to trace her editorial signature in individual published items and in the magazine as a whole, to challenge the idea that she 'tamed' the *Dial* and that it lost its 'continental flavor' during her tenure, it does so by conceptualising editorial agency as a creative social practice.[2]

As Sean Latham has pointed out, it is important, given the tendency to overlook the contribution that women have made to the formation and dissemination of modernism, to recognise how the women who edited modernist magazines 'helped fashion spaces that were social, commercial and political in order to create provocative, unsettling and interactive juxtapositions that operated on, while standing outside of, individual items like poems, essays, stories and letters'.[3] Harriet Monroe's astute business acumen, combined with her energy and commitment, launched *Poetry* magazine and kept it alive when other magazines collapsed spectacularly. Margaret Anderson and Jane Heap's intrepid *Little Review* dared to publish Joyce's *Ulysses* in spite of the censorious climate policing publication, and from 1923 the *Dial*, though launched and funded by its two wealthy patrons, Scofield Thayer and Sibley Watson Jr, owed much of its reputation for style and aesthetic judgement to its two women editors: Alyse Gregory and Marianne Moore. The groundbreaking work of Jayne Marek's *Women Editing Modernism* established the importance of women editors, including Moore, well before the study of modernist magazines transformed our understanding of the formation and dissemination of modernism.[4] Drawing on and adapting Marek and Latham's studies of women editors, I examine how Moore fashioned the spaces of modernism through her role at the *Dial* but also how 'Miss Moore' was fashioned as an editor, styled by the magazine, marketed as a 'literary beacon' of aesthetic integrity.[5]

In order to understand more fully the magazine as a particular kind of social space, I have drawn extensively on the work of Pierre Bourdieu. I am by no means the first scholar to do so. Bourdieu's studies of the social production of culture have been particularly influential as a way of accounting for modernism's rise to cultural legitimacy. In the context of modernism, what Bourdieu refers to as a sub-field of restricted production, is an 'economic world inverted' where the 'pure artist [. . .] cannot triumph on the symbolic terrain except by losing on the economic terrain'.[6] Edward Bishop examines modernist magazines in the context of this 'paradoxical universe', arguing that the founding of the *Criterion* rather than the publication of *The Waste Land* marks the seminal moment in modernism's institutionalisation.[7] The publication of the art object becomes, in Bishop's account, less important than the establishment of a magazine with the power to consecrate the art object. Lawrence Rainey adopts a similar approach examining the transactions that took place over the publication of *The Waste Land* in the *Dial* as the seminal moment in modernism's institutionalisation. It is worth returning to Rainey's account of modernism in terms of the formation of a distinctive social space created by modernist magazines:

> The actualization of this space within the commodity economy was achieved primarily through the new and unprecedented use of two institutions that had existed for some time but now became central to an emerging apparatus of cultural production: the little review and the limited edition, venues situated in a profoundly ambiguous social space simultaneously sequestered and semi-withdrawn from the larger institutions of publishing even while firmly embedded within the market economy. It was in the *Little Review*, the *Egoist*, and the *Dial* – that the principle masterpieces of the Anglo-American avant-garde would first be published.[8]

This materialist approach to the production of modernism figures the magazine itself as a productive space that includes the transnational exchanges and networks of writers, publishers, editors, artists, secretaries, advertisers, printers and readers involved in its production and consumption, the periodical communities within which the magazine operated, its 'public face' as well as its published texts.[9] In other words, reading modernism in the magazines requires a resistance to one of modernism's most influential tropes, the text as self-contained 'verbal icon'. Modernism is not made up of things, verbal and visual art objects charged with auratic resonance; it is made up of practices that shape and are shaped by social space.

To think of modernism's parameters in terms of social space connects the cultural work of the magazine with the relations of production and consumption within which the magazine was embedded; it requires us to think of modernism in terms of its material production rather than as the expression of creative genius; it requires us to think of the magazine in relation to particular forms of labour such as the downstream work of publicity and publication that Aaron Jaffe refers to in *Modernism and the Culture of Celebrity*.[10] Perhaps more importantly, it encourages us to think of the modernist magazine as emerging not just within the social space of modernity, the expansion of consumer and mass culture, technological and scientific innovations and transformations, the increasing professionalisation of culture and education, but rather that the magazine itself produces social space and is a form of social practice. The usefulness of this approach lies mainly in the emphasis it places upon the space of the magazine as a site of activity, a set of repeated and collective practices, an 'ensemble' of agents whose collective function is to consecrate the figure of the charismatic artist and the work he creates.[11]

The term Bourdieu uses to describe this form of social practice is habitus. Following Matthew Philpotts's extremely helpful discussion of Bourdieu's concept of habitus in his article, 'The Role of the Periodical Editor: Literary Journals and Editorial Habitus', I conceptualise the space of the *Dial* as an 'institutional habitus' that has its own distinctive ethos and that is ascribed an agency in its own right.[12] Philpotts's typological approach examines the editorships of Ford Madox Ford at the *English Review*, André Gide, Jacques Rivière and Jean Paulhan at the *Nouvelle Revue Française* and T.S. Eliot at the *Criterion*. It is the fusion of the personal habitus of the editor with the institutional habitus of the magazine that allows him to identify three types of editors: the charismatic editor embodied by Ford, the bureaucratic editor exemplified by the team at the *NRF* and the mediating editor characterised by the figure of Eliot.

My own analysis of Moore's role at the *Dial* draws on Philpotts's typological approach and takes into account the institutional habitus of the magazine. Aspects of Moore's editorship might be understood in terms of all three types of editors identified in Philpotts's schema. There is evidence of her as both a mediating and charismatic editor as well as a sense of the significant role played by the bureaucratic apparatus of the *Dial* itself. If Moore and other women editors are to have a place in an analysis of editorial agency, however, Philpotts's typology requires some adjustments. The distinctly masculine habitus that determines the values of the cultural sub-field of modernism needs to be figured in relation to Moore's editorial strategies. Women editors, such as Moore and her predecessor at the *Dial*, Alyse Gregory, together with Monroe, Anderson, Jessie Redmond Fauset at the *Crisis* and Gwendolyn Bennett at *Opportunity* magazine, could find stimulating intellectual work that conferred upon them the powers of cultural consecration that had been, up until then, reserved for men. Nevertheless, the social space of an institutionalised modernism reproduced social hierarchies that operated to limit women's agency and marginalise their cultural contribution. Thus, while it is undoubtedly true that by 1930, as Cristanne Miller points out, women 'had assumed a leading role in public ventures associated with the new arts', a significant shift from their position before the Armory Show of 1913, these new roles were both enabling and constraining.[13] The woman editor of the modernist magazine occupied a contradictory position in the literary field; she was a 'new woman', often sexually liberated, economically independent and at the centre of the world of avant-garde art and literature, but at the same time, as a cultural arbiter of taste reinforcing modernist distinction, she was engaged in reproducing the categorical differences that supported what Bourdieu refers to as 'masculine domination'.[14]

One of the central arguments of this book is that while Moore was an editor of a magazine that served to link highbrow culture to the modernist art object, her editorial decisions often resisted the categorical distinctions that reinforced modernism's difference from its cultural others. While Moore's editorial agency was circumscribed by the 'rules of the game', there are instances where she clearly refuses to play by the rules.[15] In the case of Moore, I argue, modernism continued to be published and publicised, it retained its image of high-hat hauteur, but the poetic and ethical principles she brought with her to the magazine challenged the cultural hierarchies underpinning the production of modernism and interrogated the ethics of cosmopolitan aestheticism. If the literary field is competitive, as Bourdieu suggests, defined by conflict between a variety of dispositions, then differing views and territorial struggles function to reinforce the boundaries circumscribing the restricted field of production. As an editor, Moore continued to reproduce modernism's symbolic value through reinterpretation, revision and even, at times, resistance to its central tropes.

Conceptualising editorial agency as a creative response to the rules of the game requires some methodological flexibility that combines close-reading strategies with an awareness of the internal and external dialogics of the magazine, its material form and its periodical codes. It also requires a familiarity with Moore's poetics and what Philpotts refers to as the personal habitus of the magazine editor. Editorial agency mediates between the aesthetic and the commercial, ensuring the magazine's financial survival while also guaranteeing its aura of artistic integrity, aligning the editor's personal dispositions with the habitus of the magazine. In other words, while I resist attributing editorial decisions to Moore exclusively, I recognise that Moore's editorial methods, her solutions to the practical problems of magazine production were underpinned by what I refer to as a compressive logic.[16] Moore's predilection for textual concentration made her particularly suited to the role of magazine editor where the limitations of page space were always a consideration. As Sibley Watson Jr was to declare to Moore within a few months of her taking over as editor, under her stewardship, the magazine 'had never been edited so creatively'.[17] Recognising that editorial agency is complex and always circumscribed by the material circumstances of magazine production does not preclude a critical discussion of Moore's editorial practice in relation to her poetics; it simply complicates that discussion.

It also requires an understanding of the space of the page and therefore necessarily owes a debt to recent scholarship in genetic and textual criticism. George Bornstein alerts us to the importance of the bibliographic codes of the little magazines first publishing modernism. Without such attention to the 'social embedding' of modernist texts, argues Bornstein, such texts become 'largely aesthetic objects existing outside of social space'.[18] The material space of the literary text becomes, in these terms, a space that extends beyond the physical boundaries of the page. McGann's notion of the 'thickened text' is the result not only of the artist's imaginative resources but also 'the textual presence and activities of many non-authorial agents'. In some instances, these non-authorial agents are not 'individuals at all'.[19] For instance, the physical constraints of the page become a determining factor in the production of the text. Correspondence between editors and contributors at the *Dial* reveals the extent to which the limitations of space frequently superseded authorial or editorial agency. Moore's repeated requests for concision become, in some instances, a practical response to the material constraints of periodical production. Those constraints extend beyond the page particularly in relation to material that might attract the attention of the censors. When explaining the publication trajectory of a text, it is not always possible to trace motives or intentions exclusively to either the author or the editor.

Moore is a particularly fascinating subject for an examination of modernist editorial practices because she was an ardent even obsessive reviser of her own work. She took every opportunity to revise at every stage of the compositional and publication processes and she also practised a form of post-publication revision. The most notorious example of this is 'Poetry' which, as Bonnie Honigsblum illustrates, initially appeared as a five-stanza poem only to be relentlessly cut, in stages, until it was a mere three lines long.[20] Moore's *Complete Poems*, as scholars working on her poetry know all too well, is by no means complete. 'Omissions are not accidents', Moore declares in the epigraph to the book in an attempt, perhaps, to assure the reader that the poet knows best. Textual scholars such as Robin Schulze and Heather Cass White are now providing facsimiles of her first collections and republishing editions that return readers to the rich complexities of Moore's work as it appeared in the first thirty years of her career.[21] Not only did Moore change poems even after they had appeared in print, her poetry manuscripts reveal that a form of textual compression was central to the compositional process itself. Like many of her modernist peers, Moore was engaged in a form of revision that has come to characterise modernism and modernist production.[22] The multiple versions of Moore's published poems provide evidence of contractility at work reinforcing the central argument of this book, the assertion that the process of revision through excision and substitution is bound up with editorial practice and is itself a creative one.

Several critics have considered Moore's editorial work at the *Dial* in relation to her poetry. Linda Leavell's *Marianne Moore and the Visual Arts* draws comparisons between the art of assemblage and the art of editing. Referring to the controversy surrounding Moore's revisions to Hart Crane's 'The Wine Menagerie', Leavell compares the poetic licence granted to Moore as a poet who frequently and strategically deploys the words of others with the condemnation she receives as an editor when asking for changes to Crane's poem.[23] Moore's poetic practice and the ethics underpinning that practice seep into her editorial approach, problematising the distinction between editorial and poetic labour. Leavell provocatively asserts that

> Moore's aesthetic of the miscellany undermines not only the conventional hierarchy between art and life but also that between artist and connoisseur. For as much imagination is demanded of the editor, the critic, the collector, as of the artist – all must see 'with piercing glances into the life of things'.[24]

The French term 'montage', of course, originally referred to the process of film editing. Moore's own poetic technique, which I have described in *Marianne Moore and the Cultures of Modernity* in terms of montage, is comparable to the editorial process of 'picking and choosing' to borrow a title from one of Moore's poems. Moore's poetry, particularly the large-scale, free-verse poems she published just before taking up her role at the *Dial,* are composed of a variety of quotations, many sourced from periodicals. Thus Moore's claim that her poem 'Marriage' consisted of 'statements that took my fancy which I tried to arrange plausibly' might be interpreted not as further evidence of her 'undermining modesty', but rather as a disruption of the gendered binaries circumscribing forms of cultural production.[25] In other words, she suggests that poetry might be read as an elaborate and creative form of editorial labour. The process of composition was bound up for Moore with what she referred to in one of her *Dial* comments as 'the science of assorting and the art of investing an assortment with dignity'.[26] Assembling and arranging textual fragments, I argue, is rather like putting together a magazine where different elements are juxtaposed in ways that produce multiple interpretive possibilities.

Catherine Paul's study of *Poetry in the Museums of Modernism* describes Moore's editorial comments in terms of an 'exhibition space' showcasing a variety of seemingly disparate objects and providing readers with the critical tools for an appreciation of such things.[27] This is a compelling argument and one that illuminates the curatorial theory and ethical principles underpinning Moore's poetics. My own approach, however, focuses on Moore's editorial methods as a practical response to the material constraints of periodical production. For instance, Paul's reading of the May 1927 issue of the *Dial* as an 'unintentional portrait' of the artist, her description of how Moore 'subtly masterminds the viewpoint on contemporary arts to which readers will be exposed' implies a degree of editorial control that was rare in the context of periodical publication.[28] By 1927 Moore was making final decisions regarding the contents of the magazine but those decisions were always circumscribed by the practical circumstances of production. While Paul reads Moore's editorial assemblage in terms of a self-portrait, I think of the editor as collector seeking to unify objects under the discursive signature of the *Dial*. As Judith Yaross Lee suggests, a magazine is a 'compendia storehouse' defined by its diversity. The editor's task is to 'create a distinctive identity for the works under their title'.[29] The *Dial* had regular features that ran at the end of the magazine, such as the theatre and music reviews, the briefer mentions and the editorial comment and there were house-rules that needed to be adhered to. The look of the magazine, its image of highbrow exclusivity had to be maintained even as its contents varied widely. At the same time, Moore had the editorial power to make decisions regarding the best way to achieve this unity.

I argue that understanding Moore's editorial practice requires understanding the institutional habitus of the *Dial* magazine, the constraints and the powers it conferred on Moore as an editor. While the impulse to condense is a characteristic of modernism, it is also, often, a characteristic of periodical culture where page space was always limited and the cost of the page itself, particularly in the *Dial*, was a financial consideration. Moore's judgements about the writing, its efficiency, its tone, its ethical stance were bound up with the material circumstances of magazine production. More specifically, as editor, Moore had a sense of what we might now refer to as the *Dial*'s discursive identity; she recognised that it served a particular market, that its readers had a certain set of expectations and values that it expected to see reflected in the magazine. A large part of the art of editing a periodical involves understanding the reader's tastes, values and sympathies, of recognising the reader not simply as a passive consumer but as an active contributor to the magazine's ethos. Often interpellated as members of an exclusive club, readers of the *Dial* might have expected something a little less lively and chic than *Vanity Fair*, a little more challenging than *Harper's* and a little less eccentric than the *Little Review*. In addition, the *Dial* declared itself to be a magazine of 'distinction' in its self-advertising and its high production values. As an editor, 'Miss Moore' confirmed that distinction bringing with her the symbolic value associated with modernist poetry.

As Lawrence Rainey has so convincingly argued, the institutionalisation of modernism was closely bound up with the *Dial*'s publication of *The Waste Land* in 1922. As a result, while the *Dial* ran from 1920 to 1929, the year 1922 has provided the focal point for discussions of the magazine when the owners, Scofield Thayer and Sibley Watson Jr, were most invested, both literally in terms of financial support and personally in terms of their involvement in editorial decision making. This limited historical perspective has persisted even with the explosion of critical interest in periodical culture and the little magazines publishing modernism. In fact, if anything, scholarship on the *Dial* has continued to attend to the early years of production and to assume that the magazine was largely the expression of Thayer and Watson's tastes and sentiments.[30] Thus, while studies of periodicals in the first half of the twentieth century have pushed against the critical parameters of modernism, testing and challenging its boundaries and exploring its relation to what Ann Ardis describes as the 'media ecology of modernity', the history of the *Dial* remains bound up with a particularly narrow conception of modernism that reproduces the discourse of highbrow exclusivity that the magazine deployed to market its own image.[31]

In addition, while both Thayer and Watson undoubtedly played important roles as editors and patrons of modernism, they increasingly relied upon the critical discriminations of their managing editors: Gilbert Seldes, Alyse Gregory, occasionally Kenneth Burke and increasingly, Marianne Moore. In fact, for the majority of the magazine's shelf life, Thayer and Watson were preoccupied with other concerns (Thayer suffered from mental health problems and officially resigned as editor in June 1926 and Watson's energies were largely devoted to his studies in medicine and his experimental film making). Seldes was managing editor from 1920 to 1923, Gregory from 1923 to 1925 and Moore, from April 1925 to July 1929. The important contribution these editors made to the magazine and, by extension, to the social production of modernism, has been largely lost in the emphasis placed on the power of Thayer and Watson's patronage. This book aims to open up and extend the discussion of the *Dial* by focusing on the years when Marianne Moore was editing the magazine.

Shifting the critical focus from the literary text to the institutional habitus of the magazine produces an alternative chronology of modernism's institutionalisation, one that locates editorial practice within a particular social milieu. In his study of the *Criterion*, Jason Harding explains T. S. Eliot's cultural influence in terms of the contacts, affiliations and periodical networks established in and through the magazine. This emphasis on location and dissemination, on the processes of production rather than the singular and authentic modernist text, provides a more nuanced and detailed account of modernism's rise to cultural legitimacy:

> In many ways, 1926 was a better marker of modernism's 'institutionalization' and 'cultural legitimacy' than Levenson's annus mirabilis. From Faber's offices in Russell Square, Eliot could cast his net more widely,

> cultivating a myriad of social connections with the nearby bohemian purlieus of Soho and the Charing Cross Road, further afield to the more bourgeois intellectual communities in Hampstead, while still maintaining a foothold in the fashionable world of the Mayfair and Chelsea patron *salonniers*.[32]

If, as Jason Harding suggests, 1926 was modernism's annus mirabilis, then it is instructive to think of Marianne Moore, by then editor of the *Dial*, in what she referred to as her 'palm tree', the office she occupied on the top floor of the Greenwich Village brownstone that served as the *Dial*'s offices. The magazine that Moore presided over had a much higher circulation than the *Criterion*, suggesting that it had successfully found the elusive middle ground that so many modernist magazines were searching for in the 1920s. The *Dial*, as Alan Golding has suggested, was not a 'little' avant-garde magazine but mediated between the quality publications such as *Harper's* and *Scribner's* and the small-scale, low circulation modernist magazines such as the *Little Review*.[33] Even at its lowest ebb, the *Dial* reached an audience of 6,500 while the *Criterion* never reached more than 1,200.[34] If Eliot presided over the intellectual communities of literary London, Moore's editorial role at the *Dial* put her at the centre of New York's cultural life. Moore cultivated connections with the activists, feminists and the radical Bohemians of Greenwich Village, the wealthy patrons of the Upper East Side, the fashionable suburbanites of New Jersey, the upwardly mobile professionals living in the towns and cities of the mid-West and the West Coast and beyond to the European readers drawn to 'New World' avant-gardes and the American expatriates living in the metropolitan centres of Europe. The *Dial* not only crossed national boundaries, but it also and perhaps ironically, as it expanded modernism's readership, began the process of crossing the class boundaries that divided high art from popular culture. Moore's principal role was to mediate between the little modernist magazines associated with a cultural elite of experts, patrons and producers and the broader and more capacious class of readers who took the respectable literary journals such as *Harper's*, *Century* and the *Atlantic Monthly*. By 1926, Moore was sitting in her palm tree with executive editorial privileges. It may not be an exaggeration to say that she was the most influential modernist editor working in the United States in the latter half of the decade. Her editorial decisions helped to fashion the spaces of modernism in ways that both contributed to its consolidation as well as challenged some of its basic tenets.

In order to understand how the *Dial* acquired its powers of cultural consecration, the first chapter, 'The Social Production of Modernism', begins with a critical perspective akin to Moore's editorial view. This overview examines the various overlapping affiliations and networks that sustained individual careers and promoted particular movements and schools of art, and it examines the social role of the magazine as a tastemaker. It traces the history of the *Dial* from 1920, when Thayer and Watson bought the magazine, to 1925, when Moore was named as Acting Editor. By focusing on the *Dial* as a site of intersecting and sometimes conflicting interests and alliances, it becomes possible to look behind its image of distinction in order to understand how it accrued and maintained the cultural prestige and authority that secured modernism's institutionalisation. It was Thayer and Watson's promotion of the *Dial* in newspapers and magazines such as the *New York Times*, the *Boston Globe*, *Harper's* and *Scribner's* that put modernism into circulation beyond the little magazine market. Thayer's marketing savvy, combined with the ample funds to pay for premium advertising spaces and the kind of connections only an Ivy League education can provide, kept modernism in the news for a number of years. In this way, readers did not have to read modernist texts nor did they even have to buy the *Dial* magazine (as the sales figures demonstrate) in order to have a sense of what the new writing and art was all about. When Moore came to take up her position as Acting Editor, her association with the radical poetry magazine, *Others*, signalled the ways in which the *Dial* mediated between the mainstream and the avant-garde, lending an edginess to the former and a legitimacy to the latter.

The second chapter, 'Editorial Agency: Performing "Miss Moore"', conceptualises editorial agency as an effect of the institutional habitus of the magazine. Editing the *Dial* required Moore to perform the role of 'Miss Moore', an embodiment of aesthetic integrity that was, from the beginning, bound up with the *Dial*'s image of distinction. I argue that Moore's editorial decisions need to be considered as interpretations of the magazine's distinct ethos rather than as direct and unmediated expressions of her own personal dispositions. Adopting Matthew Philpotts's typological perspective, one that recognises the highly influential role of the editor in the literary field by locating agency within the material circumstances of magazine production and consumption, I examine Moore's editorial role comparatively and contextually. To what extent, for instance, was Moore unusual when she made suggestions for changes and in what ways were her decisions different to her predecessors? When and why did Moore oppose Thayer and Watson, the owners of the magazine, and when she did so, how did she justify her actions? Drawing on the correspondence from the *Dial* archives, it becomes clear that she effectively saved the magazine from Scofield Thayer, who no longer trusted his co-owner, Sibley Watson, and who suspected most of his employees at the *Dial* of disloyalty and even criminal behaviour. Moore's managerial tact, her administrative efficiency, her eye for detail and her sheer hard work restored stability to the *Dial* allowing its publication to continue for another four years.

Chapter 3, 'Promotional Prose and Editorial Comments', examines the prose that Moore published in the *Dial*, arguing that certain non-hierarchical principles underpin her approach to cultural critique and endorsement. As far as I am aware, scholars have not known that Moore wrote advertisements for the magazine, though Marie Boroff perceptively detected an affinity between what she refers to as promotional prose and Moore's poetry. Comparing the advertisements Moore wrote for the *Dial* with those penned by Watson, Gilbert Seldes and Alyse Gregory reveals the extent to which Moore was resisting the kinds of categorical distinctions that were deployed precisely to sell magazines. The results are some extraordinary and distinctively modernist and Mooreish displays of textual compression and pleasure in diversity. While the advertisements have remained under the critical radar, the forty-one editorial comments that Moore published at the end of each issue (she wrote all but two of these during her tenure) have been made available in Patricia Willis's edited collection of Moore's *Complete Prose*. Having said that, Moore's comments have received relatively little attention and when they are discussed, they are often taken out of context. The last part of this chapter seeks to correct this by comparing Moore's comments to Thayer's and Seldes' in order to illustrate just how radically different Moore's approach was to the lively aestheticism that characterised the comments of her predecessors. Moore's artful, engaging and critically perceptive responses to the cultural life around her, when examined in relation to the *Dial* and its image of highbrow distinction, are agonistic, even oppositional in their refusal to denigrate.

'Hart Crane Distilled', the fourth chapter, is an examination of the controversy surrounding Moore's extensive revisions to Crane's 'The Wine Menagerie'. As is now well known, Moore did not simply revise Crane's poem, she reduced it to less than half its original length, condensing forty-five lines into eighteen lines and changing the title from 'The Wine Menagerie' to 'Again'. The central argument of this chapter is that Moore rewrote the poem because she viewed the content as being inappropriate for the *Dial*. She knew Crane was desperate for money so she went to unusual and extraordinary lengths to find a way for him to publish the poem, even if that meant radical revisions. This argument only becomes plausible if the *Dial* itself, its readership and its image of distinction are taken into account. It is important to consider the requirements of the magazine and not to assume that Moore allowed her 'scruples' to interfere with her editorial judgement.[35] While many, including and especially Crane, complained of the 'wounds' Moore's editorial cuts inflicted, I borrow the motif of 'ecstasy' from Crane's poem in order to examine the pleasures that come with textual compression. It is for this reason that I begin the chapter with a brief overview of Moore's poetic practice, paying particular attention to the ways in which she edited her own work. The multiple versions of her published poems as well as the poetry manuscripts reveal the 'compressive logic' that underpins Moore's compositional method and informs her editorial practice. I then go on to compare Moore's 'Again' with Crane's poem to argue that from Moore's perspective, there is 'virtue' and even ecstasy in 'contractility'.

In Chapter 5, 'Modernists Edited: Joyce, Stein, Lawrence and Rosenfeld', I continue to adapt the conceptual parameters of editorial agency by examining particular examples of Moore's editorial practice. In some instances, it is possible to trace Moore's editorial signature, the snail-like trails of textual compression that signal her distinctive modernist style, while in other instances, outcomes seem almost accidental in that they cannot be attributed to a single editorial or authorial agent. In the case of Moore's refusal of Joyce, Moore was clearly wary of attracting the attentions of the censor and also aware of the magazine's position in the marketplace. Moore invokes the magazine itself, arguing that it had to consider the tastes of its readers when deciding whether or not extracts from Joyce's 'Work in Progress' should be printed. The case of Gertrude Stein was different. While Moore had reservations about Joyce's late work, she was an ardent admirer of Gertrude Stein. Moore published 'Composition as Explanation' and extracts from 'A Long Gay Book', but the limitations of page space required a sampling of Stein that privileged the method she used for the much earlier novel, *The Making of Americans*. Unlike Stein, D. H. Lawrence had been a regular contributor to the *Dial*, but he tested his editor's loyalty when he sent her his last collection of poems, *Pansies*. Moore's editorial pruning of D. H. Lawrence's introduction is understandable, given the problems Lawrence was having with the censors. Here, she practises a form of modernist compression that manages to convey, succinctly and sensitively, the concerns of a much lengthier piece. Moore, we should note, was in sympathy with Lawrence's point of view and shared his opinion of censorship. The last example concerns another regular contributor to the *Dial*, the critic Paul Rosenfeld, who submitted a lengthy essay on the painter El Greco. Moore not only cut the essay, reducing it to half its length, she also suggested an alternative introduction that includes phrases bearing a resemblance to her own prose style. Here is evidence of Moore intervening, offering her own solutions to what she perceives to be Rosenfeld's unnecessary expansiveness. The exchange between Rosenfeld and Moore is instructive, revealing as it does something about the motives underpinning Moore's methods, as well as pointing to the distinct possibility that she intervened in many other instances.

Chapter 6, 'Periodical Form and the Dialogics of Gender', adopts what Sean Latham describes as an editorial view by examining the *Dial* across a number of issues in order to understand how patterns and arrangements within the magazine articulate or give voice to women's writing and art. This approach has the benefit of highlighting some lesser-known but fascinating women, including the mysterious figure of Marie/Moura Budberg, Soviet double-agent, translator and lover to Maxim Gorky, whose knowledge of Russian history and culture provided the *Dial* with a unique perspective on post-revolutionary

Russia. It also reveals the extent to which Moore concentrated women's art in clusters within single issues. The chapter explores three distinct clusters. The first of these is the May 1925 arrangement, which presented the work of writers Evelyn Scott and Jessica Nelson North, together with two paintings by Georgia O'Keeffe and Virginia Woolf's 'The Lives of the Obscure'. The second cluster appeared in the February 1927 showcasing the critic Dorothy Dudley, the poets Lola Ridge and Frances I. Wilson, and Budberg. The third arrangement, in the September 1927 issue of the *Dial*, featured work by the painter Marie Laurencin, the poet Genevieve Taggard, an extract from Stein's 'A Long Gay Book' and a painting by Vanessa Bell called *The Party*. This issue also included a critical essay by former editor, Alyse Gregory and two translations by Budberg of stories by Maxim Gorky. While Moore did not privilege the work of women artists and writers, nor did she practise a form of positive discrimination; on the other hand, these clusters suggest that she recognised the significance of patterns and arrangements, of design and layout within the magazine and that the affordances of display in magazines, while not wholly within editorial control, were, nevertheless, a vital component of editorial agency.

The final chapter, 'Poetic "Struggle" as Modernist Production', focuses on the little-known poem by William Carlos Williams, 'Struggle of Wings', published in the *Dial* in 1926. It is the 'struggle' between Moore and Williams over this poem before it was published that reveals the extent to which Williams wanted to keep alive the possibility of movement in language through a formal contingency. In other words, the central argument of this chapter is that 'Struggle of Wings' invites and resists textual analysis by repeatedly disrupting the notion that it contains within itself the meaning it set out to explore. As a result, close reading strategies alone are inadequate. The poem requires an approach which I'm referring to in terms of a dialogic formalism, an approach which moves between close textual analysis and editorial reading, between the poem and the poetry Moore published across a range of issues, and between the poem and the items in the single issue in which it appeared. The aesthetics of contingency advocated by Williams in 'Struggle of Wings' reveals the extent to which he was moving towards an understanding of the poem as a material object that became itself in and through the circumstances of its production and consumption. I conclude this chapter and the book as a whole by reflecting on Moore's influence as an editor after the closure of the *Dial* in July 1929. As Louis Zukofsky was to astutely observe, Moore was a 'constant' and important presence as a poet in the 1930s and 1940s. In *A-8* he figures Moore as 'my Lady Greensleeves', a mythical poetess who bears some resemblance to 'Miss Moore', the poet of aesthetic purity deployed to promote the *Dial*. Moore's editorial labour, I suggest in this book, has been hidden behind the figure of the charismatic poetess; the social production of modernism has, in turn, been mystified by the presence of this fabled Lady with the magic powers of cultural consecration.

Notes

1. Marianne Moore, *The Complete Prose of Marianne Moore*, ed. Patricia Willis (London: Faber and Faber, 1987), p. 357.
2. John Unterecker, *Voyager: A Life of Hart Crane* (New York: Farrar, Straus and Giroux, 1969), p. 234; Jack Selzer, *Kenneth Burke in Greenwich Village: Conversing with the Moderns* (Madison: University of Wisconsin Press, 1996), pp. 135–6.
3. Sean Latham, 'The Mess and Muddle of Modernism: The Modernist Projects Journal and Modern Periodical Studies', *Tulsa Studies in Women's Literature,* 30 (2011), 407–28 (p. 411).
4. Jayne Marek, *Women Editing Modernism: 'Little' Magazines and Literary History* (Lexington: University Press of Kentucky, 1995).
5. Scofield Thayer, 'Announcement', *Dial*, 78 (1925), 89–90 (p. 90).
6. Pierre Bourdieu, *The Rules of Art: Genesis and Structure of the Literary Field*, trans. Susan Emanuel (Cambridge: Polity Press, 1996, 2017), p. 83.
7. Edward Bishop, 'Re-Covering Modernism: Format and Function in the Little Magazines', in *Modernist Writers and the Marketplace*, ed. Ian Willison, Warwick Gould and Warren Chernaik (London: Macmillan, 1996), pp. 287–319 (p. 312).
8. Lawrence Rainey, *Institutions of Modernism: Literary Elites and Public Culture* (New Haven, CT: Yale University Press, 1998), p. 39.
9. Mark Morrisson, *The Public Face of Modernism: Little Magazines, Audiences and Reception, 1905–1920* (Madison: University of Wisconsin Press, 2001).
10. Aaron Jaffe, *Modernism and the Culture of Celebrity* (Cambridge: Cambridge University Press, 2005), p. 90.
11. Bourdieu, *Rules of Art*, p. 167.
12. Matthew Philpotts, 'The Role of the Periodical Editor: Literary Journals and Editorial Habitus', *Modern Language Review*, 107 (2012), 39–64 (p. 42).
13. Cristanne Miller, *The Cultures of Modernism: Marianne Moore, Mina Loy, and Else Lasker-Schuler: Gender and Literary Community in New York and Berlin* (Ann Arbor: University of Michigan Press, 2005), pp. 38–9.
14. Pierre Bourdieu, *Masculine Domination*, trans. Richard Nice (Oxford: Polity Press, 2001). Bourdieu examines the Berbers of the Kabylia, a culture that is both 'strange and familiar' in its reproduction of masculine domination, p. 5.
15. Randal Johnson, 'Editor's Introduction: Pierre Bourdieu on Art, Literature and Culture', in Pierre Bourdieu, *The Field of Cultural Production: Essays on Art and Literature*, ed. and intro. Randal Johnson (Oxford: Polity Press, 1993), p. 5.
16. Shawna Ross, 'Hashtags, Algorithmic Compression and Henry James's Late Style', *The Henry James Review*, 36 (2015), 24–44 (p. 28).
17. Sibley Watson Jr to Marianne Moore, 29 August 1925, Philadelphia, Rosenbach Museum and Library, Series V, Box 75, Fol. 2.
18. George Bornstein, *Material Modernism: The Politics of the Page* (Cambridge: Cambridge University Press, 2006), p. 117.
19. Jerome McGann, 'The Socialization of Texts', in *The Book History Reader*, ed. David Finkelstein and Alistair McCleery (London: Routledge, 2006), pp. 66–73 (p. 69).
20. Bonnie Honigsblum, 'Marianne Moore's Revisions of "Poetry"', in *Marianne Moore: Woman and Poet*, ed. Patricia Willis (Orono, ME: National Poetry Foundation, 1990), pp. 185–222.

21. Marianne Moore, *Becoming Marianne Moore: The Early Poems, 1907–1924*, ed. Robin G. Schulze (Berkeley, Los Angeles, London: University of California Press, 2002); Marianne Moore, *A-Quiver with Significance: Marianne Moore, 1932–1936*, ed. Heather Cass White (Victoria, BC: ELS Editions, 2008).
22. Hannah Sullivan, *The Work of Revision* (Cambridge, MA: Harvard University Press, 2013).
23. Linda Leavell, *Marianne Moore and the Visual Arts: Prismatic Color* (Baton Rouge: Louisiana State University Press, 1995), p. 134.
24. Ibid.
25. Marianne Moore, *The Complete Poems of Marianne Moore*, ed. Clive E. Driver (London and Boston, MA: Faber and Faber, 1981), p. 271, p. 151.
26. Moore, *Complete Prose*, p. 182; Moore, 'Comment', *Dial*, 82 (May 1927), 449–50 (p. 449).
27. Catherine Paul, *Poetry in the Museums of Modernism: Yeats, Pound, Moore, Stein* (Ann Arbor: University of Michigan Press, 2002), p. 158.
28. Ibid. pp. 158–91.
29. Judith Yaross Lee, 'From the Field: The Future of American Periodicals and American Periodicals Research', *American Periodicals: A Journal of History, Criticism and Bibliography*, 15 (2005), 196–201 (p. 198).
30. Nicholas Joost and Walter Sutton have provided the most extensive accounts of the history of the *Dial*. See Nicholas Joost, *Scofield Thayer and The Dial: An Illustrated History* (Carbondale: Southern Illinois University Press, 1964); Walter Sutton (ed.), *Pound, Thayer, Watson and The Dial: A Story in Letters* (Gainesville: University Press of Florida, 1994). More recently, Alan Golding's illuminating article on the *Dial* focuses on the pre-Moore years: Alan Golding, '*The Dial*, *The Little Review*, and the Dialogics of Modernism', *American Periodicals: A Journal of History, Critics and Bibliography*, 15 (2005), 42–55. Christina Britzolakis's excellent discussion of the *Dial* provides an overview of its cultural influence and includes a discussion of Moore's editorship: Christina Britzolakis, 'Making Modernism Safe for Democracy', in *The Oxford Critical and Cultural History of Modernist Magazines, Vol. II: North America, 1894–1960*, ed. Peter Brooker and Andrew Thacker (Oxford: Oxford University Press, 2012), pp. 85–102.
31. Ann Ardis, 'Editor's Introduction Mediamorphosis: Print Culture and Transatlantic/Transnational Public Sphere(s)', *Modernism/Modernity*, 19, (2012), v–vii.
32. Jason Harding, *The Criterion: Cultural Politics and Periodical Networks in Inter-War Britain* (Oxford: Oxford University Press, 2002), p. 15.
33. Golding, '*The Dial*', p. 46.
34. Moore tells Watson that they are running 6,500 copies of the magazine. Marianne Moore to Sibley Watson Jr, 24 March 1928, Yale University, Beinecke Rare Book and Manuscript Library, Scofield Thayer/Dial Papers, Series I, Box 7, Fol. 271. Jason Harding, 'The Idea of a Literary Review: T. S. Eliot and The Criterion', in *The Oxford Critical and Cultural History of Modernist Magazines, Vol. I: Britain and Ireland, 1880–1955*, ed. Peter Brooker and Andrew Thacker (Oxford: Oxford University Press, 2013), pp. 346–63.
35. William Wasserstrom, 'Marianne Moore, The *Dial*, and Kenneth Burke', *The Western Humanities Review*, 17 (1963), 249–62 (p. 256).

1

THE SOCIAL PRODUCTION OF MODERNISM

In 1924, Ernest Boyd's article, 'Aesthete: Model 1924', was published in the *American Mercury* offering a contemporary parody of the *Dial*, its editors and contributors. The Aesthete, according to Boyd, is

> already famous; at least, so it seems to him when he gazes upon his own reflection in the eyes of his friends, and fingers aggressively the luxurious pages of the magazine of which he is Editor-in-Chief, Editor, Managing Editor, Associate Editor, Contributing Editor, Bibliographical Editor, or Source Material Editor. His relationship to the press must always be editorial, and to meet the changed conditions of the cosmos, a changed conception of the functions of an editor provides him with a vast selection of titles from which to choose. The essential fact is that he has an accredited mouthpiece, a letterhead conferring authority, a secure place from which to bestride the narrow world in which he is already a colossus. Thus he is saved from those sordid encounters with the harsh facts of literary commerce which his predecessors accepted as part of the discipline of life: Meredith reading manuscripts for Chapman & Hall, Gissing toiling in New Grub Street, Anatole France writing prefaces for Lemerre's classics, Dreiser polishing dime novels for Street & Smith.[1]

The Aesthete's cultural 'authority' is 'accredited' in the 'luxurious' form of the magazine itself and this affords him a position outside the 'sordid' concerns of the literary marketplace. As an editor of a highbrow magazine, he operates within what Pierre Bourdieu describes as a 'paradoxical universe', whereby economic success is ultimately failure, where high circulation figures and large profits are evidence of a capitulation to the market and result in a loss of symbolic value.[2] Unlike writers of the previous century, the Aesthete is not obliged to compromise with his artistic principles, lowering himself to writing or publishing for profit. This economic world reversed is the result of what Boyd refers to as the 'changed conditions of the [publishing] cosmos', more specifically, the expansion of print culture and the emergence of cultural divides. The Aesthete's 'secure place' is the 'narrow world' of highbrow culture which he 'bestrides' like a 'colossus' accumulating cultural capital and conferring prestige on the select few.

As Boyd's satirical profile goes on, it becomes clear that his Aesthete is an amalgamation of a number of figures connected to the *Dial*, bearing a resemblance to the owners of the magazine, Scofield Thayer and Sibley Watson Jr, in being fabulously wealthy Harvard men with a passion for the arts. Thayer, who also edited the *Dial*, was influenced by a *Yellow Book* decadence and fashioned himself as a dandy for the jazz age. Watson, less visible but no less important, was drawn to the modernist experiments taking place both in the US and Europe and was particularly 'glamored' by the 'gaudy spectacle' of Paris. Traces of the regularly featured *Dial* poet e. e. cummings are evident in the Aesthete's poetry which is remarkable for its 'typographical and syntactical eccentricities'; like Gilbert Seldes, who is actually named in the piece, he is attracted to the 'lively arts' and his prose style, like Paul Rosenfeld's, is 'florid' and 'pedantic'.[3] Boyd's parody suggests the magazine's combination of lively aestheticism, cosmopolitanism and high-end luxury and signals the fact that by 1924, it had established a distinct brand in the crowded magazine market. Yet it also suggests that the *Dial*'s own discursive identity is a fusion of the various and often competing positions under its title. In other words, those powers of cultural consecration do not reside with one editor or even with the combination of contributors but rather with the magazine itself through its material form as well as its distinctive content.

Perhaps surprisingly, Boyd's article also points to the social production of the model Aesthete. Rather like the production of the Model T Ford, the Aesthete is designed and manufactured for an expanding consumer culture, assembled with the efficiency of mass production techniques though marketed as a commodity uniquely resistant to economic pressures. Boyd nicely captures the Thayer/Watson approach to promoting the *Dial*, which was to create the impression that the magazine did not resort to the 'sordid' tactics of the high-circulation periodicals by selling itself in the marketplace. In fact, as I will go on to discuss, in the early 1920s the owners were sinking vast sums of money into doing just that. The editor/owners successfully mediated between the commercial and the aesthetic by drawing on the latest techniques in advertising to promote the *Dial* as a 'magazine of distinction'.

Caricaturing the *Dial* as the figure of the composite Aesthete suggests the ways in which agency might be attributed to the magazine. A set of shared assumptions and overlapping interests, though not identical and often in tension, produce a sense of the magazine's discursive identity. The *Dial*'s institutional power and authority is derived from a fusion of individual agents' tastes and values, the patronage of its owners, its position in the marketplace and the changing 'cosmos' of mass print culture. Matthew Philpotts, following Bourdieu, provides a theoretical framework for understanding the literary journal as a function of ensemble performances. He describes the magazine in terms of an 'institutional habitus', a defining ethos which 'unites the members of its "nucleus" and which acts as a "unifying and generative principle" for their cultural practice'. He conceptualises the literary journal as 'an agent in its own right, participating in its various forms: literary, economic, and social; material and symbolic'.[4] Such an approach suggests that the institutional habitus of the magazine extends beyond the magazine itself and the network of writers, editors and patrons attached to the publication. It includes the ways in which the journal was positioned in the magazine market, the dialogic relations that held it in place within that market and the promotional strategies that signalled its distinction from its competitors as well as its material form, the look and feel of the magazine, its periodical codes, its style, layout and typographic design.

Extending Philpotts's argument further, the concept of habitus, a form of habitual and generative practice, suggests that it is repetition, the defining characteristic of periodicals that makes them so effective in establishing and naturalising the parameters of cultural taste. Periodical form engages producers and consumers in routine cultural rituals where the rules of the game are disseminated and practised. The *Dial*'s institutional habitus, the ensemble of agents, human and non-human that coalesced in and around the magazine, practised a form of highbrow 'distinction' that accrued symbolic value through its repeated remediation. James Mussell suggests that the repetition of formal features in a magazine, its mediating framework serves to stabilise its miscellaneous content and can 'best be understood as a form of genre that has a material effect'.[5] That effect, in the case of the *Dial*, reverberated beyond the 'little' magazines that had been publishing modernism up to that point.

This chapter examines the institutional habitus of the *Dial* as an ensemble of agents, a composite Aesthete manufactured for the modern magazine market. In the first half of the discussion, I focus on the social groups, political affiliations, personal connections and artistic alliances that coalesced to produce the modernist *Dial* in 1920. While the *Dial* presented itself as being unified by a critical consensus, a shared sense of what was worth retaining and valuing in the context of an expanding consumer culture, like most periodicals, its contents were diverse and heterogeneous. This approach suggests how the

Dial drew on existing social and cultural networks but also, as it became a more established publication, how it produced a network of writers, reviewers, editors, critics and artists some of whom were to play significant roles in the institutionalisation of modernism beyond the 1920s and some of whom were to remain manifestly resistant to modernism. It alerts us to the multiple and conflicting modernisms the magazine held together under the discursive signature of highbrow cultural exclusivity. It makes visible the transnational politics the magazine inherited from the influential *Seven Arts* magazine, the *Yellow Book* strand of aestheticism that characterised Scofield Thayer's taste in art and letters, the radical otherness of the group of writers associated with Kreymborg's magazine *Others*. It reveals the extent to which an old boys' network of Harvard graduates dominated American literary culture in the 1920s, but it also points to how contact between that world of money and privilege intersected with left politics and feminism in provocative and productive ways.

The second half of this chapter broadens this focus to include the *Dial*'s marketing strategies in the context of periodical networks beyond the restricted field of production. While the magazine's circulation figures were relatively low, its construction of an image of transcendent, timeless literary quality was mediated and disseminated in a range of periodicals during the 1920s that reached an audience well beyond the *Dial*'s own circulation figures. As a result, modernism's institutionalisation was brought about less by the actual publication of modernist masterpieces and more by the construction of those texts as masterpieces in the promotional material generated by the magazine itself. While this marketing campaign failed to attract a substantial readership and hence the necessary advertising revenue to wean it off the patronage of its owners, it did coalesce with a range of other discursive practices to reinforce modernism's reputation as exclusive, highbrow and elitist. In fact, in the context of the reversed economic world of restricted production it seems entirely appropriate that the magazine was commercially unsuccessful given that its appeal was characterised as necessarily limited.

The discussion begins with the charismatic figure of Scofield Thayer and his own editorial performance as the embodiment of the Harvard aesthete, a performance that reinforced his editorial work at the *Dial* and his discursive identity as a taste maker. Thayer was a complex and contradictory figure; while on the one hand he seemed to look backwards to the decadence of the fin-de-siècle and the art-for-art's-sake movement; on the other hand, he was forward-looking in his grasp of the modern periodical market. It was Thayer's genius for promoting the *Dial* that made highbrow culture more visible, more accessible and more fashionable in the 1920s. Thayer embodies the productive contradictions of the *Dial*, its seeming resistance to the pressures of the market coupled with a passion for selling high culture to an expanding middle-class readership. As I will go on to suggest, the formation and promotion of the *Dial* in the early 1920s generates a highbrow distinction that creates a niche in the market for modernism.

Harvard Aestheticism

The *Dial*'s status as a luxury commodity, as a form of cultural production free from economic necessity, was bound up, particularly in its first few years of publication, with the charismatic yet troubled figure of Scofield Thayer. (Sibley Watson preferred to be less visible adopting pseudonyms if he chose to publish in the magazine.) As James Dempsey, Thayer's biographer points out, when Thayer's father died suddenly in 1907, the newspapers reported that he owned the largest individual woollen manufacturing company in the United States.[6] With his vast inherited fortune, Thayer cultivated an image of the glamorous aesthete – a fusion of *Yellow Book* decadence and jazz age glitz. His letters to Elaine Orr, whom he married in 1916, provide an insight into his peculiarly privileged yet energetic and passionate faith in what he refers to, rather extravagantly, as 'the broad playground of the intellect'.[7] Always alert to the importance of making an entrance and looking the part, he describes his performance before the Cambridge Philosophical Society in 1915 when studying at Oxford. Having met up with his 'old Milton and Harvard friend, Tom Eliot', Thayer clearly enjoys recounting the moment: 'Wrapped in my most recherché mantle. I entered the club ten minutes late. This was of course duly effective. My title was "The Aesthetic Value of Orthodoxy", and I read with that deliberation which befits a philosopher from Oxford.'[8] Yet while Thayer adopted this intellectual pose, he was not simply acting the part. He had graduated cum laude from Harvard in 1913, went on to study English and Philosophy at Magdalen College and was, as is evident with his translation work for the *Dial*, an accomplished linguist with a passion for what he referred to as 'Teutonic culture' as is evident in the publication of the first translation of Thomas Mann's *Death in Venice* and translations of the work of Arthur Schnitzler, Herman Hesse, Hugo von Hofmannsthal and Gerhart Hauptmann.

Thayer began writing to Elaine Orr as early as 1913 and in these letters something of his faith in art as well as a dedication to the 'broad playground' of the intellect is evident. He advised Elaine, who was bored by her studies, to apply herself, to learn foreign languages so that she might appreciate European literature, a strategy Thayer had followed. Even for beautiful debutantes such as Orr, he argued, it was important to develop intellectually as well as emotionally. She might be able to trade on her beauty in her youth but not as she grows older. 'Perhaps', suggests Thayer,

> the purely intellectual pleasures are of less matter to a woman than to a man; they are for her more adequately supplemented and replaced by

> the wealth of personal contact and sympathy. But even in the case of women[,] I have already known too many children that were exquisite with the delicacy of youth and who are now repellent with the unrelieved vapidity of an intellectual nonentity.[9]

Thayer had not yet met Marianne Moore at this point, nor Alyse Gregory or Mina Loy. If he had, he would certainly have revised his sexist assumption that intellectual pleasures are less important to women. In these letters to his future wife, he also rails against Cook's tourists: 'I have never seen anything more hideous than a party of wall-eyed Americans dragging their eyeless bodies through one of the great galleries of France or Italy.' He criticises those who do not want to learn, yet also believes that 'modern industrialism is inimical to the finer things of life'. Friendships, and by extension, social relations, should, according to Thayer, be enriching associations based on the life of the mind. Thayer's ideas about the mass cultural consumption of 'Europe' by American tourists seep into his editorial comments and the overall ethos of the magazine he bought with Sibley Watson Jr. Underlying Thayer's critique is a resistance to what he perceives to be a rising class of cultural consumers who have the economic capital to travel but not the cultural capital to understand or appreciate what they see in the 'great galleries of France or Italy'.[10]

Thayer was not unique in these proclivities or these postures. As Malcolm Cowley remembers, the Harvard Aesthetes of 1916, influenced by Santayana, were 'trying to create in Cambridge, Massachusetts an after-image of Oxford in the 1890s'. According to Cowley, these second-generation aesthetes:

> Read the *Yellow Book*, they read Casanova's memoirs, and *Les Liaison Dangereuses*, both in French, and Petronius in Latin; they gathered at tea-time in one another's rooms, or at punches in the office of *The Harvard Monthly*; they drank, instead of weak punch, seidels of straight gin topped with a maraschino cherry; they discussed the harmonies of Pater, the rhythms of Aubrey Beardsley and, growing louder, the voluptuousness of the Church, the essential virtue of prostitution. They had crucifixes in their bedrooms, and ticket stubs from last Saturday's burlesque show at the Old Howard.[11]

While Thayer graduated from Harvard in 1913, some of this Harvard aestheticism is evident in his taste for Beardsley, his interest in religion and his enthusiasm for some aspects of popular culture. For intellectuals such as Thayer, aestheticism offered a form of resistance to what he described as 'modern industrialism'.[12] As one of the twentieth century's great taste makers, Thayer's idea of aesthetic pleasure as an end in itself was strongly connected to the aestheticism of the late nineteenth century. In her discussion of Wallace Stevens, Elizabeth Oliver points to the appeal of 'sensuous retreat and self-fashioning through aesthetic tastes and choices' as a form of opposition to the expansion of American consumer culture.[13] In other words, certainly in the context of the *Dial*, it is possible to trace a link between the modernism that emerged within its pages and the vestiges of aestheticism in circulation at Harvard.

Thayer had cut his editorial teeth as editor of the *Harvard Monthly* between 1912 and 1913 and worked alongside many who would become regular contributors to the *Dial*, including Stewart Mitchell, J. Donald Adams, Cuthbert Wright, Gilbert Seldes, e. e. cummings and Lincoln MacVeagh.[14] The Harvard connection, however, was more than simply a network of privileged vested interests; studying at Harvard in the early twentieth century meant, for many, studying under the philosopher George Santayana, whose influence, Lewis Mumford argued, is perceptible in the pages of the *Dial*.[15] Thayer had devoted a special issue of the *Harvard Monthly* to Santayana's *Winds of Doctrine* and counted Santayana as a friend and mentor during his days as a student at Harvard and Oxford. It was Santayana's critique of what he had termed the 'genteel tradition' in his 1911 lecture at Berkeley, California that was to resonate in the cultural criticism of the 1920s. According to Santayana, the twin intellectual traditions of puritanism and transcendentalism had been unable to keep pace with the expansion of modernity in the United States. The dominant 'genteel tradition' associated with derivative, second-hand culture provided no means of expressing or critiquing American 'progress'; on the contrary, that tradition stifled expression and feminised what Santayana referred to as 'the normal, practical masculine American'.[16] As Michael Kammen suggests in his critical biography of Gilbert Seldes, Santayana's influence underpins the *Dial*'s aestheticism and also its keen interest in popular culture or what Seldes referred to as the 'lively arts'.[17]

This lively aestheticism bestowed symbolic value on select forms of popular culture and characterised the magazine in the years when Thayer and Seldes were in charge. For Thayer, as for Seldes and Watson, Santayana's call for a form of artistic expression responsive to the 'spirit and the inarticulate principles that animate the community' required critics to look to indigenous forms of culture.[18] In the search for a form of artistic expression that could bridge the gap between the feminised 'genteel tradition' and the 'aggressive enterprise' of the commercial world, the writers and critics associated with the *Dial* looked to popular art forms such as comic strips, jazz, burlesque and film as vibrant alternatives to the genteel tradition. While Santayana's critique was levelled at late nineteenth-century American culture, by the 1920s a new enemy had emerged, though still one with genteel tastes. It was the middlebrow that many of the writers at the *Dial* positioned themselves in opposition to. In critical essays and editorial comments, it was the middlebrow which was characterised, like its genteel predecessor, as both feminine and fake, or what Gilbert

Seldes would describe in terms of the 'faux bon'.[19] As Seldes states in his critical study of popular culture, *The 7 Lively Arts*:

> We know that there is no opposition between the great and the lively arts.
> That both are opposed in the spirit to the middle or bogus arts.
> That the bogus arts are easier to appreciate, appeal to low and mixed emotions, and jeopardize the purity of both the great and the minor arts.[20]

Hired in early 1920 as managing editor of the *Dial*, Seldes' regular theatre column and other essays devoted to a wide range of popular culture, provided a critical framework for the analysis of the so-called 'lively arts'. Seldes valued 'highbrow' and 'lowbrow' forms of cultural production but was resistant to the expanding middlebrow, associated with literary supplements, the Book of the Month Club and, later in the decade, the *Reader's Digest*. A good example of Seldes' critical approach is his essay, 'Toujours Jazz' published in the *Dial* in August 1923. The essay responds to Santayana's call for forms of cultural expression commensurate with the experience of American modernity. While many newspapers and magazines circulated stories of the corrupting influence of jazz, Seldes found in this new music a vitality and 'liveliness' essential to the nation's cultural well-being:

> The fact that jazz is our current mode of expression, has reference to our time and the way we think and talk, is interesting; but if jazz music weren't itself good the subject would be more suitable for a sociologist than for an admirer of the gay arts. Fortunately the music and the way it is played are both of great interest, both have qualities which cannot be despised; and the cry that jazz is the enthusiastic disorganization of music is as extravagant as the prophecy that if we do not stop 'jazzing' we will go down, as a nation, into ruin. I am quite ready to uphold the contrary. If – before we have produced something better – we give up jazz we shall be sacrificing nearly all there is of gaiety and liveliness and rhythmic power in our lives. Jazz, for us, isn't a last feverish excitement, a spasm of energy before death. It is the normal development of our resources, the expected, and wonderful, arrival of America at a point of creative intensity.[21]

Rather than seeing jazz as a degraded and commercial form of culture that corrupts social values, he finds in its pulsating rhythms an expression of the experience of modernity. The emphasis here is on jazz as a cultural 'resource' that springs from American soil. It is the first flowering of a distinctly American form of culture that refuses to equate commercial success with cultural degeneration. Notably, when pitching the idea for his book *The 7 Lively Arts* to

Henry Seidel Canby, who would commission it for Harper's, Seldes constructed his position in opposition to the genteel tradition.[22] He is not only developing a critical language capable of responding to his lively subject matter, but in doing so he is offering a critique of mainstream, middlebrow culture. As he put it in an article for *Vanity Fair*: 'It is on the strange altar of refinement, indeed, that a nation usually reputed vigorous is sacrificing its robust laughter and its hearty cheers. There ought to be a law against it.'[23] The 'refinement' associated with the 'bogus' arts is also implicitly gendered as feminine.

Seldes was a critical pioneer in this area, but was by no means the only writer at the *Dial* who engaged in the cultural consecration of the lively arts. Thayer often used his editorial 'Comments' to develop appreciative responses to popular culture. For instance, in August 1920 he attacks cultural elitism, complaining of 'the mind which cannot recognize a great thing simply because it happens also to be popular'.[24] He begins his 'Comment' in April 1923 by acknowledging that 'Sport is a passion with us' and goes on to identify Grantland Rice as 'the best of sport-writers' and that, moreover, 'these writings about sport are far better critical writing than nine tenths of the criticism of art and letters published in our daily papers'.[25] In July 1920,Thayer's editorial comment ends with a lengthy appreciation of the 'wild unreality' of the cartoon 'Krazy Kat':

> Here is a veritable creation, standing cheek by jowl with all the incredibly vulgar and stupid work of our comic artists. It is as real as the Ueberbrettl', as indigenous for us as Coq d'Or is of Russia, as Jolson to the Winter Garden. The profound wisdom, the miraculous technique, the strict observance of a convention, are things of wonder, and if we have to condemn utterly the press which demoralizes all thought and makes ugly all things capable of beauty, we must still be gentle with it, because Krazy Kat, the invincible and joyous, is a creature of the press, inconceivable without its foundation of cheapness and stupidity. He is there to enliven and to encourage and to give much delight.[26]

Seldes too was a fan of 'Krazy Kat', that 'gentle monster of our new mythology'.[27] While this enthusiastic critical response to the anarchic humour and technical brilliance of Herriman's Krazy Kat might, at first glance, seem far removed from the aestheticism of the *Harvard Monthly*, embedded in the criticism of both Seldes and Thayer is not only a celebration of the work of Charlie Chaplin, vaudeville, burlesque, jazz, ragtime, comic strips, the Ziegfeld Follies, Broadway and Al Jolson, but also an aesthetic alliance against middlebrow culture. When the cosmopolitan aesthete turns his attention to popular culture, he not only finds 'beauty', he finds the expression of an 'indigenous' American culture, art forms that are produced out of the media maelstrom of modernity, the popular press. Crucially, the *Dial* critic has the cultural capital to consecrate selected items from mass culture.

While the image of lively aestheticism made the *Dial*'s modernism look unified, as Dempsey suggests, Thayer himself 'found much of the modernity celebrated by others – the city, technology, speed, mass-production – utterly horrific'.[28] He tended to prefer literary forms that retained a psychological realism: the early Joyce of *Dubliners* rather than the later, more experimental Joyce of *Ulysses;* he celebrated the work of arch-experimentalist Marianne Moore primarily as a way of putting Eliot in his place (resulting in some of Thayer's most astute critical comments). He denigrated Pound's 'silly' and 'impossible' cantos, he dismissed William Carlos Williams's poetry as 'silly pseudo verses' and regretted the publication of Eliot's *The Waste Land*, finding it 'disappointing'.[29] By 1925 Thayer would complain to Alyse Gregory that the magazine did not reflect his tastes or interests:

> [L]ooking over The Dial, the most remarkable thing about it is the fact that, although I am editor of it, no one who knew me would guess this fact. This is of course attributable to many things, but chiefly to Watson's constant and subterranean pull to the left. I myself detest all Modern Art.[30]

As Thayer's comment suggests, James Sibley Watson Jr could not have been more different both in terms of temperament and taste. Unlike Thayer, he embraced many aspects of modernity: he made several important avant-garde films, including *The Fall of the House of Usher* (1928) and *Lot in Sodom* 1933; after the Second World War he had a successful career as a radiologist, joining the faculty of the University of Rochester's School of medicine and making over 10,000 cineflurographic (x-ray) films; unlike Thayer he was enthusiastic about Joyce's work after *Dubliners* and was in favour of publishing extracts from *Work in Progress*; he liked Pound's *Cantos* and disagreed with Thayer over Pound's dismissal as Paris correspondent. While Thayer was enthusiastic about German art and literature, Watson shared a comparable passion for French culture; while Thayer was a connoisseur of visual art, he was not, like Watson, as interested in motion pictures. Watson's first appearance in the *Dial*, 'Some Remarks on Rimbaud as Magician', published in June 1920, was an appreciative essay that signals the differences between Thayer and Watson. While Watson's prose is jaunty, informative and erudite, Thayer's is frequently convoluted, combative and haughty. Watson sprinkles his essay on Rimbaud with French phrases and colloquial expressions that nicely encapsulate the *Dial*'s fusion of the local and the cosmopolitan. He writes of the colourful and charismatic character of Rimbaud with 'gusto', a term Marianne Moore used frequently to describe writing imbued with a forceful and creative energy. According to Watson, at seventeen, Rimbaud 'was in no danger of being lured by the prospects of a reputable and congenial life in the capital' successfully 'dispos[ing] of ambitions which would have lasted a talented man a lifetime'.[31]

Watson's interest in Rimbaud illustrates his aesthetic preferences for the formally experimental and informs his studies of modern poetry. His groundbreaking translations for the *Dial* of Rimbaud's *A Season in Hell* and in particular, *Illuminations*, one of the foundational texts of modernism, introduced readers to the work of this nineteenth-century avant-garde poet and also provided some textual precedents for the free verse appearing in modernist magazines, including the *Dial* itself. As Munson states in his account of the 'pivotal year of 1920', 'Watson's pioneer efforts to introduce Rimbaud to American writers and readers have not been superseded.'[32] Yet while Watson had things to say regarding modernism, he wished to maintain a low profile. He used the pseudonym of W. C. Blum for his debut at the magazine and continued to use this for all his reviews and American Letters.

From the present perspective, Thayer's tastes might look decidedly antiquated and Watson's impressively modern, but it was this combination of the established and the experimental that allowed the *Dial* to extend its readership beyond the circulations of the so-called 'little' magazines. Thus, while Thayer frequently complained about his partner (the two were often not on speaking terms), the aesthetic tensions between them produced an eclectic and diverse range of material that extended from the Victorian caricaturist, Max Beerbohm, to Mina Loy's fractured modernist poetics, from Arthur Schnitzler's psychological studies of turn of the century bourgeois life in Austria to Sherwood Anderson's flattened, emotionally reticent studies of small-town America, from the emerging 'new criticism' represented by T. S. Eliot and I. A. Richards to the impressions of George Saintsbury or the evolving social criticism of Kenneth Burke.

Seven Arts Cosmopolitanism

The *Dial*'s financial and symbolic investment in literature in translation is particularly important when it comes to discussing the political and ethical dimensions of its cosmopolitanism. The *Dial*'s cosmopolitan stance constructed a transnational modernism that reinforced the cultural hegemony of Europe and the United States; its willingness to pay for translations of texts must be viewed not simply as transatlantic acts of mutual cooperation and support but rather as forms of cultural co-option. As is evident from even the most cursory glance at the magazine, the *Dial* was impressively laden with the textual treasures of Europe as well as reproductions of the sculptures and paintings that defined the modernist visual aesthetic. In this respect, Scofield Thayer and Sibley Watson Jr were similar to a number of American patrons of the arts, such as Peggy Guggenheim, John Quinn and J. D. Rockerfeller, who all invested substantial sums of money in securing art objects from across the world for personal pleasure and public display. These vast and impressive collections are acts of appreciation, but also, of course, acts of appropriation that demonstrate the newly emergent economic spending power of the United States as well the cultural sophistication of the connoisseur as collector. Borrowing Patrick Collier's observations on the *Illustrated London News* and its colonising, imperial gaze, the cosmopolitan eye of the *Dial* might be viewed as both 'cultivated and cultivating'.[33]

But the *Dial* was not only investing in European art and literature. As numerous critics have suggested, the *Dial*'s rejection of the genteel middlebrow in favour of the lively arts is combined with a continued and keen interest in cultivating a distinctly American form of art that draws from but is not dependent upon Europe. This aim was one that Thayer and Watson inherited from *Seven Arts* magazine and, in particular, the writing of Randolph Bourne. When Seldes vacated the post of managing editor in 1923 to write *The 7 Lively Arts*, the appointment of Alyse Gregory confirmed the magazine's allegiance to the political and cultural legacy of Randolph Bourne at *Seven Arts* magazine. Gregory had been close friends with Bourne since she struck up a correspondence with him in 1912 after reading his essay 'The Excitement of Friendship'. An active suffrage campaigner and educational reformer, she had been earning her living by writing for the *Saturday Review of Literature, Vanity Fair*, the *New Republic* and the *Freeman*. By 1918 she was hosting social gatherings, or 'firesides' as Bourne would call them, that attracted the *Seven Arts* intellectuals. As Barbara Ozieblo points out, Bourne brought Thayer along to one of these gatherings and Thayer was immediately 'captivated' by his hostess.[34] Bourne also introduced Gregory to Paul Rosenfeld, another regular contributor to *Seven Arts* who would become the author of the *Dial*'s 'Musical Chronicle' from October 1921. Thus while the *Dial* was a self-declared magazine for arts and literature, eschewing an overtly political stance that was characteristic of its pre-1920 incarnation, it shared a commitment to the politics of cultural regeneration associated with the *Seven Arts*.[35] As Gorham Munson suggests, the *Seven Arts* strand underpins the *Dial*, particularly in the early 1920s when Bourne was still very much in the minds and memories of those who contributed to the magazine:

> Bourne bequeathed a renaissance role to postwar intellectuals [. . .] Scofield Thayer [. . .] had been very sympathetic to Bourne's war essays in the *Seven Arts,* and backed Bourne for a place on the fortnightly *Dial.* More or less consciously, Thayer aspired to carry out the bequest of Bourne [. . .] For several years thereafter, the *Dial* could be regarded as the continuator of Bourne's heroic endeavour to rally a new fellowship in the younger generation – the generation of Lewis Mumford and John Dos Passos and Paul Rosenfeld – that would pledge itself to the purpose of creating, in the words of Bourne's colleague Van Wyck Brooks, 'a fine, free, articulate cultural order'.[36]

Brooks's idea of a 'cultural order' is akin to Eliot's 'ideal order' articulated in 'Tradition and the Individual Talent' (1919). According to Munson, the most important role of *Seven Arts* magazine and then the *Dial* was to publish criticism capable of creating that order, of discriminating between the 'faux bon' and the art object. The reverent, almost sacred tone of Munson's description of Bourne and his cultural mission suggests the ways in which the 'fellowship' of critics emerging in the 1920s saw themselves as the nation's cultural saviours. In the transmission of cultural values there is also a sense of a spiritual regeneration of the community through the art objects it values. It was not just anyone who could offer salvation, however, but rather the select group of writers and critics with the cultural capital to make such discriminations.

That 'new fellowship', what Bourne would refer to as the 'beloved community' of *Seven Arts* writers, found a home at the *Dial*, injecting a political and social element to its lively aestheticism. Thayer and Watson published the posthumous 'Autobiographic Chapter' by Randolph Bourne in the first issue of the new *Dial*, making explicit their debt to his vision of a transnational cultural pluralism. Up until his untimely death in 1919 of influenza, Bourne had been a key contributor to the political *Dial* of the 1910s. In the same year as Royal Dixon's *Americanization*, which advocated the assimilation of immigrants into a single, unifying culture, Bourne published 'Trans-National America' in the *Atlantic Monthly*. Here he described his vision of a culture capable of accommodating rather than assimilating difference:

> America is coming to be, not a nationality but a trans-nationality, a weaving back and forth, with the other lands, of many threads of all sizes and colors. Any movement which attempts to thwart this weaving, or to dye the fabric any one color, or disentangle the threads of the strands, is false to this cosmopolitan vision.[37]

The political implications of that 'cultural order' only become visible in Thayer's strident editorials. In his 'Comment' for March 1920 he notes that some states are putting restrictions on the circulation of foreign-language publications. Tongue firmly in cheek, he then goes on to point to the hypocrisies of this attitude in a nation composed largely of immigrants:

> It is the essence of America that no foreign thing or person has ever taken root here, that the American tradition has rejected all the corruptions of Europe and, alone of all nations, has developed its life in magnificent isolation. The hated foreigner will presently learn that if he wants to write masterpieces – not to speak of reading them – he must write them in American.[38]

In the same year, the *Saturday Evening Post*, which had the largest circulation of any weekly in the United States, sponsored one of its staff members,

Kenneth Roberts, to tour Europe. The articles he wrote for the paper, collected in a book called *Why Europe Leaves Home*, stressed the dangers of the United States being used as a 'dumping ground' for 'congenital slum material'.[39] Lothrop Stoddard's racial theories, expounded in *The Rising Tide of Color Against White World Supremacy* (1920) and *The Revolt Against Civilization: The Menace of the Under Man* (1923) were popular reading on college campuses in the early 1920s. After Congress enacted a literacy test requirement for new immigrants, it went on to pass the Emergency Immigration Act in 1921 and the National Origins Act in 1924, which drastically restricted the numbers of immigrants coming into the US. Thus, while the nation became increasingly suspicious of the foreign 'other', a suspicion manifested in a wave of anti-immigration legislation, the *Dial* insisted on transnational networks of artistic production and consumption.

One of the signs of the *Dial*'s cosmopolitanism, and evidence, therefore, of its distinctive brand, was the literature in translation it published. The expert work of translators such as Kenneth Burke, Gilbert Seldes and Ezra Pound, among many others, meant that the writing of Arthur Schnitzler was featured from 1922; Louis Aragon's 'Madame à sa Tour Monte . . . ' appeared in January 1922, translated by Gilbert Seldes; Natalie Barney translated Paul Valery's 'An Evening with M. Teste' for the February 1922 issue; and while Pound's translation work ceased after Thayer fired him as Paris correspondent in 1923, he appeared regularly as a translator when he returned to the magazine under Moore's editorship. Translation of a range of material, Bulgarian, Flemish, Italian, Spanish and Russian was represented in the magazine alongside American and British modernists and those writers who have since disappeared into obscurity. No other magazine had the contacts, the resources or the ambition to publish so much work in translation.

Locating the modernist *Dial* in relation to contemporary periodical networks suggests that what Thayer and Watson were aiming for was a fusion of the *Seven Arts* with the higher-circulation 'quality' magazines such as the *Atlantic Monthly* or *Scribner's*. When it was rebranded in 1920 as a magazine for the arts, it brought with it a *Seven Arts* ethos described by Victoria Kingham as the view that art was a 'national, political and social instrument'.[40] It was not simply the case, in other words, that the *Dial* turned away from political controversy and was unwilling to engage in public debate.[41] It chose to engage in contemporary politics primarily through its assertion of cultural diversity. The *Dial*'s brand of cosmopolitanism is helpfully defined by Adam McKible in terms of both 'being at home in the world and understanding that the world is composed of myriad and discrete homes'.[42] Thus, the idea of a home-grown form of expression, of an aesthetic that emerges from what Van Wyck Brooks calls 'the indigenous voice', is combined with a renewed sense of interest and engagement with what lies outside or beyond the local environment. As

McKible points out, Maxwell Bodenheim's 'Modern Poetry', an essay which featured in the first issue of the Thayer/Watson *Dial* in January 1920, 'echoes Brooks and Oppenheim', two *Seven Arts* writers, in its assertion that the writer of new poetry must 'wrestle with the concrete forms about him'.[43]

Poetic *Otherness*

As a poet closely associated with *Others* magazine, the inclusion of Maxwell Bodenheim in the opening issue of the *Dial*, closely followed by Alfred Kreymborg, former editor of that magazine, in March 1920, Moore in April and William Carlos Williams in August of that year signals the *Dial*'s willingness to draw on the free-verse experiments that had found expression in *Others*. It also suggests that Thayer and Watson's vision of a transnational lively aestheticism intersected with a form of modernism that emerged out of a distinctly different environment from the elite social circles within which Thayer and Watson moved. That environment in Grantwood, New Jersey, where *Others* was produced offers a stark contrast to the elegance of Thayer's *Dial* dinner parties. Grantwood is vividly described by William Carlos Williams's biographer, Paul Mariani:

> [Kreymborg's hut] and the surrounding shacks became the meeting place for the younger New York artists every Sunday afternoon during the warm weather. There would be a business meeting, a picnic style lunch, a game of ball in the yard, attempts at conversation, some reading of one's own or others' poems, embarrassing silences, bad jokes, contacts. It was here in this most inauspicious of places that Williams first met some of the leading poets, painters, and critics of the day: Orrick Johns, Alanson Hartpence, Man Ray, Malcolm Cowley, Walter Arensberg, Mina Loy, Marcel Duchamp, Robert Sanborn, young Maxwell Bodenheim, and – most importantly – Wallace Stevens.[44]

Out of this unlikely and unglamorous environment came the first issue of *Others* in July 1915. Its pared down, simplistic format, the absence of extraneous material and the exclusive focus on poetry was, according to Kreymborg, 'a policy too chaste to appeal to any but the most private circles'.[45] It was not simply that the magazine was important as a way of making space for the new poetry; it was the social life that the magazine generated that proved to be so vital to poets such as Williams, Moore, Burke, Bodenheim, Loy and Kreymborg himself. As Suzanne Churchill and Ethan Jaffee point out, '*Others* enabled writers of free verse to recognize themselves and each other as poets, to identify free verse as a legitimate form of poetry, and to articulate more "sharply" the distinctive characteristics of the new form.'[46]

Though *Others* had initially been set up by Kreymborg and Walter Arensberg, a wealthy patron of the arts, Arensberg quickly gravitated towards a more European artistic milieu. Thus, in some ways, for Williams in particular and possibly for Moore, *Others* provided a social and textual space that did not privilege the European over the American. It was the shabbiness of the Grantwood environs and the no-frills, cheap production values of *Others* that functioned to signal the difference between the urbane sophistication of the Europeanised New York salon and the experiments of an emerging group of modernist poets adapting European influences to reflect upon local conditions. While many of the writers attended social events at Arensberg's apartment as well as gathering at Grantwood, the latter site of exchange indicated the ways in which the practices of the new emerging poets such as Moore, Williams, Bodenheim, Stevens and Loy were based on a publication and a collective experience that eschewed the patronage associated with salon culture.

Also, and perhaps more significantly, *Others* represented a group of writers who occupied a slightly different social class to the men connected to the *Harvard Monthly*. As Cristanne Miller has pointed out, most editors or associate editors of *Others* were either first- or second-generation immigrants. Kreymborg's father was a German immigrant, Williams's mother Puerto Rican, his father English, William Saphier was Romanian-born and Bodenheim's parents were immigrants from Germany and Alsace-Lorraine. This cultural heterogeneity was reflected in the magazine itself, which, according to Miller, 'had the closest ties to the city and [. . .] embraced a local poetics in ways distinct from some of the strains of international modernism', particularly as it was represented in the *Little Review*.[47] While the *Dial* had close ties to Bourne's transnational ideal, *Others* put that ideal into practice in its emphasis on the local as a site of energetic cultural hybridisation.

When it came into contact with the *Dial*, this local poetics worked to draw out the transnational nativism explored by Bourne and the *Seven Arts*. It served to distinguish the *Dial*'s cosmopolitanism from the *Little Review*'s internationalism. Crucially, *Others* was a magazine run by people living and working in and around New York and New Jersey. 'In contrast', Miller points out, 'many of the *Little Review*'s contributors lived outside the US, and the focus of its affiliation with foreignness resided in ancient cultures, European metropolises, expatriation or, as previously indicated, the concept of exile, not in immigrant populations'.[48] This fusion of *Seven Arts* transnationalism with native *Other*ness is best exemplified in the work of Kenneth Burke, a regular contributor to the pages of the *Dial* as well as occasional managing editor.

Burke was of the slightly younger generation of writers and critics such as Malcolm Cowley, whom he met at Peabody High School, and Matthew Josephson, whom he met at Columbia University, who were both born around the turn of the century. He studied at Ohio State, where he was tutored by Ludwig Lewisohn and worked on translations of Thomas Mann and Gustav Flaubert. He briefly attended Columbia before dropping out and moving to

Greenwich Village in 1918 to immerse himself in literary life. Yet even before he moved to the Village, he was aware of the experiments in poetry that were being published in *Others* from 1915.[49] His first publication, the free-verse poem 'Adam's Song, and Mine', was published in the magazine in 1916. Burke became part of the expanded *Others* crowd once he moved to the Village and met the writers and artists associated with the magazine (though not William Carlos Williams, whom he did not meet until 1921). Burke's main influences at this time, along with many of the writers of his generation, were the Symbolist poets whose free-verse forms, aestheticism and profound sense of alienation resonated with the post-war 'lost' generation. It was this Symbolist strain in Burke that must have attracted Watson to Burke's work, leading to his inclusion in the *Dial*. It seems appropriate that in July 1920 two of his short stories, 'The Excursion' and 'The Soul of Kajn Tafha' appeared just after Watson's translation of Rimbaud's *A Season in Hell*.

If the French Symbolist influence appealed to Watson, then Burke's profound interest and expertise in German literature, particularly the work of Thomas Mann, would have appealed to Thayer. Burke was one of the *Dial*'s most prolific translators of German material between 1921 and 1925. He not only translated Thomas Mann's *Death in Venice* in 1923, 'the hardest job of [his] life', but he also produced translations of Arthur Schnitzler, Heinrich Mann, Oswald Spengler and Hugo von Hofmannsthal.[50] It was Burke's interest in European culture along with his resistance to ex-patriotism and his engagement with free verse experimentation that signalled his *Other*ness. Yet he was not so closely allied to what Eric White refers to as the localist or indigenous avant-garde to identify fully with William Carlos Williams's aesthetic.[51] In fact, as he stated to Cowley in a letter written in December 1921, he found in Williams 'a superb adversary'.[52] Thus, while Burke and Williams were on good terms personally, Burke was more attracted to the continuities and connections across national boundaries, instinctively more transnational than Williams. Though Williams acknowledged his debt to Dada, as White has pointed out, he was determined to offer an alternative to what he saw as the *Dial*'s deference towards 'imported art'. Williams's thinly veiled attack on the *Dial* describes its cosmopolitanism as 'provincial in the worse sense because' it was 'wholly derivative'.[53] The establishment of *Contact* magazine with Robert McAlmon was an attempt to avoid the *Dial*'s superficial borrowings in the name of a false cosmopolitanism.

Burke was closer to Moore's position than to Williams's and the two formed a strong and lasting friendship when they worked together at the *Dial*. Moore recognised Burke's enormous contribution and frequently alluded to his cheerfulness and good humour in her letters. To Monroe Wheeler she noted 'his verve and enthusiastic loyalty to the office work' which she admitted was 'sometimes drudgery'.[54] It is clear that Burke often made Moore laugh. She recalls in a letter to Wheeler how Burke was able to decipher the instructions Thayer sends from Germany when no one else in the office can make sense of his handwriting, and to Glenway Wescott she describes him as a 'delightful companion-at-arms'.[55] It was Moore's idea to give Burke The Dial Award in 1929 for his 'faithfulness, discipline and literary susceptibility'.[56] Yet in addition to being willing to engage in 'drudgery', Burke's most important contribution to the magazine was his pioneering work in criticism. Not only did he offer insightful and original perspectives on Moore and Williams, he began to develop, particularly after 1925, a critical 'method' that was to offer an important alternative to the critical approaches emerging from I. A. Richards, T. S. Eliot (also included in the pages of the *Dial*) and the emerging new criticism associated with the Southern Agrarians. Indeed, if the *Dial* was a magazine of 'distinction' as its promotional material asserted, this was partly to do with its publication of a range of groundbreaking critical essays.

While Burke's age and education set him apart from the 'Dial crowd', Marianne Moore's gender set her apart. She was not from Harvard, though her Bryn Mawr education connected her to a network of influential women writers and patrons such as H.D. and Bryher. She was not from money, though, as her biographer has pointed out, her impoverished living arrangements were largely the result of her mother's frugality rather than financial scarcity. Moore met Thayer in 1920 at a party hosted by Lola Ridge, one of the *Others* poets, who had a party every time she sold a poem or an article. As Kreymborg, editor of *Others* remembers, the party went on until the early hours and at 'about two in the morning' Moore 'read something one could barely hear about "England with its baby rivers and little towns"'. Upon hearing this extraordinary poem, Thayer 'stole over to her and, after whispered consultation, induced her to part with it'.[57] Thayer may well have already had Moore in mind as a contributor, even though her work had previously been rejected; Linda Leavell speculates that Pound would have been urging Thayer to take Moore's work.[58] Undoubtedly a turning point in Moore's career, the arrival of Thayer at the party was, in a sense, prophetic. It signalled the way in which the *Dial,* a prestigious, higher-circulation magazine, began to take up the work of the 'little' modernist magazines and to promote the artists and writers who had struggled to get their work into print. As Kreymborg points out in his memoir, there was little need of an *Others* when the *Dial* had begun to publish the poetry of Moore, Williams, Kenneth Burke, Mina Loy, Maxwell Bodenheim and Kreymborg himself. Lola Ridge's modest gatherings were replaced, in Moore's social calendar, by the rather grand and formal dinner parties that Thayer hosted.

While it might be tempting to see Thayer's presence at the modernist party as evidence of the power of his extravagant patronage to colonise and co-opt the 'others', such a perspective misses the ways in which *Others* began to influence the *Dial* in subtle and significant ways. In other words, while the *Dial* was a higher-circulation magazine of 10,000 when *Others* only printed 500 copies, which Kreymborg and Williams couldn't shift, and while the former had the financial backing of Thayer and Watson, *Others* might be looked upon as a magazine that punched well above its weight; its cultural legacy was as important as the *Seven Arts* and this can be seen particularly in the issues that Moore edited.[59] Increasingly, writers such as Van Wyck Brooks, Evelyn Scott, Gilbert Seldes and Paul Rosenfeld became less prominent: Seldes contributed his regular theatre pieces but was not as closely associated with the magazine; Rosenfeld gave up his 'Musical Chronicle' in 1927; Evelyn Scott, who had been a regular from 1920, withdrew in 1928. Under Moore's editorship, William Carlos Williams was awarded The Dial prize in 1926, an emphatic statement of support for the poet who edited a number of issues of *Others* and was closely associated with the American free-verse movement that found its expression in that magazine.

Williams acknowledged the role that Moore played in the institutionalisation of modern poetry in his autobiography: 'She was like a rafter holding up the superstructure of our uncompleted building, a caryatid, her red hair plaited and wound twice about the fine skull . . . one of the main supports of the new order.'[60] That 'new order' was established through the *Dial* and, more specifically, Moore's editorial position at the magazine. While critics such as Robin Schulze and Suzanne Churchill have explored the influence of the *Dial* on Moore's career, the influence of Moore and her *Other*ness on the *Dial* has received less attention.[61] Within the pages of the *Dial* that *Other*ness was in dialogue with a Harvard aestheticism and a transnational 'lively' cosmopolitanism. As both Schulze and Churchill have pointed out, the formal elegance of Thayer and Watson's magazine effectively rebranded the modernism associated with *Others*, making poets such as Williams, Loy and Moore herself palatable to the cultural consumer more used to the conventions of regular rhyme and metre. But in turn, Moore's poetic *Other*ness underpinned her editorial practice and resisted, in subtle yet perceptible ways, the discriminations that reinforced modernism's institutionalisation.

'An Exit From the Marketplace'[62]

These discriminations, as numerous cultural historians have suggested, were bound up with what Michael Levenson describes as modernism's 'ascension to cultural legitimacy'.[63] Adam McKible sums up the importance of the magazine in terms of its ability to identify and disseminate the very best that modernism had to offer: 'Thayer and Watson's *Dial* is one of the great taste makers of the twentieth century. Its choices are still with us, and its decisions – which continue to influence literary histories, critical positions, and pedagogical practices – invite sustained interrogation and analysis.'[64] Yet how did the *Dial* acquire its powers of cultural consecration? Who or what consecrated the *Dial* and legitimised its authority? After all, its circulation figures have been estimated at 10,000 and even if we account for the common calculation made regarding periodicals, that for every person who buys the magazine you can add two more readers, 30,000 readers was still relatively low.[65] Compare this to the 2 million readers for the *Saturday Evening Post,* the most popular periodical of the 1920s.[66] Within the periodical market there were different styles of magazine and different constituencies of readers. The most popular magazines among the middle and upper classes were *Century*, *Harper's* and *Scribner's*, with circulations of around 50,000. David M. Earle provides the circulation figures of the filter magazines for modernism such as *Vanity Fair* at 81,856, *Scribner's* at 71,414 and the *Smart Set* at 31,262. But these magazines still did not reach the audiences that the all-fiction magazines of the 1920s did. As Earle points out, a number of fiction magazines came out in 1924 under the Smith and Street publication umbrella, magazines such as *Detective Story*, *Love Story* and *Western Story*, having a combined monthly distribution of 1,179,449. Earle estimates that the market percentage of the little magazines and the elite 'slicks' such as *Vogue* and *Vanity Fair* was something like 0.18%.[67]

Positioning the *Dial* in relation to the magazine marketplace of the 1920s illustrates just how unsuccessful it was in commercial terms. The 1920s saw a continuation of the expansion of print culture that had begun in the 1890s with *Munsey's Magazine*, *McClure's*, *Cosmopolitan* and the *Saturday Evening Post*. By 1923, there were over 3,000 magazines in circulation. Maureen Honey translates these figures in helpful way:

> the population of this time numbered around 114 million; only 60,000 homes possessed radios in 1922, yet as early as 1905 there was an average of four magazines to every household – a figure that increased dramatically over the ensuing twenty years. The mass-market magazine industry took root before the advent of the talking pictures in 1927, the dominance of the radio in the 1930s, and the explosion of high-quality, low-cost paperback books just prior to World War II, but these media, by all accounts, did not curtail readership, which continued to grow until the 1950s.[68]

To reiterate, the vast majority of the population were reading magazines but they weren't reading the *Dial*. As Faith Binckes suggests, however,

> even the littlest of the little magazines still participated in a textual environment that not only linked one article, or one journal to another but connected them as publications to mass-market newspapers, middlebrow literary reviews, illustrated magazines and journals devoted to self-education and improvement.[69]

In order to understand how the *Dial* became one of the most important taste makers of the twentieth century, it becomes necessary to go beyond the pages of the magazine itself to look at its image of distinction in relation to the wider print economies of modernity.

As the *Dial* correspondence reveals, while willing to invest thousands of dollars in the publication, Thayer and Watson were not intending to sink their money into a project that would have little cultural reach or impact and nor were they indifferent to the need to promote the magazine properly and to carve out a niche for themselves in a very competitive market. They borrowed techniques from their more commercial competitors recognising the importance of defining their product and stimulating consumer desire. In this respect, the *Dial*'s owners were rather like those modernist writers and editors who, as Mark Morrisson suggests, 'saw the new commercial magazine genres and the advertising that supported them as providing opportunities for modernism'.[70] The magazine constructed an image of its readers as 'cultivated', 'intelligent' consumers, reinforcing the notion of highbrow exclusivity, while at the same time, it subtly adopted the strategies of the 'standardized' publications from which it sought to distinguish itself.

The image of austere elegance it cultivated began with the magazine itself as a commodity. Its weight and texture, the smooth slickness of the half-tone reproductions and the grainy texture of the printed matter confirmed its high production values. The sober front cover, eschewing the loud graphic noise of more popular periodicals of the 1920s such as the phenomenally successful *Saturday Evening Post*, chose not to shout about its contents but simply provided the reader with a list of illustrious names that spoke for itself. Textual and visual material was presented in a format more akin to the limited-edition book than the periodical. Coloured frontispieces of modern art sat opposite the first page; generous margins, headers and footers produced a sense of space; advertisements at the front and back were discreet and subdued. The uncluttered design and muted style showcased the various and diverse forms of modernism reproduced within: The work of established visual artists such as Pablo Picasso, Paul Cezanne, Vincent van Gogh, Henri Matisse; the emerging new generation of painters, sculptors and cartoonists such as Joseph Stella, William Gropper, John Marin and Gaston Lachaise; the experiments in free verse by Ezra Pound, Marianne Moore, William Carlos Williams, e. e. cummings, Wallace Stevens and Hart Crane; the latest fiction by D. H. Lawrence, Mary Butts, Katherine Mansfield, John Dos Passos and Thomas Mann; memoirs by W. B. Yeats or Ford Madox Ford; the criticism of Kenneth Burke, Malcolm Cowley, Edmund Wilson and the regular reviews of theatre, music and art by Gilbert Seldes, Paul Rosenfeld and Henry McBride respectively.

When Thayer was in the process of buying the *Dial* in September 1918, he recognised that the magazine was 'in a worse mess than my apartment' and 'obviously bankrupt', a fact that didn't dim his enthusiasm for the venture.[71] Rather, he proposed a 'scheme of reform' which he presented to the magazine's then editor, Martyn Johnson, presumably paving the way for Thayer's eventual take-over of the magazine in 1919 with his partner, Sibley Watson Jr. The correspondence indicates that the intention was to make the *Dial* self-sustaining. As the business manager for the magazine, a Mr W. B. Marsh, explained to the owners in 1920, the magazine's income was not covering the cost of production. He suggests that an initial and very considerable investment will be required from the owners but that if managed properly, the paper can be self-supporting if not profitable. Marsh identifies advertising as the income stream capable of ensuring the magazine's success.[72] With this goal in mind, Ruth Stanley-Brown was employed as Advertising Manager at the magazine in 1920. Her education, connections and experience in the Macmillan Advertising Department recommended her for the position and is a further indication that the *Dial*, like its more commercial competitors and unlike the 'little' magazines such as *Poetry* and the *Little Review*, aimed to attract substantial advertising revenue to keep it in business.

Occupying a middle ground between the avant-garde and the middlebrow, the *Dial*, as Alan Golding suggests 'helped to canonize what the *Little Review* helped to discover'.[73] Yet as the business correspondence indicates, the aim was always to push circulation figures beyond the 'little' magazine market. The *Dial*'s circulation figures reached a peak at around 10,000, high for a 'little' magazine (the *Little Review* had a circulation of about 3,000) but low in comparison to the slicks (*Vanity Fair*) and the qualities (*Harper's*, *Century*, the *Atlantic Monthly*). The *Dial*'s business plan shows quite clearly that the ultimate objective was to make the magazine self-sustaining. Its marketing strategy was designed to sell the magazine to the luxury end of the magazine market whose readers had enough disposable income to spend on travel, high-end motor cars and high fashion clothing. The *Dial* was priced for that market, placing its advertisements in magazines that were a similar price. Ultimately, it aimed to attract the same advertising revenue as its rivals and thus, eventually, to wean itself off the patronage provided by its wealthy owners. Thus, the description of the *Dial* as 'little' has been misleading, implying as it does an indifference to the market, an indifference that reinforces that magazine's close association not only with modernism but with a particular construction of modernism as operating outside the constraints of market economics. Not only was the *Dial* rather ambitiously conceptualised as a magazine that would bring the best art and literature to a readership that extended beyond the elite coteries of little magazine culture, but paradoxically, it aimed to do this by selling modernism itself as the ultimate luxury commodity.

Re-launched in 1920, the *Dial* was branded as a magazine devoted, in Thayer's words, 'to the service of art and letters', moving away from its previous more politicised position.[74] Thayer had been involved in the magazine before he bought it in 1919 but was increasingly out of sympathy with the leftward turn it seemed to be taking, particularly in relation to Bolshevism.[75] His decision to move away from the overt political stance that the magazine had been adopting made sense as part of the wider ambition to avoid competition with the *Nation* and the *New Republic*. The former, edited by Oswald Garrison Villard, founding member of the NAACP and the ACLU, had waged war against the war-time suspension of civil liberties and offered a cogent critique of the post-war hysteria of the Red Scare. The latter, founded in 1914 by Herbert Croly and Walter Lippmann, was also one of the few magazines sympathetic to Communism and openly critical of government in the post-war period.[76] By 1920 both magazines had established formidable reputations and while their circulations were relatively low, from Thayer's point of view, there was no room for another left-leaning political journal. In other words, I would suggest that the motive for rebranding was underpinned by a desire to find a perceived gap in the magazine market.

In order to position itself in that market, however, an initial and substantial investment in advertising had to be made. Between 1920 and 1923, Thayer and Watson invested large sums of money in a promotional strategy that made the *Dial* visible to its target audience via the advertisements that appeared in a range of publications from the quality magazines such as *Harper's*, the *Atlantic Monthly* and *Century* to newspapers such as the *New York Times*, the *New York Herald*, the *New York Tribune*, the *Boston Globe*, the *Philadelphia Public Ledger*, the *Chicago Daily News* and the *Saturday Review*, as well as the *New Republic* and the *Nation*. These years also saw investment in advertising in periodicals published in Europe. For instance, advertisements appear in 1920 in *La France* and the *English Review*, in 1921 in the *Mercure de France* and the *Truam Herald*, in 1922 in the *Manchester Guardian* and *Der Querschnitt* (The Cross-Section)[77] and in 1923 in *Aufgang*. In addition, in a concerted effort to lure college students to subscribe, in 1922 the *Dial* placed advertisements in college magazines across the United States, from the *Palo Alto* at Stanford, to the *Cardinal* in Wisconsin and the *Cornell Daily Sun*. Women were also identified as potential consumers. In 1921 and 1922 advertisements were placed in *Women's Clubs in America*, the *Vassar Follies Program*, the *Woman Citizen* and *Birth Control Review*.

During this period, marketing campaigns around Christmas were devised in order to increase subscriptions. Those targeted as likely to consider such an investment were identified through Boni & Liveright lists. These literary types were sent a *Dial* Christmas card suggesting that the perfect gift for Christmas would be a subscription to the *Dial*. The tag line: 'The *Dial*: A Gift of Distinction for People of Discrimination' underlines its discursive identity.[78] While the magazine adopted, at various times, different ways of courting potential consumers, words such as 'refinement', 'authority', 'superior', 'fastidious', 'cosmopolitan', 'cultured', 'distinguished' and 'cultivated' were used consistently to reinforce that identity. A certain cultural cachet was referred to in the promotional material for the *Dial*, constructing the reader as a citizen of the arts. As an advertisement penned by Watson claimed, 'art and literature [. . .] beauty and ideas [. . .] are not a hobby for specialists but are the birthright and the deepest satisfaction of all intelligent or sensitive persons – of everyone, in short, who is worth talking to'.[79]

The subtext of this advertising copy suggests the position the *Dial* saw itself as occupying in the transatlantic marketplace; that position was somewhere between the European avant-garde 'specialist' magazine and the 'quality' magazine. Eschewing the elitism of 'specialists', yet implying that access to art and literature is only the 'birthright' of those 'worth talking to', manages to sound a democratic note while also maintaining an air of superiority. To read the *Dial* is to secure one's place within a particular cultural milieu that, according to the advertising copy, is self-selecting. Those who are 'intelligent' and 'sensitive' will require the kind of stimulation offered by the art and literature published in the magazine. Thus the consumer's identity as a citizen of culture, one capable of appreciating the best that culture has to offer is reinforced by the act of consumption itself.

Of course, this rhetoric masks the fact that a process of selection already took place at the point of purchase. Compared with other magazines, the *Dial* was an expensive product. While the *Little Review* cost 15 cents a copy, the price of the *Dial* at 50 cents per copy was considerably higher, making it a luxury item.[80] The *Dial* clearly aimed to compete not with the little magazines but rather with the higher-circulation quality magazines such as the *Atlantic Monthly* priced at 40 cents per copy in 1922 or the *American Mercury*, which cost the same as the *Dial* at 50 cents per copy. (Compare this to the most popular magazines of the day such as *Collier's National Weekly* which was 5 cents a copy.) Thus, while the *Dial* promoted itself and, by extension, art and literature as having an inherent value discernible only to the citizen of culture, that value could only be appreciated by those with the resources to subscribe to the magazine.

That there was a distinctive market for 'quality' magazines is confirmed by an advertisement placed in the *New York Times* in February 1922, which characterises the *Atlantic Monthly*, *Century*, *Harper's*, the *American Review of Reviews*, *Scribner's* and the *World's Work* as 'The Quality Group' and offers a discount to those who subscribe to all six (see Fig. 1.1). The advertisement offers a contrast in tone and style to the adverts produced by the *Dial*. Rather than emphasising cultural exclusivity, the ad for the qualities points to the large number of readers already appreciating these magazines: 'In fact, more than a million thoughtful, unusually successful people, who enjoy constructive thinking – who recognize high standards in literature and art, and the sciences,

Figure 1.1 'The Quality Group', advertisement, *New York Times*, 5 February 1922, 48.

now read these magazines.'[81] Reassuring the consumer that he or she is among a growing number of 'successful' people hints that these magazines are aimed at a middle-class consumer keen to acquire cultural capital. More importantly, the emphasis on value for money combines with a discourse that reassures the consumer that high circulations do not necessarily correlate to low status or low standards.

As David M. Earle points out in relation to his discussion of the pulps, *Century*, *Harper's* and *Scribner's* were the 'cultured triumvirate' of the magazine market and 'emulated the ideal of the educated man'.[82] In the late nineteenth century these magazines signified a 'high literary zone [. . .] targeted specifically at an elite, highly educated audience', according to Richard Brodhead.[83] By 1920, however, these magazines were also associated with what George Santayana had termed the 'genteel tradition'. The *Dial* did as much as it could to distance itself from that tradition while at the same time adopting similar marketing strategies to these magazines. Like its quality rivals, the *Dial* also offered its readers financial incentives to entice them to subscribe for a year. Rather than a simple discount, however, the *Dial* often promoted the notion that its literary expertise could benefit its readers in financial terms. For instance, recognising the attraction of a sound investment, the magazine offered 'a numbered copy of the limited first edition of Max Beerbohm's *Seven Men*. 'Max's first editions' the reader is informed, 'generally sell at high prices within a year after publication'. It goes on to add, almost as an afterthought, that Beerbohm's stories are also 'brilliant and witty'.[84] Literature, in this context, has become first and foremost a commodity capable of appreciating exponentially in value. Here the symbolic value of the art object is replaced by economic value; the reader of the *Dial* is no longer a consumer but a speculator keen to take advantage of what is presented as an insider's tip-off.

Six months after the initial report from the business manager, in July 1920 the owners of the *Dial* received an update concerning its financial viability that suggested a financial plan to cut costs. This involved cutting back on the number of free subscriptions offered as well as doubling the amount of advertising and reducing the fees for accepted manuscripts. The letter expresses 'optimism' concerning the venture, identifying the magazine's unique position in the market:

> If a continued effort can be made in this field, with true editorial sagacity, a sufficient reading public will almost certainly be developed in the course of three or four years, to make the magazine a valuable advertising medium for the modern type of books [,] paintings and other works of pure art, furniture and jewellery and other works of applied art [. . .] The life of practically every publication is dependent upon its advertising income.[85]

Thus, the challenge was to create a readership that would then provide, indirectly, the advertising revenue to keep the magazine afloat. While this may have been the theory behind the running of the *Dial*, it was, as Lawrence Rainey has shown, not the practice. He points to the deficits of $100,000 in 1920, $54,000 in 1921 and $65,000 in 1922, indicating just how much money both Watson and Thayer were pouring into the publication.[86] It is highly likely that much of this was going into the advertising budget.

While Thayer and Watson's patronage paid for the circulation of an image of modernism reinforcing its highbrow credentials, in commercial terms, this marketing strategy did little to increase circulation or attract paid advertising. This failure may well be due to the extent to which the magazine market changed between 1920, when Thayer and Watson launched the *Dial* and 1925, when Marianne Moore took over as managing editor. It was not only the *Dial* that struggled to attract high paying advertisers. *Century* magazine disappeared by the end of the decade, while *Harper's* and the *Atlantic* only survived by rebranding themselves.[87] The emergence of modernist reprints in popular digests and magazines in the 1920s meant that the qualities had considerable competition from publications such as the *Golden Book*, which was launched in 1925 and had acquired a circulation of 165,000 by 1926. It published work by Conrad, Anatole France, Katherine Mansfield, Eugene O'Neill, Lawrence, Swinburne, Anderson and Joyce.[88] By 1926, the literary supplement, the reprint digest, the Book of the Month Club and the *New Yorker* were all offering readers the 'best' literature in Europe and America, along with the expert guidance of professional reviewers and critics. The *Dial*'s commercial failure was, in large part, the result of its inability to compete with the vast array of periodicals that disseminated modernism at a more affordable price. But in an economic world upside down, this commercial failure was and continues to be the mark of the *Dial*'s success.

The response to the *Dial*'s closure in July 1929 confirms this. The news that it was going to cease publication became proof for many newspapers of its unwillingness to succumb to the pressures of the market. According to the *New York Times*, the magazine's 'great merit was that it took what it wanted and wasn't made to sell'.[89] The *Minneapolis Tribune* noted that the *Dial* 'seemed to revel in aloofness from the affairs of the mart'.[90] The *Nation* reinforced the idea of an indifference to commerce in its own tribute to the defunct magazine describing it as 'elegant, aloof, and uncompromisingly intellectual'.[91] The *Saturday Review of Literature* lamented the closure of the *Dial* in terms that the *Dial* itself frequently deployed to signal its cultural superiority:

> With the July issue, publication of *The Dial*, will be discontinued. *Miss Marianne Moore's* editorship has long conferred distinction upon it and

> we regret to hear of its passing. There has been no modern independent periodical published in America and many of its contributions in the past have been of the highest literary value.[92]

Crucially, by 1929, it is Moore who confers distinction on the *Dial* rather than the other way around. She is the cultural taste maker capable of guaranteeing 'literary value', of maintaining artistic independence in spite of the financial perils of doing so. Moore's cultural capital has increased through her association with the magazine to the point where her textual imprimatur supersedes the discursive signature of the *Dial*. The figure of 'Miss Moore', as I will suggest in the next chapter, becomes bound up with the aura of distinction that surrounded the magazine, even as Moore herself resisted the categorical distinctions reinforced by brow boundaries. That aura, cultivated in the advertising and promotion of the *Dial*, played a vital role in the institutionalisation of modernism in the 1920s and continued to reinforce modernism's symbolic value well beyond that decade. This is in spite of the fact that Thayer and Watson's journal published a great deal of material that falls outside most definitions of literary modernism.

Notes

1. Ernest Boyd, 'Aesthete: Model 1924', *American Mercury*, January (1924), 51–6 (p. 51).
2. Pierre Bourdieu, *The Rules of Art: Genesis and Structure of the Literary Field*, trans. Susan Emanuel (Cambridge: Polity Press, 1996, 2017), p. 63.
3. Boyd, 'Aesthete', pp. 54–5.
4. Matthew Philpotts, 'The Role of the Periodical Editor: Literary Journals and Editorial Habitus', *Modern Language Review*, 107 (2012), 39–64 (p. 42).
5. James Mussell, 'Repetition: "In Our Last"', *Victorian Periodicals Review* 48 (2015), 343–58 (p. 347).
6. James Dempsey, *The Tortured Life of Scofield Thayer* (Gainesville: University Press of Florida, 2014), p. 14.
7. Scofield Thayer to Elaine Orr, 5 February 1913, Beinecke, ST/Dial Papers, Series VII, Box 77, Fol. 2006.
8. Thayer to Orr, 18 March 1915, Beinecke, ST/Dial Papers, Series VII, Box 77, Fol. 2006.
9. Thayer to Orr, 5 February 1913.
10. Ibid.
11. Jonathan Freedman, *Professions of Taste: Henry James, British Aestheticism and Commodity Culture* (Stanford: Stanford University Press, 1993), p. 122.
12. Ibid.
13. Elizabeth Oliver, 'Aestheticism's Afterlife: Wallace Stevens as Interior Decorator and Disruptor', *Modernism/Modernity,* 15 (2008), 527–45 (p. 533). Jonathan Freedman makes a similar point in his study of British aestheticism arguing that a 'more self-consciously transgressive aestheticism began to grow in popularity and literary prominence, leading directly to the creation of the "modernist" avant-garde of the early nineteen twenties' (Jonathan Freedman, *Professions of Taste,* p. 123). See also Victoria Rosner, *Modernism and the Architecture of Private Life* (New York: Columbia University Press, 2005) and Jessica R. Feldman, *Victorian*

Modernism: Pragmatism and the Varieties of Aesthetic Experience (Cambridge: Cambridge University Press, 2002).

14. Dempsey, *Tortured Life*, p. 17.
15. Lewis Mumford probably had a good insight into the *Dial* as he married Sophia Wittenberg, who worked at the magazine from 1920 to 1924. Lewis Mumford, 'On The Dial', *New York Review of Books*, 20 February 1964. Available at: http://www.nybooks.com/articles/1964/02/20/on-the-dial (accessed 4 September 2018).
16. George Santayana, 'The Genteel Tradition in American Philosophy'. Available at: http://monadnock.net/Santayana/genteel.html (accessed 14 September 2017).
17. Michael Kammen, *The Lively Arts: Gilbert Seldes and the Transformation of Cultural Criticism in the United States* (New York and Oxford: Oxford University Press, 1996), pp. 86–7.
18. Ibid.
19. Gilbert Seldes, *The 7 Lively Arts* (New York: Harpers and Brothers, 1924; repr. New York: Dover, 2001), p. 319.
20. Ibid. p. 349.
21. Gilbert Seldes, 'Toujours Jazz', *Dial*, 75 (August 1923), 151–66 (p. 151).
22. Kammen, *The Lively Arts*, p. xvii.
23. Ibid.
24. Scofield Thayer, 'Comment', *Dial*, 69 (August 1920), 216–18 (p. 217).
25. Thayer, 'Comment', *Dial*, 74 (April 1923), 417–19 (p. 417).
26. Thayer, 'Comment', *Dial*, 69 (July 1920), 106–8 (p. 108).
27. Seldes, *Lively*, p. 245.
28. Dempsey, *Tortured Life*, p. xi.
29. Ibid. p. 127, p. 107.
30. Ibid. p. 149.
31. Sibley Watson, as W. C. Blum, 'Some Remarks on Rimbaud as Magician', *Dial*, 68 (June 1920), 719–32 (p. 722).
32. Gorham Munson, *The Awakening Twenties: A Memoir-History of a Literary Period* (Baton Rouge and London: Louisiana State University Press, 1985), p. 103.
33. Patrick Collier, 'Imperial/Modernist Forms in *The Illustrated London News*', *Modernism/Modernity*, 19 (2013), 487–514 (p. 496).
34. Barbara Ozieblo, 'Alyse Gregory, Scofield Thayer, and the "Dial"', *Twentieth Century Literature*, 48 (2002), 487–507 (p. 492).
35. Victoria Kingham, 'Audacious Modernity: *The Seven Arts* (1916–17); *The Soil* (1916–17); and *The Trend* (1911–15)', in *The Oxford Critical and Cultural History of Modernist Magazines, Vol. II: North American 1894–1960*, ed. Peter Brooker and Andrew Thacker (Oxford: Oxford University Press, 2012), pp. 400–19 (p. 400).
36. Munson, *Awakening Twenties*, p. 30.
37. Guy Reynolds, *Willa Cather in Context: Progress, Race, Empire* (Basingstoke: Palgrave, Macmillan, 1996), p. 93.
38. Scofield Thayer, 'Comment', *Dial*, 68 (March 1920), 408–10 (p. 409).
39. David J. Goldberg, *Discontented America: The United States in the 1920s* (Baltimore: Johns Hopkins University Press, 1999), pp. 154–5.
40. Kingham, 'Audacious Modernity', p. 400.
41. While Adam McKible's study of the transitional years of the *Dial* in *The Space and Place of Modernism: The Russian Revolution, Little Magazines, and New York* emphasises Thayer's increasing discomfort with the magazine's pro-Bolshevik stance between 1916 and 1918, he acknowledges 'that Thayer's resignation was also prompted by the magazine's staff's growing hostility toward Randolph Bourne', p. 158.

42. McKible, *Space and Place*, p. 66.
43. Maxwell Bodenheim, 'Modern Poetry', *Dial*, 68 (January 1920), 95–8, (p. 97).
44. Paul Mariani, *William Carlos Williams: A New World Naked* (New York: McGraw-Hill, 1981), p. 123.
45. Alfred Kreymborg, *Troubadour* (New York: Boni and Liveright, 1925), p. 183.
46. Suzanne Churchill and Ethan Jaffee, 'The New Poetry: *Glebe* (1913–14); *Others* (1915–19); *Poetry Review of America* (1916–17)', in *The Oxford Critical and Cultural History of Modernist Magazines, Vol. II: North American 1894–1960*, ed. Peter Brooker and Andrew Thacker (Oxford: Oxford University Press, 2012), pp. 299–319 (p. 307).
47. Cristanne Miller, 'Tongues "loosened in the melting pot": The Poets of *Others* and the Lower East Side, *Modernism/Modernity* 14.3 (2007), 455–76 (p. 456).
48. Ibid. p. 457.
49. Jack Selzer, *Kenneth Burke in Greenwich Village: Conversing with the Moderns* (Madison: University of Wisconsin Press, 1996), p. 62.
50. Kenneth Burke to Alyse Gregory, no date, Beinecke, ST/Dial Papers, Series I, Box 1, Fol. 25.
51. Eric White, *Transatlantic Avant-Gardes: Little Magazines and Localist Modernism* (Edinburgh: Edinburgh University Press, 2013), pp. 97–8.
52. Selzer, *Kenneth Burke*, p. 83.
53. White, *Transatlantic*, pp. 97–8.
54. Marianne Moore to Monroe Wheeler, 16 August 1925, Henry W. and Albert A. Berg Collection of English and American Literature, The New York Public Library, Astor, Lenox and Tilden Foundations, in m.b. Moore, M. 264 A.L.S., 13 A.N.S., 22 T.L.S. 3 T.N.S., 1 T.T. (copy), 12 postcards to Monroe Wheeler. [v.p., Feb. 24, 1923–Aug. 5, 1965]. Folder 5.
55. Marianne Moore to Glenway Wescott, 26 June 1925, Beinecke, ST/Dial Papers, Series I, Box 7, Fol. 275.
56. Marianne Moore to Sibley Watson Jr, 18 July 1928, Beinecke, ST/Dial Papers, Series I, Box 7, Fol. 273.
57. Alfred Kreymborg, *Troubadour* (New York: Boni and Liveright, 1925), pp. 332–3. Note that Churchill warns about taking Kreymborg too literally – Stevens and Moore could not have been at the same party.
58. Linda Leavell, *Holding On Upside Down: The Life and Work of Marianne Moore* (New York: Farrar, Straus and Giroux, 2013), p. 172.
59. Paul Mariani, *William Carlos Williams: A New World Naked* (New York: McGraw-Hill, 1981), p. 126.
60. William Carlos Williams, *The Autobiography of William Carlos Williams* (New York: MacGibbon and Kee, 1968), p. 146.
61. See Robin Schulze's introduction to *Becoming Marianne Moore* for a meticulous account of Moore's publication history.
62. 'An Exit From the Marketplace', *New Republic*, 12 August 1925, Beinecke, ST/Dial Papers, Series II, Box 17, Fol. 345.
63. Michael Levenson, *A Genealogy of Modernism: A Study of English Literary Doctrine, 1908–1922* (Cambridge: Cambridge University Press, 1984), p. 213.
64. Adam McKible, *The Space and Place of Modernism: The Russian Revolution, Little Magazines, and New York* (New York and London: Routledge, 2002), p. 60.
65. This figure is taken from a business report dated 23 January 1920. Beinecke, ST/Dial Papers, Series II, Box 13, Fol. 307. By 24 March 1928 the *Dial* print run was 6,500 copies, ST/Dial Papers, Series I, Box 7, Fol. 271.
66. Karen Leick, 'Popular Modernism: Little Magazines and the American Daily Press', *PMLA*, 123 (2008), 125–39 (p. 132).

67. David M. Earle, *Re-Covering Modernism: Pulps, Paperbacks, and the Prejudice of Form* (Burlington, VT: Ashgate, 2009), p. 64.
68. Maureen Honey, 'Feminist New Woman Fiction in Periodicals of the 1920s', in *Middlebrow Moderns: Popular American Women Writers of the 1920s*, ed. Lisa Botshon and Meredith Goldsmith (Boston, MA: Northeastern University Press, 2003), pp. 87–109 (p. 89).
69. Faith Binckes, *Modernism, Magazines, and the British Avant-Garde: Reading Rhythm, 1910–1914* (Oxford: Oxford University Press, 2010), pp. 12–13.
70. Mark Morrisson, *The Public Face of Modernism: Little Magazines, Audiences and Reception, 1905–1920* (Madison: University of Wisconsin Press, 2001), p. 10.
71. Scofield Thayer to Elaine Orr, 7 September and 14 September 1918, Beinecke, ST/Dial Papers, Series VII, Box 80, Fol. 2059.
72. Letter from Business Manager to Scofield Thayer and Sibley Watson, 23 January 1920, Beinecke, ST/Dial Papers, Series II, Box 9, Fol. 307.
73. Alan Golding, '*The Dial*, *The Little Review*, and the Dialogics of Modernism', *American Periodicals: A Journal of History, Critics and Bibliography* 15 (2005), 42–55 (p. 45).
74. Circular sent out from Scofield Thayer to those who had cancelled their subscriptions to the *Dial*. 11 February 1920, ST/Dial Papers, Beinecke, Series II, Box 9, Fol. 304.
75. McKible, *Space and Place*, p. 63.
76. John Tebbel and Mary Ellen Zuckerman, *The Magazine in America, 1741–1990* (Oxford: Oxford University Press, 1991), p. 204.
77. *Der Querschnitt* was a Frankfurt-based little magazine that published work by James Joyce, Ernest Hemingway and Ezra Pound, among others. See the introduction to Ernest Hemingway, *Complete Poems*, ed. Nicholas Gerogiannis (Lincoln: University of Nebraska Press, 1992).
78. 'The *Dial*: A Gift of Distinction', Beinecke, ST/Dial Papers, Series II, Box 9, Fol. 303.
79. Henry W. and Albert A. Berg Collection of English and American Literature, The New York Public Library, Astor, Lenox and Tilden Foundations, James Sibley Watson. Advertising and promotional materials (n.d.). James Sibley Watson/Dial papers. Series VII. Box 28. Versions of this advertisement appeared in *Harper's* and the *Arts* in July 1926.
80. Edward Bishop, 'Re-Covering Modernism: Format and Function in the Little Magazines', in *Modernist Writers and the Marketplace*, ed. Ian Willison, Warwick Gould and Warren Chernaik (London: Macmillan, 1996), pp. 287–319 (p. 311). Bishop compares the costs of the *Dial* and the *Little Review* but he refers to the price of the *Dial* in 1920. As Joost points out, its price had increased from 35 cents in 1920 to 50 cents by 1921 (p. 30).
81. 'The Quality Group', Display advertisement, *New York Times*, 5 February 1922, p. 48.
82. Earle, *Re-Covering Modernism*, p. 61.
83. Richard Brodhead, *Culture of Letters: Scenes of Reading and Writing in Nineteenth Century America* (Chicago: University of Chicago Press, 1993), p. 140.
84. Berg, JSW/Dial Papers, James Sibley Watson. Advertising and promotional materials (n.d.). Series VII. Box 28.
85. Henry W. Toll to Scofield Thayer, 8 July 1920, Berg, JSW/Dial Papers, Series VII. Box 28.
86. Lawrence Rainey, *Institutions of Modernism: Literary Elites and Public Culture* (New Haven, CT: Yale University Press, 1998), p. 94.
87. Tebbel and Zuckerman, *Magazine in America*, p. 200.

88. Earle, *Re-Covering Modernism*, p. 68.
89. 'Great Merit', *New York Times*, 31 May 1929, Beinecke, ST/Dial Papers, Series II, Box 17, Fol. 346.
90. 'Aloofness from Affairs of the Mart', *Minneapolis Tribune*, 7 June 1929, Beinecke, ST/Dial Papers, Series II, Box 9, Fol. 306.
91. 'The Disappearance of the Dial', *Nation*, 19 June 1929, Beinecke, ST/Dial Papers, Series II, Box 17, Fol. 346.
92. 'Publication of the Dial Discontinued', *Saturday Review of Literature*, 8 June 1929, Beinecke, ST/Dial Papers, Series II, Box 17, Fol. 346.

2

EDITORIAL AGENCY: PERFORMING 'MISS MOORE'

In her reminiscence, '*The Dial*: A Retrospect', Moore herself alludes to what might be described as the 'institutional habitus' of the magazine. As well as listing the illustrious names whose works were showcased in the magazine, Thomas Mann, W. B. Yeats, D. H. Lawrence, e. e. cummings, Ezra Pound, T. S. Eliot, Wallace Stevens and H.D., among other writers, and Arthur Dove, John Marin, Constantin Brancusi, Gaston Lachaise, Pablo Picasso, Jean Cocteau and Georgia O'Keeffe, among many visual artists, she ensures that all the regular contributors are given an honorary mention. Alyse Gregory's 'delicate lethal honesty', Henry McBride's 'punctuality and his punctuation', Ezra Pound's 'precision' as a translator, Padraic Colum's 'clemency' and the 'undozing linguistics and scholarly resourcefulness of Ellen Thayer' are noted alongside Kenneth Burke, Gilbert Seldes and Paul Rosenfeld as 'contributing editor-critics'.[1] When referring to Watson and Thayer, however, Moore produces one of those sentences that reveals much about her sense of the relation between the owner-editors and the magazine they created:

> Above all, of an inflexible morality against the 'nearly good'; for a non-exploiting helpfulness to art and the artist, for living the doctrine that 'a love of letters knows no frontiers,' Scofield Thayer and Dr. Watson are the indestructible symbol.[2]

It is the owners who become 'symbolic' while the magazine itself is 'living'. Moore emphasises working as part of a team, 'an organisation' that she, among others, represented as well as being bound to a set of 'indestructible' shared values. This is signalled in the syntax of the sentence where Moore points to the influence of Thayer and Watson. The unchanging, 'inflexible' principles underpinning the magazine and its choices, its generosity, financial and symbolic, to art and artists and its 'doctrine' supporting an unbounded faith in art precede the names of the men whose patronage paid for the *Dial*. In other words, Moore's sentence downplays the role of individuals and even the importance of money in the making of modernism; instead, she foregrounds abstract nouns, 'an inflexible morality' and 'a love of letters'. The institutional habitus of the *Dial* is reinscribed through Moore's memoir: the magazine is not simply a transparent display case showcasing modernism; it is a mediating object, a cultural agent in its own right. Marek has rightly suggested that the effect of Moore's retrospective essay is to 'effac[e] herself by posing as merely part of the staff', but she does so not out of modesty but rather to signal the enabling and constraining effects of the magazine itself as an institution with its own special and inflexible requirements.[3]

While Moore emphasises the magazine's institutional power, contributors recalling their *Dial* days remember Moore's personal authority. For instance, the poet e. e. cummings sees a photograph of Moore and is 'startled' into a memory that reveals much about her editorial style (see Fig. 2.1):

> Did either of you (incidentally) ever glimpse a remarkably flimsy 'portrait' of Miss Moore by Carl Van Vechten, which she thinks incompara-

Figure 2.1 Carl Van Vechten, *Portrait of Marianne Moore*, 1948. Library of Congress, Prints and Photographs Division, Carl Van Vechten Collection [LC-USZ62-42513]

> ble? I was really startled: until that 'cuspidor' incident jumped into my consciousness and I saw wee me friendlessly cowering in The Dial while its editor lectured (some 45 minutes) against 'spittoon.' Yet I love the lady still.[4]

Writing in 1950 to Hildegarde Watson, wife of the co-owner of the *Dial*, many years after the magazine had ceased publication, Moore's photographic image reminds cummings of a scene of chastisement at the *Dial.* Moore had objected to cummings's use of the word 'spittoon', arguing for what she perceived to be the more accurate term, 'cuspidor' as a substitute. While he checks himself, 'Yet I love the lady still', aware that Hildegarde Watson is close friends with Moore, his comic portrayal of his emasculation at the hands of this 'lady' editor strikes a familiar note. Similar anecdotes have served as evidence of Moore's fastidiousness when it came to editing the work of others, a fastidiousness that has been conflated with old-fashioned gentility. Perhaps more revealing, however, is the brief glimpse we get into Moore's editorial and managerial style: Her extraordinary eye for detail singling out the word 'spittoon' as a vulgar imprecision; her remarkable breadth of knowledge demonstrated by her ability to lecture on the word for 45 minutes and the cultural authority that comes with her position as editor. At the offices of the *Dial* it is cummings, formerly poetic doyen of the *Dial*, who is friendless, while Moore has the institutional and bureaucratic support of the magazine behind her.

Cummings must have seen the photographic portrait of Moore taken by Carl Van Vechten in 1948 (see Fig. 2.1). Moore looks just to the left of the viewer, one hand clasping the other in a pose that echoes many other portraits of her. Describing a much earlier photographic portrait taken of Moore around 1920 at the Sarony studio, Stacy Carson Hubbard notes the poet's 'impossibly curving, beautifully elongated and conspicuously posed left hand'.[5] A similar effect is achieved in Van Vechten's photograph. Sporting her signature style black cape and bow tie, hair wound tightly around her head, Moore stands before an imposing wall of books, her elegant left hand delicately clasping the right. In the right hand, as in the Sarony portrait, Moore holds a pair of gloves. Van Vechten's photograph has Moore's hands engaged in an act of double clasping: the left hand holds the right wrist while the right hand holds a pair of gloves. The effect is to contrast the delicacy of the left hand with the iron grip of the right that clenches into a fist around the gloves. As Hubbard suggests, 'the fiercely tense quality of the right hand [is] in contrast to the artful repose of the left'.[6] Perhaps the photograph reminds cummings of Moore's masculine challenge to his previously privileged position at the *Dial*, an occasion when the gloves, those emblems of feminine gentility and propriety, were off.

Hubbard draws attention to the various ways in which Moore is engaged in a form of self-styling in these photographic portraits; most suggestive is the possibility that Moore had in mind Bronzino's Renaissance portrait of a young aristocrat when she posed for the Sarony portrait. She repeatedly wore versions of the same outfit: bow tie, shirt, cloak and, particularly in her later years, a tricorn hat. She contributed to the construction of her public image in these portraits, staging an identity that was ambivalently gendered in an attempt to resist being cast in the role of prim poetess. In family correspondence, Moore adopted a masculine nickname based on the character of Mr Rat in *The Wind in the Willows*.[7] Susan McCabe suggests in her discussion of Moore's collaboration with the writer Bryher a 'mutual identification of female masculinity' between the two writers.[8] Relating these observations to cummings's scene of shame, it may be that the portrait reminds cummings of what might be described as Moore's editorial queerness. Quite literally, on the one hand, there is the delicacy and deftness of touch figured in the beloved lady's elegant, feminine fingers, and on the other, the powerful punch and masculine authority that comes with editing such an important modernist magazine. Cummings's assurance to Hildegarde Watson that even after seeing the portrait and remembering his own humiliation, he 'love[s] the lady still' takes on additional significance in this context. If Moore is still loved by a straight man, then her queerness becomes less threatening. The power of his desire restores his heteronormative privileges and puts Moore firmly in her place as the object of his platonic love.

Moore's troubling queerness has stimulated similar responses in accounts of her editorial influence. There is a need both to feminise Moore and to explain her decisions in terms of a frustrated or blocked desire. This heteronormative critical framework repeatedly emphasises what Ezra Pound referred to in a letter to William Carlos Williams as Moore's 'spinsterly aversions', contributing to the notion that her editorial interventions were expressions of a form of feminine sexual frustration.[9] This critical discourse not only pathologises Moore and serves to marginalise her contribution to modernism, but more significantly, it edits out the role the modernist magazine plays in the production of the modernist editor. 'Miss Moore', as the public face of modernism was, like her portraits, complex and collaboratively constructed. The image of Moore that was in circulation just before, during and many years after the *Dial* ceased publication, aligns with the image of distinction that the magazine deployed to promote itself and, by extension, modernism. In fact, the fetishisation of 'Miss Moore' bears some resemblance to the fetishisation of the modernist art object: both are described in term of purity, detachment and integrity.

The following discussion constructs an alternative portrait of 'Miss Moore' as both agent and effect of magazine production. While Ann Ardis considers how authorship might be conceptualised in the context of the 'deliberately and complexly authorial environment' of periodical publication, the following discussion of Moore figures editorial agency in similar terms.[10] The *Dial*'s image of distinction was partly transmitted through Moore. She maximises the *Dial*'s capital through her performance of 'Miss Moore', the intellectual high-brow whose tastes range from baseball to Milton, who refuses to take sides or to privilege one school or artistic movement and who prefers 'restraint' to self-expression. She represented to the reader an aesthetic integrity that aligned with the magazine's declaration that it was immune from the pressures of the marketplace. Moore seemed to embody the principles enshrined within the pages of the *Dial*, principles that were articulated by Thayer in the articles he wrote in the *Dial* announcing Moore as recipient of The Dial prize. In a sense, 'Miss Moore' precedes Moore's editorial performance, shaping and determining the role and critical assessments of it. Moore's decisions were bound up with the institutional habitus of the *Dial*, its image of 'distinction', its aura of high-hat sophistication. The cultural capital that came with being the editor of the magazine was enabling, as cummings's letter to Hildegarde Watson suggests, but it was also constraining. More significantly, Moore herself was caught up in the image of cultural distinction circulated in and through the magazine. Moore was thus not only making editorial decisions that were central to the production of modernism but she was also engaged in a public performance as editor of the *Dial* that aligned with its promotional material. 'Miss Moore' became the public face of modernism, the signifier of integrity and aesthetic 'intensity', the embodiment of a brand that ultimately had little to do with her own values or principles.

It is these early incarnations of Moore as charismatic modernist artist, immune from the corrupting pressures of the marketplace that signal how Moore's editorial agency intersected with and reinforced modernism's institutionalisation. The fusion of 'Miss Moore' with the magazine's ethos gave the impression of unity, a seamless alignment between editor and the institutional habitus of the magazine. But behind the scenes, Moore worked frantically to ensure the smooth running of the *Dial*. The editorial labour, what Jaffe describes in terms of 'downstream work' that circulates around the modernist art object to secure its symbolic value, is hidden behind the image of the *Dial* as a cultural taste maker.[11] The following discussion of editorial agency takes into account, therefore, not only the image of aristocratic distinction attached to Moore and the magazine but also what that image concealed: the everyday 'drudgery' of the administrative and secretarial work undertaken by Moore and those who worked in the office with her, Moore's managerial style, the editorial skirmishes with contributors as well as her resistance, in different ways, to the authority of the owners of the magazine, Thayer and Watson.[12]

'THE PALM TREE'S THE THING'

> The Palm Tree's the thing. I doubt that there's any rat in the world that so affectionates its Tree. It pores over its 'pieces,' it 'wonders?' it *b'lieves* it's got something that with 'fixing' will 'do'! Very jubilant. Then it writes; tick-tacks; sends to 'doctor' [Sibley Watson]; sends to the author; – sends to press; reads and re-reads in proof; alters; sends to author; then when the mag. is out? O me! Every ad and paragraph is scrutinized and read. It is held off and held near. It is now an exaltation – now a depth of endless descent into woe and disgrace. Were The Dial a human creature it would be honoured in having such unending solicitude bestowed upon it.[13]

In this extract from a letter by Moore's mother, she nicely captures her daughter's (rat's) absorption in the routines of periodical production, the pleasures as well as the frustrations, the emotional turmoil as well as the intellectual challenge. She also signals that from the top of her tree, Moore occupies an elevated position within the restricted field of literary production. While there is affective fall-out, 'exaltation' and 'woe' as well as intense labour, there is also a certain sense of order and efficiency. Contrast the routine of Moore's *Dial* work with the 'bohemian chaos' of Ford Madox Ford's office at the *English Review* described by Douglas Goldring in *South Lodge*.[14] It is hardly surprising that Ford's lack of organisational and financial management meant that manuscripts frequently went astray. Ford may have brought with him the kind of cultural capital few editors enjoyed, family connections to the Victorian pre-Raphaelites together with friendships with H. G. Wells, Joseph Conrad and Henry James, but his lack of practical skills proved fatal for his publication.

In his typology of editors of modernist magazines, Ford is Matthew Philpotts's example of the charismatic editor whose powers of cultural consecration are acquired largely through his affinity with the charismatic image of the pure artist. As such, Ford's lack of organisation and his notorious financial incompetency created an aura around his editorship that reinforced its symbolic value and its cultural capital. Ford's apparent ignorance of the literary marketplace perfectly suited an economic universe turned upside down. By contrast, the figure of T. S. Eliot serves as Philpotts's example of the mediating editor par excellence; one who is both charismatic but also has the skills and competencies to run a modernist magazine without incurring unforeseen costs. Eliot had commercial experience from working at Lloyds Bank; crucially, as a highbrow modernist poet, he also came with his own cultural capital and understood the inversions of the literary marketplace.

Moore, like Eliot, was better prepared for the secretarial, administrative and managerial work of running a magazine. She also came with professional competences that turned out to be very useful to her as an editor. She learnt stenography and typewriting at Carlisle Business College and in 1911 worked for Melvil Dewey at his Lake Placid Club in the Adirondacks, taking dictation, proof reading and dealing with correspondence. After this, she taught commercial arithmetic and bookkeeping, along with typing, stenography and commercial English at the Carlisle Indian School for two years. When Moore and her mother moved to Greenwich Village, she had a part-time position at the Hudson Park Library and worked there until taking up her editorial position at the *Dial.*[15] Once in post, Moore was willing and able to acquire additional skills such as working the switchboard and even helping the janitor re-upholster one of the office chairs.[16]

Adapting Bourdieu's concept of habitus, Philpotts grants more agency to the editor, concluding that the dual personage model of habitus misses the complex nature of dispositions and the plurality of social contexts within which they are performed.[17] Those complexities become particularly evident when editorial agency is gendered. In the early twentieth century, there were many women editors, particularly in the United States, engaged in the important downstream work of publishing and disseminating modernism. Harriet Monroe, Alice Corbin Henderson, Margaret Anderson, Jane Heap, Jessie Fauset, Gwendolyn Bennett, Lola Ridge, Moore and Alyse Gregory at the *Dial* all occupied editorial positions at important literary and political journals. This raises questions concerning Bourdieu's concept of habitus and Philpotts's typology. How do these women manage to develop the masculine habitus that enables them to compete in the cultural field? To what extent are these women 'passing' as men in their positions of authority as editors? To what extent, to paraphrase Toril Moi, are women editors reproducing the forms of symbolic violence that legitimate male power? [18] As editor at the *Dial*, Moore had a complex relation to her powers of cultural consecration. Unlike Thayer and Seldes, Moore used her editorial comments not to attack various 'tribes' or to denigrate the 'standardization' of culture but to list, to catalogue, to collect 'without exaggeration'.[19] The tone and content of Moore's editorials replace Thayer's *Yellow Book* aestheticism with a strikingly different attitude, one that maintains the notion of the magazine as a site of cultural consecration, akin to the space of a museum but that also challenges the hierarchies reinforcing the symbolic value of the modernist art object.

In order to think further about the relation between editorial agency and gender, it is useful to compare Moore's editorial performance to Margaret Anderson's not simply because Anderson was a woman editor but because her role at the *Little Review* has been conceptualised in relation to a performative femininity. As Elizabeth Francis suggests, Anderson,

> used her beauty, her sense of style, and her disregard of all things conventional to create a buzz – the impression that the *Little Review* was on the

> cutting edge of the cultural renaissance in Chicago and later, New York. Anderson fashioned herself and her activities into symbols of avant-garde aspirations and pretensions, an early version of what we would now call 'celebrity'.[20]

The notion of self-fashioning is pushed a little further by Alan Golding in his essay on the *Little Review* for Brooker and Thacker's *Oxford Critical and Cultural History of Modernist Magazines*. For Golding, Anderson's 'well-known charisma, insouciant charm, and radical individualism [are] not simply [. . .] personal attributes but [. . .] performative aspects of a modernist ideology'.[21] The shift from the personal to the performative opens up the subversive potential of the editorial role to challenge or disrupt the implicitly masculine cultural authority of highbrow modernism.

As Van Vechten's photograph suggests, Moore's editorial performance might look, in comparison to Anderson's, a little more staid, a little less stylish, cleaving to a conventional femininity that looks backwards to the old-fashioned virtues of propriety and decorum rather than forwards to a progressive feminism. But as cummings recognised, in some ways Moore is playing a different and to a certain extent more subversive game. While Anderson performs and modernises a new version of femininity through the aesthetics of an assertive and independent form of self-expression, Moore's editorial performance of an aesthetic purity detached from the pressures of the marketplace put into circulation a model of avant-garde feminism that challenged the misogynist tropes of modernism and, more fundamentally, queered femininity itself. While in subsequent chapters, I will discuss Moore's personal resistance to the sexist assumptions embedded in the criticism and poetry of her modernist male peers, here I am deploying the concept of performativity in order to understand the editorial role of 'Miss Moore'.

Of course, it was Judith Butler who introduced the concept of performativity as a way of thinking about agency in terms of gender. Butler's debt to Bourdieu's concept of habitus is noted by Terry Lovell in her illuminating article, 'Resisting with Authority: Historical Specificity, Agency and the Performative Self'. As Lovell suggests, both habitus and performativity recognise the 'hold of institutional norms through practice' but both also seek to retain the possibility of agency. If habitus is a form of practice then it depends upon repetition for its reproduction. Butler sees this 'logic of iterability' as a fundamental flaw or weakness in the process of socialisation. It is in the act of repeatedly performing social roles that the possibility of slippage occurs. It is unlikely that every performance is identical; in the spaces or gaps between performances, as Lovell explains, social forms 'are reproduced but may be reproduced awry, or with a difference'.[22] According to Butler, the body itself mediates and sometimes misdirects social norms: 'What is bodily in speech resists and confounds the very norms by which it is regulated.'[23] The question then is how such performances accrue an authority that makes them performative rather than simply performances, how do such acts effect change and/or become transgressive. For Butler, charismatic individual performances are capable of disrupting socially embedded performatives. Butler draws on the inspirational example of Rosa Parks for an instance of a performance that transgresses with authority.[24]

If performativity depends for its effect upon the power of social institutions as well as the habitus that reinforces that power as Bourdieu suggests, then Moore's editorial agency had a performative power. That power was not simply in the service of the social production of the cult of predominantly masculine artistic genius. Moore's charismatic editorship of the *Dial* found ways to destabilise the hierarchies underpinning categorical distinctions separating culture into high-, middle- and lowbrow. I would argue that Moore practises a form of transgressive authority through her performance of 'Miss Moore', a performance that reinforced the institutional authority of the *Dial* but that also challenged that authority. Cristanne Miller's study of Moore's poetry in terms of its various and complex questioning of authority through 'structures of negation, contradiction and multiple surfaces' suggests Moore's personal antipathy towards dominant Western literary traditions and the concepts of 'genius, nature and supernatural inspiration' that underpin those traditions.[25] My own discussion considers not only how as editor of the *Dial* Moore questioned its authority, but how the social production of 'Miss Moore' gave her, paradoxically, the institutional power to do so. The public figure of 'Miss Moore' successfully rearticulated the institutional habitus of the magazine while simultaneously and subtly undermining the rules of the game.

To return to cummings's reminiscence, it might be that Moore's queerness is related to this unsettling paradox. Cummings is startled by the photographic image of 'Miss Moore' because it reminds him of her extraordinary and disruptive power at the *Dial*. To paraphrase Butler in *Excitable Speech*, that queer image of Moore speaks eloquently, articulating something that falls outside official discourse. While 'Miss Moore' is performed, staged and arranged in such a way as to repeat some of the familiar tropes associated with her as a poet and editor: delicacy, erudition, integrity and cultural authority, in the enactment of that feminine propriety she exceeds the boundaries of its representation. Thus, while Moore's poetry and Moore herself is constructed by Thayer and Alfred Kreymborg and numerous other critics as aesthetically pure, immune from the pressures of commerce, its reiteration produces multiple and legitimate opportunities to deconstruct 'Miss Moore' as an icon of the aesthetic purity that she embodies. Periodical form, with its dependence upon repetition, becomes an ideal site within which to practise a form of transgressive cultural authority.

Editorial Queerness

Thinking about the queerness of Moore's editorial role helps to explain the critical paradigm that has emerged to explain and diminish her influence. Cummings's anecdote, gentle and humorous, has been less influential than Hart Crane's famous description of Harriet Monroe and Moore as 'hysterical virgins' an extreme example of the way in which, as Benjamin Kahan has suggested, Moore's censoring powers have been collapsed into her celibacy.[26] John Vincent has described the ways in which Moore's editorial revisions to Hart Crane's poem have been explained in terms of an overbearing, interfering feminine fussiness, a kind of 'Miss Manners gone berserk'.[27] Similar anecdotes have served as evidence of Moore's fastidiousness when it came to editing the work of others, a fastidiousness that has been conflated with a belatedness, an old-fashioned gentility. As Natalie Cecire has argued, while Pound's poetry is associated with 'sincerity' and Zukofsky's with 'objectification', Moore's 'precision' is characterised as constraining rather than enabling.[28] When it comes to assessments of Moore's editorial role at the *Dial* a similar critical paradigm emerges. Moore's editorial judgements, like Harriet Monroe's at *Poetry*, were often interpreted as evidence of a genteel resistance to the new and implicitly masculine and modernist art forms seeking venues for publication.[29] Either an uncomfortable silence surrounds her editorial decisions as if, like cummings, scholars are reluctant to cause offence by questioning the scruples of a national treasure, or, in order to contain Moore's editorial power; it is gendered as a form of feminine fussiness. The result is that Moore's passion for precision has been tacitly related to a sense that the *Dial* lost some of its institutional clout when she was its editor.

Suspicion concerning Moore's editorial judgements has reinforced the notion that 'Miss Moore' presided over and indeed contributed to the *Dial*'s decline. Referring to Moore's rewriting of Hart Crane's 'The Wine Menagerie', John Unterecker suggests that 'under the pressures of poverty, [. . .] Crane tamed his emulsion – and Marianne Moore tamed the whole magazine'.[30] In his study of Kenneth Burke, Jack Selzer comes to a similar conclusion arguing that the magazine lost its 'compelling Continental flavour' once Thayer had left, this, combined with diminishing resources, eventually led to its closure in 1929. Yet while Selzer clearly wishes to avoid attributing blame, Moore's 'celebrated misjudgements' concerning Joyce and Crane are noted.[31] William Wasserstrom also speculates that if Moore had published Joyce's 'Anna Livia Plurabelle' in 1927, the magazine's fortunes may well have been revived: 'For want of a *Dial*, we're tempted to say, *Finnegans Wake* was lost to America; for want of a Joyce, The *Dial* was lost.'[32] More recently and in the wake of the rise of periodical studies, Alan Golding asserts that the magazine was 'at its liveliest and best while Pound exercised some influence on its editorial policy and gathering of material'.[33]

Golding reinforces the general tendency, initiated by Laurence Rainey's study of the *Dial*'s role in the institutionalisation of modernism, to focus on the early years of publication. That tendency effectively bypasses the period when Moore was editing the *Dial* and, albeit inadvertently, continues to reinforce the sense that the magazine was less important under Moore's editorial leadership.

There is little concrete evidence, however, to support the notion that Moore's editorial influence contributed to a decline in quality or cultural authority. Moore's rejection of Joyce and her rewriting of Crane have obscured many other aspects of her editorship: her reinstatement of Pound, her publication of Stein and the numerous examples of editorial revisions that were gratefully received or even solicited. With the expansion of the magazine market, even modernist magazines, if they wanted to survive, were obliged to think of ways of extending their readership. This resulted in many magazines doing exactly what the *Dial* did: publishing what was traditional and familiar as well as the new. Criticism of Moore's editorship for being 'tame' look less convincing when journals such as the *Athenaeum*, the *Adelphi*, *Voices*, the *Monthly Chapbook* and even the *Criterion* were equally cautious about investing too much in art forms that might alienate their already limited readerships.[34]

The marginalisation of Moore in accounts of the institutionalisation of modernism are also probably related to a squeamishness concerning her editorial interventions. In her discussion of the *Dial* for the *Oxford Critical and Cultural History of Modernist Magazines*, Christina Britzolakis describes Moore's 'insistence on the productive role of the magazine in the final textual form of its contents', pointing out that some, though not all, contributors were 'offended by this interventionist policy'.[35] According to the editors of Moore's *Selected Letters*, she had a 'penchant for revising the work of her contributors rather than simply accepting or rejecting it'.[36] Moore's letters and the *Dial* archives reveal this to be the case. Moore not only required contributors to make the kinds of cuts necessary to conform to the limitations of page space, but she made very specific and detailed suggestions that enforced what I will go on to describe in terms of textual contractility. Moore's 'scrupulous' approach is figured here as unusual, as evidence that Moore took a different line to other modernist editors.[37]

It is difficult, however, to make such assertions without adopting a comparative approach. Undoubtedly, Moore took a different line to Watson but she was not so different to Van Wyck Brooks at the *Freeman*. Unbeknown to Moore, Thayer and Watson initially offered the editorship of the *Dial* to Brooks. In a letter to Scofield Thayer written in 1920, Sibley Watson praises the writer, Van Wyck Brooks, but disapproves of his editorial style at the *Freeman*:

> Thought Brooks very agreeable but also very much of an editorial editor. He shocked me by saying one must be very rigorous with authors and

> rewrite their stuff when necessary like Ellery Sedgwick, by God! [. . .] I am told that people complain that their stuff is considerably changed when it comes out in The Freeman.[38]

Clearly, the idea of an editor rewriting the work of contributors appalled Watson. He and Thayer had a policy of either rejecting or accepting a work without demanding extensive changes. The correspondence between Watson and Moore reveals the extent to which her approach differed from Watson's. He frequently warned her about suggesting extensive revisions, particularly when the contributor could not 'talk personally with you or comprehend easily' the changes suggested.[39] Watson tried to prepare Moore for the consequences of her 'emendations' to Crane's 'The Wine Menagerie' in November 1925, conceding that her changes are 'very fine' but that Crane may 'prove unreasonable'.[40] Likewise, though he approved of Moore's changes to Paul Rosenfeld's essay, Watson was aware that 'Mr Rosenfeld will no doubt speak hastily of us'.[41]

Thayer, however, was more inclined to interfere. There is evidence in the *Dial* archives that he would occasionally ask contributors to make significant changes that cannot be attributed to the material constraints of magazine publication.[42] Thayer was also notoriously harsh and unforgiving when it came to identifying errors in punctuation or inelegant presentation. When Kenneth Burke was temporarily covering as acting editor, Thayer wrote lengthy and critical letters detailing what was 'readable' and what was 'appalling'.[43] Thayer's editorial post-mortems became occasions when he would look through the latest issue of the magazine, point to errors and identify the culprits responsible. As Alyse Gregory recalled, Thayer would arrive at the offices of the *Dial* 'with a long sheet of paper on which he had meticulously noted down every error, and each would be remorselessly tracked to the guilty person'.[44] According to Joost, Thayer was obsessive in his pursuit of perfection:

> So relentless was [his] search for the impeccable, unassailably error-free Dial that once when a small, last-minute alteration in an essay of William Butler Yeats came as the review, already off the press, was about to be sent out to the newsstands, he had the whole issue [. . .] destroyed and a fresh one made.[45]

In comparison to Thayer, Moore's approach looks considerably less fussy. Her frequent requests for cuts and small changes were probably made in most instances to ensure alignment with the *Dial*'s image of cultural distinction. For instance, in the case of Malcolm Cowley, Moore's requests are not only for cuts but also for substitutions. She requires of him a more formal diction, reflecting the discursive signature of the magazine as much as Moore's own preferences. Thus she would like to replace 'raked over' with 'reconnoitred' and instead of 'skimps' she'd prefer 'falls short of' or 'stints'.[46] A similar request is made of Conrad Aiken, who uses the word 'colourful'. 'Here in the office, though without justification perhaps, we have banned it', Moore writes to Aiken, implying that it is not only her own preferences that are informing editorial decisions but rather the larger concerns of 'the office'.[47] In this instance, Moore's own predilection for verbal precision aligns with the magazine's reputation for formal austerity. The more colloquial 'skimps' or the vague term 'colourful' lack the exacting accuracy Moore is looking for in language.

Some suggestions are difficult to attribute to Moore herself and might better be understood as an expression of the institutional habitus of the magazine. Moore frequently downplayed her role, repeatedly foregrounding the bureaucratic nature of the magazine and the ways in which it often ran counter to her own personal preferences. For instance, when rejecting the short story, 'The House Party', by Mary Butts, she admires its 'style and workmanship' but the content of the story is not in character with '*The Dial*'s somewhat austere English taste'.[48] Moore is not simply shifting the responsibility here but rather explaining her position as an editor who operates within the social and material constraints of magazine production. Many factors limit editorial agency such as the threat of censorship. Butts's biographer suggests that Moore's rejection letter to Butts 'may well have been a coded way of saying that the explicit portrayal of homosexual relationships in the story was too risky for the time, given the legal battles faced by D. H. Lawrence and James Joyce'.[49] Particularly difficult for Moore were those occasions when close friends submitted work she felt was unsuitable. She regrets having to reject Glenway Wescott, for instance, feeling, as she writes Monroe Wheeler, 'my unusefulness to my friends'.[50] Moore was scrupulous in her decision making and never allowed her personal relations to cloud her aesthetic judgements, willing to be, in her mother's phrase, 'disliked by those who formerly were adherents'.[51]

In many cases, Moore's editorial practice aligned with the material constraints of magazine publication. Often short of page space, the editor's task was to make sure that she could accommodate all the accepted pieces within the single issue. In this sense, Moore's own poetic impulse towards contraction made her ideally suited to the role of editor. Offering advice to a would-be contributor, Moore urges 'understatement' rather than exaggeration. 'We would urge a precise use of words and a securing of force without many adjectives.'[52] The standard editorial intervention was to insert parentheses 'used to suggest omission'.[53] When answering a letter from William Wasserstrom who was curious about the *Dial*'s editorial policy, Moore replied, 'the phrase I often heard in the office was, "It must have intensity"'.[54] That intensity was achieved through omission or what Moore would describe in terms of economy, contractility and concentration, all characteristic traits of modernist writing.

Moore denied interference when questioned about it many years later by Donald Hall: 'We had an inflexible rule: do not ask changes of so much as a comma. Accept it or reject it.'[55] The correspondence suggests otherwise. She revised the contributions of others and this usually resulted in a process of excision or condensation. Attributing those revisions exclusively to Moore, however, ignores the role the magazine played in her decision-making processes. It is the fusion of the personal editorial habitus with the institutional habitus of the magazine that creates the productive tensions and even the 'intensity' that Moore describes in her letters.

'Our Beacon': Flaring 'Miss Moore'

When Moore took over at the *Dial* in July 1925, she did not bring with her the social capital of a Ford Madox Ford or the symbolic capital of an Eliot. Thayer recognised that the artist 'Miss Moore' needed to be created before her poetry could be recognised as art and before her suitability as an editor could be confirmed. In his reviews, Thayer constructed 'Miss Moore' and her poetry as immune from worldly and commercial pressures, forging a link between Moore's aesthetic integrity and the magazine's own reputation for distinction. In other words, rather than using Eliot's highbrow reputation to increase the magazine's symbolic capital, as he did when he published *The Waste Land*, Thayer produced an image of Miss Moore as 'pure artist' that signalled the magazine's powers of cultural consecration.[56] As Robin Schulze has pointed out, in the case of Eliot, Thayer and Watson were engaged in profiting from an already established reputation, while in Moore's case, they were clearly engaged in making her reputation.[57] The *Dial* had, by 1925, what Bourdieu would describe as the 'magic power of transubstantiation'; it was not only a taste maker but an 'artist maker'.[58]

This is evident in the announcements for The Dial Award that appeared from 1921. When a writer's reputation is established, the magazine sees its task as recognising 'genius' while also maintaining a critical detachment. For instance, Thayer's announcement that T. S. Eliot was to receive the award in 1922 is strangely subdued. Compliments are backhanded; Eliot is praised for managing to avoid 'the temptation not to arrive at excellence'.[59] The emphasis is placed on Eliot as a critic who has been 'of exceptional service to American letters' rather than the author of *The Waste Land* which Thayer privately thought was 'disappointing'.[60] Van Wyck Brooks, the winner of The Dial Award the following year, fares even worse. At least Eliot is given Thayer's undivided attention. While Brooks is named as the winner of The Dial prize, he has to share his limelight with 'our distinguished contributor', W. B. Yeats, who a few months earlier had received the Nobel Prize for literature. Yeats's recognition confers cultural authority on the *Dial* that has, as the editor notes, brought several Nobel prize-winning European writers to the attention of American readers.

Brooks is praised in the second paragraph, though with reservations: 'One can recognize the supreme importance of such a figure even if one fails to accept the whole body of his doctrine.' [61] The final paragraph returns to Yeats who 'has held unyieldingly to the dignity and the sacredness of his calling'.[62] Even though Brooks is referred to in the closing sentence, it is only to note that he would be encouraged by the recognition of Yeats's contribution.

In contrast to Thayer's ambivalence towards Eliot and Brooks, the announcement of The Dial Award to Moore in January 1925 is a full-blown eulogy. Recognising that his magazine serves the 'twin functions of criticism and propaganda', Thayer uses the opportunity not only to exalt Moore but also to confer upon the magazine itself the powers of cultural consecration.[63] Terms such as 'distinguished', 'virtue', 'esteem' and 'value' are deployed to reinforce the idea of Moore as a 'beacon' of literary value serving not 'that Juggernaut, the Reading Public' but rather 'the Marooned Individual'.[64] Thayer's 'flaring' of Moore served his own financial interests as well as the *Dial*'s by cementing the Moore/*Dial* union in readers' minds. As Elizabeth Gregory points out, promoting Moore made good business sense given that the New York Dial Press, Thayer's other venture, had just published Moore's *Observations* in 1924.[65] In contrast to Eliot, Moore's literary stock in 1925 had yet to accrue significant symbolic value.[66] A different tactic was required, one that involved illuminating the 'signally unacclaimed' 'Miss Moore'.[67]

Following the January 'Announcement', Thayer used his editorial comment in February, March and April to extol Moore's 'admonitory asceticisms'.[68] Drawing extensively on *Observations* for examples to support his assertions, he adopts a variety of strategies to illuminate Moore's poetry for the reader. In March, he invokes the virginal figure of 'Miss Moore' as otherworldly and rare; in April he compares the 'wildest caressing loveliness' of Moore's footnotes to Eliot's pedestrian and explanatory footnotes.[69] It is the February comment, however, that stands out for its critical perceptiveness. Here, Thayer uses the first line of Moore's poem 'To a Snail' as an epigraph: 'Compression is the first grace of style'. For Thayer, Moore's sentences are 'packed and pounded', 'solid'; they are 'rooted in, nourished from, the primal rock'.[70] As the epigraph from Moore suggests, such verbal density is achieved by compression. Tellingly, Thayer's most effective critical strategy is to imitate Moore's method in his promotion of her poetry:

> I should like here to expose certain literary fragments, torn jaggedly from the hard context, fragments which, being felt out with the hammer of our intellect, return the consistency of rock-crystal, fragments which, being thrown upon the hearth of our sympathetic understanding, betray the immense, the salt-veined, the profoundly-premeditated, chromatization of enkindled driftwood.[71]

The verbal strategies that Thayer uses are all typical of Moore. Here, nouns are deployed as pre-modifiers as in 'salt-veined', the technical language of 'chromatization' signals an interest in science and technology and the use of a prefix to transform a noun into an adjective as in 'enkindled' produces a Moore-like 'expressive density'.[72] Though Moore had not agreed at this point to becoming editor of the magazine, Thayer is providing the reader with previews of Moore's signature style. Such strategies prepare the ground for the announcement, in July 1925, that she was to take over as Acting Editor.

The critical discourse of aesthetic purity, as I have suggested elsewhere, was already in circulation by the time Thayer was preparing readers of the *Dial* for a new editor.[73] Glenway Wescott's introduction to Moore's long poem 'Marriage' in Manikin in 1923 refers to her poetry as 'aristocratic art'.[74] A year later, in a review published in the *Criterion*, Richard Aldington describes Moore 'sitting on a 'prim promontory', producing poetry that is similar to a 'fantastic museum'.[75] Like cummings, Aldington feels chastised by Moore, intimidated by her 'menacing superiority'. 'I always feel', he writes with barely concealed resentment, 'I ought to apologize for having the presumption to read Miss Moore's poems: and at the thought that I am actually trying to review them the pen trembles in my hand.'[76] The same year that Thayer was promoting Moore in the pages of the *Dial*, in *Poetry* magazine Yvor Winters was comparing Moore to the 'complete, profound, self-sufficient, bony [poetry] of Donne or Emily Dickinson'.[77] Edwin Seaver's review of Moore in the *Nation* in 1925 describes Moore's verse as 'aristocratic, severe and pure'.[78] Thayer's promotion of Moore was drawing on and contributing to an emerging discourse that constructed Moore's poetry in terms of a highbrow exclusivity.

In 1925 Moore's cultural capital was also being flared in other ways and by other critics. That Moore was peculiarly suited to making the necessary discriminations when editing a modernist magazine and that her gender made her more rather than less able to make such discriminations is suggested in Alfred Kreymborg's by now well-known anecdote concerning a trip he took with Moore to see a baseball game. Kreymborg's staging of the episode makes himself the butt of the joke and also signals Moore's signature style, her erudition, her range of knowledge and her interest in sport and popular culture. In his memoir, *Troubaour*, Kreymborg explains that he decided to take Moore to a ball game at the Polo Grounds in order to hear her 'stumped about something'. He begins by describing the journey to the Polo Grounds:

> The descent into the world of the low-brow started beautifully. It was a Saturday afternoon and the Cubs and Giants were scheduled for one of their ancient frays. The 'L' was jammed with fans and we had to stand all the way uptown and hang on to straps. Marianne was totally oblivious to the discomfiture anyone else would have felt and, in answer to a question

> of mine, paraded whole battalions of perfectly marshalled ideas in long columns of balanced periods which no lurching on the part of the train or pushing on the part of the crowd disturbed.

Once installed in their seats, Kreymborg and Moore have much to discuss:

> Without so much as a glance toward the players at practice grabbing grounders and chasing fungos, she went on giving me her impression of the respective technical achievements of Mr. Pound and Mr. Aldington without missing a turn in the rhythm of her speech, until I, a little impatient, touched her arm and, indicating a man in the pitcher's box winding up with the movement Matty's so famous for, interrupted: 'But Marianne, wait a moment, the game's about to begin. Don't you want to watch the first ball?' 'Yes indeed', she said, stopped, blushed and leaned forward. The old blond boy delivered a tantalizing fadeaway which hovered in the air and then, just as it reached the batter, Shorty Slagle, shot from his shoulders to his knees across the plate. 'Strike!' bawled Umpire Emslie. 'Excellent,' said Marianne.
>
> Delighted, I quickly turned to her with: 'Do you happen to know the gentleman who threw that strike?'
>
> 'I've never seen him before,' she admitted, 'but I take it must be Mr. Matthewson.'
>
> I could only gasp, 'Why?'
>
> 'I've read his instructive book on the art of pitching – '
>
> 'Strike two!' interrupted Bob Emslie [the umpire].
>
> 'And it's a pleasure,' she continued imperturbably, 'to note how unerringly his execution supports his theories – '
>
> 'Strike three, batter's out!' concluded the umpire.[79]

In his attempt to 'stump' Moore, Kreymborg seeks to relocate her, to transport her from her familiar highbrow bohemian setting to the lowbrow, mass spectacle of the baseball game. What the anecdote reveals is that Moore is more at home at the ball game than he is. He makes assumptions about her 'proper' place as a woman, while she challenges those assumptions through what I described earlier as her transgressive cultural authority. At the same time, however, there is something stagey about Kreymborg's account of Moore that suggests this portrait is engaged in generating what Aaron Jaffe has referred to as the 'textual imprimatur' of the modernist artist. 'At once as a distinctive mark and a sanctioning impression, the imprimatur [. . .] turns the author into a formal artefact, fusing it to the text as a reified signature of value.'[80] The 'myth of Marianne Moore' as Taffy Martin describes it, may well have been initiated by Kreymborg's entertaining anecdote.[81] That myth is engaged in a form of cultural work that reifies Moore's signature and confirms its aesthetic authenticity. From her polysyllabic, mellifluous sentences to her apparent imperviousness to her external environment, Moore is, to quote the seminal advertisement for Coca Cola, the 'real thing', the pure artist. When she becomes editor of the *Dial*, that authenticity serves to reinforce the *Dial*'s cultural capital.

All the major modernist poets were ardent admirers of Moore's work; Moore was, according to Harriet Monroe, the poet 'who Ezra Pound is adjuring us all to imitate'.[82] In her review of Moore's poems in the *Egoist* in 1916, H.D. refers to Moore as the 'perfect craftsman'.[83] Writing for the *Little Review* in 1918 Pound described Moore and Mina Loy in terms of a 'dance of the intelligence among words and ideas'.[84] In the *Egoist*, in the same year, T. S. Eliot counted Moore as a 'living writer', comparing her favourably with Laforgue and for Williams Carlos Williams 'of all American writers', Moore is 'most constantly a poet'.[85] Moore may have been less well connected than her poetic contemporaries but they all recognised the value of her work and tirelessly promoted it. As a modernist poet Moore had, like Eliot, the symbolic capital that came with a lack of readership and a scarcity of product. In a letter to Pound in 1919, she writes, 'I do not appear. Originally, my work was refused by the *Atlantic Monthly* and other magazines and recently I have not offered it.'[86] Moore recognised the significance of being refused by the *Atlantic Monthly* but accepted by the low circulation, modernist magazine, the *Egoist*. This assertion reinforces Jaffe's point that modernism's cultural value is predicated not on its availability or accessibility but rather on its inaccessibility, what he refers to as its 'meticulous scarcity'.[87] At first glance, this seems to run counter to the fact that the *Dial* wished to increase circulation, making modernism more available rather than scarce; clearly, the intentions of the magazine's editors were to have more readers in order to attract lucrative advertising revenue. Yet as Thayer's critical response to Moore in the pages of the *Dial* attest, 'Miss Moore' embodied the allure of the unattainable. This is most clearly illustrated in Thayer's March comment where he focuses his attention on the poem 'Sea Unicorns and Land Unicorns'. In jovial terms, he takes Moore to task for reinforcing the myth that only a virgin can capture a unicorn alive. Even though Moore would have been aged 38 in 1925, he repeatedly emphasises her 'youth and sex', referring to her as 'our young authoress' and a 'young woman of unusual parts'.[88] In doing so, he relates his discussion of the mythical power of virginity to Moore herself and to the 'hard context' of her verse.[89] The fetishisation of the poet aligns the body of 'Miss Moore' with the impenetrable textual body of the modernist poem.

Editorial Labours

Once in post, Moore's textual imprimatur became a form of editorial imprimatur, reinforced by the institutional habitus of the *Dial* itself. This cumulative cultural power exceeded even the authority of the owners themselves, Thayer and Watson. The result was that when Moore took over as editor, what she lacked in financial capital was more than made up for in symbolic capital making her the equal of the owner/editors and more than capable of opposing them when she felt that the interests of the magazine required her to do so.

While Moore was named Acting Editor in July 1925, she had been working at the *Dial* in an official capacity since April of that year. As Moore's biographer notes, however, as early as January 1923, when Alyse Gregory was appointed as editor in 1923 to take over from Gilbert Seldes, Thayer was trying to recruit Moore as her understudy. Gregory herself asked Moore to help at the magazine and in February 1924, Moore began to attend make-up meetings.[90] Gregory enjoyed only a brief period of stability as editor before her personal circumstances began to make her professional life increasingly difficult. Gregory's partner, the writer Llewelyn Powys, suffered from tuberculosis and after a restorative trip with Sibley Watson to the Rocky Mountains, Gregory and Powys decided to relocate to upstate New York for Powys's health. Gregory attempted to resign from her position at the magazine but Thayer persuaded her that she could manage by working remotely and commuting to the city when she needed to. This arrangement, as the correspondence in the fall and winter months of 1924 reveal, was far from satisfactory. The running of the magazine was often left largely to the stalwart Sophia Wittenberg, who had been at the *Dial* since 1920, Miss McMillan and after McMillan's resignation, Dorothy Elise DePollier.[91]

The correspondence between Gregory in Montoma and the women working at the *Dial* offices during this period reveals the difficulties that ensued because of this arrangement. McMillan is frequently wondering about the whereabouts of Sibley Watson, who was, for much of late 1924, semi-detached from *Dial* business. [92] Relying heavily on the efficiency of the postal service, packages were sent between Edgartown and New York to Thayer and Montoma and New York to Gregory containing galleys as well as the make-up of the magazine. Edmund Wilson described the chaotic arrangements at the *Dial* during this period: 'so far as I could see, the contributions were never read, the editors were never in their office, and the magazine knocked itself together every month without human intervention except on the part of the proof readers and stenographers'.[93] Wilson prefers to credit the magazine's production to mysterious non-human forces rather than recognise that at this point the *Dial* was relying heavily on the critical discriminations of 'stenographers and proof readers'. Clearly, McMillan felt that much of what she was being asked to do was well above her pay grade. For instance, when Gregory asked her to write biographical notes on D. H. Lawrence and Moore, McMillan was horrified at the prospect and resisted doing so. Exchanges between McMillan and Gregory became increasingly tetchy by the end of 1924 and at some point in February 1925 McMillan must have resigned or been replaced by Dorothy Elise DePollier.

If McMillan and Gregory struggled, so too did the eminently reliable and efficient Sophia Wittenberg, who had risen to the rank of assistant editor, having started as a stenographer in 1920. According to Gregory herself, Wittenberg was both beautiful and capable. She worked two jobs; her role as Gregory's assistant was supposed to be part-time but it is clear that in Gregory's absence, Wittenberg's workload increased. Among her many duties, Wittenberg had the unenviable task of overseeing the editorial comment which was written by Thayer, who by then had retreated to his family home in Edgartown. McMillan describes Wittenberg's frenzied exchanges with Thayer over the editorial comment.[94] When McMillan struggled with the index, Gregory suggested asking Wittenberg to help, only to find out in the next letter that Wittenberg had already completed the index. Unsurprisingly, by October of that year, Wittenberg was forced to resign from her other job in order to keep up with her work at the *Dial*. In December of that year, a note of exasperation seeps into Wittenberg's letters when she points out the incompatibilities between the magazine's schedule and Gregory's.[95] She then goes on to offer a solution, making it clear, however, that this would delay the appearance of the magazine for two days. Wittenberg left the *Dial* in April 1925 as assistant editor and was replaced temporarily by Kenneth Burke on the understanding that Thayer's cousin, Ellen, would take up the post in September of that year.

When Moore arrived in April 1925, she not only had to deal with the administrative chaos caused by the absence of a full-time editor, she also had to deal with the increasingly paranoid behaviour of Thayer, who was convinced that his personal secretary, Miss Parker, together with the newly appointed Miss DePollier, were submitting manuscripts to the *Dial* under false names. Moore dealt with the situation as best she could, trying to carry out Thayer's wishes while also attempting to treat employees at the magazine as fairly as possible. Clearly, Miss DePollier was offended by these accusations and resigned from her post, against Moore's advice, in June 1925. The fall-out from this, however, extended beyond the office, creating a difficult situation for Moore and a potentially libellous situation for Thayer. When DePollier resigned in anticipation of being dismissed, Thayer asked Moore for clarification about what had happened, fearing a battle in the courts with his former employee. With Moore as a witness for the defence, he need not have been concerned. DePollier had visited Moore at her apartment to discuss what had happened. In the wake of that meeting, Moore wrote to Thayer providing him with a verbatim account of all that was said:

> I made her welcome and said that I had expected her to come to see me at The Dial until Mrs Eveline had told me that she felt that I was hypocriti-

> cal in my surprise at her resigning and that she thought an apology was due her. I asked if she had felt that an apology was due her and if so, from whom and for what? She said from Thayer because of his searching her scrapbasket. I said: 'Miss DePollier, Mr Thayer didn't even know of our waste-basket's being searched; I asked to have it searched that I might recover envelopes which had brought doubtful manuscripts. If there is anything to apologize for in having done that, I apologize heartily; I remember your speaking of your waste-basket's having been searched and my not replying and feeling that it had been a disrespectful act but without significance.'

Moore then asks if that was what DePollier felt required an apology.

> 'Yes,' she said, 'it was; I thought it had to do with Mr Thayer. I thought he thought that I might have destroyed some of his papers or was keeping some of them back.' She said, 'And in our conversation, you said, "we don't know you" and said you thought I was going to be asked to give up my job.' I of course, reiterated what I had said and she reiterated that the above is what I had said. I then said, 'Miss DePollier, I couldn't have said I thought you were going to be asked to give up your job; I never use the word "job". What I did say was, "The atmosphere has been strange; I am not surprised that you should have thought of leaving". Then you asked, "Do you think I should resign" and I said, "No, Miss DePollier, I do not."' She said, 'Well – there has been a misunderstanding; I see that you were thinking of one thing and I was thinking of another'.[96]

Moore's mind, operating like a steel trap, not only recalls her original conversation with DePollier in extraordinary detail but also the conversation she then has with her former employee concerning that earlier conversation. DePollier is forced to admit that she resigned against Moore's advice, even though her fear about losing her job was entirely justified. As Burke writes to Thayer in July 1925, 'With Miss Moore's triumphant settling of the Affair de Pollier, we all relax a little and settle down into sloth and contentment.'[97] Little did Burke know that Thayer would then direct his paranoia towards Burke himself, much to Moore's distress. While the plan had been, all along, to have Ellen Thayer in the position of assistant editor, Moore had become reliant on Burke in the office and was keen to keep him on. Thayer had launched a vitriolic attack on Burke in a letter printed in the *Dial* in December 1925, criticising the 'Comment' that Burke wrote for the October issue of that year. As Moore noted to Gregory, fortunately the 'cryptic character' of Thayer's letter 'somewhat nullified' its content.[98] Moore had tried to give Thayer what Watson referred to as a 'moral shakedown' but to no avail.[99] She wrote to Thayer in December 1925 threatening to resign:

> In matters yet more acute, is not this need for unanimity as great? I have felt indeed, that rather than intrude, it might be better for me – as I shall tell Dr Watson – to withdraw entirely from a relationship in which I might need to disagree; although to even contemplate withdrawing pains me, attached as I am to the work of The Dial and to each of those associated with it.[100]

Watson persuaded her to stay on and she continued to resist Thayer's efforts to cull all those he suspected of disloyalty at the magazine.[101] It is no exaggeration to say that had Moore not arrived as managing editor, the *Dial* would have collapsed. Her tact and diplomacy, together with her managerial and interpersonal skills, equipped her to deal with the turmoil created by Thayer's behaviour. Ironically, the cultural capital she had acquired through her association with the *Dial*, and in part the result of Thayer's critical 'flaring', gave her the authority to defy Thayer himself.

By 1925, Moore had acquired an unusually powerful position as editor of the *Dial* bestriding, to paraphrase Ernest Boyd's caricature of the *Dial* editor, the 'narrow world' of restricted production. Unlike Monroe, Eliot and Anderson, Moore was not involved in the founding of the magazine she worked for, nor was she, like Thayer and Watson, investing her own money in the venture. Given the circumstances, it might be safe to assume that she had less autonomy compared to these founding editors and that she was less personally wedded to the publication than the magazine's owners, who had invested such vast sums of money into producing and promoting it. Ironically, in the case of Moore, her relative freedom from financial concerns was liberating. She did not have to court sponsors or seek patronage from wealthy investors. The magazine's financial position was relatively secure, due to Thayer and Watson's substantial investments. In theory, this might have resulted in the owners continuing to press their aesthetic preferences on their managing editor, but in practice, this was not the case. While Moore was required to follow the style guidelines set out by Thayer and Gregory in the 'General Instructions for Editorial Department', these guidelines provided effective and stable structures within which to work. A detailed description of the processes for dealing with manuscripts, the duties of the Acting Editor (Moore) and the Assistant Editor (Ellen Thayer), rates of pay for various forms for prose, verse and translations, as well as general rules concerning layout, the placing of advertisements and the relation between visual and verbal material, were all described in as much detail as possible.

For a few years, Thayer tried to maintain control of the half-tone reproductions of art and also the coloured frontispieces for each issue, but in January 1927 he suffered a complete mental breakdown, and from that point until the magazine's closure was no longer directly involved in decisions relating to content. His taste in European and American art, however, informed the magazine through his extensive collection, which served as the source for much of the work on display in the magazine throughout the 1920s. With Thayer incapacitated and Watson largely absent, Moore presided over the magazine, receiving guests in her 'palm tree' and allowing her to mix the business of running the *Dial* with the pleasures of socialising with its contributors. In her reminiscence of her *Dial* days she remembers Padraic Colum's visits to 152 West Thirteenth Street, where he transformed the 'routine atmosphere' of the office to 'one of discovery'.[102] The correspondence bears testimony to Moore's position of cultural authority. The emerging critic, Malcolm Cowley, writes lengthy letters to Moore but also is a regular visitor to the offices. He clearly called on Moore at the *Dial* to seek her unique perspective on literature and ethics.[103] The critic, Paul Rosenfeld, is a regular visitor telling Moore of the latest plays, discussing other writers and, it seems, seeking Moore's opinions. Moore often wrote to her brother, Warner Moore, providing an insight into the extent to which she was respected, even revered at the magazine: 'As I said to Mole [Moore's mother], Paul sat there meditatively asking me questions as if he were Buddha & I Socrates.'[104] Professional correspondence mingles with personal anecdotes, indicating the fluid nature of literary labour. Witter Bynner, one of the perpetrators of the Spectra hoax in 1916, was also a regular contributor to the *Dial* and signs off to Moore by referring to mutual friends, Glenway Wescott and Monroe Wheeler.[105] Henry McBride, the regular art critic for the *Dial*, refers to Moore's family at the *Dial* as well as to her family at St Luke's Place in a letter to Moore in 1928. Thus, while Linda Leavell, Moore's biographer, observes that Moore rarely ventured out to social gatherings, parties and performances when working at the *Dial*, it might be argued that a social life came to her as editor of the magazine. Responding to Paul Morand's request for increased payment for the Paris letter, Moore exchanges fond memories of his visit to New York: 'I too, remember with the utmost pleasure, our iced-tea in the Dial office.'[106] For Moore, the *Dial* was 'like a second home'.[107] For Alyse Gregory, work as managing editor placed her at the centre of a lively social circle: 'Young men took their hats off in the street and invitations to parties poured in.' She recalls with fondness being 'surrounded by sympathetic people', who were both intellectually stimulating and creative, making life at the office 'delightful'.[108] Perhaps also for Moore, the office space at the *Dial* offered her some respite from her domineering mother and enabled her to establish a network of friends and associates separate from her domestic arrangements.

Though Moore never complained about the amount of labour involved in editing the magazine, the fact that she wrote no poetry during her period as editor testifies to the all-consuming nature of the work. Watson and Thayer were both aware of Moore's dedication to the journal and tried to persuade her to do less. In 1925, Thayer wrote to Moore, clearly concerned that her work at the magazine was 'curtailing [her] observational output' and suggesting that she might approach her editorial work at the *Dial* more 'cavalierly'.[109] Moore's mother makes her own observations regarding her daughter's punishing schedule when she writes to Monroe Wheeler in 1926:

> Were you with us a single day you would not say 'poetry' to Marianne. You could not understand – without seeing it, the steadiness of her devotion to the present task. Our one great sacrifice in it, is that we neither can go to Warner's nor have the children and Constance here. The giving up of writing is a sacrifice too, no slight one; but the other we feel more poignantly. This is not saying that her work is a hardship. It is truly an absorbing interest, but it excludes other interests as completely as winter does, nearly every bit of gardening.[110]

In a letter to William Carlos Williams, Moore declines the invitation to contribute to *The Contact Collection*, explaining 'I have not one hour at my command.'[111] While Eliot also complained of being exhausted by his editorial duties, he continued to write poetry, something Moore was either unwilling or unable to do when editor of the *Dial.*[112] In the case of Eliot, the cultural capital attached to the *Criterion* helped to further his career as a poet, as Philpotts points out.[113] After the closure of the *New Criterion* in 1939, Eliot remained at the centre of the literary publishing world, maintaining a very high public profile and continuing to play a significant role in modernism's institutionalisation. By contrast, Moore and her mother moved away from Greenwich Village to the relatively quiet suburbs of Brooklyn once the *Dial* ceased publication.[114] Yet as she informed her brother, her association with the *Dial* had bestowed on her a 'public confidence'.[115] Work at the *Dial* conferred prestige on Moore that would help to secure her status as a 'durable' poet in the 1930s, a word Eliot used to describe Moore's poetry in his introduction to *Selected Poems* published in 1935.[116] Moore continued to exercise editorial influence, not only on the work of individual poets such as Elizabeth Bishop and Marsden Hartley, but also in an advisory capacity to Morton Zabel, who took over as editor at *Poetry* magazine in 1936.

As I will go on to suggest in the following chapter, while modernism continued to be published and publicised under Moore's editorship and retained its image of high-hat hauteur, Moore's personal habitus, the particular dispositions she brought with her to the magazine challenged the cultural hierarchies underpinning the production of modernism and interrogated the ethics of cosmopolitan aestheticism. If the literary field is competitive, defined by conflict between a variety of dispositions, then differing views and territorial struggles function to reinforce the boundaries circumscribing the restricted field of production. As an editor, Moore continued to reinforce modernism's symbolic value through reinterpretation, revision and even, at times, resistance to its central tropes.

Notes

1. Marianne Moore, '*The Dial*: A Retrospect', in *The Complete Prose of Marianne Moore*, ed. Patricia Willis (London: Faber and Faber, 1987), pp. 357–64 (pp. 358, 362).
2. Ibid. p. 363.
3. Jayne Marek, *Women Editing Modernism: 'Little' Magazines and Literary History* (Lexington: University Press of Kentucky, 1995), p. 141.
4. e. e. cummings, *Selected Letters of E. E. Cummings*, ed. F. W. Dupee and George Stade (London: Andre Deutsch, 1972), p. 207.
5. Stacy Carson Hubbard, 'Mannerist Moore: Poetry, Painting, Photography', in *Critics and Poets on Marianne Moore: 'A Right Good Salvo of Barks'*, ed. Linda Leavell, Cristanne Miller and Robin G. Schulze (Lewisburg, PA: Bucknell University Press, 2005), pp. 113–36 (p. 113).
6. Ibid. p. 118.
7. Linda Leavell, *Holding On Upside Down: The Life and Work of Marianne Moore* (New York: Farrar, Straus and Giroux, 2013), pp. 126–7.
8. Susan McCabe, '"Let's Be Alone Together": Bryher's and Marianne Moore's Aesthetic–Erotic Collaboration', *Modernism/Modernity* 17 (2010), 607–37 (p. 615).
9. Ezra Pound, *The Letters of Ezra Pound, 1907–1941*, ed. D. D. Paige (London: Faber and Faber, 1950), p. 157.
10. Ann Ardis, 'Staging the Public Sphere: Magazine Dialogism and the Prosthetics of Authorship in the Twentieth Century', in *Transatlantic Print Culture, 1880–1940: Emerging Media, Emerging Modernisms*, ed. Ann Ardis and Patrick Collier (Basingstoke: Palgrave Macmillan, 2008), pp. 30–47 (p. 31).
11. Aaron Jaffe, *Modernism and the Culture of Celebrity* (Cambridge: Cambridge University Press, 2005), p. 90.
12. Marianne Moore to Monroe Wheeler, 16 August 1925, Berg, in m.b. Moore, M. 264 A.L.S., 13 A.N.S., 22 T.L.S. 3 T.N.S., 1 T.T. (copy), 12 postcards to Monroe Wheeler. [v.p., Feb. 24, 1923–Aug. 5, 1965]. Folder 5.
13. Leavell, *Holding On*, p. 230.
14. Jason Harding (ed.), *Ford Madox Ford, Modernist Magazines and Editing* (Amsterdam and New York: Rodopi, 2010), p. 28.
15. Leavell, *Holding On*, p. 167.
16. Ibid. p. 245.
17. Matthew Philpotts, 'The Role of the Periodical Editor: Literary Journals and Editorial Habitus', *Modern Language Review*, 107 (2012), 39–64 (pp. 61–2).
18. Toril Moi, 'Appropriating Bourdieu: Feminist Theory and Pierre Bourdieu's Sociology of Culture', *New Literary History*, 22 (1991), 1017–49 (p. 1030).
19. Moore, *Complete Prose*, p. 215; Moore, 'Comment', *Dial*, 86 (February 1929), 179–80 (p. 179).
20. Elizabeth Francis, *The Secret Treachery of Words: Feminism and Modernism in America* (Minneapolis: University of Minnesota Press, 2002), p. 40.
21. Alan Golding, 'The *Little Review* (1914–29)', in *The Oxford Critical and Cultural History of Modernist Magazines, Vol. II: North America, 1894–1960*, ed. Peter Brooker and Andrew Thacker (Oxford: Oxford University Press, 2012), pp. 63–85 (p. 67).
22. Terry Lovell, 'Resisting with Authority: Historical Specificity, Agency and the Performative Self', *Theory, Culture and Society*, 20 (2003), 1–17 (p. 2).
23. Judith Butler, *Excitable Speech: A Politics of the Performative* (New York and London: Routledge) 1997, p. 142, cited in Lovell, 'Resisting', p. 4.

24. Terry Lovell, 'Thinking Feminism with and against Bourdieu', *The Sociological Review*, 1 (2000), 27–47 (p. 31).
25. Cristanne Miller, *Marianne Moore: Questions of Authority* (Cambridge, MA: Harvard University Press, 1995), pp. 38, 3.
26. Benjamin Kahan, '"The Viper's Traffic-Knot": Celibacy and Queerness in the "Late" Moore', *GLQ* 14 (2008), 510–33 (p. 510).
27. John Emil Vincent, *Queer Lyrics: (Difficulty and Closure in American Poetry)* (New York: Palgrave, 2002), p. 63.
28. Natalia Cecire, 'Marianne Moore's Precision', *Arizona Quarterly: A Journal of American Literature, Culture and Theory,* 67 (2011), 83–110 (p. 84).
29. John Timberman Newcomb, 'Poetry's Opening Door: Harriet Monroe and American Modernism', *American Periodicals: A Journal of History, Criticism, and Bibliography*, 15, (2005), 6–22 (p. 8).
30. John Unterecker, *Voyager: A Life of Hart Crane* (New York: Farrar, Straus and Giroux, 1969), p. 234.
31. Jack Selzer, *Kenneth Burke in Greenwich Village: Conversing with the Moderns* (Madison: University of Wisconsin Press, 1996), pp. 135–6.
32. William Wasserstrom, 'Marianne Moore, The *Dial*, and Kenneth Burke', *The Western Humanities Review*, 17 (1963), 249–62 (p. 256).
33. Alan Golding, '*The Dial*, *The Little Review*, and the Dialogics of Modernism', *American Periodicals: A Journal of History, Critics and Bibliography* 15 (2005), 42–55 (p. 52).
34. Peter Brooker and Andrew Thacker, 'Editors and Programmes', in *The Oxford Critical and Cultural History of Modernist Magazines, Vol. I: Britain and Ireland, 1880–1955*, ed. Brooker and Thacker (Oxford: Oxford University Press, 2009), pp. 339–45 (p. 343).
35. Christina Britzolakis, 'Making Modernism Safe for Democracy', in *The Oxford Critical and Cultural History of Modernist Magazines, Vol. II: North America, 1894–1960*, ed. Peter Brooker and Andrew Thacker (Oxford: Oxford University Press, 2012), pp. 85–102 (p. 101).
36. Marianne Moore, *The Selected Letters of Marianne Moore*, ed. Bonnie Costello, Celeste Goodridge and Cristanne Miller (London: Faber and Faber, 1998), p. 212.
37. Britzolakis, 'Making Modernism Safe', p. 101.
38. Walter Sutton, *Pound, Thayer, Watson and The Dial: A Story in Letters* (Gainesville: University Press of Florida, 1994), p. 119.
39. Sibley Watson Jr to Marianne Moore, 12 September 1925, Philadelphia, Rosenbach Museum and Library, Series V, Box 75, Fol. 2.
40. Sibley Watson Jr to Marianne Moore, 5 November 1925, RML, Series V, Box 75, Fol. 3.
41. Sibley Watson Jr to Marianne Moore, 8 October 1926, RML, Series V, Box 75, Fol. 3.
42. Dorothy DePollier to Alyse Gregory, 6 March 1925, Beinecke, ST/Dial Papers, Series I, Box 3, Fol. 86. Thayer asked his assistant DePollier to write to Elizabeth Coatsworth asking her to change one of the lines in her poem.
43. Scofield Thayer to Kenneth Burke, 12 May 1923, Beinecke, ST/Dial Papers, Series I, Box 29, Fol. 763.
44. Nicholas Joost, *Scofield Thayer and The Dial: An Illustrated History* (Carbondale: Southern Illinois University Press, 1964), p. 104.
45. Ibid.
46. Marianne Moore to Malcolm Cowley, 2 April 1926, Beinecke, ST/Dial Papers, Series I, Box 1, Fol. 44.

47. Marianne Moore to Conrad Aiken, 9 September 1927, Beinecke, ST/Dial Papers, Series I, Box 1, Fol. 3.
48. Marianne Moore to Mary Butts, 2 November 1927. Berg, JSW/Dial Papers, Series VI. Box 20.
49. Nathalie Blondel, *Mary Butts: Scenes from the Life: A Biography* (New York: McPherson & Co., 1998), p. 150.
50. Marianne Moore to Monroe Wheeler, 18 September 1925, Berg in m.b. Moore, M. 264 A.L.S., 13 A.N.S., 22 T.L.S., 3 T.N.S., 1 T.L. (copy), 12 postcards to Monroe Wheeler. [v.p., Feb. 24, 1923–Aug. 5, 1965]. Folder 5.
51. Mary Warner Moore to Monroe Wheeler, 6 June 1925, Berg, in m.b. (Moore, M.) Moore, Mary Warner, 70 A.L. S. to Monroe Wheeler. [v.p.] April 6, 1923–[June 28, 1946] Folder 3.
52. Marianne Moore to Mrs William Zimmerman, 21 November 1927. Berg, JSW/ Dial Papers. Series VI. Box 20.
53. Marianne Moore to Meridel Le Sueur, (no date), Berg, JSW/Dial Papers, Series VI. Box 19.
54. Marianne Moore to William Wasserstrom, 3 December 1963, Berg, JSW/Dial Papers, Series VI. Fol. 30.
55. Linda Leavell, *Marianne Moore and the Visual Arts: Prismatic Color* (Baton Rouge: Louisiana State University Press, 1995), pp. 48–9.
56. Pierre Bourdieu, *The Rules of Art: Genesis and Structure of the Literary Field*, trans. Susan Emanuel (Cambridge: Polity Press, 1996, 2017), p. 135.
57. Marianne Moore, *Becoming Marianne Moore: The Early Poems, 1907–1924*, ed. Robin Schulze (Berkeley, Los Angeles, London: University of California Press, 2002), p. 31.
58. Bourdieu, *Rules of Art*, p. 137.
59. Scofield Thayer, 'Comment', *Dial*, 73 (December 1922), 685–7 (p. 685).
60. James Dempsey, *The Tortured Life of Scofield Thayer* (Gainesville: University Press of Florida, 2014), p. 107.
61. Scofield Thayer, 'Comment', *Dial*, 76 (January 1924), 96–7 (p. 96).
62. Ibid. p. 97.
63. Scofield Thayer, 'Announcement', *Dial*, 78 (January 1925), 89–90 (p. 89).
64. Ibid. p. 90.
65. Elizabeth Gregory, 'Flaring Moore: The Revisionist Reviewed', in *The Critical Response to Marianne Moore*, ed. Elizabeth Gregory (Westport, CT: Praeger, 2003), pp. 1–17.
66. Aaron Jaffe, *Modernism and the Culture of Celebrity* (Cambridge: Cambridge University Press, 2005), p. 72.
67. Scofield Thayer, 'Announcement', *Dial*, 78 (January 1925), 89–90 (p. 89).
68. Ibid. p. 90.
69. Scofield Thayer, 'Comment', *Dial*, 78 (March 1925), 265–8; Scofield Thayer, 'Comment', the *Dial*, 78 (April 1925), 354–6 (p. 356).
70. Scofield Thayer, 'Comment', *Dial*, 78 (February 1925), 174–80 (pp. 179–80).
71. Ibid. p. 174.
72. Marie Boroff, *Language and the Poet: Verbal Artistry in Frost, Stevens, and Moore* (Chicago: University of Chicago Press, 1979), p. 84.
73. Victoria Bazin, *Marianne Moore and the Cultures of Modernity* (Burlington, VT: Ashgate Publishing Company, 2010), pp. 39–44.
74. Moore, *Becoming*, p. 285.
75. Richard Aldington, 'Review of Observations', *Criterion*, 3 (1924), 588–94 (pp. 589–90).
76. Ibid.

77. Yvor Winters, 'Holiday in the Day of Wrath', *Poetry*, 26 (1925), 39–44 (p. 41).
78. Edwin Seaver, 'A Literalist of the Imagination', *Nation*, 18 (1925), 297–8 (p. 297).
79. Alfred Kreymborg, *Troubadour* (New York: Boni and Liveright, 1925), pp. 244–5.
80. Jaffe, *Modernism*, p. 20.
81. Taffy Martin, 'Portrait of a Writing Master: Beyond the Myth of Marianne Moore', *Twentieth Century Literature*, 30 (1984), 192–209.
82. Harriet Monroe, 'A Symposium on Marianne Moore', in *Critical Essays on Edna St. Vincent Millay*, ed. William B. Thesing (New York: G. K. Hall, 1993), p. 45.
83. H.D., 'Marianne Moore', *Egoist*, August (1916), 3–4 (p. 3).
84. Ezra Pound, 'Marianne Moore and Mina Loy', *Little Review*, 10 (1918), 57–8 (p. 57).
85. T. S. Eliot, 'Observations', *Egoist* (May 1918), 69–70 (p. 70); William Carlos Williams, *Collected Poems I 1909–1939*, ed. A. Walton Litz and Christopher MacGowan (Manchester: Carcanet, 2000), p. 230.
86. Moore, *Selected Letters*, p. 123.
87. Jaffe, *Modernism*, p. 90.
88. Scofield Thayer, 'Comment', *Dial*, 78 (March 1925), 266–8 (pp. 267, 268).
89. Scofield Thayer, 'Comment', *Dial*, 78 (February 1925), 174–80 (p. 174).
90. Leavell, *Holding On*, p. 212.
91. McMillan seems always to be referred to in the correspondence in formal terms as 'Miss McMillan'. I haven't been able to find her first name.
92. Miss McMillan to Alyse Gregory, 20 September 1924, Beinecke, ST/Dial Papers, Series I, Box 3, Fol. 81.
93. Dempsey, *Tortured Life*, p. 15
94. Miss McMillan to Alyse Gregory, 23 September 1924, Beinecke, ST/Dial Papers, Series I, Box 3, Fol. 81.
95. Sophia Wittenberg to Alyse Gregory, 19 December 1924, Beinecke, ST/Dial Papers, Series I, Box 3, Fol. 84.
96. Marianne Moore to Scofield Thayer, 27 June 1925, Beinecke, ST/Dial Papers, Series I, Box 35, Fol. 978.
97. Kenneth Burke to Scofield Thayer, 2 July 1925, Beinecke, ST/Dial Papers, Series I, Box 29, Fol. 767.
98. Moore, *Selected Letters*, p. 220
99. Dempsey, *Tortured Life*, p. 164.
100. Marianne Moore to Scofield Thayer, 10 December 1925, Beinecke, ST/Dial Papers, Box 35, Fol. 980.
101. Leavell, *Holding On*, p. 234.
102. Moore, *Complete Prose*, p. 362.
103. Malcolm Cowley to Marianne Moore, 4 March 1926, Beinecke, ST/Dial Papers, Box 1, Fol. 44.
104. Moore, *Selected Letters*, p. 241.
105. Witter Bynner to Moore, 30 July 1925, Beinecke, ST/Dial Papers, Series I, Box 1, Fol. 31.
106. Marianne Moore to Paul Morand, 16 December 1925, Beiñecke, ST/Dial Papers, Series I, Box 4, Fol. 144.
107. Marianne Moore to Monroe Wheeler, 28 June 1925, Berg in m.b. Moore, M. 264 A.L.S., 13 A.N.S., 22 T.L.S., 3 T.N.S., 1 T.L. (copy), 12 postcards to Monroe Wheeler. [v.p., Feb. 24, 1923–Aug. 5, 1965]. Folder 5.
108. Barbara Ozielblo, "Alyse Gregory, Scofield Thayer, and the "Dial"' *Twentieth Century Literature*, Vol. 48, No. 4 (Winter 2002), 487–507 (pp. 494, 504).
109. Scofield Thayer to Marianne Moore, 6 December 1925, RML, Series V, Box 65, Fol. 4.

110. Mary Warner Moore to Monroe Wheeler, 28 January 1926, Berg in m.b. (Moore, M.) Moore, Mary Warner, 70 A.L.S. to Monroe Wheeler. [v.p.] April 6, 1923–[June 28, 1946] Folder 4. Leavell points out that Mary was involved in 'the daily workings of the magazine'; *Holding On*, p. 229.
111. Moore, *Selected Letters*, p. 219.
112. T. S. Eliot, *The Letters of T. S. Eliot, Volume 2: 1923–1925*, ed. Valerie Eliot and Hugh Haughton (London: Faber and Faber, 2009), p. 292.
113. Philpotts, 'Role', p. 56.
114. Leavell describes how Warner Moore, Moore's brother, moved his sister and mother to Brooklyn without proper consultation and that both were most unhappy about this. Leavell, *Holding On*, pp. 250–3.
115. Ibid. p. 247.
116. Marianne Moore, *The Selected Poems of Marianne Moore*, ed. T. S. Eliot (London: Faber and Faber), pp. 5–12 (p. 12).

3

PROMOTIONAL PROSE AND EDITORIAL COMMENTS

As editor of the *Dial* between 1925 and 1929, a relatively long time for a non-commercial magazine, Moore occupied a position of considerable institutional power and influence. The forty-one editorial comments she wrote for the *Dial* would have been circulated beyond a 'little' magazine readership, many of the selections she made for publication were republished in newspapers and magazines across the nation and the news in circulation around the *Dial* conflated editor and magazine, meaning that Moore herself had become news.[1] Moore reached an even wider audience with the advertisements she wrote for the magazine, advertisements that were placed in a range of periodicals, from the qualities such as *Harper's* to the *Modern Quarterly* and specialised magazines such as *Drawing and Design*. It is no exaggeration to assert that Moore was, in the United States in the late 1920s, the public face of modernism.

While the monumental achievement of Patricia Willis's *Complete Prose of Marianne Moore* published and made accessible for the first time all of Moore's critical reviews, 'briefer mentions' and editorial comments, reading them in the context of the institutional habitus of the *Dial* reveals the extent to which Moore had a complex relation to her powers of cultural consecration. Unlike Thayer and Seldes, Moore used her editorial comments not to attack various 'tribes' or to denigrate the 'standardization' of culture, but to practise what she described as the 'science of assorting and the art of investing [the] assortment with dignity'.[2] Moore's editorials replace the insouciant air of superiority associated with the *Yellow Book* aesthete with a strikingly different attitude, one that maintains the notion of the magazine as a site of cultural consecration, akin to the space of a museum, but that also challenges the hierarchies reinforcing the symbolic value of the modernist art object.

Moore's editorial otherness, her resistance to the cultural hierarchies reinforcing modernism's institutionalisation are in evidence not only in her reviews and comments but also in the advertisements she wrote to promote the magazine and its ethos. Even in the promotional prose she produced for the *Dial*, I argue, Moore was queering the pitch, playing the game while simultaneously questioning its rules. This only becomes apparent, however, when a comparative approach is taken. Reading Moore's advertisements and comments alongside those penned by Thayer, Seldes, Gregory and Watson reveals the extent to which she pushed against the institutional habitus of the magazine even as her own image of highbrow authority reproduced the charismatic ideology of the editor/poet.

Early critical assessments of Moore's prose contributions to the *Dial* have tended to miss the significance of what Suzanne Churchill has described as Moore's 'conversity'.[3] Celeste Goodridge's important study of Moore's criticism recognises that 'it is dangerous to assume that *The Dial*'s values were her own' but the focus on Moore's responses to Pound, Eliot, Stevens and Williams leaves the question of her editorial comments untouched.[4] Nicholas Joost observes that Moore's 'Comments' were less 'combative' than Thayer's and Taffy Martin agrees, though sees in these essays a subversive element in Moore's resistance to 'synthesis'.[5] Evan Kindley recognises the importance of contextualising Moore's critical stance and suggests that she resisted modernist modes of engagement and critique, modes that were characterised by 'violence of expression, an outer-directed ethic of competitiveness and mutual contest or exchange, and a public or exhibitionistic quality'.[6] What Kindley describes in terms of an agonistic critical approach was also a characteristic of magazine publication and is evident in the editorial comments of Thayer, Watson, Seldes and Burke. Kindley rightly points out that Moore 'seems allergic to argument, reluctant to take up or defend abstract positions, and to go in fear of negative evaluations and judgments'.[7] Moore was criticised for this by critics such as Donald Hall, Bernard Engel and, when Moore was still editing the *Dial*, Gorham B. Munson.[8] Extending Kindley's argument and further contextualising it, I will argue that the public performances Moore enacted as editor of the *Dial* through her promotional prose and her editorial comments refuse to denigrate, to exclude and to instruct didactically. In opposition to Thayer and, more widely, the editorial practices that characterise periodical culture, the public fisticuffs that kept magazine and newspaper readers interested, Moore appeared not to take sides. Yet in the context of the antagonisms in circulation within modernism and deployed to promote modernism, Moore's refusal to adopt a position is itself agonistic and functions to expose the symbolic violence reinforcing masculine literary and critical authority. Moore's comments, I would suggest, have fangs, to borrow an image Moore uses with reference to T. S. Eliot's *Prufrock and Other Observations*.[9] While she herself disapproved of Pound's 'promptness with the cudgels', as she told him at the beginning of their correspondence, she did not withdraw from the fight; she preferred to use scalpels rather than weapons.[10]

Queering the Pitch

The *Dial*'s institutional habitus, its defining ethos was bound up with its powers of cultural consecration, more specifically, its promotion of literary genius or what Pierre Bourdieu refers to as the 'charismatic ideology'.[11] In 1922 and 1923, Thayer and Watson were clearly following the advice of their business manager and investing heavily in advertising in an attempt to promote their publication beyond the 'little' magazine market. A number of display ads appeared in high-circulation newspapers such as the *New York Herald*, *Theatre Magazine*, the *Literary Review*, the *New York Evening Post*, the *New York Times Book Review* and the *New York Tribune* all featuring a column of illustrious heads announcing forthcoming work by authors such as Anatole France, Thomas Mann, Katherine Mansfield, Knut Hamsun, Henry James and Van Wyck Brooks. These adverts occupied a single column. The advertisement that appears in the *Yale Daily News* in 1922 and again in 1923 in the *New York Times Book Review* as well as the *Literary Review* and *Theatre Magazine*, however, is an expensive, high-impact, full-page ad displaying the illustrious 'men of genius'. By comparing the literary 'men of genius' published in the *Dial* to well-known Ivy League football players, the advertisement fetishises the figure of the author, while simultaneously maintaining an aura of privilege and exclusivity associated with the Ivy League colleges (see Fig. 3.1). The design places the title of the *Dial* centre-stage, framed by the photographs of literary figures. The headline, 'Men of Genius' is followed by some name-dropping: 'The Conrads and Santayanas of literature are as rare as the O'Hearns and Buells of football.' John 'Jack' O'Hearn, a graduate of Cornell, played for the Cleveland Tigers in the early 1920s and Charley Buell was a quarterback for Harvard's football team. By yoking the names of two canonical writers to the names of two Ivy League football players, the advertisement hails the reader in terms of gender, race and social class. The reader of the *Dial*, it is assumed, is familiar with these names and is, by association, linked to the privilege and power of an expensive, private college education. This is not necessarily to assert that the magazine wished to appeal only to Ivy League graduates, but rather that it wanted to maintain an image of exclusivity. At the same time, it offers consumers, 'people of intelligence and sophistication', the opportunity to join this exclusive club, to rise above 'the welter of mediocrities and commercial reputations' that characterise modern culture by buying the magazine and

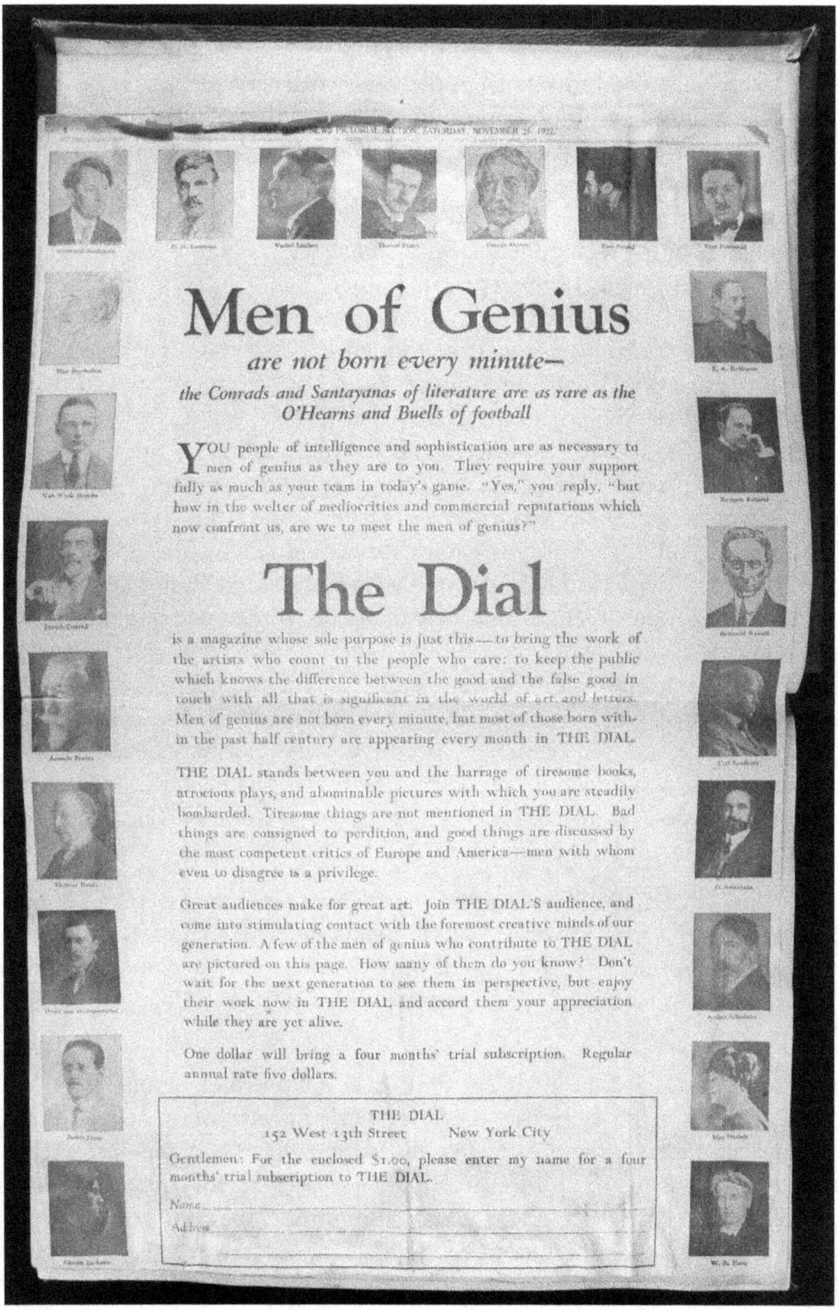

Figure 3.1 'Men of Genius', *Yale Daily News*, 25 November 1922, ST/Dial Papers, Box 14, Fol. 340.

thereby supporting the great writers of their generation. Thayer and Watson's promotional tactics are underpinned by an understanding of the literary field as a 'select club' sustained by a faith in the value of artistic genius.[12]

The concluding paragraph continues to suggest that the audience for great art is as important as art itself, an echo of *Poetry* magazine's masthead which it borrowed from Walt Whitman, 'To have great poetry we must have great audiences.' It then goes on to challenge the reader to a game of guess the author: 'A few of the men of genius who contribute to THE DIAL are pictured on this page. How many of them do you know?' The suggestion that the reader might be ignorant of such literary greatness raises the spectre of social embarrassment, a familiar advertising strategy that exploits the reader's social and personal insecurities.[13] The 'cure', however, is not directly related to reading, but rather to 'knowing' great writers. As Jaffe, following Rainey, points out, modernism's circulation did not depend on the reading of modernist texts, but rather the 'promotion of the author's reputation among non-readers'.[14] In other words, the *Dial*'s advertisements offer a short cut to the acquisition of cultural capital, a way of not-reading modernist texts while simultaneously acquiring the prestige capital associated with them.

What might be surprising is that in January 1923 the 'men of genius' would not include T. S. Eliot, whose much talked-about poem, *The Waste Land*, had been published in the *Dial* in November 1922. The publication of *The Waste Land* two months earlier had signalled the magazine's canon-making status, its ability to recognise Eliot's genius. The omission of Eliot may be evidence that the editors were assuming his name was already associated with the *Dial* in the mind of the reader, reinforcing his own literary reputation as well as that of the magazine. As Aaron Jaffe points out,

> during [the 1920s], Eliot's name represented more than a coterie concern, more than a fringe avocation in bohemian quarters and among the literary intelligentsia [. . .] as a cultural signifier, Eliot's name represented more than the sum of those intimate with his works.[15]

This was, of course, the reason why Thayer and Watson agreed to publish *The Waste Land* without having read it. Eliot's name had acquired, by 1922, what Bourdieu refers to as the 'magic power of transubstantiation'.[16] In the promotional context, the aim of the advertisement was to generate the kind of collective frisson, the allure and mystique associated with the figure of the celebrity. The modernist text was less important than the construction of authorial 'genius', as a number of the *Dial*'s early advertisements suggest. The modernist author is constructed as unique in the context of a culture that the *Dial* referred to as 'standardized'.

In spite of the presence of one lone woman writer, May Sinclair, the charismatic ideology visualises literary genius as masculine. Women are capable of playing the game, acquiring the 'values, virtues and competences' that allow them to succeed in the literary field, but at the same time, the game serves to reinforce the power and privilege of men.[17] The absence of women intimates their presence elsewhere, contributing to the 'barrage' of cultural clutter that is implicitly associated with mediocre literary non-entities. The literary superstars whose disembodied heads represent artistic genius in all its timeless and transcendent splendour operate to secure the purity of the art object. In subscribing to the *Dial*, the Ivy League graduate, plays for the same 'team' as the 'men of genius'. This is a select and exclusive old boys' club, whose cultural hegemony was, by the early 1920s, being threatened by the middlebrow.

As I have already suggested in the previous chapter, what becomes crucial in this context is not the distinction between mass culture and modernism, but rather the less discernible differences between modernism and the middlebrow. The subtext of many of the *Dial*'s advertisements is that the privileges of whiteness and maleness can be maintained only by being able to distinguish between modernism and middlebrow culture. The *Dial* is, according to an advertisement placed in the *New York Evening Post*, 'where discrimination survives', its 'divining rod of judgement' is capable of discerning 'aesthetic excellence' amid 'standardized fiction, standardized special articles, standardized criticism'.[18] In order to make those discriminations, consumers require the mediating and interpreting guidance of the magazine and its critics, reviewers and editors. As numerous cultural historians have pointed out, the 'problem' for the literary consumer in the 1920s was the sheer proliferation of books available in the marketplace. The response to this problem was to invoke the figure of the expert, who was capable of managing this textual tsunami for the reader. The *Dial* presents itself as being able to distinguish between middlebrow mediocrity and 'the classics of To-day and Tomorrow'. It helps the reader to recognise the 'faux bon', the 'literary imposter', a publication that might appear 'well-groomed' but in fact 'compromises with the semi-popular highbrow standards of good form and good taste'.[19] Echoing Margaret Anderson's tag line for the *Little Review*, 'Making no Compromise with the Public Taste', the copy asserts that 'the *Dial* makes no such compromise', claiming an allegiance to 'lasting, artistic values'.[20] As a magazine, the *Dial* is actively engaged in the production of the symbolic value of the work of art and also in the production of 'consumers capable of recognising the work of art as such'.[21]

It is worth briefly comparing the *Dial*'s advertising copy to copy generated by its rival magazines as evidence of its use of language to embody the idea of an enduring and stable tradition. The *Atlantic Monthly*, for instance, places an ad in the *Dial* in 1924 that is addressed to the consumer in letterform. Here the reader is invited to play the game by joining a club slightly less exclusive than the one the *Dial* puts into circulation. The strategy of flattery is employed in the opening paragraph – the consumer has been 'chosen' because she/he has 'a definite regard for good reading and fine literature'. The magazine offers the potential consumer the opportunity to read well-known writers, as well as writers 'whom you are going to know'. The work of emerging writers is only included if it 'measures up' and this colloquial turn of phrase is placed in quotation marks to indicate a self-consciousness concerning its use. It goes on to promise that as a reader of the *Atlantic*, 'you enjoy right off the press many things that others will be trying to look up later on'.[22] Though the sentiment is the same, it is expressed in a language that is distinctly different to the tone the *Dial* adopts. Compare the relatively forthright and punchy prose of the *Atlantic* with the pose Alyse Gregory adopts in her advertisement foregrounding the *Dial*'s aestheticism:

> Just as the Yellow Book, while laughed at by the vulgar, misunderstood by the illiterate, and despised by the reformer, is not passionately sought for by the sagacious connoisseur as representative of all that was most daring and original in the great epoch to which it belonged, so THE DIAL – the magazine of the *Illuminati* – will become a precious monument to the taste of the cultivated minority of the 'twenties, where that taste has responded to the boldest and least conventional of modern men of genius.[23]

Appearing in a number of venues in 1924, including *Century* magazine, the *Bookman Advertiser*, the *Forum* and *Future Historians*, Gregory's language repeatedly insists upon the exclusive and sophisticated nature of its audience, not only in its references to a 'cultivated minority' and its return to the monumental 'men of genius', but also in its generation of a Jamesian sentence of syntactical complexity that signals its erudition. The *Atlantic*, as its penultimate paragraph implies, is aimed at the upper-middle class whose friends include: the 'college classmate, family physician, business partner, minister [and] hostess of the summer'. While the *Atlantic* publishes the 'finest' literature of the day and benefits from the presiding 'genius' of its editor, Gregory's *Dial* out-cultivates the qualities. Its emphasis on passion, taste and daring deliberately distances itself from its staid, genteel competitors.

Compare Gregory's advertisement to one written by Moore in 1924:

> SERIOUS PLEASURE
>
> 'The more vivid and overwhelming pleasure becomes, the more absolutely serious a thing it is.' If you have time to spend upon near literature, there is plenty of it, but there is nothing more wasteful than mock erudition 'nor more frivolous than pedantry.'
>
> In THE DIAL you will find chiselled prose, accurate sculpture, witty painting, prismatic poetry, sensitive fiction, perspicuous criticism.
>
> Bertrand Russell, the most unforbidding philosopher, will discuss in a forthcoming issue of THE DIAL, Civilization and Ethics.

> Arthur Schnitzler, who exemplifies the mastercraftsman's ambition to present life without taking sides, and Thomas Mann, the perfect exponent of sage, romantically iridescent imagination, will contribute fiction; as will Glenway Wescott in a poetically perfect vignette, decorously simple, authentically American.[24]

Gregory had written to Moore in February 1924 asking for two advertisements. Even without this evidence, the taut precision of the language reflects Moore's signature style. Moore deploys some favourite terms here – including 'chiselled' and 'perspicuous' (which she'd also used in 1924 essays on H.D. and Francis Bacon, respectively).[25] The promise of 'prismatic poetry' echoes her own poem 'In the Days of Prismatic Color'; pleasure as serious is, indeed, the theme of her 1921 poem 'When I Buy Pictures', published in the *Dial*.[26]

Unlike Gregory, Moore's advertisement seems less concerned with positioning itself in relation to its competitors and less concerned with establishing its highbrow credentials. Moore's poems are full of borrowed phrases and in this advertisement, headlined 'Serious Pleasure', she refers to the 'absolutely serious' pleasure of museums from Benjamin Ives Gilman's *Museum Ideals of Purpose and Method*, implicitly comparing museum collections to magazines. Through the Ives borrowing, Moore frames the *Dial* as a showcase for aesthetic diversity. Underpinned by her own poetic principles of 'connoisseurship', Moore emphasises the distinctive qualities of each writer she alludes to. Schnitzler is the 'mastercraftsman' unwilling to 'take sides', Mann, the 'perfect exponent of sage, romantically iridescent imagination' and Wescott, 'decorously simple, authentically American'. Moore distils each writer's stylistic qualities within one dense paragraph, attaining what Boroff describes as an 'expressive density' that is typical of the lyrical advertisement and many of Moore's poems.[27]

Though Moore deploys terms that signal erudition, her copy makes no assumptions here concerning who is 'worth knowing'. Instead, the textual pleasure of reading the *Dial* is invoked through Moore's dexterous language. Moore makes the advertisement itself a thing of pleasure, a strategy that reinforces her resistance to the categorical divides separating art from commercial language. Moreover, the advertisement emphasises valuing the diversity of writing within the magazine, not creating cultural hierarchies. Even her opening quotation, which might elsewhere serve as a highbrow authority claim, she handles playfully, in a manner that blurs boundaries (here between frivolity and pedantry), rather than enforcing them.

Moore displays a similar resistance to reinforcing the high/low cultural divide in her poetry. In 'People's Surroundings' Moore imports an advertisement from the *New York Times* to describe 'paper so thin that one thousand four hundred and/ twenty pages make one inch'.[28] Thirty years later in 'The

Artic Ox (or Goat)' the speaker points to the absences of 'distinction' between commercial and poetic language: 'If you fear that you are/ reading an advertisement,/ you are.'[29] As Elizabeth Gregory suggests, Moore 'neither fears nor feels embarrassed about crossing the line into commerce'.[30] This resistance to brow boundaries informs Moore's curatorial understanding of the *Dial*, which in many ways undercuts the *Dial*'s own marketing strategies.

Moore's aesthetics of display does not value one thing at the expense of another. Her compact list making, laden with adjectival phrases, seeks to delete evidence of an interpretive or critical framework that might reproduce the cultural hierarchies reinforcing what she describes in her poem 'When I Buy Pictures' as 'that which is great because something else is small'.[31] Crucially, however, the 'serious pleasure' of 'picking and choosing', to borrow another Moore title, is formally bound to the poetics of compression and virtuous editing: In both instances, there is a resistance to making connections.[32] This resistance to connections might also be understood in terms of what Natalia Cecire refers to as 'grammatical subordination'. Cecire argues that in 'To a Snail' Moore achieves 'precision' by 'grammatically decentralizing meaning'. Drawing on and extending Paul's discussion of Moore's curatorial approach, Cecire holds that Moore's poetics of precision intersects with 'tensions that are already present in the practices of natural history – the tensions, in particular between thing and name, between category and specimen, and between detail and comprehensibility'.[33] In 'To a Snail', Cecire suggests, Moore 'defer[s] abstract categories in favor of naming some solid, intractable thing'.[34]

This deferral of the abstract foregrounds the discrete item, what Gilman calls the *unicum*. This is evident in Moore's advertisement. Whereas Watson and Gregory foreground the magazine's ethos, Moore's foregrounds the unique characteristics of each writer, paring these down until they sit within her sentences like 'chiselled ivory', hard, distinct and radically different from each other. Moore strives to maintain the integrity of the singular item and the heterogeneity of the collection.[35] As I will suggest in the next two chapters, editorial compression is a strategy deployed to accomplish this by dispensing with semantic terms that join, fuse and integrate.

Moore practises a form of compression in the other advertisements she wrote for the magazine; for instance, in this advertisement used repeatedly from 1927 to 1929 in a range of magazines from *Harper's* to *The Modern Quarterly*, *Creative Art*, *The Arts* and *The Menorah Journal*:

> THE DIAL is that fastidious, unaverage instance of substantial judgement you have wished for – an aesthetic Gibraltar manifesting love for art and an expertness to present it. The elsewhere defrauded reader finds here a fearlessness which both assails and saves him – a sympathy with

> unacknowledged excellence and unsympathy with carelessness, confusion, and insensibility paraded as 'consistency.'
> THE DIAL is generous, agile, unencased, and open to conviction. It has a fondness for learning, not for a leaning towards learning. Its unique importance as a journal of art and letters is attested each month by the poems, essays, articles, and reproductions which appear in it.[36]

The compression achieved through formations with 'un' as in 'unaverage', unsympathy', 'unacknowledged' and 'unencased' and the addition of a suffix as in 'expertness' is evident in many of Moore's poems. For instance, the poem 'England', first published in 1920 in the *Dial*, refers to America as 'grass-less, links-less, language-less' producing the strange effect of invoking something while simultaneously denying its presence. The 1919 poem 'In the Days of Prismatic Color' refers to the 'fineness' and 'obliqueness' of the days before 'complexity'. Such strategies of condensation are particularly evident in the poems Moore wrote in the 1930s. In 'Virginia Britannia' insect sounds are 'unEnglish', the nation's 'first flag' is 'undiffident', the terrapin 'unpoisonous'. In 'Bird-Witted' the 'sun-lit' air is 'unenergetic', in 'The Pangolin' the titular animal 'draws/ away from/ danger unpugnaciously' and if 'unintruded on' will 'come slowly down the tree'.[37]

The use of polysyllabic latinate words is also a stylistic feature Moore carries over from her poetry into her promotional prose. One of her favourite words, 'fastidious', is frequently deployed to designate verbal clarity. 'Consistency', 'insensibility', 'defraud', 'manifest' 'substantial' and 'attest' all have Latin origins and all convey in precise terms Moore's intended meaning. Nouns often serve adjectival functions. For instance, the magazine is 'that fastidious, unaverage instance of substantial judgement'. Rather than being merely descriptive, Moore's complex noun phrases convert things to other things. In this instance, the magazine is 'that instance', which then carries with it a slew of characteristics that define it further.

The use of lists, something particularly evident in what Leavell refers to as the 'aesthetic of the miscellany' in Moore's long poems such as 'An Octopus' and 'Marriage', is also evident in the advertisement that was circulated in the last two years of the magazine's run. Here Moore's finale is oddly anticlimactic, a feature that Boroff identifies as a form of 'uninsistence':

> Without Respect of Persons
>
> The popular taste is at war with aesthetics. A dominator, a suppliant, a patron of impermanence, it thrusts upon us what we are not able to regard as prophecy and what we have no wish to own. THE DIAL is not patronizing, nor domineering, nor at the service of feebleness. Without respect of persons, for the honour of letters, it holds severely to its independence. It has at no time concerned itself with the place of

a contributor in any movement backward or forward. If you can enjoy the accepted and the unaccepted and are not inclined to cage off either group; if you are a reader, a critic, an artist, who relishes 'daring and invention' and has 'no special objection to being slightly in advance of his friends,' you will wish to take THE DIAL, which publishes with regularity the best work of known and unknown Americans, together with the best work produced in Europe.[38]

Here is an example of what Marie Boroff refers to as Moore 'pushing in the stops'.[39] The claim for the magazine is that it puts the reader 'slightly in advance of his friends', hardly an arresting tag line. In her poems, according to Boroff, Moore frequently practised a form of self-effacement, a 'descent from flights of eloquence to the ground of prose'.[40] In her promotional prose, Moore practises a similar strategy. The *Dial* is a magazine that does 'not wish to own', that does not support any particular movement or group, that does not push any particular philosophy or aesthetic approach. Moore attempts to promote the *Dial*'s neutrality in neutral terms, eschewing the familiar lexicon of 'discrimination' and 'distinction' deployed by Thayer, Watson, Seldes and Gregory. The repeated use of negatives in 'no wish to own', 'not patronizing, nor domineering, nor at the service of feebleness' and in 'having no time', and being 'not inclined' signals Moore's desire to mimic the display strategies she attempted to deploy in the contents of the magazine itself; the presentation of a diverse range of verbal and visual material without reproducing hierarchical distinctions.

Editorial Agonism

As we have seen, in 'flaring' Moore, Thayer adopts a chivalrous and at times flirtatious tone, performing a role that both consecrates Moore and confirms his own institutional power as editor of the *Dial*. In many ways, his treatment of Moore was unusual in that the majority of his editorial comments were responding to or initiating dialogue, debate and sometimes outright hostilities with other publications, editors, critics and authors. Thayer's tone shifts from highbrow critic to lowbrow enthusiast, from chivalry to misogyny (though the two are not that far apart), from witty, cultural connoisseur and man about town to sneering snob impatient with perceived mediocrities and from formal, aristocratic dignity to emotional, overblown near-hysterical outbursts. Undoubtedly, Thayer's deteriorating mental health meant that there were times when he sacrificed the interests of the magazine for his own personal desire for public retribution. On these occasions, Moore stepped in to block Thayer's destructive actions. Nevertheless, Thayer's editorial comments must be understood as public-facing performances, concluding each issue with a statement that reminded the reader of the magazine's distinct discursive signature. The editorial comment, even more than the single items included in each issue or the regular Theatre, Music or Art sections, was bound up with the institutional habitus of the magazine. Unsigned, these short observation pieces further complicate notions of authorship in the context of magazine publication and must be read in relation to the internal and external dialogics of the magazine.

In many ways, Thayer conforms to the charismatic model of editing described by Philpotts and exemplified by Ford at the *English Review*. Thayer, unlike Ford, however, did not come from a family of bohemian artists and writers. What Thayer lacked in cultural capital, he more than made up for in the kind of connections and education that only wealth can buy. He inherited a fortune from his father's wool business, making it possible for him to sink vast sums of money into his prestigious but commercially unsuccessful magazine. The *Dial* dinner parties he hosted gathered the artists and writers linked to the magazine and were designed not only to cultivate sophisticated banter and artistic cross-fertilisation, but also to showcase Thayer's impeccable taste and ample largesse. Hildegarde Watson, recalling these lavish affairs, describes them as 'an institution' and recalls Thayer's fastidiousness when planning such social occasions. Thayer's 'magnetic looks and personality [. . . turned] heads' according to Watson.[41] Moore herself had her head turned at the beginning of her friendship with Thayer. He 'has a gorgeous library, about 3 walls full of light calf bindings or blue bindings', she wrote excitedly to her brother after taking tea with Thayer at his rooms in the Benedict Club. Moore marvelled at Thayer's collection of Beardsleys, cubist paintings and other 'art treasures' she saw hanging on his walls, together with the various pieces of furniture, 'a red lacquer cabinet three little benches and a smoking stand in front of the fireplace' that populated his rooms.[42]

Thayer cultivated an image of cosmopolitan aestheticism in his life and in his editorial comments. His editorials performed the role of the sophisticated connoisseur, a well-connected patron of the arts, a dilettante and a modernist dandy. His editorial comments engage in sparring with a range of magazines, high-profile critics and newspaper columnists. Readers of the *Dial* would often have been privy to Thayer's vituperative swipes, amused perhaps by his mocking jibes, amazed at his audacity. His awareness of the importance of publicity, even bad publicity, informs his editorial comment and in this, he was much like many of his rival editors. As Jason Harding points out in his discussion of the periodical networks within which the *Criterion* operated, there was mutual benefit for magazine editors in stoking controversy:

> *The Criterion* and the *Adelphi* were not really in direct competition and aimed, for the most part, at discrete audiences. They did, however, propound rival cultural politics, capitalizing upon the existence of the other

> as a catalyst, or as a foil, to issue an opportunistic *prise de position* or to boost flagging fortunes.[43]

As an example of the internal dialogics of the magazine and the relation between the editorial comment and the content, the March 1924 issue of the *Dial* is, in some ways, typical. The issue headlines with the first instalment of Kenneth Burke's translation of Thomas Mann's *Death in Venice.* The first page of Mann's novel sits opposite the coloured frontispiece, 'Rue à Nesles' by French Fauvist, Maurice de Vlaminck. Paul Morand writes the Paris letter, there is a review of *Some Unknown Drawings of Aubrey Beardsley*, a review by Bertrand Russell, as well as reproductions of American paintings by John Marin and a sketch by e. e. cummings of Charlie Chaplin. This is an issue that showcases exactly what the *Dial* did so well; it brings together the work of American modernists with a range of European art, criticism and literature. Thayer's comment for this issue takes the opportunity to reassert the cultural prestige of his magazine through an attack on the *New York Times.* Thayer's comment, benefiting from the symbolic value of the contributions preceding it, is engaged in illustrating the limited expertise and resources at the disposal of the *New York Times.* What is particularly striking, however, is the way in which gender becomes the focus of Thayer's criticism and how this is linked to the professionalisation of criticism and the emerging discipline of literature. He begins his attack by naming the columnist in question and then cracking a joke at her expense:

> Miss Elizabeth Luther Cary is the art critic of an exotic sheet which I myself do not come across so often as I should wish. I believe it goes by the name of 'The New York Times.' I am further informed that for a good many years now Miss Elizabeth Luther Cary has there been breaking silence – and in a dignified manner – weekly.[44]

Cary had the misfortune to be assigned to review the *Dial* folio, *Living Art*, a collection of reproductions from Thayer's art collection. Thayer admits in his comment that the review is expansive and also that he was advised not to name the reviewer in question because of 'the delicate matter of her sex'.[45] He justifies the naming and shaming of Cary by pointing out that 'these days [. . .] ladies are all about us'. Cary's article is surrounded by advertisements for 'Women's silk full-fashioned lace clocked hose' and 'High grade refrigerators', signalling that women are no longer excluded from the public sphere and need no protection from the vulgarities of the marketplace.[46] Chivalry, in the context of a mass consumerism associated with 'ladies' and their undergarments, is now dead. Unlike Moore, who shines like a beacon above the sordid materialism of the commercial world, Cary is already compromised by writing in a mass-circulation periodical. She is, to put it simply, fair game for public ridicule having placed herself in an already compromising position.

Thayer's critique of Cary's review is all the more devastating for its aloof and superior tone. Miss Cary, according to Thayer, will have been familiar with the painting called *September Morn* by Paul Emil Chabas because it appeared in a number of shop windows of department stores. The painting had won a gold medal of honour in 1912 at the Paris Salon but, when reproductions were shipped to the US, it caused a controversy for its depiction of nudity. Charges of indecency by Anthony Comstock led to art dealers in New York and Chicago being prosecuted.[47] According to Thayer, this particular painting is in Cary's mind when she is writing about André Dunoyer de Segonzac's *The River Morin in Spring*, a pen-and-ink drawing that appears in *Living Art*. This, together with her lack of familiarity with the geography of France, leads to an embarrassing mistake:

> Miss Carey read the title of this picture, The Morin in Spring. Not being familiar with the chief rivers of France, and apparently not being furnished by this journal, The Times, with a map of that country, and harbouring in her unconscious a potent and indelible image of that masterpiece, September Morn, and being, after all, but a poor human woman, she brightly and automatically assimilated 'Morin' to 'morn'.[48]

It is not only Cary, but the periodical she writes for, according to Thayer, that lacks the cultural competency to offer meaningful critical insights into art. Cary, like the young woman and her mother, whom Thayer mentions in his comment of November 1920, who think jealousy an unfitting subject for the theatre, exemplify the bland taste of the middlebrow. It is the 'kindly tap water of the New York Times' among other publications that Thayer objects to.[49] These women are comparable to the 'eyeless' Cook tourists Thayer complained about in his letters to Elaine Orr, the 'women who come and go/ Talking of Michelangelo' in Eliot's 'The Love Song of J. Alfred Prufrock' and Pound's more blatantly misogynistic description of a 'botched culture' as 'an old bitch gone in the teeth' in *Hugh Selwyn Mauberley*. The implication being that most women do not have the cultural competence to engage critically with highbrow culture and have no business reviewing the publications of connoisseurs such as Thayer.

Even though this issue of the *Dial* includes reviews of Edith Wharton's *A Son at the Front*, Elinor Wylie's *Jennifer Lorn*, poems by Jessica Nelson North and Mabel Simpson and 'Briefer Mentions' of *Their Heir* by Vita Sackville-West, Charlotte Perkins Gilman's *His Religion and Hers* and Louise Bogan's *Body of This Death*, the symbolic violence enacted in Thayer's comments reinforces the cultural divides separating modernism from the 'faux bon'.[50] Intimately bound up with modernism and its institutionalisation is an opposition to what is perceived to be a middlebrow mediocrity that is compromised by its commercial popularity and its limited cultural capital. The comment is as an editorial performance that is deliberately provocative in order to incite a response from the higher circulation periodical. This was certainly one of the ways Thayer ensured that his magazine was talked about in the popular press.

It is no surprise then that in April of that year, the *New York Times* took a swipe at the *Dial* applauding its engagement with the 'lively arts', while also pointing out that by taking pleasure in popular culture, the *Dial* was simply catching up to what most of the American public already knew, that popular entertainment is entertaining:

> Steadily the gap between the common people and the subtle intelligences is being filled up. The latest step in this happy rapprochement has been made by one of the editors of The Dial, who finds that there is something to be said for a number of things in which the common people take pleasure, such as Charlie Chaplin, vaudeville shows, comic strips, colyumists, clowns, jugglers and musical comedies. Some day we may yet have the select spirits discovering that there is something deserving of approval in the popular view on such subjects as three meals a day, eight hours of sleep, marrying, bringing up children, and being fond of them, and similar ordinary practices.[51]

The *New York Times*'s response exemplifies exactly why Thayer may have been impatient with consumers more familiar with the controversies of nudity in art than in art itself. The bourgeois institution of marriage and the family, the regularity of a working day and the 'natural' love for one's children, the very 'ordinary practices' that the *New York Times* assumes are central to American life and values, remain untouched by the seismic aesthetic quakes of the Armory Show or the *Ulysses* trial. While Thayer and his writers at the *Dial* immerse themselves in the maelstrom of modern forms, seeking to challenge American values through visual art and literature, the *New York Times* and presumably the majority of its readers, remain comfortably immune to Thayer's highbrow assaults.

Thayer did not limit himself to criticising one publication though. Many of his comments were aimed at rival journals, such as the *New York Tribune* or the *Atlantic*, Jane Heap at the *Little Review* or Clive Bell writing for *Vanity Fair*.[52] He complains more generally about what he refers to as 'colyumism', an impressionistic, undisciplined and ill-informed approach to interpreting and understanding art and literature. Sentiment and feeling underpin this approach, signalling its attachment to femininity. As numerous cultural historians have pointed out, the institutionalisation of modernism coincided with the emergence of the discipline of literature and the increasingly professionalised role of the critic. The *Dial* itself played an important part in disseminating and debating the various critical approaches that might be adapted and, more importantly, taught to students of literature. Moore presided over a golden age of criticism, bringing I. A. Richards into conversation with T. S. Eliot, continuing to publish Seldes' analyses of the lively arts and introducing the important but neglected critical method of Kenneth Burke. Crucially, this emerging discipline was also framed by the institutional habitus of the magazine reinforcing its difference from the sentimental and subjective critical responses of newspaper and mass magazine critics.

Exacting Sincerity

Moore's comments offer a marked contrast to Thayer's. While unsigned, they bear her stylistic signature: list-laden, compact, formal in tone yet often barely containing a delight in the plethora of things that, 'give pleasure' to borrow a phrase from Moore's poem, 'When I Buy Pictures'.[53] The reader of Moore's comments is often flung from the familiar to the obscure with bewildering speed. John Ashbery's description of the white knuckle nature of reading poems by Moore might easily be transferred to the experience of reading her editorial comments:

> They start smoothly enough ('The monkeys winked too much and were afraid of snakes'), like a ride on a roller coaster, and in no time at all one is clutching the bar with both hands, excited and dismayed at the prospect of 'ending up in the décor' as the French say of a car that drives off the road.[54]

Moore's succinct editorial comments move with breathtaking swiftness between items, categories, ideas and images deploying the 'force of omission', dispensing with connectives and 'too academic adverbs', achieving what she describes as 'compactness compacted'.[55] Many of Moore's promotional strategies are deployed in these essays in an attempt to display or exhibit the object world in all its 'expressive density' to borrow Boroff's phrase again.

Moore's first comment in July 1925 announces a very different editorial approach to Thayer's. Amy Lowell had died the previous month, making it necessary to acknowledge her achievements and to pay respect. Moore's tribute is gracious yet unsentimental, recognising that Lowell was 'cosmopolitan but isolated'.[56] Lowell had incited Pound's wrath by taking a leading role in the promotion of Imagism; in his opinion, taking over and diluting the modernist poetry associated with that school. His public attacks on Lowell and her brand of 'Amygism' as well as his private personal quips of her as a 'hippopoetess' effectively 'isolated' Lowell from those poets with whom she felt most aligned.[57] Moore's comment had to achieve a delicate balancing act, refraining too obviously from taking sides either against Pound or Lowell, but also having the *Dial* pay its respects to a poet and anthologist who made a significant contribution to the promotion of the new poetry. She begins by introducing questions that revolve around what we might now think of in terms of influence and intertextuality. Acknowledging that poets might be unaware of their influences, or even that, at times, literary texts are produced in an echo chamber that resonates with the words of writers who came before and who will come after, Moore prepares the ground for a reconsideration of Lowell's poetic achievements, which were often dismissed as derivative. Moore implicitly questions the concept of originality itself, that the author is the sole source or origin of the work of art. Thus H.D. is, according to Moore, 'unequivocally Greek', Stevens sports French plumage, Pound wears 'the cloak of medieval romance', cummings betrays the 'courtly' atmosphere of the fourteenth and sixteenth centuries and Eliot 'recalls to us, the verbal parquetry of Donne'.[58]

When Lowell is then introduced as a poet 'genetic[ally]' related to Keats, she is in good company and has been ushered, symbolically and posthumously, into the club that had excluded her. No longer is her poetry denigrated for being overly indebted to Romanticism or for cynically switching between imagism, vorticism and polyphonic prose. What unifies her work is her love of Keats, illustrated in extracts from some of Lowell's poems. Moore is careful; Lowell is only 'sometimes modern' but always 'self-dependently American'. She does not admire Lowell's poetry as much as she admires Pound's or H.D.'s, but she does question the concept of authenticity and, by implication, the charismatic ideology of the author as genius that consecrates poets and their traditions. Traces of Moore's own sense of isolation might be detected in her closing sentence. Drawing on the familiar trope of self-protection, Moore notes that Lowell's 'armored self-reliance' has 'obscured a generosity, a love of romance, the luster of chivalry'.[59] The need for protection in the context of the public sphere and the aggressive hard-sell tactics deployed by Pound in particular, requires some poets, particularly women poets, to adopt defensive strategies.

In her editorial comments, Moore puts into practice her ethical and aesthetic principles. This means avoiding taking a consistent critical position or offering instruction or engaging in acts of denigration. Nothing could be further from Thayer's stridently aggressive editorial posturing and this might be why so many critics have dismissed her critical reviews and comments as vague, lacking in analytical rigour and seeming to rely too much on Moore's own rather quirky tastes. Donald Hall describes them as 'impressionistic and unaimed' and Bernard Engel refers to them as 'graceful presentations of observations and impressions, the kind of statement one might expect from a good reader rather than from a professional critic'.[60] This resistance to critical agonism, as Evan Kindley brilliantly argues, is complex, sometimes tinged with envy, sometimes rejecting the aggressive stance of the critic but ultimately, adopting a position somewhere between the critic and the connoisseur. At the

Dial, Moore 'preserves some of the active authority and prestige of the agonistic poet-critic without forcing her to compromise her natural reticence'.[61] Reading 'When I Buy Pictures' as a metaphor for the activity of editing a little magazine, Kindley asserts that Moore's editorial practice allows her to perform the role of the disinterested connoisseur whose selections are made 'on behalf of a cultural institution and a grateful public: The *Dial* and its readers'. This allows Moore to 'short-circuit [. . .] all of that untidy agonistic activity that made Moore so ill at ease; the speaker can, at last, simply pick and choose the good from the bad without worrying at all about "intellectual emphasis" or rational justification'.[62]

The public role of the editor, however, complicates the metaphor of Moore's acquisition of imaginary pictures. In many ways, as editor of the *Dial*, Moore would have been conscious of occupying a position in the public sphere that gave her cultural authority and influence beyond the small readership her poems may have had at the beginning of the 1920s. In other words, even if Moore had wanted to adopt the role of connoisseur, simply picking and choosing, her choices would resonate profoundly within public-sphere debate concerning the value of art and the role of cultural institutions in supporting that art. Moore's impressionistic essays, interpreted within the context of the critical agonism in circulation within modernism and as a means of circulating modernism, become themselves, agonistic and critically provocative. Controversially, Moore adopts the sentimental tropes associated with the reviews Thayer denigrates as 'colyumism'. For Moore, 'instinct' and 'feeling' are the triggers for critical and creative work allowing her to refuse the choices made on her behalf and, crucially, on behalf of others. Moore lays critical landmines in her editorial comments that may well have remained undetected and undetonated because she seemed so ardently wedded to not taking sides or positions. Yet interpreted within the literary field, a field in which small but significant acts of symbolic violence operate to discriminate, divide and categorise, Moore's refusals suggest that matters of taste and selection are never disinterested and that they have material, social and ethical consequences.

A good example of one of these critical landmines is the comment Moore wrote for the November 1925 issue of the *Dial*. Given the magazine's ties to Harvard, it is striking that she begins with the words of Dr Eliot, President Emeritus of Harvard:

> Dr. Eliot, the President Emeritus of Harvard, regards as our foremost educators during the last 2300 years, Aristotle, Galen, Leonardo da Vinci, Sir Francis Bacon, Milton, Shakespeare, John Locke, Immanuel Kant, Sir Isaac Newton, and Ralph Waldo Emerson. Advantaged by his fearlessness to choose, one acknowledges that one might choose

> similarly, and is reluctant to remember that one's predilection for these justly celebrated persons has in some measure been instructed.[63]

Unlike Dr Eliot, Moore is fearful of making such choices, aware that they are not so much choices as instructions passed on from one generation to the next. It is this process of instruction and dissemination she then goes on to explore. She compares Dr Eliot's decemvirs to 'lesser sages' in a series of rhetorical questions that deconstruct Eliot's canon. Roger Ascham, one of Moore's favourites, is compared to Aristotle, both achieving a 'compactness' of thought in their writings on education. More unlikely is the comparison she draws between Ralph Waldo Emerson and Maria Edgeworth, the nineteenth-century Anglo-Irish novelist. Both writers should be equally celebrated for avoiding platitudes. Her third comparison not only introduces another woman but also undermines the generic boundaries reinforcing Dr Eliot's tradition. Moore compares Leonardo da Vinci with the children's book illustrator and writer, Kate Greenaway. For Moore, both achieve an 'indelible simplicity'. Galen's influence on medicine is compared to the lesser-known work of Doctor Goldsmith. Luther Burbank's experiments, which have historically been denigrated as 'witchcraft', are compared to the scientific observations of Sir Isaac Newton. Moore concludes this series of comparisons by attributing the 'educational ideal embodied in the phrase "a sound mind in a sound body" as much to the influence of *The Compleat Angler* as to the philosopher John Locke'.[64]

Moore's second sentence begins with a subordinate clause, 'Advantaged by his fearlessness to choose'. The word 'advantaged' signals not only Dr Eliot's lack of hesitancy concerning his choices of literary classics but also his social privilege. It is the cultural capital that comes with Dr Eliot's Harvard connection that makes him 'fearless' and that also points to the connection between judgements concerning literary value and the social production of the literary canon. Like many Americans, Moore would have been familiar with Dr Eliot's consecration of the Harvard Classics in 1910 where a range of books were repackaged by the Book of the Month club and sold along with Dr Eliot's five-foot book shelf, 'a handsome quartered oak bookrack which will ornament any library table'.[65] Moore admires the writers Dr Eliot has chosen, but questions the processes by which one writer is privileged over another. When she goes on to name those on her own list of literary favourites, it is no surprise that women's writing, writing for children and popular writing are prominent.

As Moore signalled in her poem, 'Picking and Choosing', published in the *Dial* in April 1920:

> Literature is a phase of life: if
>   one is afraid of it, the situation is irremediable; if
> one approaches it familiarly,
>   what one says of it is worthless.[66]

While choices must be made, the approach taken to such choices must also be examined. As Cristanne Miller suggests, 'Moore rejects falsifying 'familiar[ity]' that takes a privileged stance or interpretation as its due'. This form of 'alternative authority' is, for Miller, central to understanding Moore's refusal to identify as a 'poet', to adopt a position of assumed authority that 'sets itself up as absolute'. Miller points out that Moore saw herself as a 'compiler or editor rather than as "poet"'.[67] As editor of the *Dial*, Moore practises a transgressive authority. In her editorial comments, as in her poetry, Moore consistently interrogates the assumptions embedded within the processes of 'picking and choosing'. She relies upon what she refers to in this poem as 'a right good salvo of barks' to 'put us on the scent' of what is to be valued. Bypassing the institutions and traditions supporting cultural authority, Moore compares herself to the 'Small dog, going over the lawn, nipping the linen and saying// that you have a badger'.[68] Instinct and spontaneity, the scent rather than the sense triggers her responses to art. As Robin Schulze has argued more recently, Moore's pursuit of the 'genuine' in poetry is an attempt to return it to 'the original moment of instinctual response'.[69] In this way, she seeks to resist 'instruct[ing]', or what she refers to in a letter to her brother as an 'Alvin E. Magary condescension and insulting didacticism'.[70] Instinct rather than instruction underpins Moore's engagement with the object world and her selection process.

Moore's poetic manifesto, the poem 'Poetry', exemplifies as Schulze argues, this desire to 'reclaim a lost immediacy by getting back to the concrete roots of language itself – the pre-discursive, pre-interpretive 'genuine' response to 'raw' material.[71] In Moore's editorial comments, the concern that poetic gardens are over-cultivated, artificial and enervating is linked to the critical strategies Moore adopted in her editorial comments. Those who study the natural world such as Charles Darwin, W. P. Pycraft in the *Illustrated London News* or John James Audubon, offer a critical model of observation that relies on scientific methods capable of challenging received opinion. In one of Moore's most-discussed comments, published in the May 1927 issue, she provides an insight into her own editorial method by describing the process of compiling an 'assortment' as both a science and an art:

> Academic feeling, or prejudice possibly, in favor of continuity and completeness is opposed to miscellany – to music programs, composite picture exhibitions, newspapers, magazines, and anthologies. Any zoo, aquarium, library, garden, or volume of letters, however, is an anthology and certain of these selected findings are highly satisfactory. The science of assorting and the art of investing an assortment with dignity are obviously not being neglected, as is manifest in 'exhibitions and sales of artistic property,' and in that sometimes disparaged, most powerful phase of the anthology, the museum.[72]

As Catherine Paul has so convincingly argued, from as early as 1915, Moore had become deeply interested in curatorial theory and was a regular visitor to many of her local galleries and museums, in particular the American Museum of Natural History. Paul interprets Moore's poetry and her editing of the *Dial* as forms of 'creative assembling' comparable to the practices of the museum curator. The pages of the magazine become 'an exhibition space' where Moore 'conveyed her own ideas through curation'.[73] In this editorial comment, Paul suggests, Moore recognises the value of the miscellany but also the role that the 'connoisseur' plays in the selection process; she must have a 'genius for differences' and be skilled in the 'art of comparison and synthesis'.[74] Moore herself concludes her argument by pointing to the 'distinct unity' of a collection as the 'unintentional portrait given, of the mind which brought the assembled integers together'; signalling to the reader that 'the miscellany [. . .] she has assembled in the pages of the *Dial*' is an 'unintentional portrait' of her own aesthetic tastes and discriminations.[75]

While convincing, Paul's emphasis on the mind misses the significance of the body in Moore's argument. In the penultimate two sentences of Moore's comment, she suggests the importance of the collection as 'documents of feeling' and compares it to a 'body' that 'curiously evoke[s] the past'.[76] The diverse things contained within the anthology stimulate sensations and bodily affects capable of bypassing 'academic feeling'. For Moore, I would argue, 'academic feeling' is a form of fake feeling suppressing natural and instinctive responses in its attempt to enforce 'continuity'. In the same comment, Moore reflects on those who have direct access to the experience of things through feeling. 'Persons susceptible to objects of extreme significance' are persons alive to the auratic power of the non-human world. Such persons remember 'with gratitude' various collections on display at the Anderson Galleries. Moore then goes on to provide a characteristically detailed, object-laden descriptive catalogue of some of her own highlights of these collections recalling the 'albino tortoise shell decorated in scrimshaw with an American clipper sail in full sail [. . .] a remarkable Gothic forged iron gate' foregrounding the effect which such displays have on the senses:

> a two-edged Dresden rapier from the armory of the Fortress Hohenwerfen [. . .] seemed to one, super-eminent – the serpent-like nudity of the interlacing spirals about the grip suggesting Swinburne's comment upon Rossetti's *The Song of Lilith*: 'It has the supreme luxury of liberty in its measured grace and lithe melodious motion of rapid and revolving harmony, the subtle action and majestic recoil, the mysterious charm as of soundless music which hangs about the serpent when it stirs or springs.' One cannot be dead to the sagacity inherent in some specimens of sharkskin, camellia-leaf, orange-peel, semi-eggshell, or sang-de-boeuf

> glaze; nor be blind to the glamour of certain 'giant,' 'massive,' 'magnificent' objects in pork-fat or spinach-green jade as show last winter in the collection of Mr. Lee Van Ching at the Anderson Galleries.[77]

It is not only the speaker's mind that is susceptible to the power of objects; it is her body. The accumulation of detail and the resonant intensity of her descriptions suggests such things have an affective power producing a Swinburnian textual excess supposedly alien to a modernist poetics. And of course, this is exactly the point that Moore is making here. Moore signals an aesthetic allegiance not to the phallic forms of a hard-edged masculinist modernism but to its declared 'other', the decadence, aestheticism and suspect romanticism of Swinburne. As Ellen Levy suggests in her reading of this editorial comment, Moore is wary about critical methods that claim authority through objectivity recognising that 'literature's pose of detachment also carries with it the potent threat of exclusion'.[78] Moore's passage emphasises how she is deeply moved by the objects on display, unable to detach herself from the affective force field they generate. The collector and perhaps the editor might be glossed, in these terms, as overly susceptible and sensitive to things. It is not the case of too little feeling but rather too much: 'the deepest feeling shows itself in silence/ not in silence but restraint' as Moore suggests in her poem 'Silence'. The role of the collector or the magazine editor is to display objects with such precision and clarity that the viewer or reader can experience them directly, through the stimulation of feeling rather than through instruction.

It is worth momentarily pausing at this juncture to fully appreciate Robin Schulze's reappraisal of the significance of feeling, instinct and emotion in 'Poetry', Moore's most explicit statement concerning the function of poetry in the context of contemporary anxieties concerning the degenerative effects of modernity. Schulze points to the influence of Darwin's *The Expression of Emotions in Man and Animals* as well as William James's *Psychology*. For Darwin, human emotion is a bodily impulse comparable to the instinctive responses of animals. Examples of this can be seen when fear makes the hair bristle or when teeth are exposed in anger. James also asserts that emotions are bodily reflexes that 'follow directly the perception of the exciting fact and that our feeling of the same changes as they occur IS the emotion'.[79] In other words, rather than going through a thought process that leads to the emotion, the stimulated body produces the emotion. If this is the case, argues James, then each new stimulus, each response to an always changing, living environment produces a multiplicity of distinct and unique emotions that resist categorisation. Understood in these terms, poetry becomes possible for Moore, if poets can bypass 'academic feeling' in order to channel instinct. As Schulze explains it, each poet must 'record his or her unique responses to experience exactly as they occur, without resorting to derivative tropes that, in their separation from the roots of each poet's physiological changes, express nothing intelligible or valuable'.[80]

As an editor, Moore's task was to stimulate her readers, to produce sensations through her display of items in the magazine. Moore knew that such objects did not need to be encountered first hand to achieve such effects. Moore's engagement with the natural world was often mediated. She responded instinctively to things displayed in museums, observed in art galleries, found in magazines or newspapers. These unnatural encounters with the natural world were as 'genuine' as if she were seeing the animal or object first hand. It was the response Moore sought to capture as well as the animal or object observed. As Moore explains in her essay 'Feeling and Precision', 'when we think we don't like art it is because it is artificial art'.[81] She approves of art that is 'artless', that conveys 'emotion intact'. She explains her own fondness for the unaccented rhyme as deriving from 'an instinctive effort to ensure naturalness'.[82] Crucially, 'naturalness' leads to concentration, what Moore describes as the 'force of omission'. Her own objection to connectives is explained in terms of a desire to convey an unmediated, instinctive response that is 'genuine' and to construct a language that does not seek to make connections for the viewer but that allows the viewer to make a connection herself.

In practice, Moore's desire to get at something original, native and natural means that she repeatedly questions all forms of received wisdom, the didactic, the instructive, the canonical and the traditional. It also means that her criticism is an attempt to get outside the discursive frames of criticism itself in order to allow the viewer to connect with the object observed. As Moore suggests in her poem 'Critics and Connoisseurs', she prefers the 'unconsciously fastidious' approach of the connoisseur to the critic.

Feeling becomes central to Moore's uncritical method, ironic given the great lengths critics have gone to construct her poetry as unemotional. In 1924 Richard Aldington argued that Moore 'avoids all appeal to the emotions', in 1927, Laura Riding and Robert Graves's *Survey of Modernist Poetry* suggests that Moore resists 'the temptation to write an emotional poem' and Thayer's promotion of Moore in the *Dial,* as we have seen, emphasises the concrete precision of Moore's verse.[83] Feeling functions in this context to offer what Burke would describe as a 'counter-statement', one that adapts and responds to other statements and repeatedly refuses a fixed critical position. This is where the scientific method becomes particularly important for Moore as a model for learning. In her comment of September 1925, Moore marvels at the 'diverting' and 'enriching' exhibition of children's art at the Metropolitan Museum. Before doing so, she considers the meaning of the term 'education'. She begins the comment with a quotation from the librarian at The Astor Library dating from 1854, which notes how 'the young fry of today', when not studying at school read 'trashy current fiction such as Scott, Cooper, Dickens, Punch and The Illustrated London News'. Moore sees this as evidence that young people are 'spontaneously attracted to that which is educative'. Defined as 'any activity which we value not for its direct results but for its indirect effects upon the capacity of the man who is engaged therein', education is opened up beyond the baneful forms of 'compulsory study' to channel the 'energy and imagination' of children.[84]

The results of this inspiring pedagogic practice can be seen in the 'utmost exactitude, [. . .] the accuracy of the printing; the feeling for scale and texture' of the artwork on display. Many of Moore's key terms are present here. She admires the children's' artwork for its 'instinctive' accumulation of detail, the 'restraint' evident in the lack of decoration and the 'force of omission' achieved in particular designs. Instructed according to the theories of Dr Denman Waldo Ross, there is an instinctive pleasure but also, crucially a 'sense of order' that comes with a particular kind of educational method. According to Ross's manual, *A Theory of Pure Design*, this educational process 'is one of experimenting, observing, comparing, judging, arranging and rearranging, taking no end of time and pains to achieve Order, the utmost possible Order, if possible the Beautiful'. Moore's concluding remarks substitute order for Beauty but reiterates Ross's thesis: 'one is assured that the creating of beauty is, like the appreciating of beauty, in part the result of instruction'.[85]

'Instruction', in this context is active and ongoing, signalled in Ross's use of present participles, 'experimenting, observing'. It is flexible and responsive rather than fixed and pre-determined. This fluid and adaptive method is modelled in the sciences and is also evident within nature itself. In other words, the 'science of assorting' a collection relies upon a continual testing, practicing and experimenting until 'order' is achieved. The practice of compiling an issue of a magazine is comparable in that it requires a method capable of adapting to the material constraints of publication as well as continually testing one's own assumptions and inherited traditions.

As a result, Moore's comments explore a range of cultural material from the illustrated natural history books of John James Audubon, to Lewis Carroll's *Alice in Wonderland*, as well as text books and manuals such as *Mind Your P's and Q's* by Jerome S. Meyer, *Universal Indian Sign Language of the Plains Indians of North America* by William Tompkins, *The Religion of Undergraduates* by Cyril Harris and Alexander Johnson and James Albert Woodburn's *American Orations: Studies in American Political History.* Moore could find textual elegance, the adroit turn of phrase, the pithy, crackling epithet in advertising copy, technical manuals and in travel brochures. In the 'Comment' for February 1929, she suggests that if the reader is willing to look beyond the 'literary', a world of 'serious pleasure' opens up:

> The semi-confidential impartial enthusiasm of the pre-auction descriptive catalogue suggests a desirable mechanics of eulogy and the same kind of honor without exaggeration is seen occasionally in guide-books and travel bureau advertisements. Though somewhat unguarded and uncompactly eager in comparison with Karl Baedeker's contagious impassivity, certain handbooks of the University Travel Department of The North German Lloyd Company pictorially and with characteristic abundance, are a little cyclorama of engaging remarkableness.[86]

In describing commodities for sale, the auction catalogue achieves an impartiality in its language, a way of 'honoring' things without exaggeration. Marie Boroff connects 'the conventional self-presentation of the "expounding I"' in promotional prose to the apparent self-effacement in many of Moore's poems. In both instances, there is withdrawal, a 'retreat from centre stage' designed to draw attention to the object itself.[87] Auction catalogues, feature articles and advertisements are not as prone to exaggeration as they remain focused on the objects displayed or the information conveyed rather than the perspective of the seeing 'I'. 'Egoism', as Moore writes in her comment of March 1927, 'is usually subversive of sagacity' before praising Darwin and Audubon's 'faithfulness to the scene'.[88] The ego, the framing consciousness has a tendency to create a barrier between the object represented and the feelings it stimulates. As Moore writes in her *Dial* poem, 'A Graveyard', 'it is human nature to stand in the middle of a thing'.[89] The scientific writers Moore is influenced by, Darwin and the ornithologist Audubon stand to the side of the scene depicted, as does the copywriter or the catalogue compiler. Moore seeks to adopt a similar strategy by eschewing textual excess and exaggeration in language. 'I have an objection to the word "and" as a connective between adjectives', she explains in her 1944 essay 'Feeling and Precision'. She prefers the seemingly natural effect of the unaccented rhyme and dislikes what she refers to as 'too conscious adverbs'.[90] Moore's method mimics writers she admires, seeking to develop the 'artless art of conveying emotion in tact'.[91]

Standing to the side, showcasing items and arranging them to draw out their unique and distinctive properties, artlessly conveying the sense that the contents of the magazine have chosen themselves, was Moore's principle task as an editor. Her editorial comments, like her poems are a series of lists, catalogues, quoted fragments and 'observations' that seek to reconnect human feeling to the non-human world. Informed in part by Gilman's curatorial theory, Moore's comments sought to foreground the discrete item, to display diversity and to stimulate the 'deepest feeling' in her readers.[92] It might be tempting to think of Moore's work at the *Dial* as a distraction from the 'real' and implicitly more valuable work of writing poetry but this would ignore the ways in which Moore disrupts such categorical distinctions in her promotional prose and editorial comments. Following Moore's own impulse to resist such distinctions, I would argue that editing the *Dial* extended rather than constrained Moore's curatorial poetics with far-reaching consequences. Sitting in her 'palm tree', picking and choosing material for publication, 'Miss Moore' followed her instincts, challenged the critical discriminations of her peers and questioned the cultural authority of established traditions.

Notes

1. Beinecke, ST/Dial Papers, Box 17, Folder 345. The archives at the Beinecke contain evidence of numerous articles from the *Dial* republished in newspapers across the United States.
2. Marianne Moore, *The Complete Prose of Marianne Moore*, ed. Patricia Willis (London: Faber and Faber, 1987), p. 182; Moore, 'Comment', *Dial*, 82 (May 1927), 449–50 (p. 449).
3. Suzanne Churchill, *The Little Magazine Others and the Renovation of Modern American Poetry* (Burlington, VT: Ashgate, 2006), p. 137.
4. Celeste Goodridge, *Hints and Disguises: Marianne Moore and Her Contemporaries* (Iowa City: University of Iowa Press, 1989), p. 4.
5. Nicholas Joost, *Scofield Thayer and the Dial: An Illustrated History* (Carbondale: Southern Illinois University Press, 1964), p. 124; Taffy Martin, 'Comment as Aesthetic Equivalent', *Missouri Review* 7 (1983), 213–22 (p. 215).
6. Evan Kindley, 'Picking and Choosing: Marianne Moore Among the Agonists', *English Literary History*, 79 (2012), 685–713 (p. 687).
7. Ibid. p. 688.
8. Ibid. p. 690.
9. Moore, *Complete Prose*, p. 35; Moore, 'A Note on T. S. Eliot's Book', *Poetry*, 12 (April 1918), 36–9 (p. 36).
10. Marianne Moore, *The Selected Letters of Marianne Moore*, ed. by Bonnie Costello, Celeste Goodridge and Cristanne Miller (London: Faber and Faber, 1998), p. 123. I am drawing on Moore's own poem here, 'Those Various Scalpels': 'We grant you that, but why/ dissect destiny with instruments which/ Are more highly specialized than destiny itself?', Marianne Moore, *Becoming Marianne Moore: The Early Poems, 1907–1924*, ed. Robin G. Schulze, p. 262.
11. Pierre Bourdieu, *Distinction: A Social Critique of the Judgement of Taste*, trans. Richard Nice (London: Routledge and Kegan Paul, 1979), p. 29.
12. Pierre Bourdieu, *Pierre Bourdieu: The Field of Cultural Production: Essays on Art and Literature*, ed. Randal Johnson (Oxford: Polity Press, 1993), p. 77.
13. The most-discussed example of this marketing strategy is the Listerine campaign, which coined the term 'halitosis" to describe bad breath. As Frederick Brogger notes, these advertisements 'played heavily on people's personal and social insecurities': 'Grinding the Gears of Production and Consumption: Representational vs. Nonrepresentational Advertising for Automobiles in the Mid-1920s', *Prospects* 15 (1990), 197–224 (p. 204).
14. Aaron Jaffe, *Modernism and the Culture of Celebrity* (Cambridge: Cambridge University Press, 2005), p. 72.
15. Ibid.
16. Pierre Bourdieu, *The Rules of Art: Genesis and Structure of the Literary Field*, trans. Susan Emanuel (Cambridge: Polity Press, 1996, 2017), p. 167
17. Bourdieu, *Distinction*, p. 77.

18. *New York Evening Post*, 27 September 1924, Beinecke, ST/Dial Papers, Series II, Box 17, Folder 345.
19. 'Against the Faux Bon', *London Mercury*, July 1926, *Program Magazine*, 23 October 1926, 25 October 1926, the *Arts*, September 1926, the *Modern Quarterly*, May 1926, *Harpers Magazine*, December 1926, the *Arts*, March 1927, April 1927, February 1928, *Oriental Magazine*, February 1927, the *Arts*, August 1927, September 1928, *Virginia Quarterly Review*, October 1927, *Creative Art*, February 1928, April 1928, July 1928, Beinecke, ST/Dial Papers, Series II, Box 17, Fol. 345.
20. It seems probable that Gilbert Seldes wrote this particular advertisement as he refers to the 'faux bon' in some of his critical reviews and in his book, *The 7 Lively Arts* (New York: Harpers and Brothers 1924; repr. New York: Dover, 2001).
21. Bourdieu, *Rules*, p. 229.
22. 'The *Atlantic Monthly*', *Dial*, October 1924, Beinecke, ST/Dial Papers, Series II, Box 9, Fol. 308.
23. Alyse Gregory, 'A Modern Yellow Book', *Century Magazine*, September 1924, Beinecke, ST/Dial Papers, Series II, Box 14, Fol. 340.
24. Marianne Moore, 'Serious Pleasure', Beinecke, ST/Dial Papers, Series II, Box 14, Fol. 340.
25. Moore, *Complete Prose*, p. 81, p. 99; Moore, 'Sir Francis Bacon', *Dial*, 76 (April 1924), 343–6 (p. 344); Moore, 'Hymen', *Broom*, 4 (January 1923), 133–5 (p. 135).
26. Marianne Moore, *Becoming Marianne Moore: The Early Poems, 1907–1924* (Berkeley, Los Angeles, London: University of California Press, 2002), pp. 242, 255.
27. Marie Boroff, *Language and the Poet: Verbal Artistry in Frost, Stevens, and Moore* (Chicago: University of Chicago Press, 1979), p. 84.
28. Ibid. p. 269.
29. Marianne Moore, *New Collected Poems: Marianne Moore*, ed. Heather Cass White (London: Faber and Faber, 2017), p. 222.
30. Elizabeth Gregory, 'Combat Cultural: Marianne Moore and the Mixed Brow', in *Critics and Poets on Marianne Moore: 'A Right Good Salvo of Barks'*, ed. Linda Leavell, Cristanne Miller and Robin G. Schulze (Lewisburg, PA: Bucknell University Press, 2005), pp. 208–21 (p. 218).
31. Moore, *Becoming*, p. 255.
32. Ibid. p. 249.
33. Natalia Cecire, 'Marianne Moore's Precision', *Arizona Quarterly: A Journal of American Literature, Culture and Theory,* 67 (2011), 83–110, p. 95.
34. Ibid. p. 91.
35. Moore, *Complete Prose*, p. 81; Moore, 'Hymen', *Broom*, 4 (January 1923), 133–5 (p. 135).
36. Beinecke, ST/Dial Papers, Series II, Box 15, Fol. 341.
37. Moore, *New Collected Poems*, pp. 132, 134, 137, 141, 142.
38. 'Without Respect of Persons', *Creative Art*, August 1928, *Drawing and Design* in December 1928, *The Arts* in January 1928 and *World Unity* in February 1929. Beinecke, ST/Dial Papers, Series II, Box 17, Fol. 345.
39. Boroff, *Language*, p. 131.
40. Ibid.
41. Hildegarde Lasell Watson, *The Edge of the Woods: A Memoir* (South Lunenburg, VT: Stinehour Press, 1979), p. 90.
42. Moore, *Selected Letters*, p. 135.
43. Jason Harding, *The Criterion: Cultural Politics and Periodical Networks in Inter-War Britain* (Oxford: Oxford University Press, 2002), p. 43.
44. Scofield Thayer, 'Comment', *Dial* 76 (March 1924), 291–2 (p. 291).

45. Ibid.
46. Ibid.
47. Elizabeth Lunday, *Modern Art Invasion: Picasso, Duchamp, and the 1913 Armory Show That Scandalized America* (Guilford, CT: Lyons Press, 2013), p. 96.
48. Scofield Thayer, 'Comment', *Dial*, 76 (March 1924), 291–2 (p. 292).
49. Scofield Thayer, 'Comment', *Dial*, 69 (November 1920), 557–8 (p. 558).
50. Gilbert Seldes, *The 7 Lively Arts* (New York: Harpers and Brothers, 1924; repr. New York: Dover, 2001), p. 319.
51. 'Steadily the Gap', *New York Times*, 27 April 1924, Beinecke, ST/Dial Papers, Series II, Box 17, Fol. 345.
52. Scofield Thayer, 'Comment', *Dial*, 74 (February 1923), 213–14; Thayer, 'Comment', *Dial*, 73 (August 1922), 239–40; Thayer, 'Comment', *Dial*, 76 (May 1924), 469–73 (p. 471).
53. Marianne Moore, *Becoming Marianne Moore: The Early Poems, 1907–1924* (Berkeley, Los Angeles, London: University of California Press, 2002), p. 255.
54. John Ashbery, *Selected Prose*, ed. Eugene Richie (Ann Arbor: University of Michigan Press, 2004), p. 110.
55. Moore, *Complete Prose*, pp. 400, 153; Moore, 'Comment', *Dial*, 79 (September 1925), 264–6 (p. 266); Moore, *Complete Prose*, p. 367; Moore, 'Compactness Compacted', *Nation*, 15 November 1941, 486.
56. Moore, *Complete Prose*, pp. 149–50; Moore, 'Comment', *Dial*, 79 (July 1925), 87–8 (p. 88).
57. For an account of Imagism as a form of advertising, see Timothy Materer, 'Make it Sell! Ezra Pound Advertizes Modernism', in *Marketing Modernisms: Self-Promotion, Canonization, and Rereading*, ed. J. H. Dettmar and Stephen Watt (Ann Arbor: University of Michigan Press, 1997), pp. 17–36.
58. Moore, *Complete Prose*, p. 149; Moore, 'Comment', *Dial*, 79 (July 1925), 87–8 (p. 87).
59. Moore, *Complete Prose*, p. 150; Moore, 'Comment', *Dial*, 79 (July 1925), 87–8 (p. 88).
60. Evan Kindley, 'Picking and Choosing: Marianne Moore Among the Agonists', *English Literary History* 79 (2012), 685–713 (p. 690).
61. Ibid. p. 691.
62. Ibid. p. 706.
63. Moore, *Complete Prose*, pp. 154–5 (p. 154); Moore, 'Comment', *Dial*, 79 (November 1925), 443–4 (p. 443).
64. Moore, *Complete Prose*, p. 155; Moore, 'Comment', *Dial*, 79 (November 1925), 443–4 (p. 443).
65. Joan Shelley Rubin, *The Making of Middle/Brow Culture* (Chapel Hill: University of North Carolina Press, 1992), p. 95.
66. Moore, *Becoming*, p. 249.
67. Cristanne Miller, *Marianne Moore: Questions of Authority* (Cambridge, MA: Harvard University Press, 1995), pp. 30–3.
68. Moore, *Becoming*, p. 250.
69. Robin G. Schulze, *The Degenerate Muse: American Nature, Modernist Poetry, and the Problem of Cultural Hygiene* (Oxford: Oxford University Press, 2013), p. 175.
70. The Reverend Alvin E. Magary held pastorates in New York, New Jersey, Iowa and Detroit. Moore may well have known of his work because his Men's Sunday School was broadcast on the radio between 1926 and 1929. 'Alvin E. Magary, Clergyman Dead', *New York Times*, 15 June 1964. Available at: https://www.nytimes.com/1964/06/15/archives/alvin-e-magary-clergyman-dead-pastor-emaritus-of-lafayette-ave.html (accessed 9 August 2018).

71. Schulze, *Degenerate Muse*, 176.
72. Moore, *Complete Prose*, p. 182; Moore, 'Comment', *Dial*, 82 (May 1927), 449–50 (p. 449).
73. Paul, p. 147, p. 158, p. 153.
74. Paul, p. 158.
75. Ibid.
76. Moore, *Complete Prose*, pp. 182–3; Moore, 'Comment', *Dial*, 82 (May 1927), 449–50 (p. 449).
77. Moore, *Complete Prose*, pp. 182–3.
78. Ellen Levy, 'Borrowing Paints from a Girl: Greenberg, Eliot, Moore and the Struggle Between the Arts', *Modernism/Modernity*, 17 (2010), 1–20 (p. 9).
79. Schulze, *Degenerate Muse*, p. 173.
80. Ibid. p. 175.
81. Moore, *Complete Prose*, pp. 398, 399. Moore, 'Feeling and Precision', *Sewanee Review*, 52 (Autumn 1944), 499–507 (p. 505).
82. Moore, *Complete Prose*. p. 399; Moore, 'Feeling and Precision', *Sewanee Review* 52 (Autumn 1944), 499–507 (p. 505).
83. Richard Aldington, 'Review of Observations', *Criterion*, 3 (1924), 588–94 (p. 589); Robert Graves and Laura Riding, *A Survey of Modernist Poetry* (London: William Heinemann, 1927), p. 112.
84. Moore, *Complete Prose*, pp. 152–3, p. 152; Moore, 'Comment' *Dial*, 79 (September 1925), 264–6 (p. 264).
85. Moore, *Complete Prose*, p. 153; Moore, 'Comment' *Dial*, 79 (September 1925), 264–6 (p. 266).
86. Moore, *Complete Prose*, p. 215; Moore, 'Comment', *Dial*, 86 (February 1929), 179–80 (pp. 179–80).
87. Boroff, *Language*, p. 131.
88. Moore, *Complete Prose*, pp. 177–180 (p. 178); Moore, 'Comment', *Dial*, 82 (March 1927), 267–70 (p. 267).
89. Moore, *Becoming*, p. 258.
90. Moore, *Complete Prose*, pp. 401, 400; Moore, 'Feeling and Precision', *Sewanee Review*, 52 (Autumn 1944), 499–507 (p. 505).
91. Moore, *Complete Prose*, p. 399; Moore, 'Feeling and Precision', *Sewanee Review*, 52 (Autumn 1944), 499–507 (p. 503).
92. Moore, *Becoming*, p. 309.

4

HART CRANE DISTILLED

The story of Marianne Moore's rewriting of Hart Crane's poem, 'The Wine Menagerie', has taken centre-stage in accounts of Moore's editorship of the *Dial* and, as a result, the four-and-a-half years of her editorial tenure have been distilled into this one incident. The clash between poet and editor is appealing in that it pits Hart Crane, a notorious insolvent alcoholic, against 'Miss Moore' or 'the Rt. Rev. Mountjoy' as Crane called her.[1] Crane embodies all those romantic ideas we have about the artist: sexually promiscuous, edgy and dangerous, driven by his demons, a creative genius. Moore, on the other hand, is much more prosaic, living as she does with her mother, leading a quietly devout life. The interpretation of this clash focuses on the poets' personalities, on their eccentricities rather than on the motives underpinning Moore's radical revisions and Crane's agreement to publish a poem that was so transformed as to be no longer his. Affect flows, like the alcohol in Crane's poem, clouding critical judgement, reinforcing a familiar gendered paradigm that ignores the role the *Dial* played in the rewriting of the poem. As John Vincent has argued, the episode has been interpreted in ways that reinforce the notion that Moore was motivated by 'a psychopathology, a kind of quiet megalomania'.[2] As a result, Crane's accusation that Moore is an 'hysterical virgin', whose editorial decisions are the result of her unfortunate condition – that of being a single, celibate woman – are tacitly reinforced.[3] Here is the reverse, or perhaps the logical conclusion, of Thayer's eulogistic comments where Moore's 'virtue' was her strength. For Crane it is her weakness, even her illness.

This is not to deny what Vincent describes as the 'violence' of Moore's revisions, nor is it to ignore the pain they caused. After all, Moore reduced Crane's poem to less than half its original length, condensing forty-five lines into eighteen lines and changing the title from 'The Wine Menagerie' to 'Again'; rather it is to acknowledge first, that this pain relates to the constraints of periodical publication and second, that for some writers, including Moore, such constraint produced pleasure or even a form of ecstasy. The following discussion examines the textual pleasure, even the ecstasy of compression. Vincent's detailed and remarkably insightful account of both Crane's poem and Moore's revision of that poem has revealed much about the intersections and disjunctions between these poets. According to Vincent, ecstasy is present in both 'The Wine Menagerie' and Moore's revision of the poem re-titled 'Again', though in 'fundamentally different' ways.[4] What Vincent describes as the 'clash of poetics' between Moore and Crane over 'The Wine Menagerie', I understand in terms of a collision involving the author and a number of non-authorial agents, including the editor and the magazine itself.[5] In other words, while Vincent's account is a brilliant reading of Crane's poem and Moore's revisions to that poem, my own approach seeks to return to the scene of Moore's supposed crime against Crane in order to understand Moore's motives as well as her editorial method.

What Moore referred to as her 'transgressions' as an editor were motivated by a concern to maintain the *Dial*'s reputation for highbrow distinction.[6] Crane's poem explores a moment of intimacy between strangers in a bar. Not only that, the bar itself is the scene of a poetic transcendence, transformed into a 'glozening' jewel reflected from the slightly blurry perspective of the inebriated speaking persona. Moore would have undoubtedly disapproved, but that is beside the point. As an editor of a magazine occupying the space between the qualities and the modernist 'little' magazines, Moore knew that most of her readers would also disapprove. Her solution was to edit out the bar scene while retaining the moment of transcendence, not only making the poem more palatable to the *Dial* reader, but also making ecstasy more accessible. The compressive logic of Moore's revisions, as Vincent suggests, eliminates the narrative sequence of events as well as the location of the bar where these events take place. Without this sense of a narrative located in time and place, Moore's poem 'Again' examines ecstasy without any distractions, stripping away the objects and the subjects, the 'menagerie' that constitutes Crane's poem.

Taking into account the institutional role that the *Dial* played, its readership and its position in the market points to Moore's motives for revising Crane's poem but does not explain her method of revision. For that, we need to return to Moore's own poetry and the editorial work she undertook to adapt her own poetry for publication in the *Dial*. What Suzanne Churchill has described as the scrappy modernism associated with the poetry of *Others* magazine needed to be refined for readers of the *Dial*. According to John Slatin, Moore changed the form of her poems from syllabic to free verse as a way of paying 'a debt of gratitude to the magazine itself' for launching her career.[7] Once she began publishing in the *Dial* she started taking out the sharp angles and disruptive syntax produced by her syllabic stanzas in order to produce poems that, in Slatin's words, 'look less forbidding' on the page.[8] The effect of revising for publication for the *Dial* produced some of Moore's most extraordinary poems. For Moore, the intense pleasures of poetry are bound up with formal constraint or as she suggests in 'The Past is the Present', '"Ecstasy/ affords/ the occasion and expediency determines the form".'[9] The requirements imposed by external pressures produce formal innovation, new methods and techniques capable of achieving what is referred to in this poem as a 'sort of heightened consciousness'. As a poet, this meant adapting to the material circumstances of periodical publication. Like the chameleon in 'You Are Like the Realistic Product of an Idealistic Search for Gold at the Foot of the Rainbow', Moore's poetry demonstrates what Schulze describes as its 'evolutionary fitness' by transforming in order to survive.[10]

A new phase of poetic production ensued when Moore's predilection for 'contractility' came into contact with the *Dial*'s image of highbrow distinction. From 1920 to 1924, Moore turned from syllabics to free verse, publishing almost exclusively in Thayer's magazine and producing a distinct body of poetic work for the *Dial*. In the large-scale, free-verse montage poems Moore wrote in the mid-1920s ('Marriage', 'An Octopus', 'Sea Unicorns and Land Unicorns'), she pushes together clauses, pares down phrases and cuts out ornament. Patricia Willis, Susan McCabe and Carolyn Burke have all described this technique in terms of 'splicing', a form of 'hyper-montage' that eschews connectives and embraces radical juxtaposition.[11] The splicing technique Moore uses in her own poetry is extended into her editorial practice. For Moore, as an editor and a poet, poetic ecstasy requires and indeed is predicated on formal constraint.

The following discussion begins with the modernist art of revision before going on to consider the pleasures and the pain of editorial cuts. The assumption that textual compression is necessarily painful is one that underpins many accounts of Moore's editorial practice. The late work of Henry James, one of Moore's favourite writers, dispels the notion that editing is always and inevitably wounding. On the contrary, for both James and Moore, magazine publication 'affords' creative opportunities to produce what Shawna Ross refers to as a 'delicious, desirable restriction'.[12] For Moore, publication in the *Dial* became the 'occasion' for a set of radical revisions that release textuality from the constraints of the syllabic stanza. These free-verse explosions are, I argue, the product of an encounter between poetic agency and the institutional habitus of the *Dial*. In the last part of the chapter, I look more closely at 'The Wine

Menagerie' and Moore's revision of that poem, 'Again'. Drawing on Vincent's emphasis on ecstatic utterance in both poems, I suggest that in many ways it is 'distillation', in all its punning potential that explains Moore's revisions.

The Pleasures of Compression

> To A Snail
> If 'compression is the first grace of style,'
> you have it. Contractility is a virtue
> as modesty is a virtue.[13]

The 'virtue' of 'contractility', embodied in the snail and practised in Moore's poem 'To a Snail', signals a certain kind of 'grace' for the speaker, a 'method' of compression. A few lines on, the poem values the 'principle that is hid in style, and Moore's verbally compressed poem suggests its own hidden principle: that language achieves its ethical energy, or what she refers to elsewhere as 'gusto', when it is formally constrained. Moore valued the 'force of omission', the 'vigilant exactness' achieved in poetic language through the process of extraction and ellipsis.[14] For Moore, 'a poem is a concentrate', a form of 'compressed energy' that yields spiritual force.[15] As Kenneth Burke was to point out to Moore herself, 'your typical way of proceeding is to get revision by condensation, and condensation by omission (plus whatever new transition may happen to be needed)'.[16]

Moore was not alone in her predilection for compression. As many have already observed, accounts of modernism's origins often begin with narratives of compression. The now well-known occasion when Pound identified H.D. as an Imagist is remembered by H.D. herself in terms of a violent editorial intervention when Pound 'slashed with his creative pencil', urging her to 'cut this out, shorten this line'.[17] But Pound was willing to be just as ruthless with his own work, reducing the thirty-line poem 'In a Station of the Metro' to the elliptical couplet that marks the arrival of a 'new' poetic form. [18] The seminal moment of modernism's emergence is often characterised in terms of Pound's radical excisions to *The Waste Land*, 'one of the greatest acts of editorial intervention on record', according to Lawrence Rainey.[19]

Ezra Pound figures prominently in Hannah Sullivan's account of modernism in *The Work of Revision*. Pound made Eliot's poem more modernist with his 'bold, excisive editing' describing himself as a surgeon performing a 'caesarean Operation' on Eliot's poem.[20] Hemingway, having learnt much from Pound, practised the modernist edit on his novel *The Sun Also Rises*, reducing the original manuscript by 15 per cent. As Sullivan points out, Hemingway's advice to himself had been to cut away ornament and to avoid including the paraphernalia of introductions or presentations. [21] As we will see with Moore's editing of her own work and the work of contributors to the *Dial*, she follows the same principles. The splicing effect of Moore's revisions is also comparable to Pound's technique of 'super-position', a form of layering images, pressing clauses together, allowing fractured phrases to collide in order to keep language lean and efficient.[22]

It is not surprising, then, given Moore's desire for contraction, that Ezra Pound should recognise her gifts as an editor. Pound was tempted back to the *Dial* by Moore in 1927.[23] She relied heavily upon his advice, particularly when it came to translations. He thought Moore one of the few writers capable of editing a magazine in the United States that could showcase work that was new and innovative.[24] Even though Moore had admonished Pound in her first letter to him for his 'promptness with the cudgels', the two poets engaged in productive and creative forms of revision, not only on their own work but on the work of others.[25] They shared a critical vocabulary: for Pound, the new poetry needed to be 'austere, direct, free from emotional slither' and for Moore poetry should display 'accuracy', 'compression' and 'controlled emotion'.[26]

However, Pound was not the only modernist writer who practised this form of modernist contraction. Scholars working on Henry James recognise that a 'compressive logic' drives even the long late novels.[27] While Hannah Sullivan recognises that James, like his fictional character Dencombe in 'The Middle Years' is a 'passionate corrector', she lingers over the pain of these revisions. This contrasts with the approach of Shawna Ross, who has suggested that, for James, the constraints of word length that came with periodical publication could be enabling and compression itself could provide 'textual pleasures'.[28] But Ross also demonstrates something else that is worth bearing in mind in terms of thinking about the relation between Moore's method of composition and her editorial interventions; she points to the effect of compression not simply in terms of textual contraction. Compression can accommodate and in fact, makes possible the long imagist poem, as Rainey suggests in his discussion of Pound's revisions to *The Waste Land*. In July 1922, before the publication of Eliot's poem, Moore began collecting material for her own modernist long poems, 'Marriage' and 'An Octopus'. She too was thinking about how to achieve intensity and economy while also expanding her vision beyond discrete objects or particular scenes and locations. She had begun to do this with her poem 'People's Surroundings', but it was, as most critics believe, in 'An Octopus' that Moore created an imagistic collage balancing specificity with diversity. This provided a microscopic lens capable of honing in on the ecosystem of Mount Rainier, together with a macroscopic perspective framing that diversity.[29] Drawing on and adapting Ross's reading of Jamesian compression, I argue that like James, Moore's impulse to concentrate and distil is not simply a means of reducing length. According to Ross, James responded enthusiastically and creatively to the constraints imposed upon him by periodical publication; in fact, such constraints led to the experiments in point of view characteristic of James's late work. James compares 'the "squeeze" of a skillfully compressed narrative to the "last squeeze of the gold orange"' in the preface to *The Middle Years* signaling, as Ross points out, a 'delicious, desirable restriction'.[30]

In addition, what Ross refers to as the 'compressive logic' underpinning James's revisions enables the long-form to maintain intensity even as it stretches, expands and extends through multiple points of view.[31] For Ross, this is achieved through a tension between the compact and the dispersed: 'As James internalizes the external calls for discipline, he enacts a dialectical reversal that transforms an antipathy for the terse into a voluptuous, covetous jealousy for the compressed.'[32] Moore describes this dialectical reversal in terms of 'restraint' and 'gusto', which she too finds in the work of Henry James, one of the writers she most admired. In her essay on James, 'Henry James as a Characteristic American', Moore identifies a combination of 'diffidence, reserve, and strong feeling', emotional intensity and a lack of artifice that signals that it is both instinctive and 'real':[33]

> Things for Henry James glow, flush, glimmer, vibrate, shine, hum, bristle, reverberate. Joy, bliss, ecstasies, intoxication, a sense of trembling in every limb, a shattering first glimpse, a hanging on the prolonged silence of an editor; and as a child at Mr. Burton's small theater in Chambers Street, his wondering, not if the curtain would rise, but 'if one could exist till then'; the bonfires of his imagination, his pleasure in the 'tender sea-green' or 'rustling rose-color' of a seriously best dress, are too live to countenance his fear that he was giving us 'an inch of canvas and an acre of embroidery.'[34]

The idea of 'things' as sensuous objects, of places as sites of almost unbearable emotional intensity, of the writer as embodied subject, 'trembling' and 'hanging', suggests the powerful affective pull of James's writing. James is a writer capable of returning to and capturing what Schulze refers to as 'the original moment of instinctual response'.[35] Moore clearly identifies with James's responsiveness and sensitivity to the object world but there is also a danger here. He worries as she does that the creative response is unrestrained and overly elaborate. Compression becomes a way for both writers to maintain this genuine, immediate, impulsive response to external stimulation. But what Moore's passage also reveals is not only the importance of 'restraint', which signals 'the deepest feeling', as Moore suggests in her poem 'Silence', but also the aesthetic pleasure inherent in the process of trying to achieve restraint.

Contraction Pains

It is the pain, however, rather than the pleasure of editorial compression that has dominated discussions of Moore's revisions to the work of others. Moore's 'victims' as she describes them, undoubtedly felt the pain of Moore's cuts.[36] Emily Setina, discussing Moore's editorial work on Marsden Hartley's poetry in the late 1930s, has argued that Moore gave Hartley 'a kind of correspondence class in poetic revision', signalling the relation between Moore's editorial practice and modernist revision.[37] Moore's editorial advice, she suggests, 'could feel painfully disciplinary'.[38] In Hartley's poem, 'Marianne Moore', Moore, like Pound, wields a scalpel but, rather than bringing the infant poem out of the womb, she tends to the wounded sentence: 'like a surgeon at the drugged decisive/ table/ opening the cicatrice carefully – to find/ what ails the sentence'.[39] Moore's scalpel might have cleansed and sutured the wound but the fact was that her 'revisions hurt'.[40] Moore's mentorship of Elizabeth Bishop also reveals the extent to which editorial revision could test even her most ardent admirers. Between 1936 and 1940 Moore was reading, revising and even typing out the final drafts of poems that Bishop sent to her. It was Moore's editorial interventions with the poem, 'The Roosters', however, that led to a cessation of this practice and a slowing down of exchanges between the two poets. At this point, according to Betsy Erlikka and Rosanne Wasserman, Bishop declared her independence from Moore.[41] Up until then, Moore had been revising Bishop's poetry, pressing upon the younger poet the 'advantages of economy', as Bonnie Costello notes.[42]

Moore repeatedly refers to compression as a desirable effect in the poetry and prose she admires. H.D.'s poetry has a 'compressed energy'; in William Carlos Williams's poetry there is 'compression, color, speed, accuracy and that restraint of instinctive craftsmanship'; Alfeo Faggi's sculptures have a 'distilled impersonal spiritual force'. In her essay, 'Humility, Concentration, and Gusto' (1949) Moore describes a poem as a 'concentrate'.[43] The effect of textual concentration is to 'heighten gusto' as is evident in William Cowper's poem 'The Snail', to which she dedicates her own 'To a Snail'. From an editorial point of view, the limitations of page space provided the opportunity or even the excuse to practise a form of compression on work submitted for publication. Such a strategy, I would argue, is not necessarily about finding the poem or the prose passage among unnecessary verbiage, as if it already exists; for Moore, compression is a process that generates intensity and gusto.

As editor at the *Dial*, Moore took the opportunity to practise a form of compression whenever she could, not only as a practical response to the limitations of page space but also to achieve the textual gusto or energy she finds in the writers she admires. Moore's compression is not identical to James's or to Pound's or to H.D.'s, but it bears a resemblance and might be understood as the distinctly modernist form of revision that Hannah Sullivan describes in *The Work of Revision.* While Pound's radical excisions were gratefully accepted by Eliot, who dedicated his poem to 'Il miglior fabbro' (the better craftsman), and while these editorial cuts have attained a mythical status in accounts of the formation of modernism, Moore's interventions often came silently into the pages of the *Dial*, many of them barely noticeable.

The Passionate Corrector

Rather than being cautious or careful in our estimations of Moore's contribution as an editor, I would suggest that a certain bravado is necessary. Moore was an energetic, enthusiastic even 'passionate corrector' to borrow Henry James's phrase. She revised with guts and gusto. She wielded the editorial pencil with conviction in the firm belief that contraction produced the textual density necessary for the kind of 'intensity' she associated with art.

Nowhere was she more passionate than when correcting her own work. Particularly instructive is the poem, 'Poetry', which, as its title suggests, provides us with something as close as Moore can get to an explanation of her poetics. Moore practised a form of radical post-publication revision on this poem, producing four basic versions: a five-stanza syllabic poem; a thirteen-line free-verse version; a fifteen-line, three-stanza syllabic poem; and the final three-line, free-verse incarnation that was included in *The Complete Poems*. To make things a little more complicated, however, Moore published the five-stanza version of the poem in the notes to *The Complete Poems*, thus showing readers that it had been drastically cut. Bonnie Honigsblum has discussed the versions of 'Poetry' extensively, arguing that 'a modernist application [. . .] underlies Moore's method of revision' and I would concur. Choosing not to abandon either version, Moore 'carefully distinguishes between them'. [44] The key point that Honigsblum makes is that Moore 'intended the revision to have meaning for the readers'; she wanted the reader to interpret the significance of revision as a practice. More specifically, she is demonstrating the ways in which a poem is produced through textual compression.[45] A poem might contain any number of objects, such as 'business documents and school books', but what makes it a poem is its ability to compress such things into itself. Such things may even disappear entirely from the poem in terms of its content but they are present in a distilled form. In addition, the more the poem practises compression, the more it can contain.

To illustrate further, we need look no further than the poem 'To a Snail'. Its first appearance in *Observations* makes it unusual, having not been published in a periodical at any point in its publication history. 'To a Snail' was composed around the same time as the long free-verse montage poems, 'An Octopus', 'Marriage' and 'Sea Unicorns and Land Unicorns' and, as Bonnie Costello has already pointed out, comparing the first version in syllabic verse to the free-verse version reveals Moore's 'process of self-instruction'.[46] Costello works on the principle that, through revision, Moore achieves greater clarity and precision; that 'To a Snail' is extracted from the rather convoluted and clumsy phrases that Moore initially deployed in syllabic form. She also points

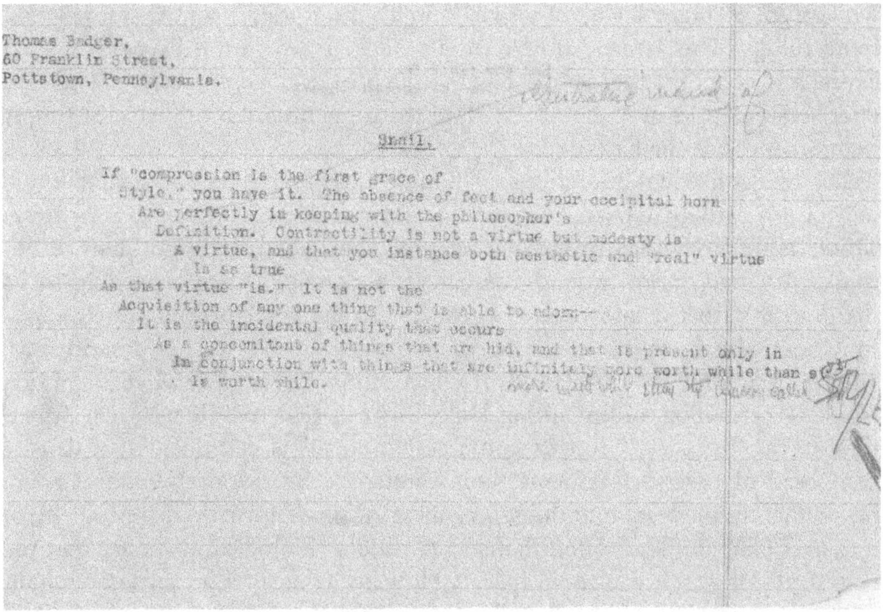

Thomas Badger,
60 Franklin Street,
Pottstown, Pennsylvania.

Snail.

If "compression is the first grace of
Style," you have it. The absence of feet and your occipital horn
Are perfectly in keeping with the philosopher's
Definition. Contractility is not a virtue but modesty is
A virtue, and that you instance both aesthetic and "real" virtue
Is as true
As that virtue "is." It is not the
Acquisition of any one thing that is able to adorn--
It is the incidental quality that occurs
As a concomitant of things that are hid, and that is present only in
In conjunction with things that are infinitely more worth while than s
Is worth while.

Figure 4.1 Marianne Moore, 'Snail', in Bonnie Costello, '"To a Snail": A Lesson in Compression', *Marianne Moore Newsletter*, 3 (1979), 11–15 (p. 12).

to the fact that if the poem is about anything, it is about William Cowper's poem, 'The Snail', which Moore greatly admired. While it is hard to deny that the free-verse poem is more succinct, my own interest is in the compositional process itself as much as the end product (see Fig. 4.1).

Moore's syllabic version of the poem splits it into two stanzas of 9, 11, 13, 14, 11 and 3 syllables. This draft, probably produced in 1924, suggests that syllabics were still central to her method of composition even though she had not published a syllabic poem since 1920.[47] In terms of its typographical layout, the syllabic structure seems to encourage the use of the width of the page. The poem's longer lines push out towards the page margins, particularly when the staggered and increasingly indented first word of each line becomes more indented as the stanza progresses. Thus, the first line of each stanza is hard up against the left-hand margin but by the final line of each stanza, the indentation is about ten spaces inside the margin. This staggered effect alerts the reader to a visual pattern. The syllabic stanza cuts open the quotation so that it runs into the second line: 'If "compression is the first grace of/ style"'. The revised version and the one that appeared in *Observations* in 1924, abandons this 'style' in favour of something more discreet and integrated. The free-verse version reduces three sentences to two, while at the same time adding two more quotations. What 'To a Snail' demonstrates, therefore, is that while a poem might shrink in terms of its length, it might contain more ideas, more things. This is an example of the dialectical relation between textual excess and economy that is so central to the poetics of compression. While the later version looks more compressed, at the same time, Moore has not simply reduced and cut, she has added.

The two additional quotations, as Bonnie Costello points out, can be found in Moore's reading diaries. These are taken from Duns Scotus in *The Medieval Mind*: 'Is theology then properly a science? Duns Scotus will not deny it, but thinks [it]/ may more properly be called, a *sapienta,* since according to its nature it is rather a knowledge of principles than a method of conclusions.' In Moore's final version of the poem what is valued in style is described as, among other things '"a method of conclusions"';/ "a knowledge of principles"'.[48] Extracting and adapting Duns Scotus's text to suit her own principles, in this instance, Moore's compression creates a certain textual density composed of diverse fragments. For Natalia Cecire, Moore's modest poem has rather immodest ambitions, engaging as it does with the problem of 'the overwhelming and often monstrous scale of biological diversity that the empirical enterprise makes visible'.[49] How to achieve compression without simply reducing the poem to a haiku-like impression, how to be expansive and inclusive while also maintaining linguistic precision and economy, became a crucial question for both Moore and Pound in the 1920s. Moore's response to this question came as she was also responding to the requirements of the *Dial*, the magazine that published ten of the thirteen poems she published between January 1920 and January 1925.

New editions of Moore's poetry have allowed scholars to examine Moore's post-publication revisions and to trace the variants of individual poems. Robin Schulze's edition of Moore's early poems, *Becoming Marianne Moore*, and Heather Cass White's *A-Quiver with Significance: Marianne Moore, 1932–1936* suggest that each new publication was seen by Moore as an opportunity to revise. Particularly intriguing from the perspective of periodical publication are the poems that appeared in the *Dial* between 1920 and 1924. When Thayer invited Moore to contribute to the *Dial*, Moore sent him two poems in syllabic stanzas, 'England' and 'Picking and Choosing'. The syllabic stanza had been a formal innovation initiated by Moore with the poem 'Critics and Connoisseurs' in 1916 for *Others*. Having corresponded with both Thayer and Watson and sending them multiple versions of poems, Moore then moved to free verse, a dramatic formal shift indicating that the *Dial* required something different, something that had a little of the dazzling qualities of the magazine itself, a certain textual extravagance, a 'pleasure' in things as well as a sense of the ethical imperatives that accompany such pleasures.

'Picking and Choosing' and 'England' appeared in April 1920 in the *Dial* in syllabic stanzas and also in *Poems* and *Observations* as syllabic poems.

By July 1921, however, with the publication of 'When I Buy Pictures' and 'A Graveyard' in the *Dial*, Moore was converting all her poems to free verse. As its publication history reveals, 'When I Buy Pictures' was originally in syllabic stanzas and published in this form in *Poems*, a collection edited by H.D. and Bryher, apparently without Moore's permission. Schulze speculates that Moore must have sent Thayer the syllabic version, which he then sent to H.D. and Bryher for *Poems*.[50] Moore then revised the poem extensively, transforming it from syllabics to free verse for publication in the *Dial*. Two different versions of the poem appeared in 1921 but the free-verse version was the one that had Moore's blessing.[51] Again, according to Schulze, 'A Graveyard' was drafted as a 'work of symmetrical syllabic stanzas' and then converted to free verse before its publication in Thayer and Watson's magazine. In December 1921, 'The Labors of Hercules' and 'New York' appeared in free verse. All the poems Moore published in the *Dial* subsequently were free verse, though early unpublished versions suggest that she was still composing in syllabic stanzas: 'People's Surroundings' appeared in June 1922, 'Novices' in February 1923, 'Silence' in October 1924, 'Sea Unicorns and Land Unicorns' in November 1924, 'An Octopus' in December 1924 and 'The Monkey Puzzler' in January 1925.

This formal shift was signalled when Moore published *Observations* in 1924. As Vicki Graham points out, the volume is divided into more or less two halves: the first half consists of the visually patterned poems in syllabic stanzas and the second half consists of free-verse poems.[52] The arrangement is chronological but it also divides the collection into *Dial* poems and the poems published in the little modernist magazines such as *Others*, *Poetry* and the *Little Review*. Clearly for Moore, there was something about publishing in the *Dial* that prompted her temporarily to abandon what she referred to as her method of 'patterned arrangement[s]'.[53] She would return to syllabics when she started to write poetry again in the early 1930s.

Slatin's suggestion that Moore's free-verse poems are more public-facing than her earlier syllabic verse indicates that Moore became particularly conscious at this time that she was writing for an audience, the 'wholesale trade' that was the magazine market.[54] The print run of the first edition of *Observations* was 250; compared to the circulation of the *Dial*, this was relatively limited public exposure.[55] It is likely that Moore revised her poetry for this wider audience, assuming that the reader of the *Dial* would find the subordination of semantic meaning to the spatial and visual rhythms of the poetic line somewhat alienating. Comparing the syllabic version of 'When I Buy Pictures' to the later free-verse version published in the *Dial*, Vicki Graham provides a helpful account of these different forms and their effects in language:

> Up to line twelve, the most striking difference between the two versions is in the line breaks. In the earlier, visually pattered version, Moore

> breaks lines in the middle of phrases, as well as in the middle of words. In the later version, Moore breaks the lines (with one exception) at the ends of phrases or clauses, after commas, semicolons, periods, or dashes. Each line forms a separate and complete rhetorical unit. In the patterned version, most of the lines do not contain whole phrases. A line either consists of a fragment or a single image or it contains fragments of two different images which depend on the lines before and after for completion. Line breaks occur in unexpected places: after an article, 'the' in the second line, between the parts of a verb, 'would/give,' and in the middle of words, 'medi-/aeval.' Though the first stanza is a separate unit, the next three are not: images and words are broken at the ends of each.[56]

The geometrical patterns of the syllabic stanza break up syntactical rhythms, splice individual words and dissect phrases. As a result, the discrete items, the people and the animals that populate these poems become fractured, cubist portraits that reflect as much on the processes of seeing such things as on the things themselves. The free-verse poems, by contrast, as both Graham and Leavell suggest, foreground the object world in all its diversity. For Leavell this poetic practice is more akin to 'selecting' rather than 'making', as the 'I' recedes to make way for 'the proliferation of appropriated things'.[57] Rather like the magazine itself, the 'compendia storehouse' capable of containing a multiplicity of objects, Moore's *Dial* poems shift attention away from the observing subject towards the object observed.[58] More specifically, they reflect something of the *Dial*'s image of highbrow distinction in their smoothing out of the sharp edges with which Moore's poetry had come to be associated.

Moore may well also have been aware that the look of her jagged syllabics was too formally radical for the *Dial*. Thayer was very particular when it came to the design of the magazine, as Kenneth Burke, Alyse Gregory and Moore herself knew only too well. Kenneth Burke remembers that Thayer was:

> very strict about the number of lines allowed to a page; also he wanted to avoid such breaks as would make a stanza end at the bottom of a page, for unless the new stanza was marked by a subtitle, it would look as though it were a continuation of the previous stanza.[59]

Moore solved this design problem by avoiding stanzas altogether when she published with the *Dial*. This is not to suggest that she slavishly conformed to what she thought was Thayer's preferred style, but rather that Moore may well have felt that the free-verse poems travelled more easily and elegantly across the pages of the *Dial*. Particularly in the case of 'An Octopus' and 'Sea Unicorns and Land Unicorns', long poems that consist mainly of quoted fragments, the syntactical rupture of the syllabic stanza would have added another considerable challenge to the reader. While the magazine is now known for its publication of Eliot, Pound, Loy, H.D. and Williams, modernist poets who 'broke the pentameter', the majority of the verse that the magazine published adhered to the conventions of regular rhyme and metre. Seeing the jagged lines of 'Picking and Choosing' and 'England' in the April 1920 *Dial* may have compelled Moore to think again about form and structure. It is revealing to see her poems beside Djuna Barnes's 'To the Dead Favourite of Liu Ch'e' and 'Pastoral' published in the same issue (see Figs 4.2 and 4.3).

Moore's syllabic verse stretches across the pages of the *Dial*, while Barnes's poems sit neatly inside ample margins providing a luxurious expanse of expensive textual real estate. Even cummings, whose leggy, loose-limbed poems often swaggered down the middle of the page, cleaves to a lilting cadence that stands in marked contrast to Moore prose-like stanzas. Also intriguing is the fact that Moore's debut in the *Dial* coincides with Hart Crane's. 'My Grandmother's Love Letters' appears a few pages after Barnes's poems. Aligned along the left-hand margin, Crane's poem is in free verse and sits, formally speaking, somewhere between Barnes and Moore. Crane's light-touch use of rhyme, repetition and sibilance, the sense of space produced by the long vowel sounds in 'room', 'loose' and 'roof', the echo of 'memory' and the sibilance of 'soft', 'stars', 'pressed', 'steps' and snow' creates a lyrical 'music' that

ENGLAND

with its baby rivers and little towns, each with its abbey or its
        cathedral;
   with voices—one voice perhaps, echoing through the
        transept—the
criterion of suitability and convenience; and Italy with its equal
      shores—contriving an epicureanism from which the grossness
        has been

extracted and Greece with its goats and its gourds, the nest of
        modified illusions·
   and France, the "chrysalis of the nocturnal butterfly" in
whose products, mystery of construction diverts one from what was
        originally one's
      object—substance at the core· and the East with its snails, its
        emotional

Figure 4.2 Marianne Moore, 'England', *Dial*, 68 (April 1920), 422.

TWO POEMS

BY DJUNA BARNES

TO THE DEAD FAVOURITE OF LIU CH'E

The sound of rustling silk is stilled,
With solemn dust the court is filled,
No footfalls echo on the floor;
A thousand leaves stop up her door,
Her little golden drink is spilled.

Her painted fan no more shall rise
Before her black barbaric eyes—
The scattered tea goes with the leaves.
And simply crossed her yellow sleeves;
And every day a sunset dies.

Figure 4.3 Djuna Barnes, 'To the Dead Favourite of Liu Ch'e', *Dial*, 68 (April 1920), 444.

would have been familiar to the ear, even though Crane's stanzas are uneven and his metre irregular:

MY GRANDMOTHER'S LOVE LETTERS
BY HART CRANE

There are no stars to-night
But those of memory.
Yet how much room for memory there is
In the loose girdle of soft rain.[60]

It is only when returning to the pages of the *Dial* that Moore's radical otherness becomes legible. Ironically, given her reputation for prudery and temperance, it is Moore's modernism that appears most formally disruptive, most resistant to the conventions of verse, most unpoetic in both sound and sense. Aware of this difference, Moore adjusted to her new circumstances, loosening her verse from the constraints of the syllabic stanza. In doing so, however, she did not produce poems any more accessible than her syllabics. As Kenneth Burke observed, 'she could be extraordinary even in the attempt to be average'.[61] Increasingly, the effect of free verse on Moore's poetics was to open up the poems to quotation, to allow a 'cavalcade' of textual fragments to accumulate and thereby push the poetic speaker to the edges of the verse.[62] If the syllabic poems destabilise language, creating rifts between signifier and signified, Moore's free-verse collages stifle the lyric subject in vacuum-packed poems where the non-human objects seem to take up all the oxygen.

As she continued to compose with the *Dial* in mind, she began to expand her use of quotation, producing 'An Octopus', 'Marriage' and 'Sea Unicorns and Land Unicorns', poems where the lyric voice is subsumed by multiple quoted fragments. Once again, Moore was pressing against the conventions of the lyric poem. When she sent 'An Octopus' to Thayer she was worrying that the poem 'was in no way suited to a magazine' and she even wondered whether it would be 'a little heavy' for *Observations*, which was being prepared for publication at this time.[63] Thayer published 'An Octopus', Moore's 'longest observation', even though Moore herself had doubts about its suitability for the magazine. It is to his credit that rather than baulking at Moore's quotations, he pressed her in his correspondence to explain her sources. When she did so, he suggested she include these notes in *Observations*.[64] When Moore was awarded The Dial prize, Thayer used one of his comments to compare Eliot's 'pedestrian' use of footnotes in *The Waste Land* to the 'wild caressing loveliness' of Moore's notes.[65]

This shift into free verse also resulted in Moore using the quoted fragment more extensively, a poetic method that involved her editing the work of others. Of the sixteen lines of 'Silence', for instance, a mere two-and-a-half lines are outside quotation marks. In 'An Octopus', as Patricia Willis points out in her meticulous account of that poem's composition, 'nearly two-thirds of the two hundred and thirty lines in the manuscript can be accounted for by various sources'.[66] Moore was editing the words of others in the sense that she was adapting quotations to fit their new poetic environment. This practice was, for Moore, bound up with what she repeatedly refers to in terms of 'restraint': 'The deepest feeling always shows itself in silence;/ not in silence, but restraint."[67] Restraint is formally tied to the principle of contractility practised in 'To a Snail', but is also evident in the way the long montage poems press together and condense a proliferation of textual extracts from a wide range of sources. It is intertextually bound to Henry James, who figures prominently in the poems that Moore wrote for the *Dial*. In 'An Octopus' James is '"damned by the public for decorum";/ not decorum but restraint;' a quotation drawn from Moore's mother who had been reading Carl Van Doren's review of James in *The American Novel*.[68] While 'restraint' and 'compression' are not identical, the former signalling 'feeling' and the latter referring to a form of textual practice, one is the expression of the other. Moore's mother thought her daughter dangerously intoxicated by James. Writing to her son in 1910, she described Moore's reaction to reading *Roderick Hudson*:

> As one bad fellow says of another with a head-shake, 'He's been drinking heavily,' so may I mention that he [Marianne] has been pouring heavily potations of Henry James . . . The little wretch stood under the light with his book, one night, motionless; yet with a Sarah Bernhardt look at me, he said: 'I tremble from head to foot when I read a book like this.'[69]

The intensity of feeling described here by Moore's mother is similar to Moore's impressions of James in 'A Characteristic American'. Not only does restraint signal deep feeling, when put into practice as a form of textual compression, it is capable of stimulating deep feeling or what Moore refers to as 'gusto'. For Celeste Goodridge, Moore identifies with James because he seems to revel in 'the gap between the moment of anticipation and the thing itself'. Restraint is, in these terms, a form of 'partial disclosure', a delight in the unattainable.[70]

Reading 'Again' Again

As John Vincent notes in his reading of both 'The Wine Menagerie' and Moore's edited version, 'Again', 'it seems more than coincidental that the very poet being accused of overstepping bounds and putting words in other poets' mouths is the same one whose corpus is full of the words of others'.[71] He notes Moore's use of quotation, particularly in the poem 'Marriage', which Moore herself described as 'statements that took my fancy which I tried to arrange plausibly'.[72] That Moore should deploy the term 'fancy' with its Romantic connotations retains a sense of the pleasure of the found fragment. Such pleasures were, I argue, entwined with the poetics of restraint and the desire for a modernist form of compression. This becomes evident in Moore's editing of Crane.

It is worth reminding ourselves of the details of the exchanges between Moore and Crane over 'The Wine Menagerie'. Logan Esdale notes that on 10 November 1925 Moore wrote to Crane with the following proposal:

> We should like to publish your poem, 'The Wine Menagerie', if you could permit us to make certain changes in it which we are venturing to present to you separately. It is so much our wish not to distort or interfere with an author's concept, that we had thought to take no liberty and to relinquish the poem; we feel, however, that you may concur with us in the changes we suggest. In that case, we might use 'Again' as a title?'[73]

Crane wrote back to Moore on the same day agreeing that 'the condensed version of "The Wine Menagerie" contains the essential elements of the original poem' and accepting the changes.[74] Yet even as he agreed to the revisions, he regretted his decision, a decision, he explained to Yvor Winters, made 'not only because I was penniless at the time but because I owed money to others at the time equally penniless'.[75] According to Matthew Josephson, Crane wept over Moore's 'mutilation' of his poem.[76] John Vincent's reading of Josephson's rather stagey and over-dramatic account of the incident suggests a considerable amount of embellishment on Josephson's part. A few years earlier, in 1923, Josephson and Moore were involved in what Moore's mother described as a 'carnage of skin and fur', where he was 'disintegrated' by Moore in an argument about what Moore liked and disliked about modern poetry.[77] Having been severely admonished by Moore, he may well have relished the opportunity to act as the defender of artistic integrity. When he offered to buy the poem back from the *Dial*, Moore summoned Crane to the office for an explanation. Crane backed down and the poem appeared in May 1926.

As the *Dial* archives reveal, it was not only Crane who was subject to Moore's editorial cuts and substitutions. Her approach was perceived as interference by some and by others as a poetic masterclass gratefully received. In July 1925, Witter Bynner sent Moore a number of poems, reminding Moore that they had met and making sure she knew that they shared mutual friends in Monroe Wheeler and Glenway Wescott. In her response, Moore reassures Bynner that she remembers him well but sends back all the poems he has submitted for consideration. A few years later, however, Bynner tried again, submitting 'A Love Song' for publication in the *Dial* in February 1928. Moore accepts but only if certain changes are made. Bynner does not reply until July of that year suggesting an initial reluctance to agree to the revisions but, having had time to reflect on Moore's proposals, he is eventually willing to approve them.[78] John Cournos, who Pound had recommended to Moore as a translator, was happy to make revisions which he thinks are an improvement.[79] Lola Ridge is quick to accede to Moore's suggestions, judging that the omission of five lines helps rather than hurts the poem.[80] Other contributors, such as Malcolm Cowley, clearly enjoy a form of linguistic sparring with Moore on literary ethics.[81] Evelyn Scott, on the other hand, is offended by Moore's revisions to her poem 'The Eaglet' in 1928 and, though she had enjoyed a friendly relationship with the magazine since its early years, she severed ties with the *Dial* at that point.[82]

Moore was very careful concerning how she phrased her requests for cuts. She repeatedly urged contributors not to agree to changes unless they felt that they improved their work. Moore attempted to maintain a collaborative relationship with those who submitted work for publication. Her comments, as Emily Setina points out in relation to Moore's revisions of Marsden Hartley's poetry, often took the form of questions 'keeping alternate readings alive rather than merely, and more expediently, cancelling and replacing existing lines'.[83] This is evident in Moore's exchanges with many contributors: She uses a question when suggesting changes to Kenneth Burke's essay on H. G. Wells: 'Should you lose impact if you allowed us to make the "Wellsian concept." The "H. G. Wells Concept"?' And as if aware of accusations of over-zealous editing, she allows Burke the choice: 'If it seems prim please restore the original when the proof comes.'[84]

When writers like Crane were under considerable financial pressure, however, there may not have been any alternative. The *Dial* paid its contributors handsomely compared to other modernist magazines.[85] Publication in the magazine brought with it a cultural prestige that could make or break reputations. So while Moore may have increasingly couched her requests in language that almost begged her contributors to avoid compromising on aesthetic grounds, as editor of a magazine that promised cultural consecration, those requests were hard to refuse. Most modernist writers, operating in an economic world turned upside down where little capital was flowing in their direction, still required an income and some, like Crane, could not afford to refuse prestigious magazines like the *Dial*.[86]

But as I have suggested, for Moore, cultural consecration brought with it a certain pressure to adhere to the *Dial*'s image of austere elegance. Her requests for changes look less remarkable when read alongside the changes she made to her own poems for publication in the *Dial*. Moore's revisions to Crane's 'The Wine Menagerie', for instance, bear a resemblance to her revisions to poems such as 'Picking and Choosing', 'When I Buy Pictures' and 'To a Snail'. As early drafts of 'Picking and Choosing' illustrate, Moore began to push against the syllabic form, truncating the stanzas and moving towards free verse. The original eight stanzas are reduced to five. The first two stanzas are unceremoniously cut for the *Dial* version so that the poem begins with: 'Literature is a phase of life'. The omitted stanzas and the work they do in the poem are worth dwelling on:

> The half of what is written is not like a play
> for enjoyment nor is it rich in material that one can use after-
> ward and it is permissible to
> say so; if one must give one's opinion, it is per-
> missible that one should know what one likes and criticism is the
>
> result of knowing, but to be dogmatic is
> to be no longer scientific. "I am fascinated by Benson's ser-
> iousness" but whoever it is
> that understands the matter, must not say this for fear
> we might misunderstand. To me who knows nothing, it is very
>
> simple; literature is a phase of life; if [87]

In order to deploy words constructively, to paraphrase the poem, to avoid the 'opaque allusion – the simulated flight// upward', a 'racoon-like curiosity' is required. Approaching literature directly, 'picking and choosing' involves instinct. Like the dog at the end of the poem 'nipping the linen' able to sniff out the badger, Moore's speaker eschews 'opinion' resolving instead simply to acknowledge what she likes. This relates to Moore's resistance to what she refers to as 'insulting didacticism' and reinforces Schulze's assertion that Moore seeks a form of language that is prismatic rather than opaque, immediate rather than mediating. As the later poem 'New York' suggests, literature should offer 'accessibility to experience'; it should open up without colonising or plundering the 'wilderness'.[88] The way to provide this 'accessibility' is to plunge the reader into the poem in media res, to immerse her in the experience rather than providing her with an introduction or an explanation of the subject. As a result, in Moore's revisions to her own work, as well as to the work of others, she cuts sentences and lines that explain or introduce subject matter. The opening stanzas of the first draft of 'Picking and Choosing' set up the argument and announce the theme, thereby preparing the reader for the necessity of 'picking and choosing'. In doing so, the poem performs the mediating role of which it complains. In Moore's attempt to eradicate all simulation, the explanations framing the ensuing discussion disappear, forcing the reader to tackle the first elliptical line of the poem, 'Literature is a phase of life; if' with little assistance. This is a strategy typical of many Moore poems and one which she also adopts in her revision of Crane's poem.

Here is 'The Wine Menagerie' as Crane wished it to be published, followed by 'Again':

The Wine Menagerie

Invariably when wine redeems the sight,
Narrowing the mustard scansions of the eyes,
A leopard ranging always in the brow
Asserts a vision in the slumbering gaze.

Then glozening decanters that reflect the street
Wear me in crescents on their bellies. Slow
Applause flows into liquid cynosures:
– I am conscripted to their shadows' glow.

Against the imitation onyx wainscoting
(Painted emulsion of snow, eggs, yarn, coal, manure)
Regard the forceps of the smile that takes her.
Percussive sweat is spreading to his hair. Mallets,
Her eyes, unmake an instant of the world . . .

What is it in this heap the serpent pries –
Whose skin, facsimile of time, unskeins
Octagon, sapphire transepts round the eyes;
– From whom some whispered carillon assures
Speed to the arrow into feathered skies?

Sharp to the windowpane guile drags a face,
And as the alcove of her jealousy recedes
An urchin who has left the snow
Nudges a cannister across the bar
While August meadows somewhere clasp his brow.

Each chamber, transept, coins some squint,
Remorseless line, minting their separate wills –
Poor streaked bodies wreathing up and out,
Unwitting the stigma that each turn repeals:
Between black tusks the roses shine!

New thresholds, new anatomies! Wine talons
Build freedom up about me and distill
This competence – to travel in a tear
Sparkling alone, within another's will.

Until my blood dreams a receptive smile
Wherein new purities are snared; where chimes
Before some flame of gaunt repose a shell
Tolled once, perhaps, by every tongue in hell.
– Anguished, the wit that cries out of me:

'Alas, – these frozen billows of your skill!
Invent new dominoes of love and bile . . .
Ruddy, the tooth implicit of the world
Has followed you. Though in the end you know
And count some dim inheritance of sand,
How much yet meets the treason of the snow.

'Rise from the dates and crumbs. And walk away,
Stepping over Holofernes' shins –
Beyond the wall, whose severed head floats by
With Baptist John's. Their whispering begins.

'– And fold your exile on your back again;
Petrushka's valentine pivots on its pin.'[89]

AGAIN
BY HART CRANE

What in this heap in which the serpent pries,
Reflects the sapphire transepts round the eyes –
The angled octagon upon a skin,
Facsimile of time unskeined,
From which some whispered carillon assures
Speed to the arrow into feathered skies?

New thresholds, new anatomies,
New freedoms now distil
This competence, to travel in a tear,
Sparkling alone within another's will.

My blood dreams a receptive smile
Wherein new purities are snared. There chimes
Before some flame a restless shell
Tolled once perhaps by every tongue in hell.
Anguished the wit cries out of me, 'The world
Has followed you. Though in the end you know
And count some dim inheritance of sand,
How much yet meets the treason of the snow.'[90]

In 'Again', Moore's revised version of Crane's poem, the first three stanzas of the original have entirely disappeared. Crane's first line, 'Invariably when wine redeems the sight' is particularly important, providing as it does a sense of the poem's main theme: the effect of alcohol on the subject and on poetic creativity, though this précis hardly does justice to Crane's lush locutions. Moreover, the dazzling verbal effects of the reflective surfaces of the bar, the 'glozening decanters that reflect the street/ wear me in crescents on their bellies', the subject's sense of losing his integrity as the alcohol flows, feeling 'conscripted' to the 'shadows' glow' are all lost in Moore's rewriting.[91] It is not only the wine that has been taken out of 'The Wine Menagerie' but the features of the poem that are characteristic of Crane, the affect that flows between the subject and his environment, the ways in which feelings melt, like snow into the object world and return to 'assert a vision'.[92]

Moore's 'Again' begins with a slightly revised version of the first line of the fourth stanza of the original. Unsurprisingly, she omits the adverb, 'invariably'. For her, 'concentration avoids adverbial intensives such as 'definitely', 'positively', or 'absolutely'.[93] The further changes she makes to this line are intriguing: 'What is it in this heap the serpent pries' – becomes 'What in this heap in which the serpent pries'. Moore's version starts, characteristically, with a subordinate clause. Note how many occasions Moore deploys this tactic. In

'Black Earth', for instance, the whole of the first stanza is subordinate. Moore's use of an adverb here, unusual for her, has to wait until the second stanza for the finite verb that it qualifies:

> Openly, yes,
> With the naturalness
>   Of the hippopotamus or the alligator
>   When it climbs out on the bank to experience the
>
> Sun, I do these
> Things which I do, which please
>   No one but myself.[94]

This tactic of suspension is apparent in many of Moore's poems. Frequently titles are part of the poem:

> When I Buy Pictures
>
> or what is closer to the truth,
> when I look at that of which I may regard myself as the imaginary
>   possessor,
> I fix upon what would give me pleasure in my average moments:[95]

Though the verb 'to buy' is contained in the title of the poem, the act of buying takes place off-stage, at another time and place. The reader waits for the finite verb, the fixity of 'I fix upon', predicated on the doubled 'when'. Buying pictures is a contingent activity, one that 'depends upon' to paraphrase William Carlos Williams, other things. Moore enjoys hanging lines on conjunctions or prepositions: 'If "compression is the first grace of style" (To a Snail), 'When I Buy Pictures', 'If external action is effete' ('The Past is the Present'), 'In "taking charge of your possessions when you saw them"' (To the Peacock of France'). The sensation of waiting in a queue suspends activity so that the reader experiences the effect of accumulation. The suspense produces compression allowing clauses to pile on top of each other. This is the splicing effect described by critics such as Susan McCabe in terms of montage. By forcing the reader to wait for the main verb in 'When I Buy Pictures', the title must be held in mind, and then the first line with the qualification of 'or' and then the second line with the noun phrase, 'imaginary possessor'. As Marie Boroff notes, the stative quality of Moore's language is partly the consequence of the paucity of finite verbs. Her poems are replete with content words, 'squadrons of nouns march through Moore's poetry' rather than words that signal an action that takes place in time.[96] Moore's poems are places where the reader waits for *things to happen*. As she waits, textual pressure builds up producing the concentration required imaginatively to possess pictures, a concentration that stimulates an intense pleasure for the reader. This is not vicarious pleasure mediated through the speaker's response to pictures, but it is the new pleasure generated by the poem's precise observations.

In Moore's 'Peoples Surroundings' the environment moves into the foreground. Even when Moore is wary of the seductive pleasures of aestheticism, as Robin Schulze suggests in her reading of the poem, the accumulation of flora, fauna, birds and reptiles associated with the distinct ecosystem of the island of St Thomas produces a 'shiver', a bodily sensation akin to 'the touch of a hand'.[97] The pleasure of such things, 'compact' yet diverse, the subtle distinctions registered in the discernible shades of red: 'crimson, [. . .] copper, and [. . .] Chinese vermilion' together with the 'fifty shades of mauve/ and amethyst' in the 'obedient chameleon' signal Moore's interest in what Douglas Mao describes as the 'feeling of regard for the physical object as object – as not-self'.[98] Moore's solid objects have their own integrity but in the context of a poem, they affect the reader in particular ways. More specifically, she is thinking about how the poem might be a thing capable of stimulating feeling. To what extent does the poem 'surround' the reader by accumulating, listing, describing and delineating things peculiar to certain environments? Moore continued to ask this question in her long poems, particularly 'An Octopus', which was a recreation of the ecosystem of Mount Rainier. At this point in her career, Moore is particularly interested in developing a poetic method capable of 'maintaining many minds', a phrase deployed in 'An Octopus'.[99] In poems such as 'An Octopus', 'Marriage' and 'Sea Unicorns and Land Unicorns' Moore was to address the distinctly modernist problem of how to maintain the intensity associated with close observation while expanding that vision, a problem that Pound had engaged with in the 'Homage to Sextus Propertius' and was continuing to explore in the 1920s in the *Cantos*.

Another way of thinking about this is to consider the question of what holds things together in a poem by Moore. Examining the effect of the shift from syllabics to free verse helps to explain how Moore achieved compression even when she inserted additional material. It also helps to explain how she might have thought that her cuts to 'The Wine Menagerie' expanded rather than contracted Crane's vision of ecstasy. In 'When I Buy Pictures' five stanzas of between eight and ten lines are reduced to twenty-seven lines. The most dramatic change is the addition of two quotations in the two last lines of the poem in the *Dial* version:

> It comes to this: of whatever sort it is,
> it must acknowledge the forces which have made it;
> it must be 'lit with piercing glances into the life of things'
> then I 'take it in hand as a savage would take a looking-glass.'[100]

The first quotation is attributed to A. R. Gordon in *The Poets of the Old Testament* in Moore's notes in *The Complete Poems*. The second quotation has no attending note to reveal its origins. Both versions repeatedly use the word 'it' in the last lines of the poem building up a specificity and intensity around the indefinite pronoun. 'It' is 'taken in hand' in the free-verse poem, grasped finally in a looking-glass by the speaking persona who, like the 'savage', sees him or herself reflected as if for the first time. That 'it' rhymes with 'lit' in the penultimate line and then the lilting 'l' is alliteratively picked up in the word 'life' creates a connection between 'it', 'lit' and 'life'. As Schulze suggests more widely in relation to Moore's poetics, what 'it' is might best be understood in terms of imaginary art forms that offer connections to the 'genuine', original moments that awaken the subject to a direct and unmediated relation to things that 'give pleasure'.[101] In the syllabic version, the poem concludes with the sentence, 'It must be a voluntary gift with the/ name written on it' whereas in the free-verse version, the poem returns to the reflective trope of the poetic speaker regarding her 'self' in the pictures. The free-verse poem suggests that pictures have an effect on the subject's way of seeing herself and it emphasises the agency of things, their ability to act on the subject.

If Moore is engaged in thinking about how things surround and affect the subject, for Crane, the subject's feelings and sensations are reflected in things and in their surroundings.

In Crane's poetry, verbs proliferate indicating a form of action that most often takes place within the speaker's sponge-like sensing consciousness. Dramatic tension is often produced by the shift of tone as the poem registers the speaker's various states of mind as well as his feelings. 'The Wine Menagerie' begins in a reflective, controlled mood that shifts in the second stanza to the excitement of immersion and then is followed by dissolution as the subject is 'conscripted' by alcohol. The longer five-line stanza that follows intimates the sense of threat, of menace that seems to be connected to an erotic entanglement in the bar. The fourth stanza, the one that Moore uses as the beginning of her poem shifts again as the speaker looks for something in 'this heap' that carries him beyond the temporal and spatial limitations of the bar itself. Shedding a skin like the serpent, the speaker begins to experience a clarity as the constraints of his sober and conscious mind 'unskeins'.

In stanza five, as if now outside the bar and looking in, the speaker gazes through the windowpane at the interior scene newly attuned to its affective resonances, the 'guile' and 'jealousy' of those both inside and out. The following stanza builds on this affective cluster of associations merging the economic transactions of the bar with the sexual transactions that accompany the consumption of alcohol. What Crane achieves here and more so in the poems that constitute *The Bridge* is both that sense of being at the scene as well as looking at the scene, of an embodied, affective immersion together with moments, albeit elliptical and sporadic, of ecstatic transcendence. The ecstasy in 'The Wine Menagerie' occurs in the seventh stanza with the intricate and intimate image of the speaker seeing himself reflected in another's tear. This form of 'competence – to travel in a tear' as Vincent argues, 'acknowledge[s] one's own image in any affective attachment to an other, but also [. . .] maintain[s] the intense clarity and attention that would allow one first to find and then follow a welling, spilling, sprinting, and, then, stalling, tear'.[102] Being 'alone' yet also 'within another's will' allows the speaker to 'travel' or to cross the boundaries that circumscribe individual experience. Both erotic and transcendent, the exchange of bodily fluids signals a transgression as well as a transfusion for the poetic speaker as he merges with and then separates from the other.

This moment of intense intimacy is then followed by what Vincent refers to as 'dispersal' and this is what Moore cuts from the poem. She retains almost all of stanza eight, which registers the ensuing anguish that follows the ecstasy, but she excises half of stanza nine and omits the entire final stanza with its images of floating severed heads. Both Crane and Moore end their poems with a quotation from the 'wit', a voice that 'cries out from' the speaker and who picks through the 'dim inheritance' of the ecstasy. All the 'glow' associated with initial inebriation, the 'sweat' of erotic transgression and the 'sparkle' of transcendence turns to sand and then melts figuratively into something less substantial – snow. Crane's version, however, has the wit refer to both Holofernes and John the Baptist, both Old Testament figures who lose their heads and who, as Gregory Woods suggests, refers to the severed head of the singing Orpheus who was punished for recommending love between men.[103] For Vincent, 'these figureless heads' do not signify the song of the poet as it echoes throughout history, but rather 'a pile up of failure that is powerfully hallucinatory and therefore, in its own entirely new way, transcendent'.[104] If we follow Vincent's argument, then by removing the heads, Moore removes the 'pile up of failure' as well as the association between that failure and a new form of transcendence.

By excising the whispering heads of John the Baptist and Holofernes, Moore also severs the poem from a queer tradition of poets who are punished for what are perceived to be their sexual and textual transgressions. In addition, as Vincent suggests, the heads float through the concluding stanzas of the poem, reminding us of the speaker who has figuratively lost his head in desire. In her suggestive reading of Crane's 'queer intimacy', Julie Taylor notes the ways in which intimacy is uncontainable but sees, like Vincent, that this failure is a form of 'unintegration' that has its own ecstatic possibilities.[105] For Moore, 'unintegration' is exactly what the poet should avoid. If concentration produces gusto, if 'contractility' is a 'virtue', then dispersal dilutes the poem's affective power and even pollutes its ethical integrity. It does this by getting in the way of the reader's access to ecstasy.

Moore's idea of intoxication is very different to Crane's. It is worth returning to 'A Characteristic American', to remind ourselves that for Henry James, according to Moore, things 'glow, flush, glimmer, vibrate, shine, hum, bristle, reverberate'. His writing conveys and also shares with the reader a sensuous and affective intensity capable of producing bodily sensations: 'Joy, bliss, ecstasies, intoxication, a sense of trembling in every limb'.[106] Such writing produces the effect of the 'shattering first glimpse', providing the reader with an unmediated sensation, a direct and genuine feeling that is instinctive rather than learnt. And this is the reason why Moore resisted so emphatically Crane's poetics. What she perceived in his poetry was a lesson in feeling rather than genuine feeling, an instruction by the poet that informed the reader what ecstasy looked like and felt like. In response to this, rightly or wrongly, Moore's revisions are designed to make ecstasy available to the reader through the process of poetic distillation rather than dispersal. For Moore, the poem is too explicit, not in the sense of being lewd or distasteful, but in the sense of being too instructive. Vincent is right to summarise the differences in this way: 'Crane is zoomed in on ecstasy in order to enact it for his reader, and Moore produces a wide-angle shot that shows where ecstasy is so that her readers can go and experience it themselves.'[107] At the same time, his explanation misses a sense of what was at stake for Moore. From her perspective, Crane gets in the way of the reader experiencing ecstasy by trying to explain it to those who, it is tacitly assumed, will never have direct access to the places, experiences and even, perhaps, the feelings articulated in the poem.

It is worth returning to the 'carnage of skin and fur' between Josephson and Moore in order to dispel the notion that Moore's revisions were motivated by prudery.[108] In 1923, Josephson, recently established as editor of the Dada magazine *Broom*, visited Moore in her apartment in Greenwich Village hoping to recruit her as a possible editor or contributor. In that conversation, Josephson asked Moore for her opinion on a number of writers, including William Carlos Williams and his friend, Slater Brown. With her usual candour, Moore said she thought that Brown 'lacked discipline' and that she 'loathed and abhorred [Williams's] lewdness and told him so many times'. As for Josephson's own recent book of poems, she disliked all but two of them. When asked what she disliked in particular, 'excrement' was the response and 'armpits'. She went on to clarify, 'Sherwood Anderson says he likes the smell of excrement. I do not, and I refuse to be made to think of it. Armpits would not interest me if you were the first to mention the subject, but it's done to death.'[109] Moore complained repeatedly that many of her male modernist peers included subjects in their writing that lacked what she referred to as 'decorum'. Writing to Williams in 1935, she explains her position:

> I cannot see that art is in any way different from the rest of life, from conversation or from the strategies of solitude; and it is an unending query to me why a person would say on the page what he has never been known to say to your face.[110]

According to Moore, when reflecting on the carnage, 'all my stinging legs stand out like the fretful porpentine [. . .] when I am told that if I were cosmopolitan I'd like lewdness better'.[111] What Josephson perceived as Moore's lack of cosmopolitan sophistication signals the underlying social discriminations that were being made in the production of the modernist aesthetic. In other words, Josephson implies that if Moore had travelled, if she were a woman of the world, if she had seen things as he had done, then she would have a very different attitude to art. Twelve years her junior, it is easy to see why Moore's 'stinging legs' came up in response to this criticism of her values and, implicitly, her lifestyle.

The 'carnage' between Moore and Josephson is related to her textual collision with Crane. What she objects to in the work of some of her modernist contemporaries are the lessons they seem to be offering in how to feel about art. As Schulze suggests, for Moore, 'the artist must be willing to follow his or her instincts at all costs'.[112] This meant putting instinct at the centre of poetry and maintaining individuality as well as diversity. As an editor, Moore carries this philosophy with her when making aesthetic discriminations. This is not, as Josephson and others assumed, to reinforce a normative and genteel set of conventions; it is just the opposite, it is to challenge the notion that art should provide instructions in feeling. Moore aims to bring the erotic frisson of the illicit sexual encounter out of the bar and onto the page, to 'intoxicate' her readers, to make them 'tremble' with desire, to stimulate an unmediated and intense ecstasy through the process of aesthetic distillation.

The differences between Crane and Moore unfold through a comparative analysis of their poems. Such an analysis does not seek to privilege Moore, the more experienced and established poet over Crane, the second-generation modernist, resisting, in many ways, the austerity implied in a 'dieted down modernism'.[113] Nor does it suggest that Moore's rewriting of Crane's poem can simply be explained in terms of a clash of poetics. Moore's position as editor of the *Dial* required her to make decisions with the magazine in mind. Thus while her omission of the first three stanzas of Crane's poem enacts a distinctly modernist revision akin to Pound's cutting of the original opening of *The Waste Land*, it also removes the explicit reference to alcohol, 'Invariably when wine redeems the sight'. Without that opening line providing an explanatory framework for the poem, the ecstasy of 'Again' becomes a form of poetic transcendence with little connection to an embodied and affective subject. Undoubtedly, Moore's version is less seedy, less sweaty and less sexy. The removal of this line and the subsequent revision by Moore must be understood not as Moore's prissy objection to Crane metaphorically 'slumming it', but in relation to the *Dial* as a periodical serving a particular constituency. Moore, ever alert to the dangers of alienating her readership, was keen to maintain a sense of the magazine's image of distinction. She may well have come to the conclusion that to have a poem meditating on the ecstasies of inebriation would be out of place in a magazine aimed at a respectable upper-middle class, even genteel, audience. Her response was to practise a form of distillation on Crane's poem, thereby solving the problem of Crane's desperate need for money while maintaining the magazine's image of distinction.

The case of Crane, however, is provocative not only because it allows us to more fully understand the material pressures circumscribing modernism's dissemination, but it also draws attention to the limitations of positing Moore's 'austere' modernism against Crane's textual excesses. We can learn as much about Moore from reading Crane as we can learn about Crane from reading Moore. Not only that, the critical construction of a 'lean modernism' reacting violently against the 'sentimental slither' of late Victorian poetry obscures the many and various ways in which poets like Moore and Crane were indebted to the poetic ornamentation associated with poets such as Swinburne.[114] As Elisabeth Oliver suggests, making it new was associated with a 'model of a newly purified poetry, stripped of all its gaudy remnants', yet for Moore the decorative impulse was equally important and shaped the patterns of her syllabic stanzas.[115] On the other hand, as Brian Reed suggests, Crane took a 'contrary path' to the first-generation modernists like Moore, who eschewed overt displays of emotion and who seemingly rejected the decorous and ornate language of late nineteenth-century poetry. Reed's tracing of the influence of Swinburne on Crane reminds us of Moore's delight in some aspects of the late Victorian lyric.[116] She takes T. S. Eliot to task in her review of *The Sacred Wood* in the *Dial* in March 1921:

> Mr Eliot allows Swinburne, perhaps, a sufficiently high place as a poet; to imply that he does not, is to disregard the positively expressed acceptance of his genius; nevertheless, in the course of the essay on Swinburne the Poet, he says, 'agreed that we do not (and I think that the present generation does not) greatly enjoy Swinburne,' et cetera. Do we not? There is about Swinburne the atmosphere of magnificence, a kind of permanent association of him with King Solomon 'perfumed with all the powders of the merchants, approaching in his litter' – an atmosphere which is not destroyed, one feels, even by indiscriminate browsing – and now in his verse as much as ever, as Swinburne says of the Sussex seaboard, 'You feel the sea in the air at every step.' There is seeming severity in stripping a poet of his accepted paraphernalia and bringing him forth as he is.[117]

Moore resists relinquishing Swinburne. The 'atmosphere of magnificence' evident in the nineteenth-century poet signals the textual excesses and extravagances that are present in Moore's poems, though distilled. She also objects to Eliot taking Swinburne 'to pieces', echoing a similar criticism she levelled at Eliot's *Prufrock and Other Observations*, which she admired but which required, in her opinion, sweetening for 'the gentle reader'.[118] According to Reed, Crane 'supersaturated his poetry with the perceived vices of the late Victorian lyric'. His debt to Swinburne, in particular, was as important as his debt to Walt Whitman. Yet rather than interpreting Crane as outside the modernist frame, Reed suggests we read his poetry as 'differently modern'.[119] Crane's modernism looks less 'different', however, if the austere aesthetics associated with poets such as Moore is also revised. As Jessica Feldman and Victoria Rosner have suggested and as a perusal of the *Dial* further reinforces, modernism and aestheticism were intimately related. Moore looks less 'austere', Crane looks less different and modernism looks less lean if examined in the context of the magazine associated with its rise to cultural legitimacy.

The case of Crane has come to define Moore's editorship and confirm suspicions that Moore's motives were underpinned by her 'hysterical' approach to modernism's supposed 'obscenities'. A gendered critical discourse emerges in response to the wounds inflicted on male writers by women editors like Moore and Monroe. According to Pound, these editorial impositions threatened to 'emasculate literature utterly'.[120] As Pound was all too aware, however, modernism itself was conceived in terms of a textual compression that required writers to submit their work to radical excision and revision. A double standard lingers, one that constructs Pound's editorial interventions as profound and sensitive interventions central to the formation of modernism, while women editors are associated with the practical, pedantic and even prudish preoccupations of the magazine market. In the following chapter, I will argue that we need to understand editorial agency as occupying a space somewhere between the high art of the modernist poet/editor and the material constraints of periodical publication.

Notes

1. Marianne Moore, *The Selected Letters of Marianne Moore*, ed. Bonnie Costello, Celeste Goodridge and Cristanne Miller (London: Faber and Faber, 1998), p. 213.
2. John Emil Vincent, *Queer Lyrics: (Difficulty and Closure in American Poetry)* (New York: Palgrave, 2002), p. 63.
3. Natalia Cecire, 'Marianne Moore's Precision', *Arizona Quarterly: A Journal of American Literature, Culture and Theory*, 67 (2011), 83–110 (p. 85).
4. Vincent, *Queer Lyrics*, p. 69.
5. Ibid. p. 60.
6. Marianne Moore to Sibley Watson Jr, 1 January 1927, Beinecke, ST/Dial Papers, Series I, Box 7, Fol. 267.
7. John Slatin, *The Savage's Romance: The Poetry of Marianne Moore* (University Park: Pennsylvania State University Press, 1986), pp. 99–102.
8. Slatin, *Savage's Romance*, p. 101.
9. Marianne Moore, *Becoming Marianne Moore: The Early Poems, 1907–1924* (Berkeley, Los Angeles, London: University of California Press, 2002), p. 74.
10. Robin G. Schulze, *The Degenerate Muse: American Nature, Modernist Poetry,*

and the Problem of Cultural Hygiene (Oxford: Oxford University Press, 2013), p. 179.

11. Marianne Moore, *The Complete Prose of Marianne Moore*, ed. Patricia Willis (London: Faber and Faber, 1987), p. vii; Susan McCabe, *Cinematic Modernism: Modernist Poetry and Film* (Cambridge: Cambridge University Press, 2005), p. 190; Carolyn Burke, 'Getting Spliced: Modernism and Sexual Difference' *American Quarterly*, 239 (1987), 98–121.
12. Shawna Ross, 'Hashtags, Algorithmic Compression and Henry James's Late Style', *The Henry James Review*, 36 (2015), 24–44 (p. 30).
13. Moore, *Becoming*, p. 65.
14. Moore, *Complete Prose*, pp. 153, 165; Moore, 'Comment', *Dial*, 79 (September 1925), 264–6 (p. 265); Moore, 'Comment', *Dial*, 80 (May 1926), 444–8 (p. 444).
15. Moore, *Complete Prose*, p. 80; Moore, 'Hymen', *Broom*, 4 (January 1923), 133–5 (p. 133).
16. Kenneth Burke to Marianne Moore, 12 April 1957, RML, Series V, Box 8, Fol. 22.
17. H.D., *End to Torment: A Memoir of Ezra Pound*, ed. Norman Holmes Pearson and Michael King (New York: New Directions, 1979), p. 40, cited in Suzanne Raitt, 'The Rhetoric of Efficiency in Early Modernism', *Modernism/Modernity*, 13 (2006), 835–51 (p. 840).
18. Ezra Pound, *Gaudier-Brzeska* (New York: John Lane, 1916), p. 108. Available at: https://archive.org/details/gaudierbrzeska00pounrich (accessed 15 October 2017).
19. Lawrence Rainey, *The Annotated Waste Land with Eliot's Contemporary Prose* (New Haven, CT: Yale University Press, 2005), p. 23.
20. Hannah Sullivan, *The Work of Revision* (Cambridge, MA: Harvard University Press, 2013), pp. 132, 121.
21. Ibid. p. 114.
22. Ibid. p. 110.
23. Jayne Marek, *Women Editing Modernism: 'Little' Magazines and Literary History* (Lexington: University Press of Kentucky, 1995), p. 157.
24. Writing to Harriet Monroe from Rapallo in 1931, Pound thought Moore the only person capable of taking over the editorship of *Poetry*. Ezra Pound, *The Letters of Ezra Pound*, ed. D. D. Paige (New York: Harcourt, Brace and Co., 1950), p. 315.
25. Moore, *Selected Letters*, p. 123.
26. Moore, *Complete Prose*, pp. 56, 74; Moore, 'Kora in Hell by William Carlos Williams', *Contact*, 4 (January–March 1921), 5–8 (p. 5); Moore, 'Is the Real Actual?', *Dial*, 73 (December 1922), 620–2 (p. 621); Ezra Pound, *The Literary Essays of Ezra Pound*, ed. and intro. T. S. Eliot (London: Faber, 1954), p. 12.
27. Ross, 'Hashtags', p. 28.
28. Sullivan, *Work of Revision*, p. 82; Ross, 'Hashtags', p. 30.
29. For interpretations of this poem, see Fiona Green, '"The magnitude of their root systems": "An Octopus" and National Character', in *Critics and Poets on Marianne Moore: 'A Right Good Salvo of Barks'*, ed. Linda Leavell, Cristanne Miller and Robin G. Schulze (Lewisburg, PA: Bucknell University Press, 2005), pp. 137–49 and Patricia Willis, 'The Road to Paradise: First Notes on Marianne Moore's "An Octopus"', *Twentieth Century Literature*, 30 (1984), pp. 242–66.
30. Ross, 'Hashtags', p. 30.
31. Ibid. p. 28.
32. Ibid. p. 30.
33. Moore, *Complete Prose*, p. 317; Moore, 'Henry James as a Characteristic American', *Hound and Horn*, 7 (April–May 1934), 363–72 (p. 364).
34. Ibid.
35. Schulze, *Degenerate Muse*, p. 175.

36. Moore, *Complete Prose*, pp. 361, 364.
37. Emily Setina, '"Mountains being a language with me": Marianne Moore, Marsden Hartley, and Modernist Revision', *Modernism/Modernity*, 22 (2015), 153–82 (p. 156).
38. Ibid. p. 173.
39. Cited in Setina, '"Mountains"', p. 160 and published in *Marsden Hartley: Selected Poems*, ed. Henry W. Wells (New York: Viking, 1945), p. 107.
40. Setina, '"Mountains"', p. 173.
41. Betsy Erkilla, 'Elizabeth Bishop and Marianne Moore: The Dynamics of Female Influence' and Rosanne Wasserman, '"A Tutelary Muse": Moore's Influence on Bishop', both in *Marianne Moore: Woman and Poet*, ed. Patricia C. Willis (Orono, ME: National Poetry Foundation, 1990), pp. 335–50 (pp. 351–70).
42. Bonnie Costello, 'Marianne Moore and Elizabeth Bishop: Friendship and Influence', *Twentieth Century Literature*, 30 (1984), 130–49.
43. Moore, *Complete Prose*, pp. 80, 56, 75, 424, 426; Moore, 'Hymen', *Broom*, 4 (January 1923), 133–5 (p. 133); Moore, 'Kora in Hell By William Carlos Williams', *Contact*, 4 (January–March 1921), 5–8 (p. 5); Moore, 'Is the Real Actual?', *Dial*, 73 (December 1922), 620–2 (p. 622); Moore, 'Humility, Concentration, and Gusto', *Grolier Club Gazette*, 2 (May 1949), 289–300 (p. 291). Available in New York Heritage Digital Archives at: https://cdm16694.contentdm.oclc.org/digital/collection/Grolier01/id/652 (accessed 6 September 2018).
44. Bonnie Honigsblum, 'Marianne Moore's Revisions of "Poetry"', in *Marianne Moore: Woman and Poet*, ed. Patricia C. Willis (Orono, ME: National Poetry Foundation, 1990), pp. 185–222 (p. 197).
45. Ibid. p. 201.
46. Bonnie Costello, '"To a Snail": A Lesson in Compression', *Marianne Moore Newsletter*, 3 (1979), 11–15 (p. 11).
47. For a lucid account of Moore's use of the syllabic stanza, see Linda Leavell, *Prismatic Color*, pp. 68–80.
48. Moore, *Becoming*, p. 65.
49. Cecire, 'Marianne Moore's Precision', p. 90.
50. For a full account of Moore's publication history up to 1925, see Moore, *Becoming*, pp. 18–38.
51. Moore, *Becoming*, pp. 256–7.
52. Vicki Graham, '"The Power of the Visible": Marianne Moore and the "Mimetic Faculty"' *Sagetrieb*, 12 (1993), 33–50 (p. 37).
53. Moore, *Complete Prose*, p. 644.
54. Slatin, *Savage's Romance*, pp. 118–19.
55. Moore, *Becoming*, p. 36.
56. Graham, '"Power"', p. 40.
57. Leavell, *Prismatic Color*, p. 126.
58. Judith Yaross Lee, 'From the Field: The Future of American Periodicals and American Periodicals Research', *American Periodicals: A Journal of History, Criticism and Bibliography*, 15 (2005), 196–201 (p. 198).
59. Kenneth Burke to Marianne Moore, no date, 1944, RML, Series V, Box 8, Fol. 22.
60. Hart Crane, 'My Grandmother's Love Letters', *Dial*, 68 (April 1920), 457.
61. Linda Leavell, *Holding On Upside Down: The Life and Work of Marianne Moore* (New York: Farrar, Straus and Giroux, 2013), p. 245.
62. Moore, *Becoming*, p. 315.
63. Marianne Moore to Scofield Thayer, 25 September 1924, Beinecke, Dial/ST Papers, Box 35, Series IV, Fol. 975.
64. Moore, *Becoming*, p. 327.

65. Scofield Thayer, 'Comment', *Dial*, 78 (April 1925), 354–6 (p. 356).
66. Willis, 'Paradise', p. 251.
67. Moore, *Becoming*, p. 124.
68. Willis, 'Paradise', p. 259; Moore, *Becoming*, p. 317.
69. Cited in Linda Leavell, 'Marianne Moore, the James Family, and the Politics of Celibacy', *Twentieth Century Literature*, 49 (2003), 219–56 (p. 236).
70. Celeste Goodridge, 'Towards a Poetics of Disclosure: Marianne Moore and Henry James', *Sagetrieb*, 6 (1987), 31–43 (p. 35).
71. Vincent, *Queer Lyrics*, p. 63.
72. Marianne Moore, *The Complete Poems of Marianne Moore*, ed. Clive E. Driver (London and Boston, MA: Faber and Faber, 1981), p. 271.
73. Cited in Logan Esdale, 'The Saintsbury Years of Marianne Moore', *Textual Cultures: Texts, Contexts, Interpretations*, 5 (2010), 46–75 (p. 60). William Wasserstrom makes a similar point in 'Marianne Moore, The Dial, and Kenneth Burke', *The Western Humanities Review*, 17 (1963), 249-62 (p. 253).
74. Esdale, 'Saintsbury Years', p. 60.
75. Cited in Vincent, *Queer Lyrics*, p. 64.
76. Vincent, *Queer Lyrics*, p. 60.
77. Leavell, *Holding On*, p. 209. The Moore family frequently used nicknames taken from Kenneth Grahame's *The Wind in the Willows*. Moore was known as Rat, while her mother was Mole and her brother Badger.
78. Witter Bynner to Marianne Moore, 16 July 1928, Beinecke, ST/Dial Papers, Series I, Box 1, Fol. 31.
79. John Cournos to Marianne Moore, 5 December 1928, Beinecke, ST/Dial Papers, Series I, Box 2, Fol. 41.
80. Lola Ridge to Marianne Moore, 29 June 1929, Beinecke, ST/Dial Papers, Series I, Box 5, Fol. 175.
81. Malcolm Cowley to Marianne Moore, 4 March 1926, Beinecke ST/Dial Papers, Series I, Box 2, Fol. 44.
82. Evelyn Scott to Marianne Moore, 18 February 1928, Beinecke, ST/Dial Papers, Series I, Box 6, Fol. 206.
83. Setina, '"Mountains"', p. 158.
84. Marianne Moore to Kenneth Burke, 16 June 1926, Beinecke, ST/Dial Papers, Series I, Box 1, Fol. 25.
85. As Vincent points out, Crane received $20 for 'Again' (*Queer Lyrics*, p. 65).
86. Hart Crane, *The Letters of Hart Crane, 1916–1932*, ed. Brom Weber (Berkeley: University of California Press, 1965), p. 220.
87. Moore, 'Picking and Choosing', RML, Series 1, Box 3, Fol. 32.
88. Moore, *Becoming*, p. 267.
89. Hart Crane, *The Complete Poems of Hart Crane*, ed. Marc Simon (New York: Liveright, 1986), pp. 23–4.
90. Hart Crane, 'Again', *Dial*, 80 (May 1926), 370.
91. Crane, *Complete Poems*, p. 23.
92. Matthew Josephson famously quipped that Moore had taken all the 'wine' out of 'the menagerie' as Vincent points out (*Queer Lyrics*, p. 75), cited from Matthew Josephson, *Life Among the Surrealists* (New York: Holt, Rinehart and Winston, 1962), p. 296.
93. Moore, *Complete Prose*, p. 421; Moore, 'Humility', p. 291.
94. Moore, *Becoming*, p. 237.
95. Ibid. (*Dial* version), p. 255.
96. Marie Boroff, *Language and the Poet: Verbal Artistry in Frost, Stevens, and Moore* (Chicago: University of Chicago Press, 1979), pp. 95, 99.

97. Moore, *Becoming*, p. 270.
98. Douglas Mao, *Solid Objects: Modernism and the Test of Production* (Princeton: Princeton University Press, 1998), p. 4.
99. Moore, *Becoming*, p. 314.
100. Ibid. p. 255.
101. Schulze, *Degenerate Muse*, p. 176.
102. Vincent, *Queer Lyrics*, p. 73.
103. Ibid. p. 74. Gregory Woods, *Articulate Flesh: Male Homo-Eroticism and Modern Poetry* (New Haven, CT: Yale University Press, 1987), p. 148.
104. Vincent, *Queer Lyrics*, p. 74.
105. Julie Taylor, 'On Holding and Being Held: Hart Crane's Queer Intimacy', *Twentieth Century Literature*, 60 (2014), 305–35 (p. 317).
106. Moore, *Complete Prose*, p. 317; Moore, 'Henry James', p. 364.
107. Vincent, *Queer Lyrics*, p. 70.
108. Leavell, *Holding On*, p. 209.
109. Ibid. p. 208.
110. Marianne Moore to William Carlos Williams, 17 October 1935, RML, Series V, Box 77, Fol. 25.
111. Leavell, *Holding On*, pp. 208–9.
112. Schulze, *Degenerate Muse*, p. 203.
113. Sullivan, *Work of Revision*, p. 105.
114. Ibid. p. 112.
115. Elisabeth Oliver, 'Redecorating Vorticism: Marianne Moore's "Ezra Pound" and the Geometric Style', *Journal of Modern Literature*, 34 (2011), 84–113 (p. 88).
116. Brian Reed, *Hart Crane: After His Lights* (Tuscaloosa: University of Alabama Press, 2006), p.17.
117. Moore, *Complete Prose*, p. 53; Moore, 'The Sacred Wood', *Dial*, 70 (March 1921), 336–9 (p. 336).
118. Moore, *Complete Prose*, p. 35; Moore, 'A Note on T. S. Eliot's Book', *Poetry*, 12 (April 1918), 36–9 (p. 36).
119. Reed, *Hart Crane*, p. 40.
120. Pound, *Letters*, p. 54.

5

MODERNISTS EDITED: JOYCE, STEIN, LAWRENCE AND ROSENFELD

In Moore's exchanges with Sibley Watson, she described some of her editorial interventions as 'trespassing', implying that there were boundaries that ought to be respected by the editor and limits to editorial influence.[1] What these limits were, exactly, is difficult to ascertain, not because Moore interfered so extensively, but because editorial agency is itself bounded by the institutional habitus of the magazine. While we know that Moore was not always in sympathy with the *Dial*, that in her comments she challenged some of the assumptions underpinning the critical assessments of her predecessors, at the same time, editorial judgements are so embedded within material and social circumstances that to identify them as 'judgements' or even to refer to 'motives' becomes problematic. Testing the boundaries of editorial agency becomes a matter of examining particular examples of the ways in which texts appear or do not appear in print as well as reading closely for evidence of Mooreish contractility.

To add a further layer of complexity, we might add the periodical form to the list of agents contributing to the production of modernism. Seriality and repetition, as James Mussell has argued, mediates content in ways that are only just beginning to be explored.[2] To what extent, we might ask, is Moore's editorial style and the signature of the *Dial* magazine itself as well as the author's intention usurped or superseded by the formal constraints of periodical publication? Possibly the most well-known non-event in the publication history of the *Dial* is the refusal to publish extracts from Joyce's *Work in Progress*, later to become *Finnegans Wake*. The exchanges between Moore and Watson in 1926 and then again in 1927 reveal the extent to which size mattered. The length of Joyce's submission made it difficult to accept without significant cuts. Even then, Moore was not convinced that publication was worth the risk of attracting the censors.

In the case of Stein, for instance, a writer Moore very much admired, publication in the *Dial* also meant sampling extracts from longer prose pieces. In the process of sampling Stein, however, the *Dial* gave readers the impression that her work culminated in *The Making of Americans*. The complexity of the decision-making processes around the publication of 'A Long Gay Book' suggests how Stein endeavoured to anticipate Moore's editorial decisions. While Stein's work was necessarily sampled for publication, Moore's own remarkable review of *The Making of Americans* provided readers of the *Dial* with a lucid and compressed articulation of Stein's modernist method of accretion, illustrating not only that she had read and understood Stein's novel but that for Moore, Stein practised a form of compression even as her work expanded. Moore did not solve the problem of how the periodical might publish the long modernist text but she was one of the few reviewers of Stein able to explain the method underpinning Stein's genealogy of an American family.

In the case of D. H. Lawrence, it was the threat of censorship that played a significant role in determining the form of publication. Lawrence sent Moore his last collection of poems, *Pansies*, which included a heartfelt, provocative and potentially libellous introduction attacking the censors. Moore was moved by the poems and Lawrence's introduction though she knew she had to be circumspect in what she chose to publish. The friendly exchanges between Moore and Lawrence belie the notion that Moore's editorial practice was motivated by prudery but also reveal the extent to which both editorial and authorial agency had to adapt to the social circumstances of periodical publication.

There are instances, however, where Moore appears to exercise a form of editorial authority that supersedes other factors. When editing the work of Paul Rosenfeld, Moore's predilection for contractility is evident. Snail-like trails of Mooreish compression are evident in the cuts and interventions Moore makes to Rosenfeld's essay on the painter El Greco. Archival evidence clearly illustrates in this instance that Moore made substitutions and alerts us to the possibility, even the probability that she intervened frequently at the textual level in ways that are no longer traceable. In other words, while this chapter argues that editorial agency is limited and that some editorial effects might be accidents, it also argues that in the context of periodical publication, editorial agency sometimes exceeds the limits that we ascribe to the editor. Once we begin to look for contractility, traces of Moore's own signature style appear everywhere and it becomes difficult to discern the boundaries of the editor's agency.

Refusing Joyce

Undoubtedly, Moore held profound and deeply felt ethical principles concerning art and adhered to those principles throughout her life. When it comes to her editorial practice, however, it is important to move beyond the seemingly personal beliefs of the editor to the institutional habitus of the magazine. Anecdotes concerning Moore's eccentricities abound and while Moore is often perceived to be out of place in the context of New York's avant-garde circles, she was not out of place as a magazine editor in terms of her values and her tastes. As the notes to Moore's poems indicate, she was an avid reader of magazines. Her poetry is composed out of the textual fragments of a variety of textual sources; many of them mass circulation magazines such as *National Geographic*, the *Illustrated London News* and the *Literary Digest*. In the quarrel with Josephson referred to in the previous chapter, she expressed her preference for the *Spectator* or the *Natural History Magazine* over the *Dial*, signalling an allegiance not to the 'little' magazines associated with experimental modernism but with the publications read by what Thayer disparagingly referred to as the 'juggernaut of the reading public'.[3] Moore was more likely to discriminate against forms of highbrow culture that denigrated or devalued in any way the subject matter that it represented. This resulted in an editorial policy that resisted publishing overwhelmingly negative criticism. Moore makes it clear in a letter to Conrad Aiken in November 1926 that the *Dial* is not interested in publishing reviews of books that are wholly negative.[4] In many of her letters to aspiring young writers, Moore offers advice that reveals much about the principles underlying her editorial decisions suggesting that 'readers have a right to see life triumphant or to see that it could have been so but for this or that mistake'.[5] In correspondence to other contributors, Moore repeatedly states that the magazine will not publish material that she describes as 'degraded'. She asks Robert Hillyer to omit the critical refrain 'liar' from a poem.[6] She rejects material that denigrates its subject matter. 'At the risk of offering comment which is gratuitous,' she writes to Harry C. Tuttle in 1929, 'may I say that there are many persons who would be pained by a portrayal of old age to the discredit of the subject'.[7] Yet crucially, Moore attributes these preferences to a collective pronoun, signalling that her decision is bound up in the ethos of the magazine.

In some instances, Moore found herself in opposition to the owners of the magazine. Her policy of refusing the derogatory informs her decision to omit two stanzas from Scofield Thayer's bad-tempered poem about Leo Stein, 'Leo Arrogans', expressly against Thayer's own wishes.[8] In 1926, Moore writes to Thayer in an unsuccessful attempt to try to persuade him not to print that he is 'happy' to announce his resignation from the *Dial* in the June issue. In that letter, she recalls sharing her unease with Thayer about the contents of the magazine and hearing that he too did not like everything that appeared. What becomes evident in the correspondence is that editorial decisions are based on how best to maintain the magazine's discursive identity. Moore often interpreted this as maintaining a certain 'propriety and elegance'.[9]

Moore's most serious quarrel with Watson was over the publication of an extract from Joyce's 'Work in Progress', what would eventually be published as part of *Finnegans Wake*. Moore's decision concerning Joyce's manuscript is worth returning to as evidence not of Moore's moral 'scruple[s]' getting in the way of Joyce's 'daring' modernism but more practically in terms of the institutional habitus of the *Dial*.

On 12 July 1926, Sylvia Beach sent a letter offering the *Dial* 30,000 to 34,000 words of 'Work in Progress'; the manuscript, Beach assured Moore, contained no material that might attract the unwanted attentions of the censor. While Moore admired *Dubliners*, she had not been particularly enthusiastic about *Ulysses*, admitting to Pound that she had not been able to read it.[10] The manuscript arrived in the *Dial* offices when Moore was on holiday in Maine and a tentative acceptance had been sent out in her absence. When she returned, Lincoln MacVeagh, who ran the Dial Press, warned Moore that the extract contained sexual content and that it would be risky to publish. Moore informed Watson, who agreed to some cuts and she then quickly made it clear to Beach that she might have to reduce the manuscript 'by one third – perhaps a half'.[11] In the end, Moore decided to publish twelve pages, but by that time, Joyce had withdrawn the manuscript. It is worth pointing out that extracts from 'Work in Progress' appeared in Ford Madox Ford's *Transatlantic Review*, Eliot's *Criterion* and *This Quarter* between February 1924 and late 1925, but none of these editors chose to publish further instalments after that.[12] As Linda Leavell points out, the *Dial* received another part of 'Work in Progress' in February 1927. With this second extract, Moore was decidedly against publication and was singularly unimpressed, declaring to Watson quite categorically in March 1927: 'I [. . .] feel that the manuscript is bad material intrinsically.'[13] Watson was more inclined to publish, arguing in its favour and urged Moore to reconsider. Even after reading it again, Moore remained unconvinced, laying out her objections and even invoking Thayer in support:

> In the letter [. . .] you make it plain I think, by your emphasis on 'protest,' that the decision with regard to the Joyce manuscript is open, so I have read it again and recognize in it, literary ability that I had missed; but surely it lacks what originality and distinction parts of the longer manuscript had; and in so far as readers will be able to catch the author's meaning, we should be discredited I think. We have elected to exclude obscenity when it was dull, and even the advance guard couldn't think that we consider this piece brilliant. You permitted me to oppose Scofield

> when he fell below what we felt to be his own standard; so for us to like this would be exceedingly grievous to him, the more that he resists Joyce's present method.[14]

Moore argues that when she 'opposed Scofield' by taking certain editorial decisions, she was, in fact, adhering to standards that he himself had established. Now she invokes these, not as her own exacting standards, but as those that have been set in stone at the *Dial* itself, what might be understood in terms of the magazine's institutional habitus. Watson would be doing a disservice to Thayer and to the magazine if he were to accept Joyce's work. But what is more significant about this non-event in modernist history is the way in which Moore's refusal of Joyce in 1927 has been interpreted in terms of an editorial discontinuity, a break with the Watson/Thayer policy of setting out to buy up (and perhaps buy out) avant-garde writing even if it came at a high cost. Moore's defence of her own position needs to be considered more carefully. It is worth noting that she does not simply refuse on the grounds of obscenity, but on the grounds of a lack of 'originality and distinction'. Joyce's extract, more specifically, does not have the mark of 'distinction' associated with the institutional habitus of the *Dial* magazine.

Moore was acutely aware of the position the magazine held in the marketplace, of its readership, and of its role in disseminating what the editors thought to be the best of modernist culture. Further on in Moore's response to Watson, she reminds him not only of the legal risks of publishing such material, but also of the distinct possibility of alienating the *Dial*'s readership:

> Private publication could take what risks courage would recommend, but remembering that I felt detached from *The Dial* by certain juxtapositions of material when I was a subscriber to it, and sometimes a contributor, I am aware of the way the content of the magazine might affect some of our contributors and readers.[15]

Moore suggests that her own personal dislike of Joyce's obscenities is, in a sense, beside the point. What underpins her motives for refusing Joyce is her awareness that many of her readers would share her distaste. In this context, Moore's refusal of Joyce's 'Work in Progress' was not only entirely consistent with the magazine's marketing strategies and ethos, but it was based on an identification with the magazine's target audience. The editors of Moore's *Selected Letters* describe Moore's editorial work in terms of a synthesis of Thayer's desire for the 'aesthetically crafted' and Watson's interest in new art forms.[16] Perhaps more crucially, Moore brought with her a sense of the magazine's ambitions to occupy the middle ground between the avant-garde and mass-circulation periodicals. It was Moore, one might argue, who recognised the ways in which the *Dial* was not a 'little' magazine and should therefore not behave like one.

Sampling Stein

The letters between Ezra Pound, Thayer and Watson reveal the tensions between Thayer and Pound in the early 1920s. Thayer's refusal to publish any more of what he referred to as Pound's 'silly' Cantos (the *Dial* had published *The Fourth Canto* in 1920 and *Cantos V, VI* and *VII* in August 1921) and his dismissal of Pound as the Paris correspondent in 1923 resulted in a rift between the magazine and one of modernism's most important and influential poets. The omission of Pound greatly disturbed Moore and she recognised that with Thayer no longer making editorial decisions, she had the opportunity to repair the rift. Jayne Marek meticulously reconstructs Moore's negotiations with Pound, arguing that Moore was fully aware of the quarrel between the *Dial* and Pound but that she feigned ignorance in order to avoid opening up old wounds. It was Moore who suggested that Pound receive The Dial Award in 1927, which resulted in the ensuing publication of 'Canto XXVII' in January 1928. Equally important, however as Marek points out, is Moore's reclamation of Gertrude Stein, who, like Pound, had found Thayer disagreeable. It was Pound, in fact, who brought Thayer to 27 rue de Fleurus in 1923 to visit Stein, a meeting Stein describes in *The Autobiography of Alice B. Toklas*:

> But to come back to Ezra. Ezra did come back and he came back with the editor of The Dial. This time it was worse than Japanese prints, it was much more violent. In his surprise at the violence Ezra fell out of Gertrude Stein's favourite little armchair, the one I have since tapestried with Picasso designs, and Gertrude Stein was furious. Finally Ezra and the editor of The Dial left, nobody too well pleased.[17]

In *The Autobiography*, 'Alice' also recalls meeting Glenway Wescott, who was on his first trip to Europe. On returning to New York, Wescott made sure he visited 14 St Luke's Place to tell Marianne Moore of his overseas adventures. As Moore writes to her brother in August, 1923, Wescott reported that, 'Scofield Thayer is in wrong everywhere, refused an article by M. Loy on G. Stein, was offensively aggressive and insolent when calling at Gertrude Stein's and that she "showed him the door."'[18] Even when Sibley Watson called upon Stein a year later, she had not forgotten the incident involving her 'favourite little armchair' and Thayer's aggressive behaviour. Watson received a frosty welcome from Stein who, he writes Thayer, 'hates you extraordinarily [. . .] because the Dial refused her poems and because you came to see her introduced not by her "dear friend," Henry McB[ride], but with an "almost total stranger."'[19]

Stein's opinion of the *Dial* would certainly have changed after reading Moore's review of *The Making of Americans* in February 1926. Having assigned the review to one of the *Dial*'s regular critics, Moore was obliged to write it herself when she was let down at the last minute. Though she had read extracts of Stein's novel in the *Transatlantic Review* in 1925, it was, as Moore's mother attested, a 'breathless race' to finish the novel and the review for the February issue. Mrs Moore forgives Stein her verbal excesses, however, writing to Monroe Wheeler that there 'is not a stupid page from first to last'.[20] Clearly Moore agreed with her mother; the review gave her the opportunity to acknowledge Stein's achievement and in doing so, repair another rift between a monumental modernist and the magazine that claimed to represent the best of the new writing in Europe and the United States.

It is only when comparing Moore's reviews of Stein to her criticism of other modernist writers such as Pound, Eliot, Williams and cummings that it becomes evident just how enthusiastic Moore was about *The Making of Americans*. Of the modernist writers, only Wallace Stevens's poetry excites such lavish praise and, while there is always in Moore's reviews a note of caution or hesitation as she identifies the perceived limitations of the work, the overwhelming impression given is that of admiration. After having managed to smuggle Stein into her lukewarm review of Vachel Lindsay's *Collected Poems* in the November 1923 issue of the *Dial*, Moore wrote 'The Spare American Emotion', her review of *The Making of Americans*, which appeared in the *Dial* in February 1926. Here Moore declares that the 'chiselled typography and an enticing simplicity of construction are not those of ordinary book-making'. She describes Stein's epic history of an archetypal American bourgeois family as a 'kind of living genealogy', one she finds 'romantic, curious, and engrossing'.[21] Moore quotes extensively from Stein, a tactic the poet used to showcase language she found particularly powerful. Thus often, Stein's work is allowed to speak for itself in that repetitive, evocative and circuitous style that was distinctly her own.

Moore also acknowledged, albeit in subtle terms, Stein's enormous influence on other writers. For instance, in her essay '"New" Poetry Since 1912' for the *Dial*, Moore makes sure that those who were first to experiment are acknowledged as the pioneers of modernism. Thus Arensberg's poem 'Ing' is given an honourable mention but only as it 'corroborated the precisely verbal exactness of Gertrude Stein's "Tender Buttons" – a book which had already appeared'.[22] Clearly for Moore, Stein was one of the most important modernists of her generation, little understood but widely influential.

The *Dial*'s rejection of Stein's work does seem rather strange, given that Stein was so central to modernism as both a patron of the visual arts and as an experimental writer herself. In a letter to Thayer in February 1921, Pound finds Stein 'intelligent' when discoursing on Picasso and Matisse and suggests she write something on art for the *Dial*.[23] Thayer ignored Pound but so too did Watson, who concurred with his partner's estimation. After reading Moore's review of *The Making of Americans*, Watson wrote to her complimenting the essay but offering his own critical judgement. For Watson, Stein is not only 'patronizing' but also, adopting a word frequently deployed to condemn the woman writer, 'sentimental'.[24]

Moore had first-hand experience of being rejected by the *Dial* and was, perhaps, conscious that acceptance had as much to do with the writer's personality as it had to do with the quality of the writing. 'I am a little in doubt as to the exact nature of the editorial policy', she writes to Bryher in 1920.[25] Aware that her own work was considered dense and difficult, Moore recognised that all too often such experiments in language were deemed too radical even for the supposedly radical little magazines publishing the new writing. Both Stein and Moore's work looked decidedly strange in the context of a consolidated modernism, so much so that Thayer and Watson initially turned Moore's own eccentric verse away and persisted in rejecting Stein.

Moore may well have been conscious that editors of the modernist little magazines seemed to look more favourably upon the innovations of Joyce and Eliot than those of Moore or Stein. It was only upon meeting Moore herself that Thayer recognised there might be something in her work even if he did not know what it was. While he could act as Moore's patron, take her under his wing, showing her his world-class collection of art and his 'gorgeous' library, Stein was not so easy to impress. In fact, she was one of the few art collectors who could compete with Thayer, not only in terms of material acquisitions, but also in terms of her extensive knowledge of modern art. Moore's decision to publish 'Composition as Explanation' in 1926 and in September 1927 an extract from 'A Long Gay Book' must be read in the context of her own experience as a woman writer and, more widely, in relation to the subtle and not so subtle discriminations operating at an institutional and personal level to marginalise women's writing.

Moore's promotion and perhaps her identification with Stein did not, however, prevent her from requesting 'that we [. . .] omit a portion' of the manuscript of 'A Long Gay Book' and in 1928 rejecting *Lucy Church Amiably*, albeit in the most tactful terms.[26] The *Dial* published only a small portion of 'A Long Gay Book', about 10 per cent of the whole.[27] It was not Moore, however, who made the drastic cut; it was Stein herself. Knowing the delight Moore took in *The Making of Americans*, Stein selected the first part of 'A Long Gay Book', the part that resembles most closely the experiments in the slightly earlier text. Here is evidence, then, of a writer recognising the limitations of the magazine format, paring down her work to fit its requirements and radically revising the text in the process of doing so. Stein's own editorial interventions, moreover, are clearly designed to anticipate Moore's, selecting as she does the part she knows will appeal to the editor. Moore's editorial influence, then, extends beyond the decisions she made concerning texts submitted for publication at the *Dial*. Some writers, those like Stein, who found it particularly difficult to find publication venues, were willing to cut their own work in order to appear in print. The consequences of doing this, however, created the impression that 'A Long Gay Book' was simply an extension of *The Making of Americans*.

'A Long Gay Book' was completed in the early spring of 1913 just after *The Making of Americans*. Indeed, the first two-thirds of the text adopts the familiar repetitive style of that text. Yet as Ulla Dydo points out, it is only in the last third of the book that Stein 'records the discovery of [a] new reality.'[28] In other words, the book represents a conceptual shift that is registered towards its end by a shift in style as Dydo suggests: 'Within some ten pages the manner, the matter, and the very nature of Stein's enterprise change radically'.[29] Typical of the first two-thirds of the book are the chunky, dense paragraphs characterised by repetition:

> Each day being a day Nettie was telling that thing, was telling that any day is a day, that every day is a day. Nettie telling that any day is a day is telling that any day is a day. Nettie telling that again and again is telling often that any day is a day.[30]

In contrast, the last third of the book looks and sounds distinctly different as it increasingly adopts a fragmented, elliptical language as a response to the 'new reality':

> A whole cow and a little piece of cheese, a whole cow openly.
> A cousin to a cow, a real cow has wheels, it has turns it has eruptions, it has the place to sit.
> A wedding glance is satisfactory. Was the little thing a goat.
> A, open, Open.[31]

Stein did not publish 'A Long Gay Book' until 1933. Up until then, those who had seen it in the *Dial* would have assumed that it adopted the same narrative technique as *The Making of Americans*. The stylistic and conceptual shift recorded in the slightly later text was omitted in the extract Moore used for publication, making it largely irrelevant as a record of Stein's progress as a writer. This omission, however, was not of Moore's making but rather Stein's, an 'accident' that was largely the result of Stein's decision to send Moore work that she knew Moore would approve of together with the inevitable limitations of periodical page space.

In the context of magazine publication, extracts were often used to provide a flavour of the writer's work. The part would stand in for the whole. Even poems occasionally had to be pruned in order to fit neatly into the available space. The *Dial* correspondence shows how often editorial requests for cuts were based on limited page space. It is worth noting, however, that Thayer and Watson were willing to print long prose pieces by established authors. Sherwood Anderson's increasingly lengthy short stories, D. H. Lawrence's travel essays and stories, W. B. Yeats's lively memoirs all ran in instalments. Moore was less willing to adopt this policy, though nowhere does she articulate this explicitly. Instead, she simply resists the dominance of one author. As mentioned above, approximately 10 per cent of 'A Long Gay Book' was published in the *Dial*; a chapter of Elizabeth Madox Roberts's forthcoming novel, *The Time of Man*, appeared in 1926; and Moore only published extracts from William Carlos Williams's *A Voyage to Pagany* as 'Five Prose Sketches' in 1928. While this policy may well have reinforced the notion that the *Dial* did not favour any one writer or school, something Moore repeatedly insisted was the case, it also may have led to a shortage of material at times.[32]

Stein's 'unreadability' has been repeatedly remarked upon by critics from Edmund Wilson to the more recent work by Tanya Clement. In the context of the *Dial*, Stein became a little more legible not only through 'Composition as Explanation' but also through Moore's review of *The Making of Americans* in February 1926, which emphasises not only the stylistic qualities the poet most valued, 'the chiseled typography' of Stein's language, but also the 'enticing simplicity of construction [which] are not those of ordinary book-making'.[33] Unlike so many critics of Stein, Moore finds nothing particularly strenuous or sticky about Stein's prose; on the contrary, she shows her admiration by quoting extensively from the novel to illustrate key points. For Moore, Stein achieves a clarity and precision in her language that is in no need of glossing or explanation.

Perhaps reading Stein's book is not as important as seeing it, a point Moore makes when she compares the novel to

> early German engravings in which Adam, Eve, Cain, and Abel stand with every known animal wild and domestic, under a large tree, by a river. *The Making of Americans* is a kind of living genealogy which is in its branching, unified and vivid.[34]

Rather than a painting or a sketch, the novel is likened to an engraving, something carved of solid, dense material. For Moore, such an effect is highly desirable as when she praises H.D.'s poetry as the 'chiseled ivory of speech'.[35] Stein achieves the kind of precision and clarity that Moore associates with the German tradition of engraving. The biblical reference Moore makes also suggests that Stein treats the subject of the bourgeois American family as comparable to the bible's first family. Stein presents an alternative history of the human family, one that explores relations between humans as well as between humans and the non-human world. For Moore, there is a 'firmness in [Stein's] method' that affords the opportunity to depict her historiography of America as branching, evolving and yet firmly rooted.[36] While Stein's method operates through expansion and accretion rather than compression, Moore finds here an underlying principle that unifies this sprawling epic novel.

As Karen Leick has pointed out, the popular press circulated stories about Stein, produced parodies of 'Steinese' and provided readers with extracts from her work.[37] For instance, the *Chicago Daily Tribune* published nine poems from *Tender Buttons*, as did the *Chicago Evening Post*, the *Boston Transcript*, the *Baltimore Sun* and the *Saint Louis Post Dispatch*. Although there was a great deal of interest and even enthusiasm for Stein in the newspapers and magazines of the 1920s, there were few concerted efforts to understand her work. Having been let down at the last minute by the writer assigned to review Stein's novel, Moore not only read it but she compressed its concerns in her own review. Stein offers a 'psychological exposition of American living' that seeks to assort different phenomena into '"an ordered system"'. The 'different phenomena' are the character and behaviour of the two American families the novel describes. To produce that system, the novel uses repetition. Repetition and the permutations that evolve out of repetition, like branches of a tree, become the means by which to explore the history of the Herslands and the Dehnings, a history that Moore describes as a 'curious backward kind of progress'. Moore then goes on to explore the use of repetition in Stein in two quotations. In the first, Moore points to Stein's use of repetition as producing difference, '"Sometimes I like it" Miss Stein says, "that different ways of emphasizing can make very different meanings in a phrase or sentence I have made and am rereading."'[38] Here repetition points to the slippery nature of language, its uniterability. Other forms of repetition point to a sameness evident in the way in which national identity is produced through the repetition of a perceived difference:

> It's a great question this question of washing. One can never find any one who can be satisfied with anybody else's washing. I knew a man once who never as far as any one could see ever did any washing, and yet he described another with contempt, why he is a dirty hog sir, he never does any washing. The French tell me it's the Italians who never do any washing, the French and the Italians both find the Spanish a little short in their washing, the English find all the world lax in this business of washing, and the East finds all the West a pig, which never is clean with just the little cold water washing. And so it goes.[39]

Moore then points to this passage as evidence of the importance of repetition as Stein's method: 'Repeating has value then "as a way to wisdom".' What, the reader might ask, is the wisdom gleaned from these nationalistic prejudices concerning the unclean 'other'? Clearly, the 'wisdom' concerns not the knowledge of the 'other' but rather the ways in which repetition itself becomes a way of knowing and then not knowing. This relates to what Stein, following William James, refers to as 'habits of thinking'. Habits are formed that produce knowledge, in this instance, knowledge of national identity, but as soon as those habits become settled, they block knowledge. As Jennifer Ashton helpfully points out:

> Learning something, in other words, requires both an initial act of attention, that is, a sufficient burst of nervous energy to overcome the brain's resistance, and enough repetition to establish pathways for the new knowledge. But as soon as that knowledge submits to habit, it sets, becomes that which resists rather than accommodates the efforts of attention required to learn.[40]

Repetition is necessary for a 'curious backward kind of progress' but it can ossify into fixed prejudices that then block understanding. For both James and Stein, character is constructed through habit. Moore, familiar with James's work, would have been acutely aware of his influence on Stein and of how *The Principles of Psychology* informed Stein's understanding of American character. The habits that form character are like the engraving Moore alludes to at the beginning of her article. They appear fixed and permanent and can be traced back to characters in the bible, Adam and Eve, Cain and Abel. If examined closely, they reveal a history of human character and its formation. This is what Moore refers to in her review of *The Making of Americans* as 'a psychology that is universal'. Stein's 'history of a family's progress' explores identity through patterns and repetition that are the same and changing.

For Moore, the 'living' part of this 'genealogy', the 'branching' part suggests that while character is formed through habit, this 'universal' psychology contains within it many differences. Stein is engaged in an activity close to Moore's heart, that of 'assorting phenomena' into an 'ordered system'.[41] To return to Moore's editorial comment of May 1927, this involves the 'science of assorting and the art of investing an assortment with dignity'.[42] Moore values the science of psychology underpinning Stein's novel but also 'a sense of the dignity of the middle class', which is, according to Stein herself, 'the one thing always human, vital, and worthy'.[43] Crucially, for Moore, Stein's method is one that is capable of accommodating multiplicity and difference. It is 'universal' yet it also provides a 'picture of life which is distinctly American'.[44]

Moore's appreciation of Stein frames the pieces that are published in the *Dial* in subsequent issues. Under Moore's editorial reign, Stein is not an oddity nor is she a celebrity, but rather a writer and one who is eminently readable. This treatment of Stein contrasts with the critical reception of Stein which constructed her work as unreadable. More specifically, as Natalia Cecire has suggested, the impossibility of reading Stein is discursively linked to Stein's body. Her textual corpus becomes confused with the body of Stein herself. In *Axel's Castle*, for instance, Edmund Wilson describes Stein as a 'human seismograph whose charts we haven't the training to read'.[45] This is, according to Cecire, 'typical of a reception history that has always understood Stein's writing as an emanation of her body'.[46] B. F. Skinner's article of 1934 in the *Atlantic Monthly*, 'Has Gertrude Stein a Secret?', makes a similar move, suggesting that Stein's style is simply a form of automatic writing, transforming her into the object of her own experiments rather than a conscious writing subject. This also results in the tendency to sample Stein and to imply that her texts are interchangeable.

In the context of not reading Stein, Moore's critical insights are very important. Stein's mediation in the *Dial* engages with the possibility that her method is underpinned by scientific research, that her use of repetition more specifically, is a way to explore and explain the habits of thinking, attention and perception that constitute subjectivity. Without citing William James directly and through a judicious deployment of quotations from Stein, Moore compresses Stein's history into a compact three pages of exegesis based on her own reading.

It is productive to consider Moore's role here in relation to Stein and, more widely, her relation to Edmund Wilson who emerges as one of modernism's central mediators in the 1920s. While Wilson declares Stein unreadable largely because her soporific prose style tends to lull the reader to sleep, Moore finds a 'simplicity' and a 'great firmness' in Stein's method. For Moore, in other words, Stein is entirely legible. Rather than falling asleep, Moore is stimulated, finding in the pages of Stein's novel a narrative that is 'romantic, curious and engrossing'.[47] Moore's review of Stein, however, appears only as a result of being left in the lurch by the critic who had originally promised to produce it. Behind the scenes at the *Dial*, there were those who read Stein and those who did not. For both Moore and her mother, the monumental labour that went into reading *The Making of Americans* was amply rewarded. As Cecire suggests, the supposed 'unreadablility' of Stein has provoked a critical debate about the value of certain kinds of labour, particularly the labour involved in reading the unreadable and the rewards for doing so. For Cecire,

> while not reading is the only possible response to what is unreadable, designating a corpus 'unreadable' always amounts to a judgement about the kind of labor that would go into reading it: a suggestion that that reading would be drudgery, a kind of worthless work unrewarding or unrenumerable or both.[48]

As editor of the *Dial*, Moore was in the position where she could culturally consecrate works that might otherwise be dismissed as unreadable. At the same time, as the *Dial*'s own sampling of Stein reveals, in the context of periodical publication, expediency often determined the form.

Beheading Rosenfeld

In September 1925, when Paul Rosenfeld submitted his essay on the painter El Greco, he was the *Dial*'s resident music critic. He had been part of the *Seven Arts* circle associated with Randolph Bourne's vision of cultural pluralism, and through that group also became involved with the *Dial* even before its modernist reincarnation in 1920. Having been so long affiliated with the magazine, Rosenfeld must have been taken aback by Moore's request for extensive cuts: 'If you can be so generous as to allow us to have your essay on El Greco's Portrait of Himself with omissions and a change of I think three words, we shall be most grateful', she writes on 15 September.[49] Recognising that she is testing Rosenfeld's loyalty, she assures him that her revisions are not in order to 'improve your paper', only to make it conform in length to the *Dial*'s requirements, an unconfirmable claim. While Moore downplays the significance of the omissions and the change of just 'three words', the instructions that follow indicate the extent of her cuts, which actually amounted to excising half the essay.

Rosenfeld was clearly offended by Moore's suggestion that so much of his essay exceeded requirements. Such treatment must have been particularly painful given his great admiration for Moore; he'd praised her poetry in his book *Men Seen* for its 'keenness of perception' that same year.[50] His indignant reply, however, reveals more than a sense of wounded pride. Having thought about what he refers to as Moore's 'ultimatum' concerning his essay, he writes a detailed exposition of his argument and method, thereby throwing into relief Moore's own tendency to eschew explanatory frameworks. He is willing, however, to acknowledge Moore's superior verbal dexterity even as he resists her editorial pressure to condense:

> I find in all the coolness of September that I cannot decapitate my piece even for the sake of The Dial. The introductory sentence which you have salvaged from the wrecks of mine is, I am ready to acknowledge, lovelier than anything in my article, and I know I shall be very much tempted to lift it if I ever reconstruct the piece. But in conjunction with the two or three others which you allow me out of the first paragraph, it does not cover the idea of the page, and that happens to be the central one of the entire article. I am at a loss to understand how you would propose to get along without that statement. The point of the piece is that Greco communicated his personal life through the dynamism of shapes, consciously or unconsciously; and permitted us to refer to his communication to himself personally, by painting a portrait of himself. If then, you deprive me of all indications of the architecture of shapes in my opening paragraph, the remainder of the article merely answers the 'how?'. I am

> prepared to concede that the article could stand bloodletting in one or two places, as long as the central ideas remained; but I cannot see who is to benefit by a headless fowl, not even the Flamen Dialis; I am sure you are disgusted; but I find myself dramatically inclined to repeat the speech of Luther in Strindberg's play, when the fiend approaches him at the Diet in the satins of a cardinal and he cries (historically enough) 'Hier stehe Ich! Ich ann nicht anders!'[51]

In a dramatic flourish at the end of the paragraph, Rosenfeld compares himself to Strindberg's Martin Luther, who declares: 'Here I stand. I can do no other', indicating his unwillingness to compromise. Rosenfeld's main objection seems to concern what Moore does to the opening paragraph of the essay. Here, he argues, Moore has excised so many crucial sentences that the main argument is no longer in evidence. For Rosenfeld, the introduction requires a statement of intent, something most of us expect from a critical essay. He is following the conventions of critical reviews and essays, adhering to a set of principles concerning structure and exegesis that were followed and continue to be followed by most critics. For Rosenfeld, it is El Greco's 'dynamism of shapes' that reveals the contours of the artist's life, his concerns, his values. It is this 'architecture' that provides the structuring principle of Rosenfeld's own argument. Without that, the article simply conveys a sense of El Greco's methods rather than the underlying impulses driving artistic creation. It becomes a headless chicken, an essay without a thesis, a description rather than a critical analysis.

Unfortunately, Rosenfeld's original manuscript does not appear to have survived, so we do not have a direct comparison between his submitted manuscript and Moore's revisions but what we do have is the article itself, which was published, in spite of Rosenfeld's initial resistance to Moore's suggestions, in the December issue of the *Dial* in 1925. We also have a version of the essay he published in *By Way of Art* in 1928 that signals Rosenfeld's intentions, his divergence from Mooreish contractility as well as his recognition of its powerful textual effects. It is instructive to compare the *Dial* 'El Greco' to Rosenfeld's later version. This later 'authorized' version embeds Moore's 'salvaged' sentence but retains what must be more of the original introduction:

> 'Greco's Portrait of Himself' (*Dial* version, 1925)
> The movement of the ears unlocks his life to you, letting the world slip with a precipitous gesture of falling shoulders, erecting the seeing head solitary as a lighthouse in the night.[52]
>
> 'El Greco's Portrait of Himself' (*By Way of Art* version, 1928)
> At a distance, the picture is a ghost shooting to heaven, constrained and projected by two flanking earth-brown masses. Closer, the ghost becomes a high-domed, fine-whiskered head; the brown: fur and velvet

> of a rich robe; and background. It is the portrait of a man wise at sixty, setting you midmost forces. The movement of the ears unlocks his life to you, letting the world slip with a precipitous gesture of falling shoulders, erecting the seeing head solitary as a lighthouse in the night.[53]

In the later version, Rosenfeld resists opening the essay with Moore's pithy, elliptical sentence (we can't know how much of it was his originally) but cannot bring himself to edit it out altogether. His opening sentences, by contrast, provide two distinct perspectives, one 'at a distance' and one 'closer' to the portrait. As he pointed out in his letter to Moore, his introduction sought to establish the 'dynamic shapes' in El Greco's work; it was this idea that provided the 'architecture' for his own argument. As the painting comes into focus, shapes solidify, revealing the details of the portrait itself, of a man 'wise at sixty'. Now that the subject of the essay has been identified, Rosenfeld inserts Moore's 'salvaged sentence'. He had complained to her that she had effectively excised so many crucial sentences that the main argument disappeared. Rosenfeld fears that the interpretive framework has been eradicated, resulting in a textual corpus without cognitive functions, what he described in his letter to Moore as a 'headless fowl'.[54] Rosenfeld fears that the interpretive framework has been eradicated, leaving the textual corpus drained of life.

The traces of Mooreish compression in the opening sentence of the *Dial* version of Rosenfeld's essay become particularly evident compared to other opening sentences written by Rosenfeld for earlier essays published in the *Dial*. For instance, Rosenfeld's essay on Alfred Stieglitz begins:

> Alfred Stieglitz is of the company of the great affirmers of life. His photographs bear witness to the presence in him of a sense of the significance of animate and inanimate things as catholic as any which man has ever possessed.[55]

The critic provides a statement that asserts Stieglitz's significance as an artist and in doing so, provides the reader with a critical framework for the ensuing discussion. A slightly different approach is taken in his essay 'American Painting', which might seem, at first glance, to begin in a similar way to Moore's sentence on El Greco: 'The Ryders hang dark on the museum walls. They are pools of very dusk, many of them so low in key that for a while they resist the scrutiny.'[56] The reader is invited to look at the Ryder paintings as they hang in the museum, their darkened gloomy hues initially resisting the viewer's gaze. In his article on Sherwood Anderson, a similar strategy is taken:

> They pass us every day, a grey and driven throng, the common words that are the medium of Sherwood Anderson. In the thick ranks of the newspapers they go drab and indistinct as miners trooping by grim factory walls in latest dusk.[57]

Rosenfeld, quite sensibly, includes the subject's name within the first two sentences of the article; he orients the reader providing a succinct synopsis of his thesis within the first few sentences. Thus Stieglitz's willingness to treat the inanimate and the animate object equally is foregrounded, Ryder's mysticism is implied in the murkiness of his paintings, Sherwood Anderson's lean, spare prose style as a 'hard surface' speaks of the American quotidian.

As in her revisions of 'The Wine Menagerie', Moore omits Rosenfeld's statement of theme entirely. Her opening sentence dispenses with exegesis, presses clauses together and eschews connectives. This method of prose construction, which Patricia Willis refers to as 'inventive splicing',[58] closely resembles Moore's poetic technique of splicing and juxtaposition, a feature of her verse that Carolyn Burke and Susan McCabe consider in detail. Moore, as William Carlos Williams points out, 'despised connectives'.[59] Rosenfeld is happy to insert 'and', whereas Moore's use of a series of present participles – 'letting', 'falling', 'erecting' and 'seeing' – allows clauses to pile up on top of each other to produce what McCabe refers to as 'dynamic rupture and disjunction', a form of 'hyper-montage' that compels the reader to provide the connectives.[60] Such a technique reminds us of 'Sea Unicorns and Land Unicorns', which deploys the present continuous to maintain momentum in its opening ten-line sentence. Poems such as 'New York', 'Those Various Scalpels', 'An Octopus' and 'Marriage' also operate in this fashion, building up and layering to dazzling effect. Describing the ecosystems and wildlife on the slopes of Mount Rainier, 'An Octopus' is a knotty, complex, seemingly 'endless skein' of 'miniature cavalcades', 'home' to 'a diversity of creatures'.[61]

Rosenfeld's approach imagines the viewer gradually moving closer to the portrait, placing emphasis on the movement of the mind as it perceives and decodes the accumulating visual information. Moore's sentence, however, presents the portrait itself as an image of moving parts, a form of dynamic disclosure. Following McCabe, Moore's compression gives the portrait a cinematic quality in order to bring it to 'life'. In her reading diary, Moore extracted phrases from Sergei Eisenstein's translated essays, 'The Cinematographic Principle and the Ideogram' and 'The Dialectic Approach to Film Form', including lines that McCabe suggests are 'descriptive of her own poetic method': "Synthesis constantly arising in the process of opposition between thesis and anti-thesis [. . .] For art is always conflict.'[62] If montage achieves its effect through the collision and explosion of forms, Moore's own adaptation of this technique exerts pressure on the sentence, constraining and compressing verbal images through superimposition. This method of layering and juxtaposing serves two editorial functions: It allows Moore as editor to adapt texts to fit within the limited page space of each issue and it provides her with the opportunity to practise a form of modernist revision. In doing so, Moore seeks to showcase the object perceived (El Greco's self-portrait) rather than the perceiving subject (Paul Rosenfeld).

The effect of compression is to reverse the subject/object relation and to foreground the object itself as an 'intractable thing'.[63] Returning to Moore's controversial revisions to 'The Wine Menagerie', we can see a similar process take place. Moore cuts away the transitions between the various stages of the speaker's movement towards what Vincent describes as ecstasy. The connections between one state of mind and another and the contexts where these connections are made, the scene of the bar itself, are omitted in order to focus on the distilled and singular moment of ecstasy. What Moore refers to as 'serious pleasure' in her advertisement for the *Dial* is more intense if undiluted by semantic connections. This is not to assert that Moore's revisions were always improvements. In the case of 'The Wine Menagerie', the process of distillation that produced 'Again' cut away the tonal shifts, reflective imagery and erotic charge of Crane's original, in service to an ethical compression alien to Crane's poetics. The cases of Crane and Rosenfeld are instructive, however, not simply as a means of illustrating Moore's editorial interventions, but for thinking more broadly about the role of the periodical editor. Moore's editorial practice provides a set of terms and 'principle[s]' that respond with 'gusto' to the pressures of periodical production, complicating the idea that art is necessarily constrained or limited by the exigencies of mechanical reproduction. On the contrary, for Moore, the compositional process is itself intimately tied to editorial compression and makes a 'virtue' of the material constraints of magazine publication.

Yet it is more than connectives that Moore objects to. While Rosenfeld's prose is replete with adjectives like 'grey', 'common', 'thick', 'drab', 'indistinct', Moore keeps such words to a minimum. Those adjectives she does use, 'solitary' and 'precipitous', function less in descriptive terms and more as conceptual markers, signalling the presence of El Greco as artistic genius. In the revised version of Rosenfeld's essay in the *Dial* with this image of the artist's head as a lighthouse, one can't help but wonder whether Moore has in mind Gaudier-Brzeska's sculpture of Pound's head, his 'Hieratic Head of Ezra Pound', dubbed by Wyndham Lewis as 'Ezra in the form of a marble phallus'.[64] It is ironic then, that Moore's own verbal sculpture of El Greco with its phallic image of the artist's head 'erecting' like 'a lighthouse in the night', should come at the expense of Rosenfeld's own head. As we saw earlier, Rosenfeld complains to Moore that she has decapitated his essay turning it into a headless chicken, rather than a fighting cock. In other words, while the link between masculinity and creative genius is implied in the phallic imagery Moore deploys, at the same time, her exchanges with Rosenfeld signal an unwillingness to allow any one 'genius' to dominate the pages of the magazine.

Before Moore became managing editor at the *Dial,* Rosenfeld's essays tended to be much longer than the five-page essay on El Greco: 'Stieglitz' is twelve pages; 'Sherwood Anderson' is thirteen pages long; 'American Painting' a generous twenty pages. In fact, in the years before Moore's editorial reign,

Rosenfeld enjoyed the kind of textual expansiveness usually reserved for headline acts such as Eliot, cummings, Anderson and D. H. Lawrence. This ended abruptly when Moore took over as managing editor. Rosenfeld's articles are drastically reduced after 1925 and never extend beyond five pages. It seems that after this particular exchange Rosenfeld did not publish any more review essays, though he continued to write the 'Musical Chronicle' until March 1927. More significantly, as Linda Leavell points out, in early 1927 the editors of the *New Republic* launched a scathing critique of what they perceived to be the *Dial*'s failure to introduce 'any new American writer'. Rosenfeld was named, along with Van Wyck Brooks, Lewis Mumford and Alfred Kreymborg in relation to a new competing journal, *American Caravan*. It is not surprising, then, that Rosenfeld stops writing the 'Musical Chronicle' in March of that year.

Identifying traces of Moore's textual contractility in Rosenfeld alerts the reader to other similar instances and, more broadly, to Moore's extensive influence across the magazine and in a range of individual items. Once tuned into the textual effects of compression, Moore's interventions are thrown into relief. For instance, Moore mentions in correspondence with Watson 'trespass[ing]' with submissions by Llewelyn Powys and Charles Trueblood. Trueblood's review of Hardy is a 'great disappointment', requiring omission and condensation of 'redundancies'.[65] With this correspondence as corroborating evidence, reading the article as it was published in the *Dial* points to Moore's textual presence. In the opening paragraph, the use of negatives combined with the verbal density so characteristic of Moore's style suggests that she did more than cut; that she made strategic textual interventions: 'It is surely not often that one finds in the ranks of the merely affirmative such extremity of consciousness, such magnitude and delicacy of sentience as is implied in Thomas Hardy's courageous and sombre honesty of question.'[66] The compressive logic found in Moore's poems is evident here as the reader is compelled to wait for the subject of the sentence, suspended momentarily among the abstract nouns. We are in the familiar syntactical waiting room so characteristic of Moore's style where she accumulates and concentrates to produce a verbal 'gusto' capable of transmitting to the reader a sense of Hardy's creative force. When Moore complains to Watson that Edwin Seaver's review of Alfeo Faggi's 'The Way of the Cross' is a 'fiasco' but one that is 'redeemable', then evidence of editorial 'trespassing' becomes apparent. Who else but Moore could write the following sentence:

> Personal revelation, as in the work of Giotto, is independent of time and we are permitted to know the flower of Christianity no less in Alfeo Faggi's vision of the road to Calvary than in the frescos of that other primitive describing the life of St Francis.[67]

Suspended in time, Moore's sentences convey a sense of stillness by downgrading the finite verb in preference for nouns. Moore has practised a form of editorial compression that only becomes perceptible through the practice of close reading. Similar interventions are apparent in the work of John Cowper Powys. The first paragraph of his review of Dreiser's *An American Tragedy*, for instance, betrays itself in the prefix 'un' so often used by Moore: 'The pleasure to be derived [from the novel] is grim, stark, austere, a purely aesthetic pleasure, unpropitious to such as require human cajolery in these high matters.'[68] We'll never know the extent of Moore's textual 'trespasses' but it seems fairly safe to assume, given the evidence in the archives and in the magazine itself, that she was routinely practising a form of modernist revision on material submitted for publication.

Pruning Lawrence

In the anecdotal accounts of Moore as an editor and critic, her puritan sensibilities are often foregrounded to comic effect, creating the impression that Moore was out of step with her contemporaries. Yet if she were so wedded to old-fashioned scruples, if she were unable to approve of any art of a sexual nature or references to bodily functions there would not have been many modernist texts that she could have read. Moreover, she would not have been the editor that D. H. Lawrence chose to send his poems to in 1929. After the private publication of *Lady Chatterley's Lover* in 1928, Lawrence's writing was receiving a great deal of unwanted attention from the censors in Britain. In January 1929, two manuscripts of his poetry collection entitled *Pansies* were intercepted in the post and confiscated by Scotland Yard. In the retyping of the manuscript, Lawrence made important changes and, he thought, improved the poems considerably. He then sent this revised manuscript, not to Martin Secker or Curtis Brown, publishers being watched by Scotland Yard, but to Moore at the *Dial*'s offices.[69] By March, Moore had notified Lawrence that the magazine would take some of his poems and was clearly enthusiastic: 'One can hardly express the enjoyment given by poems in this book, as feeling and as form of expression, and that we should have for the Dial what we have selected, is an eager delight.' But she goes on to add some reservations: 'I admit, there are lines in the book, that are the outcome of certain hurts, and I am not saying that in every case the lines themselves leave no shadow of hurt.'[70]

Lawrence replies,

> I like the group you chose – some of my favourites. [. . .] I knew some of the poems would offend you. But then some part of life must offend you too, and even beauty has its thorns and its nettle-stings and its poppy-poison.[71]

Lawrence's strategy paid off. Recognising that Moore would be able to choose and appropriately present the poems without attracting unwanted attention, Lawrence managed to place his poems in the prestigious magazine while also continuing to protest vociferously against the censorship of his writing. But what this episode also reveals is that Lawrence knew that even if Moore took offence, she would not refuse publication on that basis. She selected those poems she felt most accomplished, poems that Lawrence himself regarded as his best. Thus in the last issue, July 1929, Moore managed to publish the work of one of modernism's earliest practitioners. Even if the poems did not break any new ground, they represented Lawrence's last significant output.

True to form, the most revealing aspect of Moore's last exchange with Lawrence concerns Moore's textual interventions. It is hardly surprising that Moore steered clear of poems such as 'Leave Sex Alone' and 'Obscenity', the latter asserting that 'the body itself is clean, but the caged mind/ is a sewer inside, it pollutes'.[72] The original introduction by Lawrence was not included in the trade edition of *Pansies* published by Martin Secker, nor were some eleven poems considered likely to incite the censors. As Christopher Pollnitz points out in his study of the complicated publication history of *Pansies*, Lawrence prepared a second typescript to send to Moore at the *Dial* after the Home Office had seized his first unexpurgated version.[73] Moore published 'When I Went to the Circus' in June 1929 and ten further poems in July 1929.[74] Her decision to include the poem, 'Censors', is one that signals her sympathy for Lawrence's position. In that poem the censors are described as 'dead men' who attack anything that is 'alive'. Moore also included a condensed version of the introduction to the poems, an introduction that Lawrence had already decided to withdraw from the Secker edition for fear it would attract further unwanted attention. It was this introduction that became the four introductory lines preceding the ten poems published in the July *Dial*:

> Pensées, like pansies, have their roots in the earth, and in the
> perfume there stirs still the faint grim scent of under-earth.
> Certainly in pansy-scent and in violet scent it is so: the blue of
> the morning mingled with the corrosive smoulder of the ground.[75]

Moore took these four lines largely from one particular paragraph of Lawrence's text:

> The fairest thing in nature, a flower, still has its roots in earth and manure; and in the perfume there hovers still the faint strange scent of earth, the under-earth in all its heavy humidity and darkness. Certainly it is so in pansy-scent, and in violet scent; mingled with the blue of the morning the black of the corrosive humus. Else the scent would be just sickly sweet.[76]

It is probably the case that it was the introduction, more than the poems themselves that led to the confiscation of the first two manuscripts of *Pansies*. Lawrence used it to attack those who called his work 'obscene', provocatively asserting that 'the word arse is as much god as the word face'. It is not words such as 'arse' that are dirty, he argues, but the minds that 'drag in a filthy association'.[77] Such sentiments would have been offensive to Sir William Joynson-Hicks, the Home Secretary, who, according to Pollnitz, 'ran an unofficial but state-directed system of censorship' between 1924 and 1925.[78] And indeed, there is much evidence pointing to Marianne Moore's own resistance to what she describes in her letter to Lawrence as 'certain hurts'. It is hardly surprising that Moore does not include words such as 'arse' and 'shit' in her version; she even omits the word 'manure' from her four-line introduction.

After the trouble with 'The Wine Menagerie', Moore made sure she had Lawrence's permission to excise and to rewrite. She did not want to risk offending Lawrence, but nor did she want to risk the wrath of the censors. Her creative solution to this was to judiciously prune and rewrite Lawrence's text. Having seen what Moore proposed, Lawrence approved, writing in April 1929, 'you just keep my part of [the introduction] you wish, and use it with your group of poems, as you wish'.[79] Recognising that the essence of the argument remained, Lawrence had no objections to Moore's editorial interventions. While initially it appears that she has simply sweetened the scent of Lawrence's sentiments and revised according to her own instincts for economy and her own distaste for the vulgar, the changes she makes reveal her willingness and indeed her eagerness to have the *Dial* publish Lawrence's attack on censorship. Two crucial interventions point not only to Moore's sympathy with Lawrence's argument but also her understanding of the poetic sensibility at work in the poetry.

Moore changes the 'faint strange scent of earth' to 'faint grim scent of under-earth'. The word 'grim' is, in fact, more emphatic, more harsh and repellent than the 'strange scent' that Lawrence refers to. Thus without direct reference to 'manure' the soil transmits the odour of something unpleasant. In Moore's text, the reader picks up on the scent without having to have her nose rubbed in it. Moore also changed the line 'mingled with the blue of the morning the black of the corrosive humus' to 'the blue of the morning mingled with the corrosive smoulder of the ground'. It is a seemingly innocuous and puzzling change but one that makes sense when the whole of Lawrence's essay is considered. The word 'smoulder' is inserted, while 'black' and 'humus' are extracted, presumably because Moore did not think either word was working hard enough to convey Lawrence's point. 'Smoulder' meaning to suffocate or smother points to the suppression that Lawrence discusses in the rest of the essay. 'For by pretending to have no roots', he writes, we are in danger of 'starving and stifling' them. These roots 'now need a little attention, need the hard soil eased away from them, and softened so that a little fresh air can come to them, and they can breathe'.[80] Moore's insertion of the words 'smouldering' and 'grim' capture Lawrence's meaning succinctly. For Lawrence it is the 'sensual, instinctive and intuitive body' that connects us to our roots, that sustains and nourishes us. The earth is grim because it is unyielding, packed too tight on the roots stifling life and suppressing instinct. Thus albeit in a rather compact form, Moore's lines manage to convey the sense of the earth not simply as that which nurtures life but also as that which can bury or suppress life. Moore's own textual revisions and omissions might seem to some evidence of suppression rather than nurture. Yet in the case of Lawrence, Moore was able to retain the essence of what was a highly controversial and incendiary essay while avoiding the threat of prosecution.

Notes

1. Marianne Moore to Sibley Watson Jr, 1 January 1927, Beinecke, ST/Dial Papers, Series I, Box 7, Fol. 267.
2. James Mussell, 'Repetition: "In Our Last"' *Victorian Periodicals Review*, 48 (2015), 343–58.
3. Scofield Thayer, 'Announcement', *Dial*, 78 (January 1925), 89–90 (p. 89).
4. Marianne Moore to Conrad Aiken, 10 November 1926, Beinecke, ST/Dial Papers, Series I, Box 1, Fol. 2.
5. Marianne Moore to Jack Wood, 3 May 1926, Berg, JSW/Dial Papers, Series VI, Box 20.
6. Marianne Moore to Robert Hillyer, 7 June 1926, Berg, JSW/Dial Papers, Series VI, Box 20.
7. Marianne Moore to Harry C. Tuttle, 13 March 1929, Berg, JSW/Dial Papers, Series VI, Box 19.
8. Marek, pp. 191–2.
9. Marianne Moore to Scofield Thayer, 1 May 1926, Beinecke, ST/Dial Papers, Series IV, Box 35, Fol. 982.
10. Marianne Moore, *The Selected Letters of Marianne Moore*, ed. Bonnie Costello, Celeste Goodridge and Cristanne Miller (London: Faber and Faber, 1998), p. 162.
11. Linda Leavell, *Holding On Upside Down: The Life and Work of Marianne Moore* (New York: Farrar, Straus and Giroux, 2013), p. 238.
12. Katherine Mullin, 'Joyce Through the Little Magazines', in *A Companion to James Joyce*, ed. Richard Brown (Chichester: Wiley-Blackwell, 2008), pp. 374–89 (p. 384).
13. Moore, *Selected Letters*, pp. 229–30.
14. Ibid. p. 230.
15. Ibid.
16. Ibid., p. 212.
17. Gertrude Stein, *The Autobiography of Alice B. Toklas* (London: Penguin, 1966), p. 218.
18. Moore, *Selected Letters*, p. 202.
19. Walter Sutton (ed.), *Pound, Thayer, Watson and The Dial: A Story in Letters* (Gainesville: University Press of Florida, 1994), p. 244.
20. Mary Warner Moore to Monroe Wheeler, 3 January 1926, Berg in m.b. Moore, M. 264 A.L.S., 13 A.N.S., 22 T.L.S., 3 T.N.S., 1 T.L. (copy), 12 postcards to Monroe Wheeler [v.p., Feb. 24, 1923–Aug. 5, 1965]. Folder 6.
21. Marianne Moore, *The Complete Prose of Marianne Moore*, ed. Patricia Willis (London: Faber and Faber, 1987), p. 128; Moore, 'The Spare American Emotion', *Dial*, 80 (February 1926), 153–6 (p. 153).

22. Moore, *Complete Prose*, p. 121.
23. Sutton, *Pound, Thayer, Watson*, p. 207.
24. Sibley Watson to Marianne Moore, February 1926, RML Series 5, Box 75, Fol. 3.
25. Moore, *Selected Letters*, p. 136.
26. Jayne Marek, *Women Editing Modernism: 'Little' Magazines and Literary History* (Lexington: University Press of Kentucky, 1995), pp. 160–1.
27. I would like to thank Eva Guggemos at the Beinecke Library for pointing out that Stein only submitted a small portion of the full manuscript of 'A Long Gay Book'. Beinecke ST/Dial papers, Series I, Box 6, Fol. 233.
28. Gertrude Stein, *A Stein Reader*, ed. Ulla Dydo (Evanston, IL: Northeastern University Press, 1993), p. 152.
29. Ibid. pp. 151–2.
30. Ibid. p. 176.
31. Ibid. p. 252.
32. In a letter to Sibley Watson, Moore says she has not got enough reviews for the September issue of the *Dial*. Marianne Moore to Sibley Watson, 10 July 1928, Beinecke, ST/Dial Papers, Series I, Box 7, Fol. 273.
33. Moore, *Complete Prose*, pp. 128–31 (p. 128); Moore, 'Spare', p. 153.
34. Ibid.; ibid.
35. Moore, *Complete Prose*, p. 81.
36. Ibid. p. 129.
37. Karen Leick, 'Popular Modernism: Little Magazines and the American Daily Press', *PMLA*, 123 (2008), pp. 125–39.
38. Moore, *Complete Prose*, p. 129; Moore, 'Spare', p. 155.
39. Ibid. pp. 129–30; ibid.
40. Jennifer Ashton, 'Gertrude Stein for Anyone', *ELH*, 64 (1997), 289–311 (p. 307).
41. Moore, *Complete Prose*, p. 129; Moore, 'Spare', p. 154.
42. Moore, Complete Prose, p. 130; Moore, 'Comment, Dial, 82 (May 1927), 449–50 (p. 449).
43. Moore, 'Spare', p. 182.
44. Moore, 'Spare', p. 131.
45. Edmund Wilson, *Axel's Castle: A Study in the Imaginative Literature of 1870–1930* (New York: Scribner's Sons, 1931), p. 239. Cited in Natalia Cecire, 'Ways of Not Reading Gertrude Stein', *ELH*, 82 (2015), 280–98 (p. 284).
46. Ibid. p. 290.
47. Moore, *Complete Prose*, pp. 128, 129; Moore, pp. 154, 153.
48. Cecire, 'Ways', p. 102.
49. Marianne Moore to Paul Rosenfeld, 15 September 1925, Beinecke, ST/Dial Papers, Series I, Box 5, Fol. 183.
50. Emily Setina, '"Mountains being a Language with Me": Marianne Moore, Marsden Hartley, and Modernist Revision', *Modernism/Modernity*, 22 (2015), 153–82, p. 167.
51. Paul Rosenfeld to Marianne Moore, 18 September 1925, Beinecke, ST/Dial Papers, Series I, Box 5, Fol. 183.
52. Paul Rosenfeld, 'Greco's Portrait of Himself', *Dial*, 79 (December 1925), 485–90 (p. 485).
53. Paul Rosenfeld, 'El Greco's Portrait of Himself', in *By Way of Art: Criticisms of Music, Literature, Painting, Sculpture, and the Dance* (New York: Books for Libraries Press Inc., 1967), pp. 99–110 (p. 99).
54. Paul Rosenfeld to Marianne Moore, 18 September 1925, Beinecke, ST/Dial Papers, Series I, Box 5, Fol. 183.
55. Paul Rosenfeld, 'Stieglitz', *Dial*, 70 (April 1921), 397–409 (p. 397)

56. Paul Rosenfeld, 'American Painting', *Dial*, 71 (December 1921), 649–70 (p. 650).
57. Paul Rosenfeld, 'Sherwood Anderson', *Dial*, 72 (January 1922), 29–42 (p. 29).
58. Moore, *Complete Prose*, p. vii.
59. William Carlos Williams, 'Marianne Moore' *Dial*, 78 (May 1925), 393–401 (p. 395).
60. Susan McCabe, *Cinematic Modernism: Modernist Poetry and Film* (Cambridge: Cambridge University Press, 2005), p. 190.
61. Marianne Moore, *Becoming Marianne Moore: The Early Poems, 1907–1924*, ed. Robin G. Schulze (Berkeley, Los Angeles, London: University of California Press, 2002), pp. 312–18.
62. McCabe, *Cinematic*, p. 190.
63. *New Collected Poems: Marianne Moore*, ed. Heather Cass White (London: Faber and Faber, 2017), p. 253.
64. Paul Edwards and Jane Beckett, *Blast: Vorticism, 1914–1918* (Burlington, VT: Ashgate, 2000), p. 44.
65. Marianne Moore to Sibley Watson Jr, 1 January 1927, Beinecke, ST/Dial Papers, Series I, Box 7, Fol. 267.
66. Charles Trueblood, 'The Poetry of Thomas Hardy', *Dial*, 82 (June 1927), 522–5 (p. 522).
67. Edwin Seaver, 'The Road to Calvary', *Dial*, 82 (April 1927), 341–3 (p. 341).
68. John Cowper Powys, 'An American Tragedy', *Dial*, 80 (April 1926), 331–8 (p. 331).
69. Nicholas Joost and Alvin Sullivan, *D. H. Lawrence and The Dial* (Carbondale and Edwardsville: Southern Illinois University Press, 1970), p. 107.
70. Moore, *Selected Letters*, p. 249.
71. Moore, *Complete Prose*, p. 360.
72. D. H. Lawrence, *The Complete Poems of D. H. Lawrence*, ed. Vivian De Sola Pinto and Warren Roberts (London: Penguin, 1964), p. 463.
73. Christopher Pollnitz, 'The Censorship and Transmission of D. H. Lawrence's *Pansies*: The Home Office and the "foul-mouthed fellow"', *Journal of Modern Literature*, 28 (2005), 44–71.
74. Moore published 'To Let Go or Hold On?', 'Things Men Have Made', 'Whatever Man Makes', 'Work', 'What Would You Fight For?', 'Attila', 'Sea-Weed', 'Lizard', 'Censors', and 'November by the Sea', *Dial*, 86 (July 1929), 543–8.
75. D. H. Lawrence, 'Introduction', *Dial*, 86 (July 1929), p. 543.
76. Lawrence, *Complete Poems*, pp. 417–18.
77. Ibid. p. 418.
78. Pollnitz, 'Censorship and Transmission', p. 45.
79. D. H. Lawrence, *The Collected Letters of D. H. Lawrence: Volume II*, ed. Harry T. Moore (London: Heinemann, 1962), p. 1142.
80. Lawrence, *Complete Poems*, p. 418.

6

PERIODICAL FORM AND THE DIALOGICS OF GENDER

> The immaculate
> conception
> of the inaudible bird
> occurs
> in gorgeous reticence . . .[1]

In the celebrated November 1922 issue of the *Dial*, the last lines of Mina Loy's poem, 'Brancusi's Golden Bird', sat opposite a luminescent photographic reproduction of Brancusi's sculpture, courtesy of the American art collector John Quinn. Loy's poem gives voice to this 'inaudible bird' articulating its 'gorgeous reticence', mimicking the sculpture's form and meditating on what 'strikes/ its significance'.

This chapter examines the striking significance of particular patterns, arrangements and clusters within the *Dial*. It seeks to make 'audible' in language, the sounds of periodical form. In her provocative book, *Forms: Whole, Rhythm, Hierarchy, Network*, Caroline Levine borrows the concept of 'affordance' from design theory, explaining how it is not only materials that have distinct properties that lend themselves to particular functions but that specific designs 'lay claim to their own range of affordances'.[2] Transferring this to the study of a wide range of forms, Levine adopts an approach that examines how forms constrain, enable, travel and do a certain kind of political work within the particular historical contexts within which they operate. She asks what seem to be fairly fundamental questions about forms in order to examine how they influence, organise or in some instances determine what it is possible to say. According to Levine,

> the advantage of this perspective is that it allows us to grasp both the specificity and the generality of forms – both the particular constraints and possibilities that different forms afford, and the fact that those patterns and arrangements carry their affordances with them as they move across time and space.[3]

Drawing on Levine's work, Sean Latham compares the affordances of the periodical to the codex book, arguing that 'the magazine affords a great many more possibilities for agents' as readers.[4] If, as Barbara Green and many others have asserted, the periodical makes its meaning through heterogeneity, then the study of patterns, rhythms and repetitions becomes one way of thinking about how the material form of the magazine makes meaning out of that heterogeneity.[5]

When examining the affordances of the magazine, it is worth considering the ways in which patterns shape what might be said or seen. In his article, 'The Mess and Muddle of Modernism: The Modernist Journals Project and Modern Periodical Studies', Latham adopts what he refers to as an 'editorial reading' that 'moves across the magazine rather than simply look[ing] deeply into individual pieces'.[6] Following Latham's advice, rather than looking for the snail-like trails of Moore's signature style in the texts published in the *Dial* as in previous chapters, this chapter adopts a wide-angle lens. This methodology identifies particular arrangements that recur, juxtapositions that produce a concatenation of sounds rather than a single melodic line. The internal dialogics of the magazine, the ways in which writing and art work were presented in relation to other texts in a single issue, the prominence of the authorial signature (briefer mentions were anonymous, editorial comments were not signed), as well as the significance of the regular slots for Music, Art and Theatre all interact within an issue and across issues. External dialogics, the periodical networks within which the magazine operated, the controversies surrounding avant-garde art such as Brancusi's legal case against the US government and more generally, the wider public sphere debate particularly as it related to gender, culture and the restricted field of artistic production, form part of an editorial perspective that extends beyond the close reading of individual items.

My interest in the role of the editor requires thinking about how Moore finds creative ways of making periodical form speak. As I have been arguing, editorial agency is complexly bound up with a range of competing dispositions that complicate the relation between editor and magazine. The periodical codes that signalled the *Dial*'s unique position in the marketplace, the storehouse of visual material available via Thayer's private collection, the presentation of image and text and their relation to each other as well as the social restrictions that came with magazine publication such as the fear of the censor were all part of the production process. Yet at the same time I wish to argue that the affordances of display, arrangement and pattern in magazines, while not wholly within editorial control, are, nevertheless, a vital component of editorial agency. In these terms, agency is understood as being expressed through the form of the magazine. That form must be understood not only in terms of heterogeneity but in terms of seriality, of how the editor has in mind not only the current issue but also previous and future issues, of how each decision is related to previous decisions and future decisions. The form of the periodical itself shapes the ways in which issues are produced and consumed. As James Mussell points out:

> No single issue exists in isolation but instead is haunted by the larger serial of which it is a part. This larger serial structure is invoked through the repetition of certain formal features, issue after issue. It insists on formal continuity, repeated from the past and projected onwards into the future, providing a mediating framework whose purpose is to reconcile difference by presenting new content in a form already known to readers.[7]

A set of stable periodical codes that are repeated from one issue to the next contains the radical heterogeneity of the magazine's content. As we have seen in relation to the *Dial*, Thayer and Watson quickly established an image of highbrow exclusivity through the look and feel of the magazine, its non-commercial ethos, its stable format and its resistance to the design features associated with high circulation newspapers and magazines. Scofield Thayer and Alyse Gregory had produced an extensive document, 'General Instructions for the Editorial Department', providing Moore with guidance concerning the procedures she should follow as editor, the layout of the magazine, the editorial comment, the Theatre, Music and Art Chronicles as well as the critical essays and the 'Briefer Mentions'. Readers would not have noticed any obvious changes to the magazine when Moore settled herself into her 'Palm Tree'. The temporal, material, economic, social and compositional codes of the *Dial* remained consistent reinforcing a sense of permanence, stability and integrity.

Rather than seeing this formal stability as a limit to editorial agency, I understand editorial agency as the effect of this formal stability. What gave the *Dial* and its editor the powers of cultural consecration was its aura of permanence, an aura at least partly transmitted through its periodical codes and its formal unity. This meant that Moore could introduce some fairly remarkable changes without upsetting the *Dial*'s reputation for distinction. She did this by concentrating women artists where possible in order to create dialogic spaces for women's art, poetry, prose and criticism. In doing so, the woman artist is no longer solitary, operating in the context of a predominantly masculine modernist aesthetic. Moore's clusters of women create critical capacity maximising not only the visibility of the feminine artistic signature but also generating a network of intertextual relations across visual and verbal texts that puts into circulation multiple and complex modernisms.

Moore's editorial decisions may not have resulted in an increase in the number of women being published in the *Dial*, but her awareness of the importance of those internal dialogic relations, of the interactions particularly between the visual and the verbal, signal a desire to create spaces within the magazine for women's art, writing and criticism. In other words, while women do not often appear, when they do appear they are frequently arranged together, as if Moore were aware that this was the only way to foreground the significance of gender in the production of modernism. Returning to Catherine Paul's idea of Moore as fulfilling a curatorial role as both editor and poet, Moore resisted privileging the unicum, the singular object, at the expense of a unified aesthetic. It might look as if by gathering together women artists, writers and critics she is reinforcing the category of 'woman' and thereby undermining her own preference for diversity rather than aesthetic unity, yet the clustering of women artists has the opposite effect. Through this arrangement, diversity is showcased. There is no category that can be labelled 'woman'; there is no aesthetic or formal unity that links women as creators and makers of modernism. Moore displays women artists through proximity to illustrate difference rather than sameness.

In addition, I would argue, these internal dialogics must be considered in relation to the external dialogics of the magazine, the periodical networks within which it operated and the social spaces within which it was produced and consumed. Women's writing and art was almost always framed by a masculine critical discourse. The case of Georgia O'Keeffe is an instructive one; her work was largely curated by Alfred Stieglitz in the 1920s and her reputation as an artist framed by Stieglitz's initial view of her as primitive, innocent and expressive. In some ways, of course, the *Dial* repeated this dynamic in the sense that its discursive signature was masculine and highbrow. The women writers and artists who appear in the magazine are discursively framed in this way. A certain cultural legitimacy is bestowed on them simply by appearing in the illustrious pages of the magazine. For instance, for Babette Deutsch, Genevieve Taggard, Mina Loy and Moore herself, appearing in the *Dial* effectively launched their careers; at the same time, the magazine as habitus is an institutional space that reproduces the structures that exclude the majority of women in its reproduction of the categorical differences between the highbrow and the middlebrow.

Judging from the numbers of women contributors to the *Dial*, it can hardly be described as a magazine particularly welcoming to women. Over the course of its modernist shelf life, the number of women contributors was approximately 14 per cent. Unlike *Others*, which devoted 38 per cent of its content to women poets, including one whole issue to Mina Loy's 'Songs to Joannes' and one all-woman issue, the space of the *Dial* was overwhelmingly dominated by male writers and artists. Perhaps more importantly, the magazine's critical framework was, until Moore's arrival, exclusively masculine. Henry McBride, Paul Rosenfeld and Gilbert Seldes wrote regular 'chronicles' on art, music and theatre. Between 1920 and 1924 the editorial comments were written by Seldes, Watson, Thayer or, occasionally, Kenneth Burke though not, significantly, Alyse Gregory, who was managing editor between 1923 and 1924. Letters from the metropolitan sites of modernism were produced by a range of writers, all of them men. All the headline acts, the texts that opened each issue, were authored by male writers. While reproductions of Marie Laurencin's paintings appeared on the first page of issues in August 1925, July 1926 and September 1927, these were the only instances where work produced by a woman was given such a prominent position. Notably this occurred under Moore's editorial reign. While Moore received The Dial Award in 1925, it was a critical essay about her poetry rather than the poetry itself that opened the January issue.

Moore herself published twelve poems between 1920 and 1925, thirteen reviews and numerous briefer mentions for the *Dial* before she became its editor. Between 1925 and 1929, she published nine reviews, forty-one editorial comments and eighty briefer mentions but no poetry. As a poet, then, Moore disappeared from the pages of the magazine when she became its editor. When thinking about Moore's editorial role it is important to acknowledge both her presence and, perhaps paradoxically, her absence. Moore's poetic signature had become, by 1925, synonymous with the *Dial*'s reputation for highbrow distinction. While she did not publish as many poems as William Carlos Williams or e. e. cummings in the magazine, the publication of two of her long poems, 'Sea Unicorns and Land Unicorns' in November 1924 and 'An Octopus' in December 1924, together with The Dial Award and the unanimous critical support she received from *Dial* reviews, brought a degree of acclaim that had been reserved, up until that point, for the modernist 'men of genius'. When she became editor of the magazine that made her reputation, however, Moore's signature was at least partially subsumed by the discursive function of the magazine.

Moore's absence as one of the most important poets of her generation had a significant impact. Simply judging by the numbers, Moore's editorial influence seems not to have made a difference to the number of women appearing in the pages of the magazine. Of the seventy-nine women contributors, she introduced twenty-seven. She used reproductions of art by women a little less often than her editorial predecessors did, but the numbers here are comparable. It is more instructive, however, to look closely at those writers she did introduce to the magazine. For instance, as Jayne Marek has already pointed out, it was Moore who not only brought Stein to the *Dial*, but who also repeatedly pointed to Stein's significance as a groundbreaking artist. Moore introduced Meridel Le Sueur, as well as Elizabeth Madox Roberts, and she continued to favour Babette Deutsch, Elizabeth Coatsworth and Lola Ridge. In addition, as I will go on to argue, Moore's arrangements of women writers, artists and critics in associative clusters reproduced in terms of design the kind of condensation that Moore desired in language. There is an expressive density, a compressive logic to Moore's treatment of women in the *Dial* that produces what she would refer to as 'gusto'.

The *Dial*, October 1921

The first and only cluster of women artists to be published in the *Dial* before Moore became its editor was in the October 1921 issue, presumably presided over by Gilbert Seldes. In this particular example, Mary Butts's short story, 'Speed the Plough' sits between Elizabeth J. Coatsworth's poem 'Reflections' and 'Poe', a poem by Mina Loy.

Coatsworth, little known today, made several appearances in the *Dial* throughout the decade. She published more than ninety books over her long and successful career. She was an established writer when she appeared in the *Dial*, having already had a collection of verse published in 1912. The poem 'Reflections' wonders at the popularity of geraniums, flowers not often associated with feminine artistry and beauty. In a series of rhetorical questions, the speaker asks whether Sappho, Cleopatra or Beatrice would have adorned themselves with this flower. The geranium is associated not with the lyrical song of the nightingale but the 'gossip of sparrows'. It is 'spinsters' who have loved them and 'living girls' who 'have felt quite festive, going/ Down vulgar streets'.[8] The speaker reflects on modern femininity, the 'unsubtle gaiety' of the prostitute and the single woman whose affections are lavished on cats and common blooms. Coatsworth's speaker is herself, perhaps, a modern woman who draws our attention to the gap between these elevated, romantic and overblown images of femininity and the ordinary and mundane lives of women who have to make do with whatever colourful flowers can be cultivated in 'tomato cans'.

Coatsworth's 'Reflection' is in free verse, eschews a regular rhyme scheme and deploys enjambment within stanzas. Syntactically, however, it is fluent and lyrical, in marked contrast to Loy's unpunctuated ode to Poe. Loy's poem seems tuned in to language itself and its strange clusters of sounds and associations. While clearly sound is important here, so too is typographic design. The ample white space surrounding Loy's poem makes it appear less solid than Coatsworth's 'Reflection'. Lines and stanzas are tenuously held together, creating a sense of the poem as a gauzy, transparent textual fabric, a delicate cobweb dedicated to capturing the essence of Poe's imaginative world. What holds the poem together within that fragile textual web is sound. Loy's delicate use of alliteration in the first line: 'a lyric elixir' requires the tongue to work its way around the words and is repeated in 'embalms' and 'glass loves'. The lilting of the 'l' is then joined by the sibilance of the 's' which recurs throughout the poem: 'spindle spirits', 'glass', 'spun', 'sets' and 'icicled'.[9] The sibilance is repeated and emphasised in the masculine rhyme between 'nights', 'lights' and 'rites'. For Loy, poetry is, in her own words, 'a music made of visual thoughts, the sound of an idea'.[10] Here she creates an echo chamber that resonates with the sounds and sensations of Poe's uncanny art. Loy's free-verse poem not only translates Poe into modernism but also hints that he was a modernist all along.

Neither of these poems occupies its own page space but rather both are used as fillers. Coatsworth's poem fills the half page left by the extract from Anatole France's memoirs while Loy's poem fills the space left at the end of Mary Butts's short story, 'Speed the Plough'. In other words, Butts's narrative is bracketed by the two poems. These juxtapositions of new womanhood construct a dialogue that resists easy assumptions about gender. It is Poe who is the 'lyric elixir' in Loy's poem, the poet's masculine muse. For Coatsworth it is the ordinary, everyday women, the spinsters and working girls who merit attention. For Butts, however, modern femininity is not exclusively the domain of women. The protagonist of 'Speed the Plough' is a soldier wounded in the First World War who is recovering in hospital. He is 'distressed' by the women working in the hospital who are so unlike the 'Kirchner girls' he looks at in the pages of his 'battered' magazine. His distress, however, is not due to his frustrated heterosexual desires but rather to the absence of a 'loveliness' associated with a more modern and sophisticated femininity. Formerly a fashion designer, he longs for the touch of fabric between his fingers, the 'velours and organdie and that faint windy stuff aerophane'.[11] His fantasies climax not with undressing women but with styling them in the 'immaculate fabrics' of high fashion. He is interested not in the fresh-faced prettiness of the nurses in the hospital but rather in 'women whose skins were lustrous with powder, and whose eyes were shadowed with violet from an ivory box'.[12]

Worried about his health, the doctors send him to work on a farm where he discovers that he is a 'natural milkman', capable of soothing the most obstreperous of cows. Yet he finds himself disgusted by the rank cowshed with its 'twenty female animals', their 'huge buttocks shifting uneasily'. While the milk is an 'amazing substance', it too begins to 'nauseate him'.[13] When out at a country pub, the perfumed smell of a woman reminds him of the fabricated femininity that he associates with 'civilization' and he cannot forget the allure of the fashionable London life. The narrative then cuts abruptly to the protagonist working once again as a fashion designer for a London atelier. We never learn how he manages to find his way back to his profession, but we realise from the look in his eyes at the end of the story that he has found solace in the sensuous pleasures of haute couture. The final scene of the story shows the protagonist

> on his knees, vertical in black cloth, and grey trousers, and exquisite bow tie. A roll of Lyons brocade, silver, and peach, was pliant between his fingers as the teats of a cow. Inside it a girl stood frowning down upon him.

She complains to him about the scarcity of lace during wartime: '"When the war starts interfering with my clothes," she said, "the war goes under . . .".'[14] On hearing this, the protagonist's 'eyes kindled', conveying in a complex image the repression of the experience of war 'under' the pleasures of his art.

Butts's story of post-war trauma has the protagonist saved not by the love of a good woman but rather by the love for a culture commonly dismissed as frivolous and gendered as feminine. The pleasures of textures and fabrics, of ephemeral fashions and fabricated femininities become, for this wounded soldier, redemptive and regenerative. That Butts draws attention to a man's desire not for a woman but for the fashionable trappings of a constructed womanhood, signals an interest in questioning the terms of hegemonic masculinity. The masculinity associated with war and aggression is reinforced by certain heteronormative assumptions as well as by its opposition to femininity. Here Butts presents the reader with a transgressive masculinity that finds pleasure not in objectifying the female body but rather in adorning and accessorising it. Such pleasures, associated with the expansion of consumer culture and the empowerment of women as desiring and consuming subjects are transferred to the masculine subject, keen to return to 'normality'. It is not that the war castrates men, as Hemingway would have it. It is rather that the catastrophic destruction of the war has challenged the values and virtues associated with hegemonic masculinity. More broadly, recovery involves replacing outmoded models of manhood with more fluid and flexible ideas about men's roles.

The *Dial*, May 1925

Moore, a regular reader of the *Dial*, may well have found in this cluster of 1921 a striking significance that, when she came to edit the magazine, she wished to reproduce. Pressing these texts together produces the impression of a wealth of women contributors rather than the meagre number of women who did actually make it into the magazine. By the time Moore became managing editor, the situation was, if anything, worse, which makes it all the more significant that such clusters occur more often in her presentation of women's work. The first cluster comes in the May 1925 issue before Moore became managing editor but at a time when she was attending make-up meetings.

Moore had been working at the *Dial* since April of that year but was not to take over officially until the July issue. Nevertheless, correspondence shows that she gave up her job at the New York Public Library and started work on 27April 1925.[15] Given that the office was in turmoil during the period when the May issue was being put together, it is difficult to assign editorial responsibility for its final arrangement. The confusion in the office around this time is evident in Elise DePollier's letters to Alyse Gregory, where she expresses her anxiety about the May issue, having witnessed the fitful and somewhat chaotic circumstances of its production.[16] I would like to suggest, however, that while Moore did not select these writers and artists for publication, it was probably Moore who decided to arrange them in a cluster.

This cluster begins with Evelyn Scott's short story, 'The Old Lady', followed by the poem 'As One Invulnerable' by Jessica Nelson North, and then a reproduction in black and white of two Georgia O'Keeffe paintings, *The Flagpole (First Painting)* and *The Flagpole (Second Painting)*, concluding with one of the rare contributions by Virginia Woolf, 'The Lives of the Obscure', an extended version of which was published in *The Common Reader* in 1925. With the exception of Georgia O'Keeffe, none of these writers reappeared in the *Dial* under Moore's editorship.

Woolf is conspicuous by her absence in Moore's critical reviews. 'Mr. Bennett and Mrs. Brown' is mentioned in Moore's editorial comment of February 1926 but otherwise, Moore remains silent on the subject of modernism's most well-known woman novelist. In private, Moore was less circumspect, admitting to Bryher in correspondence that both *Jacob's Room* and *The Voyage Out* contained 'amazing imagery' as well as 'infinite disappointment'.[17] Woolf had appeared in the Thayer/Watson *Dial* in previous issues. The short story 'Mrs Dalloway in Bond Street' was published in July 1923. It was one of a sequence of short stories with characters in common with the novel and later published together as *Mrs Dalloway's Party*. This story, as Amanda Sigler has pointed out, focuses on the activity of shopping and presents, in the context of its magazine publication, an image of the tensions between commerce and art.[18] In December 1924, 'Miss Omerod' appeared in the *Dial*, preceded by a critical essay on Woolf by Clive Bell. A year later, Woolf found it difficult to place her study of unknown writers, 'The Lives of the Obscure', as Julia Briggs points out in *Reading Virginia Woolf*; its publication in 1925 in the *Dial* suggests that the magazine was willing to support Woolf even though her appeal had not yet extended to the quality magazine market in the US.[19] Given that *Mrs Dalloway* was simultaneously published in Britain and the United States in May 1925, the inclusion of 'The Lives of the Obscure' in the May issue of the *Dial* was probably arranged to coincide with the publication of Woolf's latest novel.

Evelyn Scott had enjoyed some success at the *Dial* before Moore's editorial reign, having published twelve poems along with several articles and reviews.

While she continued to submit work to the *Dial* under Moore's editorship, Moore repeatedly rejected it. By 1928, Scott's patience had run out. She withdrew her poem, 'The Eaglet', rather than succumb to Moore's requests for revisions and turned instead to other publication venues.[20]

Evelyn Scott had published the novels *The Narrow House* in 1921 and *Narcissus* in 1922 but it was not until 1929 that she achieved popular and critical acclaim with the publication of her sprawling Civil War novel, *The Wave*. Scott's short story, 'The Old Lady', appearing in the May 1925 issue of the *Dial*, explores the thoughts of a woman who has exiled herself from her friends and family, who travels in Europe, adopting the gaze of the *flâneur*, remaining detached from the social life surrounding her. There is something akin to Mansfield and even Woolf in terms of style. In observing the sea, the woman becomes psychologically immersed in its currents and streams:

> The foam concentrated, lifted, and made a glittering edifice of snow, harsh, exquisite, and momentary, like the Gothic traceries of frost. The tower of marble, of a lacy substance, of the purity of linen left long to bleach, but with the adamant glitter of diamonds, sank easily, waned in prismatic reflections, and was no more than a pale breath, breathed on the distance of the intense sky and evaporating like mist.[21]

In the attempt to capture the ephemera of her protagonist's thoughts, Scott's prose style becomes verbose, overladen. Yet the awareness of the complex inner life of the old woman, of the extraordinary nature of the everyday is characteristic of both Mansfield and Woolf, particularly in *Mrs Dalloway*. While Scott's method might not be characterised as modernist, the engagement with daily life and the depiction of streams of thought signal a preoccupation with the inchoate and fluid nature of consciousness. The ordinary and even 'obscure' lives of women, edited out of history, become the subjects of fiction that focus on everyday lives, punctuated by the occasional Joycean epiphany: 'And the old lady was suddenly overcome by an emotion which she afterwards preferred to forget. What she felt, as she turned from her promenade, the sea-wind stinging her flaccid cheeks, was an immanence of death [. . .]'[22] This overwhelming awareness of life as loss leaves an 'austere bitterness' in the old woman that affords her, paradoxically, a 'new strength'.[23]

Scott's story finishes on the recto page and is followed by Jessica Nelson North's poem, 'As One Invulnerable', which occupies the verso page. All artwork was reproduced on the recto. To appear on the verso was, in terms of design format, to occupy a marginal position in the magazine. North's poem is there to fill the page that would otherwise have to remain blank. Imagine, for instance, Eliot's 'The Hollow Men', which appeared in March 1925, occupying the verso, or Pound's translations of Calvacanti, or Williams's 'Paterson' beginning on the left page rather than the right. In the correspondence, Moore discusses using poems as fillers, indicating that a hierarchy existed within the pages of the magazine, whereby some pieces took centre-stage while others played supporting roles. In this instance, North's poem is clearly used to avoid wasting precious page space and also segues into the next and more significant contribution.

Compared to some of the *Dial*'s favoured poets, North's four-stanza poem looks rather conventional in terms of form. Unlike cummings, she does not play with punctuation; unlike Williams, there are no experiments with typography; and unlike Moore, the syntactic arrangements of her sentences unfurl rather than contract. Eschewing the free-verse format associated with most modernist poetry, 'As One Invulnerable' is, nevertheless, elliptical. The man at the centre of the poem who buttons himself up against emotional pain refuses to lay bare his tortured soul, to make public his pain. This might be related to the modernist turn away from sentiment. If this is the case, then North provides an image of the high modernist poet adopting the 'hard, indifferent repose' of 'one invulnerable'. As Eliot was advocating the extinction of personality, as Pound described the disintegration of the ego and as Moore preferred affective 'restraint', North reflects critically on the consequences of poetry that appears to disengage from the emotions.[24]

North's resistance to the emotional reticence of the modernist poetic project sits opposite the first of two paintings by Georgia O'Keeffe: *The Flagpole (First Painting)* (Fig. 6.1) followed by *The Flagpole (Second Painting)* (Fig. 6.2). While North had been published in *Poetry* magazine by this time, she was still relatively unknown. O'Keeffe, on the other hand was, according to Henry McBride a 'newspaper personality'.[25] She had appeared in photographic portraits by Alfred Stieglitz, exhibited at the Anderson Galleries in 1921. These included graphic nude close-ups of her head, neck, breasts and torso. Several art critics, including Paul Rosenfeld in the *Dial* in December 1921, had then produced interpretations that conflated the artist's body with the body of her own work. For Rosenfeld, O'Keeffe's work articulates the feelings of her sex: 'There is registered the manner of perception anchored in the constitution of the woman. The organs that differentiate the sex speak.' More specifically, it is the womb that speaks because, according to Rosenfeld, 'Women, [. . .] always feel, when they feel strongly, through the womb.'[26] Stieglitz, well aware of the power of this sexualised imagery as a marketing strategy, encouraged this reading of O'Keeffe's work, much to her irritation. 'I wonder if man has ever been written down the way he has written woman down – I rather feel that he hasn't been', she writes to Sherwood Anderson in 1922.[27]

O'Keeffe had produced a painting entitled *The Flagpole* in 1922 which initiated a series of paintings where she began to explore the relation between the vertical cut of the flagpole, the horizontal lines of human structures like houses and barns and the natural forms of trees and clouds. *The Flagpole*

Figure 6.1 Georgia O'Keeffe, *The Flagpole (First Painting)*, *Dial*, 78 (May 1925), 381. © Georgia O'Keeffe Museum / DACS 2018.

Figure 6.2 Georgia O'Keeffe, *The Flagpole (Second Painting)*, *Dial*, 78 (May 1925), 382. © Georgia O'Keeffe Museum / DACS 2018.

(First Painting), as presented in the *Dial*, is in black and white and appears to represent a flagpole in the foreground and a house surrounded by voluminous clouds. Drained of colour, the reproductions privilege the spatial and geometric concerns of the painting over its representational terms. Without colour, the trees and bushes look like clouds surrounding the house. In the original paintings, the mauve and purples of the billowing clouds and the verdant greens of the surrounding foliage signal the difference between these forms. This painting had appeared as part of the 'Seven Americans' show at the Anderson Galleries in 1925 which Edmund Wilson reviewed for the *New Republic* in March of that year. His review includes a close visual analysis of *The Flagpole*, where he notes how colour contributes to the distinction between organic and inorganic forms:

> the actual outlines of the house have melted away into the exquisite mist of lavender and green but the rectangle of the doorway has intensified itself to black opacity and geometrical exactness in such sharp relief that is seems actually to have been projected out from the plane of the picture to hang in the air before it.[28]

If anything, the black-and-white image of O'Keeffe's painting highlights the ways in which these forms melt into each other. The lilac bushes and trees are cloud-like shapes that appear insubstantial in relation to the clean lines of the geometrical house. Without colour, these organic forms meld and merge in shades of grey, emphasising the intensity and angularity of the doorway.

Wilson repeats a gendered critical discourse in his appraisal of O'Keeffe that Stieglitz himself had initiated in the marketing of her work.[29] On display in O'Keeffe's work, according to Wilson, is a 'feminine intensity' that is distinctive from her modernist male peers. According to Wilson:

> Men, as a rule, in communicating their intensity, seem not only to incorporate it in the representation of external objects but almost, in the work of art, to produce something which is itself an external object and, as it were, detachable from themselves; whereas women seem to charge the objects they represent with so immediate a personal emotion that they absorb the subject into themselves instead of incorporating themselves into the subject.[30]

For Wilson, masculine creativity is associated with a certain objectivity, a detachment that undoubtedly connects writing and art by men to the critical discourses of emotional reticence in circulation around modernism. Eliot's notion of the 'objective correlative', Pound's determination to avoid 'emotional slither' were, as Suzanne Clark has persuasively argued, developed in opposition to 'sentimental', popular writing.[31] While clearly Wilson admires O'Keeffe's work, and admits that she 'outblazes the other painters in the exhibition', she is also associated with 'personal emotion' rather than 'restraint' and detachment. In other words, O'Keeffe's modernism does not sound or look like modernism. While women artists can produce work of 'intensity', it is essentialised as 'feminine intensity'. As she herself noted, this critical impulse represented her as 'like some strange earthly sort of creature floating in the air – breathing in the clouds for nourishment'.[32]

As Charles C. Eldridge has pointed out, many of the paintings O'Keeffe produced between 1919 and 1929, the still lifes and the nature studies, might best be viewed as abstract portraits.[33] The artist signalled this herself when writing about these paintings:

> There are people who have made me see shapes . . . I have painted portraits [of them] that to me are almost photographic. I remember hesitating to show the paintings, they looked so real to me. But they have passed into the world as abstractions – no one seeing what they are.[34]

Given the influence of Stieglitz on O'Keeffe both personally and professionally, it does not seem much of a leap to assume that the flagpole series are portraits of Stieglitz himself. Painted in Lake George, the Stieglitz family estate where O'Keeffe spent many summers, the little house depicted here is Stieglitz's darkroom, a converted shed. The flagpole cuts skywards through the canvas, dissecting forms and thrusting vertically into the horizontal lines of the house and the curves of the clouds, trees and bushes. The phallic implications are hard to miss but so too is the sense that O'Keeffe is preoccupied not only with depicting Stieglitz but with the activity of seeing Stieglitz. Stieglitz is figured, punningly, in and as the line of her vision. He intersects the shapes and colours of her seeing, dominating the picture plane, dissecting the graphic and chromatic elements of the composition.

In this, O'Keeffe is adopting a familiar modernist strategy by treating the canvas as a visual 'espace', a conceptual space distinct from representational or referential activity. She emphasises the picture plane through her use of geometric shapes and vivid colour. As Johanna Drucker summarises, for the modernist artist, 'the requirements of pictorial space came to take precedence over the illusion of representational image'.[35] O'Keeffe's visual meditations on a landscape dominated by Stieglitz bring into objective and concrete form the experience of seeing him.

The feelings bound up with that experience are, undoubtedly, signalled through O'Keeffe's use of colour. Drained of that colour in the black-and-white reproductions in the *Dial*, O'Keeffe's paintings lose the pastel hues that distinguish trees from clouds. This has a curious and not entirely negative effect. The remediation of the flagpole sequence of paintings allows the viewer to focus on the design of both paintings and their relation to each other. While in the first painting, the shed (Stieglitz's darkroom) sits squarely in the centre of the canvas dissected by a flagpole and lines (perhaps electricity cables) that shoot up beyond the frame, in the second painting, the view moves into the sky and away from the grounded structures associated with Stieglitz. In the second image, the flagpole is like a tendril that becomes finer and thinner as it reaches up into the sky. This time we see neither its base nor its tip. It cuts into the spherical forms that sit at the bottom of the canvas and then as it reaches skyward it intersects with two sets of clouds. Beside it, in the centre and in the bottom third of the painting is a small black rectangle. Slightly above this, as if blown off a weathervane, sits a black arrow pointing diagonally left. To the right, the electric wires, previously attached to the house, now appear to be attached to a cloud formation and shoot up, almost parallel to the flagpole.

The effect of 'seeing' Stieglitz in the first painting becomes the subject of the second painting. More specifically, Stieglitz's photographic way of seeing is reflected in the painting. The photographic distortions Stieglitz perfected in his own work, the use of halation in particular, which produced a blurring effect around the edges of objects, is recreated in this painting. Everything seems slightly out of focus; a halo of light emanates around the clouds creating the halation that can also be seen in many of Stieglitz's photographs. In effect, the reproduction of O'Keeffe's paintings in black and white emphasise this photographic quality by pointing to the similarities between her paintings and Stieglitz's black-and-white photographs. As many critics have noted, what Stieglitz referred to as his 'equivalents', his studies of clouds, were responses to O'Keeffe's paintings.[36] Here, O'Keeffe continues the intervisual exchange; an exchange that demonstrates not only the feelings associated with Lake George and Stieglitz but also questions the parameters of perception and form. When O'Keeffe began to paint barns and sheds in the 1920s, she moved away from the spiralling arcs and circular forms that had dominated her earlier work, as well as the iconic flowers for which she was to become so well known. The flagpole paintings reproduced in the *Dial* signal this change of direction.

It is difficult to second-guess the response of the *Dial* reader to these reproductions of O'Keeffe's paintings. What is likely, however, is that O'Keeffe would have been known as the subject of Stieglitz's nude portraits. If readers had not seen O'Keeffe's paintings first hand, they probably would have encountered reviews of her work that essentialised her paintings as expressions of an innate femininity. These black-and-white versions of O'Keeffe present, albeit accidentally, a more sober and restrained painter, one engaging with conceptual problems of perception and form. In addition, they are not the 'calla lilies, gladiolas and alligator pears' that Moore sees at the Anderson Galleries.[37] The *Dial* shows a very different painter in its pages, one less colourful and expressive, one that coincides with O'Keeffe's own reframing of her public image after 1924.

The *Dial*, February 1927

Moore's next cluster was much more of her own making. The February 1927 issue of the *Dial* might be described as the William Carlos Williams issue. In January, Moore had announced that Williams was to receive The Dial Award and the following issue led with an early incarnation of what was to become *Paterson*. Kenneth Burke's critical essay, 'William Carlos Williams, the Methods of', provides an important critical analysis of his work, which is then followed by black-and-white reproductions of three paintings by Jack B. Yeats: 'Fair Day', 'Dublin Newsboys' and 'The Funeral of a Republican'. In the wake of this celebration of Williams's poetry, is a cluster of women writers that begins with Lola Ridge's poem 'Ray', followed by Marie Budberg's 'Russian Letters', a reproduction of a Brancusi sculpture, Dorothy Dudley's essay 'Brancusi', a poem by Frances I. Wilson and concludes with a reproduction of a print by the French painter, Hermine David.

Ridge and Moore had known each other since Moore's arrival in Greenwich Village in 1918. As associate editor of *Others* in 1919 and as editor of *Broom* in 1923, Ridge published Moore before Moore published Ridge. Linda Kinnehan points to the mutual respect and friendship between the two poets, as well as a shared interest in 'a sense of the reciprocity between artistic or creative labor and social good'.[38] Ridge was not only a poet and activist; she also played a significant role in shaping literary modernism by offering alternative social gatherings to the salons of the Arensbergs or the 'firesides' of Alyse Gregory. Caroline Maun notes how it was at parties hosted by Ridge that Robert McAlmon and William Carlos Williams met, and of course, where Moore had her first and career changing encounter with Thayer. Ridge also served as a mentor to Kay Boyle who assisted Ridge at *Broom* and Evelyn Scott who found opportunities to publish largely because Ridge introduced her to a network of Greenwich Village publishers, writers and artists. Ridge was probably best known for her free-verse poetic sequence, published in the *New Republic* in 1918, called 'The Ghetto'. The poem described life on the Lower East Side in the Hester Street Jewish community. It was also published in book form and followed by a collection called *Sun-Up and Other Poems* in 1920. While the *Dial* was not averse to publishing poems that engaged with political controversy, as is evident, for instance, in the publication of Evelyn Scott's provocative anti-lynching poem 'Devil's Cradle' in the January 1920 issue, other magazines adopted a more overtly political stance.[39] Ridge selected the publication venue most appropriate for her work, sometimes favouring modernist magazines such as *Poetry*, *Others* and the *Dial*, and sometimes preferring the more overtly left-leaning magazines such as *New Masses* and the *New Republic*.[40]

The publication of 'Ray' in the *Dial* provides a good example of Ridge's poetics of activism, which suggested that there were not clear boundaries between politics and poetry. Drawing on the light imagery that is so central to her collection *Sun-Up* and that alludes to her early life in New Zealand, 'Ray' is a poem that explores what Nancy Berke has referred to as 'the politics of pain'.[41] For Berke, Ridge's poetry places the spectacle of the body in pain at the centre of much of her work drawing on religious imagery to do so. For instance, the poem 'Three Men Die' compares the execution of Sacco and Vanzetti to the crucifixion of Christ. Berke also shows how Ridge herself was willing to put her body on the line for causes she believed in. The most famous example, described in Katherine Anne Porter's autobiography, was in August 1927 when Ridge was outside Charleston Prison protesting the decision to execute Sacco and Vanzetti. Ridge refused to retreat when mounted police officers stormed the crowd of protestors and was eventually arrested, along with Edna St Vincent Millay. So when Ridge writes of suffering, she does so from the position of one who was literally willing to die for her beliefs. In the sonnet 'Ray', Ridge articulates the poet's own 'burning' desire to make something indelible as well as to make something happen. The pain associated with the physical dangers of political protest is aligned to the struggle to make a poetic mark in the imagery of Christian suffering and the Crucifixion. In the quest to hold the 'ray' to 'let [it] not slip silently back in the sun', the poetic speaker's body is marked by a painful imprint like 'A golden nailhead [. . .] in [her] palm'.[42]

There may well have been no woman more actively engaged in the making and shaping of history who appeared in the pages of the *Dial* than Marie, later known as Moura, Budberg. While Moore would have had no way of knowing about Budberg's secret life as a double agent, it is worth alluding to just a few of the stories circulating around this extraordinary woman even though the facts are difficult to verify given Budberg's apparent involvement in espionage.[43] Budberg, born Maria Ignatievna Zakrevskaia in the Poltava province of Ukraine in 1891, married a high-ranking Czarist diplomat and had three children. Her husband was killed during the Russian Revolution leaving Maria, who had been working as a translator and secretary, in St Petersburg. In the political turmoil of post-Revolutionary Russia and in a potentially vulnerable position as a widowed mother and an aristocrat, she began an affair with Bruce Lockhart, the British agent, who was the inspiration for Ian Fleming's James Bond. Lockhart and Budberg were arrested in 1918, accused of being involved in a plot to assassinate Lenin. A deal was brokered with the British that resulted in the release of Lockhart, though it is unclear how Budberg managed to escape execution. There is some evidence to suggest that this was when she agreed to become a Soviet spy.

Budberg stayed on in St Petersburg and became a secretary and translator for Maxim Gorky, with whom she had an affair. She married Baron Budberg in 1921 but appears to have continued her relationship with Gorky. To complicate matters even further, when H. G. Wells was visiting Gorky in 1920, Budberg and Wells had a brief sexual liaison that would turn into a long and, for Wells, painful affair. Lenin expelled Gorky from the Soviet Union in 1922 and Budberg followed him, acting as his secretary and translator, which is how she came to be in correspondence with Moore. During this time, however, many believe that she was an active agent for the Soviet Union. Recent biographies of Budberg have stressed her sexual allure, her hard-drinking and louche lifestyle and her aristocratic tastes. Her work for the *Dial*, and particularly for Moore, demonstrates her extensive knowledge not only of Gorky's work, but more widely, of Russian literature and culture. She offers a unique perspective on the seismic transformations that had taken place and their effect on Russia at a time when Europe and the United States were hungry for news of Soviet life. Her essay, 'Russian Letters', is the only letter from abroad by a woman writer. While Budberg had translated for the *Dial*, she had not had any of her own work published and was not a well-known author. In this context, Moore's decision to use Budberg was a bold one.

As Adam McKible points out, 'creating a Russian literary landscape was as vital to the *Dial* as were its 'England', its 'France', its 'Ireland' and its 'America'.[44] Russia was both a geographical place as well as a culturally imagined space in the pages of the magazine, a space that, according to McKible, repeatedly produced nostalgic images of pre-Revolutionary Russia.[45] Budberg's essay is an explicit critique of these nostalgic narratives. When Moore advised Budberg about the kind of material suitable for publication in the *Dial*, she pointed out that 'our general trend is toward art and literature rather than toward politics'.[46] Nevertheless, Budberg can hardly discuss Russian letters in 1927 without alluding to the seismic social changes that had been brought about by the Russian Revolution. Her opening paragraph acknowledges that the 'old standards' no longer apply, that 'the Russian letters of old – sadistic, mystical, dogmatic, and simple, and at the same time naively, childishly beautiful' are associated with another era, another time. Budberg aims to provide the reader with a 'short survey [of] the most singular metamorphosis that has ever taken place in the mentality of a nation – as reflected in the mirror of its letters'.[47]

Critical of European synopses of Russian literature, Budberg claims the authority of 'a Russian', even though she herself was born in the Ukraine. According to Budberg, the great Russian writers such as Pushkin, Gogol, Tolstoy and Dostoevsky are pathologised by the shorthand critical guides to Russian literature that Budberg encounters in the West. In an attempt to counter this outdated caricature, she offers her own view of the contemporary literary scene in Russia, a view that emphasises the impact the revolution has had on writers. According to Budberg, 'A keen, obstinate struggle with all emotions that leaves one unbalanced and unsettled, pervades everything – a struggle inspired by a wholesome instinct for self-preservation.'[48] This is not a nostalgic glance backwards. This is the perspective of someone who has become an expert in 'self-preservation', who does not stand outside the Soviet Union but who is deeply engaged with and aware of the cultural and political transformations taking place.

Budberg describes the old tradition of Russian letters as a 'glorification of wretchedness and hopelessness', a form of writing wedded to oppressive detail, to the everyday and the trivial. This 'crushing [Russian] realism' has, according to Budberg, separated Russian literature from Western literature. The emerging new forms of Russian writing are more influenced by Europe and as a result, the 'soulfulness' of Russian literature is disappearing. Yet rather than seeing this as the result of the Russian Revolution, she suggests that the loss of soulfulness is being brought about by modernity: 'But was not that bound, anyway, to disappear in the spirit of our age?' she asks. To reinforce this point she suggests that the divide in Russian literature might best be described not in terms of pre- and post-revolutionary Russia, but rather in terms of the split between the country and the city. She offers the case of the Russian poet, Sergei Yesenin, as an example of a writer who came from the country and became intoxicated with the city. When he tired of city life, when he was filled with 'the sick feeling of satiety and disappointment', he longed to return to the old world, to the pre-modern rural community that he had left behind. But of course, as Budberg points out, 'there was no "getting back"'. As a result of this extreme alienation from modern life, Yesenin hung himself in a hotel room in St Petersburg in 1925.[49]

It is the collision between the tram and the country cart, as Budberg describes it, which is so central to contemporary Russian literature. Yet at the same time, she points out that while Russia's revolutionary history has produced a dramatic and sudden transformation, that transformation is taking place across the globe as modernity brings with it the new technologies of mass production and communication. The nostalgia for a pre-Revolutionary past that McKible associates with the Russian material the *Dial* itself published is, for Budberg, a dangerous desire for something that cannot be recovered. Yesenin 'turned back once in an anguish of loneliness, and found his sister reading Karl Marx. Result: a towel round his neck and a footstool pushed aside in agony.'[50] Budberg could not be more explicit concerning the dangers of nostalgia for the artist. She finds evidence, however, that some Russian writers are resisting this temptation to look backwards. Instead of attempting to return to a mythic space untouched by modernity, these writers are developing a historical approach that engages with the present by studying rather than mythologising the past.

Adam McKible's examination of the representations of Russia in the *Dial* explores material published before Moore became editor, though he does note an item published in the last issue of the magazine that offers a 'hopeful anticipation of a Russian future'.[51] This piece chimes with Budberg's essay suggesting, perhaps, a slight shift in tone under Moore's editorial reign. In fact in September 1928 when Moore is asking Budberg to find an appropriate story by Michail Prishvin for the magazine, she asks for one 'that does not carry a heart-break with it'.[52] Moore is aware that many of the stories published in the *Dial* have in them 'distress' and is keen to provide some 'relief or contrast from time to time' to alleviate the gloom. Moore might have had in mind the tone of stories published in the *Dial* by Manuel Komroff, Ivan Bunin, Paul Morand and Aleksie Remizov. In these stories, as McKible points out, Russia can only be remembered in terms of the loss of a beloved. While Moore may have had in mind her readers' feelings, her push for stories that move away from loss, despair and tragedy have significant political implications in relation to the magazine's representation of Russia.

Following Budberg's essay is a black-and-white photograph of Constantin Brancusi's *Mlle Pogany*, providing a visual segue into Dorothy Dudley's essay, 'Brancusi'. Dudley's essay seems to be the only example of art criticism written by a woman for the *Dial* with the exception of Moore herself. While Dudley graduated from Bryn Mawr in 1905 when Moore started at the college, Moore may well have known Dudley through mutual friends. Dudley was part of the literary circle around Harriet Monroe and *Poetry* magazine. She published some poems there and also appeared in the *Nation* and the *American Magazine of Art*. Dudley is most well known for writing the first biography of Theodore Dreiser, a study riddled with inaccuracies, but, as Donald Pizer has suggested, one that offers a critique of American culture via the biographical portrait.[53] Dudley might be viewed as a writer influenced by the work of critics closely associated with the early *Dial*, such as Van Wyck Brooks, Randolph Bourne and Waldo Frank, the so-called 'Young Americans' who were offering alternatives to what was perceived to be the stifling conventions of the so-called, genteel tradition.

Dudley's article appears to be part interview, part critical overview. She begins with the 'first impression' of the nine sculptures, drawings and frescoes at the Brancusi exhibition at the Brummer Galleries in New York. This 'constellation in polished bronze, in wood, marble, onyx, and alabaster' produces a variety of shapes and textures: 'Surfaces scintillant, flaming, natural; varyingly warm and cool, not hot or cold, nor dry or lush, but living.' Dudley emphasises the organic nature of Brancusi's sculpted forms and resists the label of abstraction: 'People who call this sculpture abstract have not felt it, have not seen how the edges are vibrant, how a pulse appears to beat in each one, how they are living organisms and projects.'[54] This organicism seems vitally connected to the artwork's impact on the viewing subject's sense of herself in space. Space is transformed, Dudley implies, by Brancusi's sculptures. Translating from the French (she had lived in Paris in the mid-1920s), she quotes extensively from the artist himself, whose main concern is to allow the material he is working with to determine the way in which he will interpret his subject. Each sculpture becomes an opportunity to explore and express the affordances of the material being used:

> You cannot make what you want to make, but what the material permits you to make. [. . .] Each material has its own life, and one cannot without punishment destroy a living material to make a dumb senseless thing. That is, we must not try to make materials speak our language, we must go with them to a point where others will understand their language.[55]

Brancusi's sculptures had been attracting a great deal of media attention largely due to the legal case, C. Brancusi vs the United States, which began a year earlier, in 1926. When Brancusi had shipped his sculpture, *Bird in Space*, into the US, customs official decided to categorise it under 'kitchen utensils and hospital supplies'. As a result of defining the sculpture as a utilitarian object, it was subject to a hefty tariff upon entering the US. If it had been categorised as art it would have been allowed to enter the US tax-free.[56] In the same issue of the *Dial*, resident art critic Henry McBride devoted the majority of his short essay to the scandal of Brancusi's treatment, to the impossibility of defining art and to the success of Brancusi at the Brummer Galleries. McBride explains that according to the authorities, Brancusi's abstract streamlined sculpture did not represent the bird in its 'true proportions of length, breadth, and thickness' and therefore did not qualify as art.[57] As if in response to the customs authorities' assessment, Dudley's essay picks up on the difficulty of discerning the difference between utensils and art objects. Crucially, when describing Brancusi's studio, she points to the fact that even the sculptor's tools 'are supremely themselves. The steel of a row of saws hanging on the white wall gleams preciously; mallets and chisels on a stone table are important.' What Dudley refers to as the 'separate intentional values of material objects' is evident in the way that the tools themselves acquire an integrity of their own when placed alongside Brancusi's sculpture.[58] It may not be surprising then that US customs officials categorised *Bird in Space* as a utensil rather than an art object. Dudley's point is that such categorical distinctions become less apparent in the wake of art that foregrounds the affordances of all things, including the tools out of which things are made. Brancusi's sculpture exists in an object world not as the expression of the artist's ideas but rather as the expression of the materials themselves. The polished bronze of *Bird in Space* is itself a form of ekphrasis that speaks in non-verbal terms for the mute materials out of which it is made.

Dudley's essay finishes half way down the page and is followed by a short poem by Frances I. Wilson called 'The Shack'. A minimalist, unfussy poem that seems, at first glance, to concern a discarded shell on a beach, it is written from the point of view of the creature that makes a home of the shell. The poem may well have reminded Moore of her own 'To a Snail', which recognises the need for hard and protective forms as well as adaptability. 'The Shack' of the title is a greying shell 'dropped by a careless hand'. [59] The rhetorical question, 'Who would retrace steps/ to look for a lost shell?' suggests that nobody, no human being would bother to look for such a small, seemingly insignificant object. By contrast, the non-human world finds such things and makes use of them.

Traces of Moore's taste might also be detected in the last contribution of this cluster of women artists. Hermine David's *Le Jeu* is a reproduction of a woodcut depicting a Parisien game of boules. David (1886–1970) was accepted, at the age of sixteen to the École des Beaux Arts, an exceptional achievement at this time, considering the prohibitions placed on women artists. There she met the artist, Jules Pascin, and moved with him to New York in 1915. David exhibited in New York but returned to France in 1920 and for the following two decades established a reputation as an illustrator and print maker, specialising in dry point engraving and lithography. She illustrated Rimbaud's *Une Saison en Enfer* and Verlaine's *La Bonne Chanson. Le Jeu* is typical of David's work in that it depicts a city street scene that seems to bulge with life and activity. David's curvilinear forms and the thickness and blockiness of her lines create an inky density that works particularly well in the magazine. It is not surprising that David was most successful as an illustrator. Her work seems to lose little in being translated for the pages of the *Dial*.

Showcasing women's work, particularly women such as O'Keeffe and David, who were themselves often treated as modernist pin-ups, muses and objects of desire rather than active and creative subjects, was one way in which Moore as editor of the *Dial* used her position to resist the fetishisation of the female body. O'Keeffe may well have been more famous in the 1920s for Stieglitz's nude photographs of her than for her own work. Likewise, David had to share the limelight with her husband, the Bulgarian painter, Jules Pascin, who was a notorious drinker and party animal. David frequently sat for her husband and his portraits of her were some of his best-known work.[60] While O'Keeffe's reputation as an artist was revived in the 1970s, David has all but disappeared from the history of modernism.

The *Dial*, September 1927

The September 1927 issue features a coloured frontispiece of Marie Laurencin's *Young Girl*, the last of three Laurencin paintings that Moore featured in this prominent space. This issue also includes a cluster of women artists: an extract from Gertrude Stein's 'A Long Gay Book' followed by Genevieve Taggard's poem, 'Letter in Solitude', which sits opposite a black-and-white reproduction of Vanessa Bell's painting, *The Party*. But this issue is also noticeable for its inclusion of Marie Budberg's translation of two stories by Maxim Gorky and a critical essay by Alyse Gregory. Raymond Mortimer's letter from London identifies Virginia Woolf as one of the two most important writers in contemporary England, the other being Sacheverell Sitwell. While Moore writes one 'briefer mention', it is Sibley Watson who writes the editorial comment for this issue, a strident defence of the *Dial*, which had come under attack in the *New Republic*. Watson takes the opportunity to remind rival magazines that the *Dial*'s role as mediator between the 'small' magazine and the quality magazine means that it requires clear editorial leadership:

> On the other hand, magazines which are edited by their contributors can and must give their contributors the run of the place, and to be given the run of any place can be, for a time, a great encouragement to a writer. Magazines of this type are often more immediately encouraging to interesting new writers, not to mention movements, than magazines like The Dial. But in the long run the reader too is important. Many writers will continue to appear first in small 'group magazines.' Our business is to furnish a not too scattered public for what they write well, as others will see that they have a larger public whenever they choose to be tiresome.[61]

Watson's counter-attack argues that the *Dial* keeps the business of editing and the business of contributing separate, to do otherwise is to risk the danger of using the periodical to publish and support one's friends. Ironically, it is not the *Dial* that is a cliquish old boys' club but rather the left-leaning, progressive magazine run by Herbert Croly that gives contributors 'the run of the place'. Moore's discerning critical eye, Watson suggests, is trained on the text rather than on personal friendships and professional alliances. Any form of partisanship would compromise the integrity of the magazine. Though Watson's defence recognises the importance of Moore's impartial stance, this is somewhat undermined by the fact that the magazine was obliged to publish Thayer's poetry. Therefore, while the *Dial* claimed to be non-partisan, its open-door policy for Thayer invited criticism from other periodicals.

In this September issue, Marie Laurencin's *Young Girl* appears as the frontispiece in the soft pastel colours Laurencin preferred to use to depict her fragile, ethereal feminine figures (see Fig. 6.3). The representation of girls was a theme she returned to repeatedly throughout her career to explore, through design and colour, girlhood and its affects. The pink tones of the girl's blouse, the pompom on her hat, her delicate pink lips and the bloom on her cheeks and her right forearm emphasise the first flush of youth. Against the shades of pink is the turquoise greeny-blue of the girl's hat and collar. Her hair, by contrast, is almost colourless. It sits under her hat and behind her face and shoulders in an amorphous, light-brown cloud. It is her eyes, however, that are most striking in the context of these soft colours. Though one hand reaches across her breast in a gesture of protection, her black, almond-shaped eyes stare back at the viewer, signalling a subjectivity emboldened.

Figure 6.3 Marie Laurencin, *Young Girl*, *Dial*, 83 (September 1927), 263. © Marie Laurencin/ DACS 2018.

Laurencin had enjoyed considerable success as a painter by this time. The only woman in the Bateau-Lavoir and Cubist coterie, she exhibited at the Salon des Indépendants, the Salon d'Automne and the Salon de la Section d'Or as well as exhibiting seven works at the Armory Show in 1913. Readers of the *Dial* would probably have been familiar with Laurencin's work perhaps having encountered it first hand at the Armory Show or through regular exhibitions in the 1920s in Paris, London and New York. She designed the sets and costumes for the Ballets Russes production of Les Biches (1924) choreographed by Nijinsky and set to the music of Frances Poulenc. By the 1920s, her work was being collected by those like Thayer, Stein and John Quinn who had the resources to acquire modern European art.

Laurencin's relationship with Guillame Apollinaire between 1907 and 1913 has often taken centre-stage in assessments of her work. As with Sonia Delaunay, Käthe Kollwitz, Georgia O'Keeffe, Frida Kahlo and Natalia Goncharova, she was frequently cast as muse to a more significant male artist rather than an artist in her own right. Rather like Stieglitz, Apollinaire emphasised Laurencin's feminine style even though he saw her as an equal to Braque, Picasso, Gris and Gleizes. The American artist, Marsden Hartley, praised the work of modernist women artists like Delaunay and O'Keeffe, but singled out Laurencin for eliminating 'all severities of intellect'. In an ekphrastic poem, 'In a Frail Wood', published in *Poetry* in July 1918, Hartley gives voice to the mute subjects of Laurencin's portraits:

> Marie Laurencin!
> How she likened them to young gazelles
> Disporting in a quiet glade, with their thin legs
> And their large wondering eyes
> Full of delicate trembling – shy, tender, suspecting,
> Furtively watching for the stranger in the wood.[62]

Above all, it was the association of the decorative style with femininity that constructed Laurencin in opposition to a masculinist modernism of hard intellectual edges and emotional reticence.

The placement of Laurencin's *Young Girl* opposite Bertrand Russell's 'Things that Have Moulded Me', an introduction to the forthcoming *Selected Papers of Bertrand Russell*, might be viewed as in some way reinforcing this gendered opposition between feminine feeling and masculine intellect. Such oppositions, as W. J. T. Mitchell has shown us, are embedded within the critical apparatus framing our understanding of the differences between pictures and words.[63] However, I would argue that Laurencin's painting lends a certain expressiveness to Russell's first page and likewise, his introductory remarks cast a slightly different light on Laurencin's painting. As Russell points out, critically reflecting on his own development as a thinker would be much more straightforward if he were dead. As a subject, Russell gets in the way of his own analysis of his work, recognising that it is 'impossible to see oneself as a whole'.[64] Laurencin's portraits of young girls enact a similar problem. Repeatedly she returned in the 1920s to images of young women as if trying to construct a feminine artistic identity. The problem of seeing 'oneself as a whole' is one of the problems with which modernist artists and writers were continually grappling. What Eliot refers to as the 'unity of the soul', an integrated and stable subject position, is continually being interrogated through the fractured images and dislocated lyrics of the modernist aesthetic. Laurencin's work, displayed in this context, takes on aspects of the philosophical questions being posed on the opposite page.

The cluster of women artists within the pages of this September issue begins with an extract from 'A Long Gay Book', selected by Stein, as I have shown, for its resemblance to *The Making of Americans.* In a sense, 'A Long Gay Book' stands in for or replaces, synecdochically, *The Making of Americans*, giving the reader of the *Dial* the opportunity to encounter, first hand, the style of accumulation, repetition, variation and extension that characterises Stein's expansive novel. The extract from 'A Long Gay Book' appearing in September 1927 is followed by Genevieve Taggard's poem, 'Letter in Solitude'. Arranged in four- and six-line stanzas, the liberal use of enjambment subdues the regular rhyme scheme. The poem initially seems to assert the consistency of love, but as it develops, 'Autumn certainties' give way to 'seasonal certainties', which then give way to 'other certainties'. A tonal shift is reflected in the temporal changes of the seasons, the transformation from the 'carnival' colours of autumn to the 'gaunter' 'outlines' of winter. An apparent bleakness, the exposure of 'uncovered ground', precipitates a thinking 'into rhyme'. [65] The poem itself seems to enact a transformation, a reversal that may have reminded *Dial* readers of Wordsworth's 'A Slumber Did My Spirit Seal'. It is as if Taggard has unearthed Lucy, the 'she' referred to in Wordsworth's poem. Lifeless Lucy is 'rolled round in earth's diurnal course/ with rocks, and stones, and trees'; she is a thing that no longer feels.[66] In 'Letter in Solitude', the speaker's love transforms her into something akin to a corpse. She loves but in a 'prone// Dogged way, more like a stone', her love 'tempered [. . .] from the large fact of altering earth'.[67] Lucy becomes the poetic subject, turning 'frozen' feelings, what the poem refers to as 'winter-bound' love into 'rhyme'. Though the earth changes, alters and moves, she does not move with it as Lucy does. She is fixed and solidified in the poetic space of the letter, which seals though does not silence her spirit.

Opposite the last two stanzas of Taggard's poem is a reproduction, in black and white, of Vanessa Bell's *The Party*, which is also known as *Mrs Dalloway's Party* (see Fig. 6.4). Maggie Humm points to the fact that since Virginia Woolf owned this painting at one point, it may well have influenced the writing of *Mrs Dalloway*, serving as 'a visual impetus for the party scene at the close of the novel'.[68] Humm's analysis of the painting, with its emphasis on Bell's use of colour, points to the prominence of the portly central figure in black who stands in the foreground of the painting. Her large, dark, blurry silhouette contrasts with the splashes of colour around her. As with O'Keeffe's

Figure 6.4 Vanessa Bell, *The Party*, *Dial*, 83 (September 1927), 239. © Estate of Vanessa Bell, courtesy Henrietta Garnett.

painting, the black-and-white reproduction brings to the foreground what Clive Bell would refer to in relation to Post-Impressionist painting as 'significant form'. Here Vanessa Bell's sense of design comes to the fore, as well as her use of shadow and light. In particular, the way in which light falls on the central figure, on her facial profile, her arms and her ample décolletage draws attention to her flesh. This is not traditional chiaroscuro deployed to provide a sense of three-dimensional depth. Bell's use of light suggests an emotional and subjective response to this central figure. As Clive Bell would suggest in the opening remarks to the Second Post-Impressionist exhibition in London: 'We have ceased to ask, "What does this picture represent?" and ask instead "What does it make us feel?"'[69] The plunging neckline of the dress draws the eye to her breasts, as does the white flower that glows luminously in the centre of the painting. Her relatively small head and delicate features further emphasise the weight and density of her body. She looks into the eyes of the woman seated next to her, seemingly oblivious to the viewer. The bottom left-hand corner of the image shows the central figure's hand around the stem of a wine glass. Just below this, the hand of the seated woman appears holding a rose. The canvas severs this hand from the body it belongs to, signifying the cut between the rose as a symbol of heterosexual romance and the intimacy between the two women. Here is love composed differently.

While many of Picasso's nudes look steadily or even aggressively back at the viewer, Bell's figure is simply unaware of our presence. She is absorbed in the seated woman, her body partially protecting the other woman from the intrusive gaze of the viewer, her back decidedly against the male figure behind her. It is almost as if the two women are not with the other guests at the party but form their own alliance. Bell's composition invites viewers to the party yet also operates a kind of exclusion zone. The same-sex intimacy of the two women in the foreground combined with their lack of interest in other guests as well as the viewer resists the male gaze and the heteronormative assumptions that go with it.

The intimacy between the two women in Bell's painting, the pushing together of bodies within the composition, is a strategy Moore also adopts in the clusters she creates of women writers and artists in the *Dial.* Moore produces a textual intimacy between women artists, writers and critics, a collusion rather than a collision that points to the complex, heterogeneous and multiple bodies of work being produced by women.[70] Yet Moore's arrangements do more than simply draw attention to that heterogeneity; they operate ekphrastically, giving voice to the category of gender itself as an arrangement that underpins the critical construction and the marketing of modernism. These critical patterns, repeated in reviews of women's art and writing within periodical networks, enact a symbolic violence, one that reinforces the restricted field of artistic production as highbrow, intellectual, unsentimental, heteronormative, white and, above all, masculine. Gender as a form that shapes social life becomes visible as much through arrangements, patterns and clusters as through the individual items themselves.

Notes

1. Mina Loy, 'Brancusi's Golden Bird', *Dial*, 73 (November 1922), 507–8 (p. 508).
2. Caroline Levine, *Forms: Whole, Rhythm, Hierarchy, Network* (Princeton and Oxford: Princeton University Press, 2015), p. 6.
3. Ibid.
4. Sean Latham, 'Affordance as Emergence: Magazines as New Media', *MLA* (2013), https://seeeps.princeton.edu/wp-content/uploads/sites/243/2015/03/mla2013_latham.pdf (accessed 6 September 2018), (para. 4 of 9).
5. Barbara Green, 'Complaints of Everyday Life: Feminist Periodical Culture and Correspondence Columns in *The Woman Worker*, *Women Folk* and *The Freewoman*', *Modernism/Modernity*, 19 (2021), 461–85 (p. 462).
6. Sean Latham, 'The Mess and Muddle of Modernism: The Modernist Projects Journal and Modern Periodical Studies', *Tulsa Studies in Women's Literature*, 30 (2011), 407–28 (p. 416).
7. James Mussell, 'Repetition: "In Our Last"', *Victorian Periodicals Review*, 48 (2015), 343–58 (p. 347).
8. Elizabeth J. Coatsworth, 'Reflections', *Dial*, 71 (October 1921), 398.
9. Mina Loy, 'Poe', *Dial*, 71 (October 1921), 406.
10. Mina Loy, 'Modern Poetry', in *Modernism: An Anthology*, ed. Lawrence Rainey (Oxford: Blackwell, 2005), p. 437.
11. Mary Butts, 'Speed the Plough', *Dial*, 71 (October 1921), 399–406 (p. 399).
12. Ibid. p. 400.
13. Ibid. p. 402.
14. Ibid. p. 406.
15. Marianne Moore to Scofield Thayer and Sibley Watson Jr, 9 March 1925, Beinecke, ST/Dial Papers, Series IV, Box 35, Fol. 976.
16. Elise DePollier to Alyse Gregory, 6 April 1925, Beinecke, ST/Dial Papers, Series I, Box 3, Fol. 86.
17. Marianne Moore, *The Selected Letters of Marianne Moore*, ed. by Bonnie Costello, Celeste Goodridge and Cristanne Miller (London: Faber and Faber, 1998), p. 201.
18. Amanda Sigler, 'Expanding Woolf's Gift Economy: Consumer Activity Meets Artistic Production in The Dial', *Tulsa Studies in Women's Literature*, 30 (2011), 317–42 (p. 319).
19. Julia Briggs, *Reading Virginia Woolf* (Edinburgh: Edinburgh University Press, 2006), p. 34.
20. By May 1925, Woolf undoubtedly had a reputation as a writer of considerable talent but her most important work had yet to appear. More significantly, her biographical studies of unknown writers were difficult to place, as Julia Briggs points out in *Reading Virginia Woolf*. Woolf had originally planned to publish 'Miss Ormerod' in the *Athenaeum* and Briggs implies that Woolf had Ormerod in mind as a subject from 1919. In the end, it was only published in the States, first in the *Dial* and then in the American edition of *The Common Reader*.
21. Evelyn Scott, 'The Old Lady', *Dial*, 78 (May 1925), 369–97 (p. 377).
22. Ibid. p. 378.
23. Ibid. p. 379.
24. North would go on to edit *Poetry* magazine from 1936 after Harriet Monroe's death. She was co-editor with Peter De Vries from 1937 to 1942.
25. Henry McBride, 'O'Keeffe at the Museum', *New York Sun*, 18 May 1946, p. 9. Cited in Sarah Greenough, 'Georgia O'Keeffe: A Flight to the Spirit', in *Modern Art in America: Alfred Stieglitz and His New York Galleries*, ed. Sarah Greenough (Boston, MA: Bulfinch Press, 2000), pp. 445–67 (p. 450).

26. Paul Rosenfeld, 'American Painting', *Dial*, 71 (December 1921), 649–70 (p. 666).
27. Philip Hunter Drohojowska, *Full Bloom: The Art and Life of Georgia O'Keeffe* (New York: Norton, 2004), p. 218.
28. Edmund Wilson, 'The Stieglitz Exhibition', *New Republic*, 18 March 1925. Available as 'Georgia O'Keefe [*sic*] Outblazed Other Female Painters of Her Time' at: https://newrepublic.com/article/115597/georgia-okeefe-paintings-outblazed-contemporaries (accessed 7 August 2015; para. 2 of 4).
29. For an excellent discussion of Stieglitz's presentation of O'Keeffe and her work, see Vivien Green Fryd, 'Georgia O'Keeffe's "Radiator Building": Gender, Sexuality, Modernism and Urban Imagery', *Winterthur Portfolio*, 35 (2000), 269–89.
30. Wilson, 'Georgia O'Keeffe', para. 1 of 4.
31. Suzanne Clark, *Sentimental Modernism: Women Writers and the Revolution of the Word* (Bloomington: Indiana University Press, 1991).
32. Cited in Barbara Bubler Lynes, *O'Keeffe, Stieglitz, and the Critics, 1916–1928* (Ann Arbor: University of Michigan Press, 1989), p. 243.
33. Charles C. Eldridge, *Georgia O'Keeffe: American and Modern* (New Haven, CT and London: Yale University Press, 1993), pp. 172–3.
34. Georgia O'Keeffe, *Georgia O'Keeffe* (New York: Viking Press, 1976), opposite plate 55.
35. Johanna Drucker, *Theorizing Modernity: Visual Art and the Critical Tradition* (New York: Columbia University Press, 1994), p. 42.
36. Elizabeth Hutton Turner, 'O'Keeffe and Abstraction' in *Georgia O'Keeffe: Abstraction*, ed. Barbara Haskell (New Haven, CT: Yale University Press, 2009), pp. 65–74 (p. 212).
37. Moore, *Complete Prose*, p. 151; Moore, 'Comment', *Dial*, 79 (August 1925), 177–8 (p. 178).
38. Linda A. Kinnahan, 'Marianne Moore and Modern Labor', in *Twenty-First Century Marianne Moore: Essays from a Critical Renaissance*, ed. Elizabeth Gregory and Stacy Carson Hubbard (New York: Palgrave Macmillan, 2017), pp. 149–66 (p. 153).
39. Evelyn Scott, 'Nine Poems', *Dial*, 68 (January 1920), 71–6 (p. 74).
40. Nancy Berke, '"Electric Currents of Life": Lola Ridge's Immigrant Flaneuserie', *American Studies*, 51 (2010), 27–47 (p. 34).
41. Nancy Berke, *Women Poets on the Left: Lola Ridge, Genevieve Taggard, Margaret Walker* (Gainesville: University Press of Florida, 2001), p. 36.
42. Lola Ridge, 'Ray', *Dial*, 82 (February 1927), 118.
43. Nina Berberova, *Moura: The Dangerous Life of Baroness Budberg*, trans. Marian Schwartz and Richard D. Sylvester (New York: New York Review of Books, 2004).
44. Adam McKible, *The Space and Place of Modernism: The Russian Revolution, Little Magazines, and New York* (New York and London: Routledge, 2002), p. 67.
45. Ibid. p. xii.
46. Marianne Moore to Marie Budberg, 23 July 1928, Beinecke, ST/Dial Papers, Series I, Box 8, Fol. 24.
47. Marie Budberg, 'Russian Letters', *Dial*, 82 (February 1927), 119–22 (p. 120).
48. Ibid.
49. Ibid. pp. 121–2.
50. Ibid.
51. McKible, *Space and Place*, p. 77.
52. Marianne Moore to Marie Budberg, 28 September 1928, Beinecke, ST/Dial Papers, Series I, Box 8, Fol. 24.

53. Donald Pizer, 'Dorothy Dudley's Forgotten Frontiers: Dreiser and the Land of the Free', *Studies in American Naturalism*, 7 (2012), 193–206.
54. Dorothy Dudley, 'Brancusi', *Dial*, 82 (February 1927), 123–30 (p. 123).
55. Ibid. p. 124.
56. As Caroline Levine has pointed out, the controversial decision to categorise *Bird in Space* as non-art produced an event that disrupted the institutional rhythms in the legal definitions of artistic originality (*Forms*, pp. 68–73).
57. Henry McBride, 'Modern Art', *Dial*, 82 (February 1927), 172–4 (p. 172).
58. Dudley, 'Brancusi', p. 127.
59. Frances I. Wilson, 'The Shack', *Dial*, 82 (February 1927), 130.
60. Pascin was immortalised by Ernest Hemingway in *A Moveable Feast* in the chapter, 'With Pascin at the Dôme'. Ernest Hemingway, *A Moveable Feast* (London: Jonathan Cape, 1964).
61. Sibley Watson, 'Comment', *Dial*, 83 (September 1927), 269–70 (p. 270).
62. Marsden Hartley, 'In the Frail Wood', *Poetry*, 12 (1918), 195–6 (p. 195).
63. W. J. T. Mitchell, *Picture Theory: Essays on Verbal and Visual Representation* (Chicago: University of Chicago Press, 1994).
64. Bertrand Russell, 'Things That Have Moulded Me', *Dial*, 83 (September 1927), 181–6 (p. 181).
65. Genevieve Taggard, 'Letter in Solitude', *Dial*, 83 (September 1927), 237–8 (p. 237).
66. William Wordsworth, *Wordsworth's Poetry and Prose*, ed. Nicholas Halmi (New York: W.W. Norton and Co., 2014), p. 115.
67. Taggard, 'Letter', p. 237.
68. Maggie Humm (ed.), *The Edinburgh Companion to Virginia Woolf and the Arts* (Edinburgh: Edinburgh University Press, 2010), p. 129.
69. Jane Goldman, *The Feminist Aesthetics of Virginia Woolf: Modernism, Post-Impressionism and the Politics of the Visual* (Cambridge: Cambridge University Press, 1998), p. 131.
70. Debra Rae Cohen, '"Strange Collisions": Keywords Toward an Intermedial Periodical Studies', *English Studies in Canada*, 41 (2015), 93–104.

7

POETIC 'STRUGGLE' AS MODERNIST PRODUCTION

Preceding chapters have discussed Moore's editorial agency in terms of her textual interventions, her selections and arrangements as well as her critical reviews. The texts published in the *Dial* when Moore was editor have been interpreted in relation to the internal and external dialogics of the magazine, its institutional habitus and its position in the restricted field of literary production. The textual space of the magazine is a material space, implicated in the social processes of production. In many ways, as I have already pointed out, such an approach to the modernist text requires a resistance to one of modernism's most influential tropes, the text as self-contained 'verbal icon'. The following discussion reverses this approach, not in order to reinstate the aura of the modernist art object, but rather to think about the poem as a material object that requires or even initiates non-textual reading strategies. While reading modernism in the magazines transforms our understanding of how modernism became Modernism, the concern of this chapter is how the modernist poem might transform our understanding of how to read magazines.

More specifically, this chapter examines 'Struggle of Wings', by William Carlos Williams first published in the *Dial* in July 1926, a poem that was radically transformed as a result of Moore's editorial cuts. After reluctantly accepting the excision of two pages, Williams insisted this cut should be signalled by publishing the word 'incomplete' at the end of the version of the poem printed in the *Dial*. This indicated to the reader that another poem was waiting in the wings, a complete and authentic version that carried with it the seal of authorial approval. By the time the poem actually appeared in the *Dial*, however, Williams had realised that in some ways remaining 'incomplete' was desirable. He recognised, along with his most astute critics, Pound and Moore, that 'struggle [was] a main force' in his poetry.[1] When he came to republish 'Struggle of Wings' for *The Collected Poems* in 1934 he omitted the word 'incomplete' without restoring the original pages. In Williams's mind, the poem was no more incomplete than any of his other poetic works, indicating that he wished to retain a sense of the poem as provisional and contingent.

It is partly because it invokes this contingency that 'Struggle of Wings' both invites and resists textual analysis. A close reading of this ekphrastic poem points to the inadequacies of an approach that treats it as a self-contained linguistic object. The poem's use of ellipses as well as its use of space signals its awareness of itself as a visual 'design', a form of non-verbal signification. Following the requirements of the poem, I adopt an approach that might best be understood as a dialogic formalism, one that engages in close textual analysis but that supplements this by drawing on the internal and external dialogics of the magazine, together with approaches borrowed from the object-based methodologies of visual studies.

This is why I begin this discussion with an overview of the poetry Moore published in the magazine across multiple issues before analysing in detail the exchanges between Moore and Williams over 'Struggle of Wings' and the poem itself as it first appeared in the *Dial* in July 1926. Adopting both dialogic and close reading practices points to creative tensions within the magazine between what I have referred to previously in terms of a cosmopolitan aestheticism and a radical *Other*ness, between the representational and the abstract, the symbolic and the 'real' and between the verbal and the visual. Within the stable periodical codes of the magazine, the heterogeneity of the *Dial*'s content generates multiple and contingent meanings within and across issues. The modernist poem only becomes visible when read in relation to the formally conventional poems that dominated the pages of the magazine. In the still incipient stages of modernism's institutionalisation, the non-modernist poem holds in place its radical 'other' allowing readers to see the unsettled, seemingly formless poetry of William Carlos Williams as distinct from the lilting and occasionally lush effects of Thayer's tortured aestheticism or Joseph Auslander's elegiac romanticism. Bourdieu is instructive here reminding us of the importance of engaging with non-canonical as well as canonical modernisms:

> Everything inclines us to think that [. . .] one loses the essence of what makes for the individuality and even the greatness of the survivors when one ignores the universe of contemporaries with whom and against whom they construct themselves.[2]

In addition, the *Other*ness of Williams's poetry, I will suggest, was repurposed as Objectivism in the 1930s. The exchange with Moore over 'Struggle of Wings' provides an insight into the ways in which Williams was beginning to think of the process of writing as a way of seeing. According to Charles Altieri, this meant that the idea of a poem as a means of interpreting the world was giving way to the poem as 'a process of perception by composition'.[3] Though Williams was initially resistant to the cuts Moore made, he used the occasion to reflect on these processes of poetic production. He was, of course, a great admirer of Moore but he did not accept her changes simply because they came from her. This particular poem came to signify a conceptual shift for Williams, a struggle that resulted in a move away from the notion of 'no ideas but in things', a phrase that appears in the poem 'Paterson' published in the *Dial* in February 1927 to what Zukofsky described in terms of 'thinking with things'.[4] Moore's changes reminded Williams that the material circumstances of the poem's production and consumption were as much part of the poem as the creative energies that went into making it.

Moore recognised the significance of the motif of struggle in Williams's poetry when she reviewed his *Collected Poems* in 1934 in *Poetry* magazine. As she points out, 'Struggle is a main force in Williams Carlos Williams. And the breathless budding of thought from thought is one of the results and charms of the pressure configured.'[5] This 'budding' of thought is a form of pollination, the result of the poet's bee-like search for the 'flower' of representation. Referring specifically to 'Struggle of Wings', Moore suggests that in this poem 'likenesses are not reminders of the object, they are it'.[6] We might gloss this further by saying that for Moore, the poem does not represent the movement of thought, it is the movement of thought; the thing itself rather than its 'likeness'. Moore recognises the objectivist turn Williams takes with this poem as a 'pressure configured', a way of conceptualising poetic form as something capable of producing new ways of thinking.

The role of Moore as editor of the *Dial* and the role of the magazine itself in the production of the modernist poem tells us something about the 'objectivist nexus' that emerges in the 1930s with Louis Zukofsky at its centre.[7] In many ways, Moore has been written out of the history of objectivism largely because she chose not to be included. Even though her work was not closely associated with the objectivists, she continued to have an editorial influence on the second-generation modernists through her friendship with Morton Zabel, who took over as editor of *Poetry* after Harriet Monroe. In the final part of this chapter, I will briefly examine Moore's editorial and poetic correspondences with Zukofsky and Zabel and will conclude with Zukofsky's image of Moore as 'my Lady Greensleeves' in the poem *A-8*.[8] Zukofsky may have heard of Moore's splendid costume for the Bryn Mawr May Day festival in 1906 or he may simply have thought of Moore as a 'lady' emanating from another era.

Either way, he works Moore into his poem about the value of poetic labour at a historical moment when writing modernist poetry looked like a retreat from the economic crisis.

Poetry Edited

When Moore took over as managing editor at the *Dial*, familiar names continued to appear, such as Arthur Schnitzler, George Santayana, D. H. Lawrence and Thomas Mann, but Moore foregrounded the work of William Carlos Williams (who received The Dial Award in January 1927) and George Saintsbury, who was being published regularly in the *Criterion*. Moore continued to publish work in translation and led with stories by Dostoevsky and Schnitzler as well as a critical review of Honoré de Balzac by Hugo von Hofmannsthal in 1925; she led with a translation of Nicolai Lyeskov's story 'The Bear' in January 1926, two philosophical essays by Bertrand Russell in that year, together with more Lawrence and Yeats. Claims that the *Dial* had lost its 'compelling continental flavour' once Thayer had left seem unfounded when examining the contents pages of the magazine.[9] A glance at the year 1928 reveals that letters from Europe continued to be a regular feature. Raymond Mortimer took over from Eliot to produce the London letter, Rafaello Piccoli wrote the Italian letter, Paul Morand the Paris letter, John Eglinton the Irish letter, Thomas Mann the German letter and Hugo von Hofmannsthal the Vienna letter. The Spanish writer Azorin published five short stories in the *Dial* in that year while Piccoli also translated the work of the Italian philosopher, Benedetto Croce. Perhaps it might be more accurate to say that the magazine's definition of continental broadened to include more work in translation from Eastern Europe. For instance, the Bulgarian writer Angel Karaliycheff, the Macedonian-born Stoyan Christowe and the Russian writers Alexander Bashky, Alexander Kaun and Michail Prishvin all appear along with Maxim Gorky.

What is striking when surveying the headline acts in the *Dial* is that poetry occupies the privileged first slot more often under Moore's editorship than in the years between 1920 and 1925 when Gilbert Seldes and then Alyse Gregory were acting editors. 'The Two Houses', a poem by Thomas Hardy, appears in August 1921; *The Waste Land* is the first item in November 1922; and then it is not until the publication of Scofield Thayer's 'On a Crucifix' in April 1926 that the magazine leads with a poem. In this instance, given the problems that Moore and the staff at the *Dial* were experiencing with the unstable Thayer at that time, the publication of this poem might not represent or reflect any editorial trend but rather a desire to appease Thayer. In contrast, in February 1927 Moore led with William Carlos Williams's poem 'Paterson', which was reworked in Book I of *Paterson* eventually published in 1946. In August of that year, Moore also printed W. B. Yeats's 'Among School Children', though this was after she had received a letter from Yeats wondering why the *Dial* was declining his work.[10] 1928 was a bumper year for poetry: Pound won The Dial Award in 1928 so led with Cantos XXVII in the January issue, and Guido Calvacanti's 'Donna Mi Prega', translated by Pound, was the first item in the July 1928 issue. In addition, that year saw poetry by Joseph Auslander, Josef Bard, Robert Hillyer and Mikhail Lermontov also feature first. Kenneth Burke was awarded The Dial prize in 1929 for his enormous contribution not only to the running of the magazine but also for his work in translation and his groundbreaking critical reviews. His poem 'From Outside' led the February 1929 issue of the *Dial* and as we have seen, much to Moore's delight, the last issue of the magazine presented ten poems by D. H. Lawrence from his new collection, *Pansies*.

What is also striking is that many of the poems Moore published in the *Dial* owed more to fin-de-siècle aestheticism than the dislocations of modernism. For instance, Joseph Auslander's 'The Death of Adonis', headlining in February 1928, adopts end-rhymes, a predominantly regular metre and a slightly lilting romantic melody that most modernists, including Moore herself, would have resisted.[11] The poem took a long time to appear in the pages of the *Dial* perhaps because Moore liked the poem but Watson didn't. Moore had received a revised version of the poem in June 1925 and wrote to Thayer asking his opinion.[12] Though presumably he approved, the delay in publication signals a certain ambivalence. When Auslander's poem did appear, however, it occupied centre-stage.

Auslander was a graduate from Harvard, an anthologist and translator who studied at the Sorbonne between 1921 and 1922. Undoubtedly he was fully aware of the experiments with form undertaken by Pound, Eliot and Stein, but favoured instead poetic examples from an earlier age. His poem came with a dedication signalling its intimate subject matter: 'in memory of Morris Auslander, 1890–1901'.[13] Joseph Auslander was born in 1897, suggesting that Morris might have been his older brother. Whatever the personal circumstances to which the poem is responding, it is clear that the figure of Adonis represents the tragic circumstances of a life prematurely cut short. No doubt, Auslander was aware of Giovan Battista Marino's Renaissance masterpiece, *Adone* of 1623 and Shelley's 'Adonais: An Elegy on the Death of John Keats'. The theme is a familiar one, a meditation on the passage of time, the inevitable disintegration of matter, things 'blown to dust' with the turning of the seasons:

> Soon will the butterflies in cotton
> Sleep with suspended breath;
> The windfalls in the orchard rotten
> With rain mildew beneath;
> And the dead spring will be forgotten
> At length even by death.[14]

The human grief that accompanies death and loss is set against a natural world deaf to the 'sad paces' of those who mourn, blind to the wounds that inflict affective pain, somehow 'negligent' in forgetting. It seems that 'these things' that Adonis loved cannot love back, or remember or mourn; the bee is intent upon acquiring its 'golden loot', the thrush hunts arum root, the blackbird rummages and the cuckoo 'that serene ventriloquist [. . .] cannot hush'. Such things 'insist' while the speaker wonders: 'What is it we wait for?'[15] Echoes of Shelley's poem can be heard as spring returns but brings no relief from the painful experience of loss:

> Ah woe is me! Winter is come and gone,
> But grief returns with the revolving year;
> The airs and streams renew their joyous tone;
> The ants, the bees, the swallows reappear;[16]

This poem might at first glance look to be an unlikely candidate for publication in a magazine better known for its dissemination of high modernism. Yet the majority of the poetry that appeared in the *Dial*, like 'The Death of Adonis', eschewed free verse in favour of regular rhyme schemes and orderly stanzaic patterns. In this respect, Moore and Williams were unusual in using metrical variation and internal rhyming patterns. Auslander's poem is composed of twenty six-line stanzas alternating, in most stanzas, between lines of eight and six syllables. The modernisation of the myth of Adonis might be detected in the decentring of the speaking subject. Whereas Shelley's poem begins with a grief that declares itself immediately and in exclamatory terms: 'I weep for Adonais – he is dead!', Auslander begins with 'The thrush rustles last year's leaves', a much more muted and subdued opening.[17] The speaker in 'The Death of Adonis' uses a collective pronoun while Shelley's exploration of grief centres around the singular lyric 'I' as the locus of affect. Auslander's poem is inflected or maybe even afflicted with a sense of being left behind, left out, not 'in our time' as Hemingway would have it, but out of time, out of step with the present moment. Shelley's poetic diction is suffused with feeling suggesting at least the consolation of a grief fully expressed in language, whereas Auslander's mourners seem, in contrast to the cuckoo, hushed. References to the spilt blood of Adonis that clots on the broken stem of a flower, that drops like a purple diadem might remind the contemporary poetry reader of the myth of the Holy Grail that Eliot draws on for *The Waste Land*. In this myth, the blood of Christ contained in the Holy Grail offers the hope of regeneration and rebirth. Eliot's syncopated jazz rhythms, his appropriation of slang and everyday idioms as well as his use of complex literary allusion produced an image of modernity in a fractured form and a schizophrenic language. For Eliot, the lyric speaker is cut off from forms of collective experience, of mourning shared. While 'The Death of Adonis' finds no 'medicine' to cure the sickness, the fluid lines and elegant end-rhymes intimate a unity of feeling, a humanist faith in loss itself as a humanising experience.

Robert Hillyer, who occupied centre-stage in the *Dial* in June 1928, began publishing with the *Dial* in 1924 but also appeared in Harriet Monroe's *Poetry* magazine. Associated with the Harvard Aesthetes, Hillyer's 'Manorbier' owes much to the mystical tradition of a set of English writers such as Arthur Machen and Algernon Blackwood. Dedicated to 'To Mr and Mrs Arthur Machen', the poem refers to Manorbier Castle in Wales, a site close to Machen's birthplace and associated with the hauntings and supernatural disturbances that Machen explored in his writing. The ruins of the Norman castle are haunted by voices from the past. The speaker inhabits the spaces of the decaying structure, following 'the stairway/ That ends in the air' and leaning out of windows 'that have no top'.[18] The poetic persona is, like Manorbier, occupied by ghosts and histories, love stories and passions existing in an isolated spot in a wild and inhospitable landscape.

Ironically, the poet most resistant to modernist poetic forms was Scofield Thayer. Thayer's 'On a Crucifix' appeared in April 1926 as the first item in that issue. Placed opposite a reproduction of a twelfth-century sculpture of Christ on the cross, this four-part poem seems to be in dialogue with the carved simplicity of the sculpture. The reproduction itself is of such high quality that the figure of Christ seems almost to lean out of the page. Thayer's poetry appeared more frequently once he had relinquished editorial control. Moore published six of his poems in 1925, thirteen poems in 1926 and three poems in 1927 – in other words, he was published more than any other poet, a privilege owing to his status as owner of the magazine.

As Jayne Marek has shown, Moore brought Pound back to the *Dial* after Thayer had refused to publish any more of *The Cantos*. Once restored to the magazine, the correspondence reveals the extent to which, as editor of *Exile*, Pound collaborated with Moore to publish between them the work of new writers, such as Louis Zukofsky and established writers such as Max Beerbohm. Pound was also instrumental in getting Josef Bard published in the *Dial*. An expatriate Hungarian writer, Bard is best known for his novel *Shipwreck in Europe*, published in 1928, the year his poem 'Aurea Mediocritas' appeared in the magazine in the privileged first slot. Pound's generosity is evident here not just as a supporter of new writing but also as a colleague who is willing to help out, albeit with considerable grumbling, when Moore needs assistance. A good example of this is the publication of 'A Song' by Lermentov, translated and published in September 1928. Pound had written to Moore in January of that year concerning the Russian-born, London-based writer John Cournos, who worked mainly as a reporter and translator. Cournos was, as Pound pointed out, struggling to tend to his ailing wife and suffering from ill health himself. While Pound admits that this is not a good reason to publish work, at the same time he suggests that Moore might look favourably on the unlucky writer. Pound sends Moore Cournos's translation of Lermentov in February, but in April, she confesses to feeling disturbed by 'the rhythmic progress and diction' and asks Pound to look over the translation before it is published. Having suggested Cournos in the first place, Pound is then obliged to make editorial adjustments at Moore's request.

Pound introduced Moore to Louis Zukofsky and encouraged her to support the younger poet. Pound himself published 'Poem Beginning "The"' in *Exile* in 1928. Moore was less enthusiastic about Zukofsky than Pound was. As she admitted to him in 1932, she thought Zukofsky's prose style was limited, his poetry 'fluttered', but was willing to accede that he had 'the heart for the thing'.[19] As we have seen in previous chapters, it is misleading to assume that Moore's lack of enthusiasm for Zukofsky can wholly explain her editorial decisions regarding his poetry. It is likely that she rejected the first two movements of what was to become Zukofsky's epic 'poem of a life', *'A'*, in 1928 because she thought it would alienate her readers. She agreed to publish four short poems by Zukofsky in December 1928 as a compromise and to placate Pound. These poems represent an earlier phase of Zukofsky's poetic career and unsurprisingly, traces of what Mark Scroggins describes as 'Paterian aestheticism' are present.[20] Each poem serves to illustrate Zukofsky's formal dexterity, his testing of poetic techniques in free verse and sonnet form. In other words, as with the publication of Stein, the *Dial* published work by Zukofsky that was out of sync with his developments as a writer. Just as Zukofsky was emerging as a modernist poet with a distinct and radically different articulation of a modernist 'disjunctive' poetics, he was appearing in the *Dial* as a Harvard aesthete, alongside Hillyer, Auslander and Thayer himself.[21] In this instance, the magazine's mediating role meant that, while it sponsored Zukofsky as a new poet, it did so in a way that effaced his newness.

'Struggle' for/as Modern Poetry

Reading the poetry of Hillyer, Auslander and Thayer in the *Dial* reminds us exactly what it was that Williams was resisting when he insisted upon location, the everyday and the quotidian, adopting American idioms that, to many ears, sounded distinctly unpoetic. He first published in the *Dial* in August 1920 but was initially critical of what he perceived to be the magazine's European bias. Gilbert Seldes, the acting editor, had to reassure him in 1922 that the magazine paid the same rate to American writers that it paid to its non-native contributors.[22] Williams was, in the early 1920s, involved in his own publication enterprise with Robert McAlmon, launching *Contact* in December 1920 to counter what McAlmon described as the 'the slavish spirit of the Dial, the odiferous exoticism of a lot of the L R [*Little Review*]; the disciplined traditional politeness of Poetry'.[23]

While Williams and McAlmon were critical of the *Dial*, Williams regularly submitted poetry to the magazine and was published consistently under the editorial management of Seldes, Alyse Gregory and Marianne Moore up until the magazine's demise. As cummings was the unofficial *Dial* poet in the first few years of its modernist incarnation, Williams may well have been identified as the *Dial*'s poet in the latter stages of the magazine's life. Though he did not appear as frequently as Thayer did, he was awarded The Dial prize in January 1927 and then had 'Paterson' (its first incarnation) published at the front of the February issue alongside an essay by Kenneth Burke, 'William Carlos Williams, The Methods of'. Following this, the March issue contained not only three of his own poems, 'March is Light', 'Young Sycamore' and 'Lines on Receiving the Dial's Award', but also a critical essay by Marianne Moore on his work. When he wrote to Moore to praise the March issue, he also took the opportunity to point out that these recent successes served to highlight the failings of the magazine: 'the Dial is criticised about town as having no virility and having petered out. I too have felt that. The present issue has a distinction which goes well forward in correcting that somewhat justified fault finding.'[24] The implication is that the virility so sorely missing from the pages of the *Dial* has been supplied by Williams's poetry and the critical attention paid to it. By 1928, the problem for Williams was that now he was associated with the magazine, his own reputation was suffering. Writing to Pound, he complained: 'The Dial is a dead letter among the publisher crowd. It almost means that if you are "one of The Dial crowd" you are automatically excluded from perlite society as far as influence in N.Y. goes.' At the same time, Williams clearly felt that the magazine's editorial policy was tepid: 'I myself feel so disgusted with *The Dial* for its halfhearted ways that I am almost ready to agree with anyone concerning its worthlessness.'[25] The poet senses that the *Dial* crowd is no longer the 'in-crowd' in New York. Not only that, its perceived mediocrity threatens to engulf even Williams's radically experimental poetics. Further publications of 'On Gay Wallpaper', 'The Lily' and 'The Source' followed by a lengthy exposition of Williams's poetry by Pound in the November issue of 1928 and a sketch of Williams by Eva Herrmann did nothing to allay his fear that his association with the magazine was detrimental to his poetic reputation.

Williams probably persisted with the *Dial* because he recognised that his work reached a relatively large audience through the magazine. Even though it was not a mass publication, it offered writers such as William Carlos Williams access to a much wider readership. *Spring and All* had a print run of 300 and *Sour Grapes* had a print run of 600. Thus, the majority of Williams's readers would have encountered his work in the *Dial* first, rather than in one of the early collections of poems. Contradicting his own estimation of the disapproval of 'perlite society', Williams's biographer notes that 'it was only after he won the Dial Award [. . .] that his Rutherford friends began to take him seriously at all'.[26] Undoubtedly, the magazine's aura of distinction conferred at least some symbolic value on Williams's poetry as well as financial capital in the form of the $2,000 prize money, a sum that impressed his Rutherford neighbours.

While Williams was concerned about his work becoming tainted by what he saw as the *Dial*'s retrograde aestheticism, he nevertheless continued to send his work to Moore assuring Ezra Pound that 'Marianne [. . .] is never included by me in my condemnations; she is doing quietly all she can to warp things toward a better policy.'[27] His opinion of Moore as an editor was bound up with his deep respect for her as a poet. He published the poem 'Marianne Moore' in his own magazine, *Contact* in December 1920, which features 'sacks of rags' who cry, 'Marianne, save us!/ Put us in a book of yours'.[28] When Moore won The Dial prize, Williams's article praised her in terms that say much about his own poetics. Moore's poetry is characterised in terms of a 'rapidity of movement'. The long, montage poem 'Marriage' is 'an anthology in transit. It is a pleasure that can be held firm only by moving rapidly from one thing to the next.'[29] Rhythm becomes one way of conveying the movement of the mind in language as it reflects on the non-human world. Williams notes that Moore's use of rhythm 'does not interfere with her progress; it is the movement of the animal, it does not put itself first and ask the other to follow'.[30] A poem by Moore, for Williams, moves with the things it encounters, it is agile and responsive reminding the reader of Williams's own 'Poem', which follows the deliberate, careful movements of a cat. Such experiments for both Moore and Williams allow objects or animals to remain themselves while reflecting on how the mind is transformed by those things. To 'Miss Moore an apple remains an apple whether it be in Eden or the fruit bowl where it curls'.[31]

In 1927, Moore had the opportunity to reciprocate when Williams won The Dial Award. In her essay, 'The Poet of the Quattrocento', Moore was publicly supportive, but as the correspondence reveals, privately, she had considerable reservations. According to a letter she wrote to her brother, Thayer had made her write the review of Williams.[32] Clearly she was not comfortable doing this because she felt ambivalent about Williams's poetry. Almost incapable of literary falsehoods, Moore deployed a tactic she used frequently when she found herself in this position; she quoted other critical views of her subject. She begins her essay with Pound who sees in Williams a '"praiseworthy opacity"'.[33] In the subsequent discussion, she tends to veer around rather than engage directly with Williams's poetics. She cites Watson on Williams (as W. C. Blum) and Henry James as another American with a strong 'feeling for the place', but most often, she cites Williams himself. When she offers her own insights in the concluding paragraph, they are uncharacteristically clipped:

> and Doctor Williams is vivid. Perhaps he is modern. He addresses himself to the imagination. He is 'keen' and 'compact'. 'At the ship's prow' as he says the poet should be, he is glad to have his 'imaginary' fellow-creatures with him. Unless we are very literal, this should be enough.[34]

Hanging in the air in that last sentence is whether this *is* enough. Accompanying The Dial Award, few readers would have been aware that Moore's article expresses reservations, withholding as much as it praises. Williams's contemplation of 'old things, shabby things, and other things' with 'new eyes' recognises a new approach but also registers the impoverished nature of the 'things' contemplated. Williams, however, found Moore's words 'reassuring' evidently not aware of an ambivalent tone or maybe choosing not to notice.[35]

Given Williams Carlos Williams's deep respect for Moore, it must have been difficult to be on the receiving end of one of her letters of rejection. Williams submitted 'Struggle of Wings', 'The Five Dollar Guy' and 'Sadness' to the *Dial* sometime in late 1925 or early 1926. Moore's apparently belated response in February 1926 was surely not entirely welcome: 'Only today' she writes,

> am I able to ask you to allow us to return to you THE FIVE DOLLAR GUY and SADNESS; and to allow us to keep for The Dial STRUGGLE OF WINGS. Could you bring yourself to allow us to conclude with 'construe him,' omitting pages five and six; and could you approve of substituting for 'besmut,' 'besmirch'?[36]

Williams's swift response of 18 February is slightly tetchy: 'so be it', he writes.

> Print the poem as you please but allow me this: That the poem shall end at the line So I Say he shall be dressed and that after the name of the poem in your table of contents you will place the word (incomplete) in brackets as here. If this is not satisfactory to you I have no choice but to withdraw the poem. The decision is yours.

And then remembering Moore's desire to change 'besmut' he agrees to 'besmirch'.[37]

By 24 February, however, he had had time to reflect on the changes:

> I was disturbed by your request at first but I really believe you are right though the poem remains, for all that, incomplete. There should be some splitting, some tormenting of words at the end such as I attempted; I don't know what. Let it go – and again thank you.[38]

The correspondence between Moore and Williams over 'Struggle of Wings' and the subsequent revisions made to the poem reveal the extent to which for Williams, as Ann Ferry suggests, 'revision was an instrument for treating a poem as a process'.[39] He had the opportunity to recover the ending when he published the poem in his *Collected Poems* in 1934 but as Litz and MacGowan point out, he retained most of the apparatus that signals the poem's provisional status and never restored the deleted stanzas. In fact, the publication for *Collected Poems* is a little more complicated than Litz and MacGowan suggest. Williams changed the lineation and syntax in the first five stanzas, paring down in places and making some substitutions. More drastically, however, he omits entirely four lines in the middle of the Envoi as well as the final line of the poem, 'So I say he shall be dressed'.

As mentioned above, Williams also removed the word 'incomplete' when he came to publish the poem for *Collected Poems* and, in doing so, was acknowledging the provisional, unfinished nature of his poetics. Pound's critical essay 'Dr Williams's Position' in the *Dial* in 1928 observes that Williams 'does not conclude'; his work is often 'formless' yet Pound believes that this is essential to Williams's poetics:

> Art very possibly ought to be the supreme achievement, the 'accomplished'; but there is the other satisfactory effect, that of a man hurling himself at an indomitable chaos, and yanking and hauling as much of it as possible into some sort of order (or beauty), aware of it both as chaos and as potential.[40]

After reading this essay, Williams wrote to Pound: 'Nothing will ever be said of better understanding regarding my work than your article in *The Dial*.' More recently, Jay Ladin points to Williams's strategic use of the pause indicated by indentation, dashes and line breaks. 'By arranging his lines as he does', argues Ladin, 'Williams suspends rather than resolves the syntactical expectations created by each line.'[41] Embedded within Williams's poetry, within each line is a continual refusal of closure, a resistance to the idea of the poem itself as a unified, self-contained aesthetic object.

When Williams submitted poems to Moore, it was not simply the case that he was seeking publication; he was seeking her opinion. In a later exchange with Moore over the publication of extracts from *A Voyage to Pagany*, Williams was reminded of his altercation with H.D. in 1916 when he submitted the poem 'March' to the *Egoist*. He initially resisted H.D.'s extensive pruning but, as Litz and MacGowan point out, Williams retained the *Egoist* version for subsequent printings. Here is Williams to Moore, writing in April 1928 on her selection from *A Voyage to Pagany*:

> It is very interesting to me to read what you have chosen for reproduction in *The Dial*. The effect produced does not give an impression of the book tho' it does give a taste of the writing. It is, in effect, something like what H.D. did to a poem of mine many years ago. She (and Richard Aldington) edited the poem before publishing in *The Egoist*. I liked what

> they did but I have since wondered if they really knew what I was talking about. I really wish I could have the benefit of your careful reading throughout the manuscript before it goes to the printer. Perhaps you will let me submit sections of it here and there to you, sections that puzzle me, for your criticism before I let them have it.[42]

H.D. had radically revised 'March', editing out what she referred to as 'the hey-ding-ding touch running through your poem'.[43] Williams had included a parody of the regular rhythmical cadences of poems published in popular collections such as Palgrave's *Golden Treasury*. Whether H.D. misunderstood or whether she simply resisted, like Moore, the inclusion of the derogatory, what she refers to in the letter as 'flippancies', because they detract from the 'real beauty' is not known. Williams is clearly wondering whether Moore's cuts and/or her preferences are underpinned by a comparable sentiment. Many years after this encounter with H.D., Williams is faced with a similar editorial response from Marianne Moore, which he is clearly trying to decode. It is likely, however, that page space was the main issue rather than a fundamental resistance to Williams's poetics (see Figs 7.1, 7.2, 7.3 and 7.4).

As with the earlier ekphrastic 'Portrait of a Lady' published in the *Dial* in 1920, 'Struggle of Wings' appears to be describing a painting, most likely a Renaissance painting depicting the Ascension.[44] Divided into two halves, the poem imitates the representation of the heavenly and the earthly by being divided into two parts. The sky, clouds, wings and pigeon-like angels of the first half of the poem are contrasted with the ordinary and mundane aspects of the grounded experiences of the everyday in the second part. The nineteenth-century landscape painter, George Innes, is referred to in the second half of the poem, together with a fractured Picasso: 'Pic, your crows feet at your window sill/ asso, try and get near mine'.[45] While the Ascension scene itself is rendered comical, the 'drab trash' of ordinary life requires some infusion of imaginative energy, a 'grand chorus' that imbues experience with grandeur. As Robert Cirasa suggests, the poem posits 'the happy aesthetic imagination [. . .] as a potent transformational force and a serious remedy to the depressed sensibility that is the implicit audience for the final lines'.[46] Rather than reading the imagination as a remedy for the ordinary and sometimes depressing realities of everyday life, I see the poem as a tenser and evenly balanced struggle between forces equally valued.

The first ten four-line stanzas seem to follow a characteristic pattern for Williams of perception initially 'occluded' – a term signifying blockage or the prevention of anything passing through, a word which also has a chemical definition that Williams may well have been familiar with referring to the ability of a solid to absorb and retain a gas within its structure.[47] This sense of a blockage is reinforced by the dense cluster of difficult to enunciate consonants such

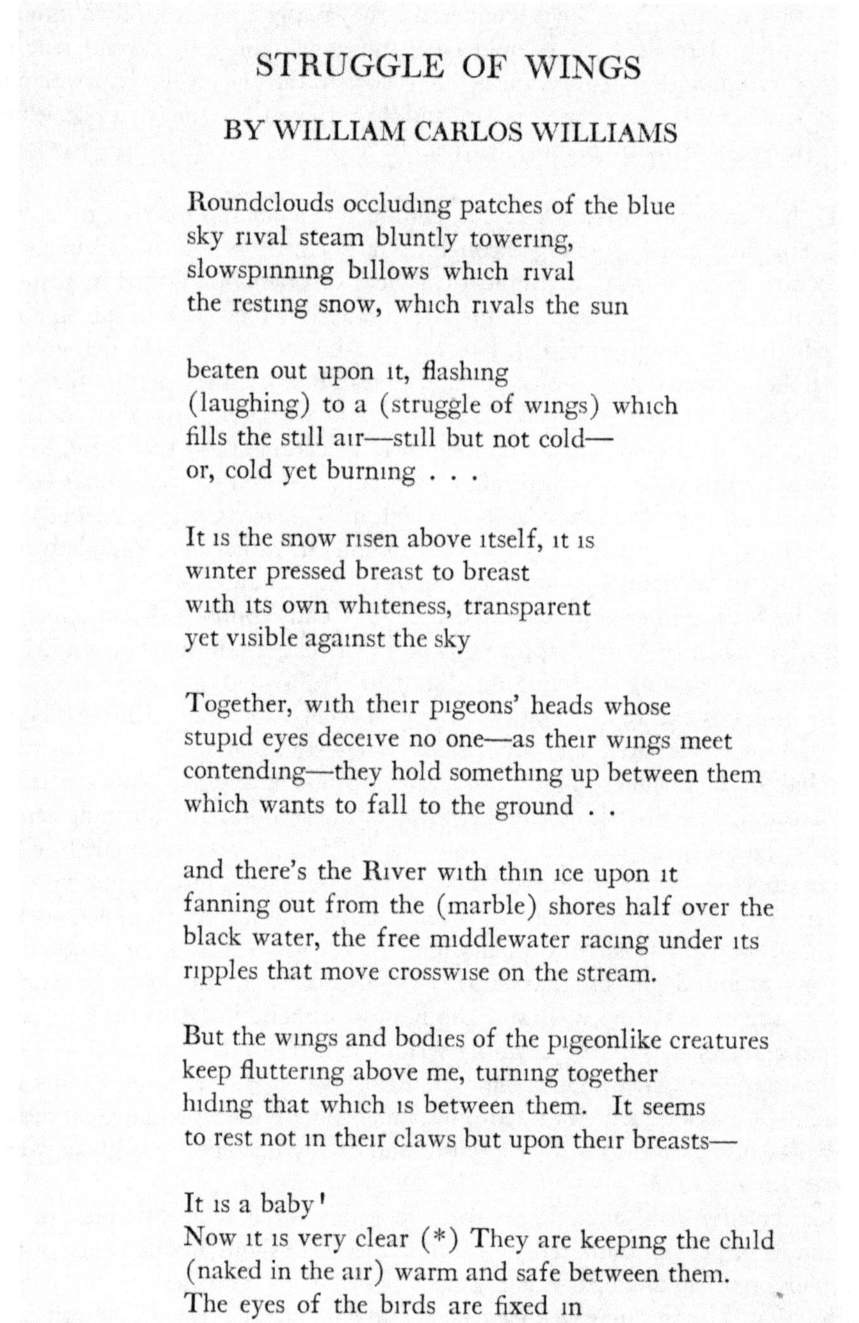

STRUGGLE OF WINGS

BY WILLIAM CARLOS WILLIAMS

Roundclouds occluding patches of the blue
sky rival steam bluntly towering,
slowspinning billows which rival
the resting snow, which rivals the sun

beaten out upon it, flashing
(laughing) to a (struggle of wings) which
fills the still air—still but not cold—
or, cold yet burning . . .

It is the snow risen above itself, it is
winter pressed breast to breast
with its own whiteness, transparent
yet visible against the sky

Together, with their pigeons' heads whose
stupid eyes deceive no one—as their wings meet
contending—they hold something up between them
which wants to fall to the ground . .

and there's the River with thin ice upon it
fanning out from the (marble) shores half over the
black water, the free middlewater racing under its
ripples that move crosswise on the stream.

But the wings and bodies of the pigeonlike creatures
keep fluttering above me, turning together
hiding that which is between them. It seems
to rest not in their claws but upon their breasts—

It is a baby!
Now it is very clear (*) They are keeping the child
(naked in the air) warm and safe between them.
The eyes of the birds are fixed in

Figure 7.1 William Carlos Williams, 'Struggle of Wings', *Dial*, 81 (July 1926), 22.

WILLIAM CARLOS WILLIAMS 23

a bestial ecstasy They strive together panting.
It is an antithesis of logic, very
theoretical To his face the baby claps
the bearded face of Socrates . .

Ho, ho! He's dropped it. It was a mask.
Now indeed the encounter throws aside all dissim-
ulation. The false birdheads drop back, arms
spring from the wingedges, all the parts

of two women become distinct, the anatomy
familiar and complete to the smallest detail
A meaning plainly antipoetical . and
all there is is won

[

It is Poesy, born of a man and two women
Exit No. 4, the string from the windowshade
has a noose at the bottom, a noose? or
a ring—bound with white cord, knotted
around the circumference designedly in a design—
And all there is is won

And it is Inness on the meadows and fruit is
yellow ripening in windows every minute
growing brighter in the bulblight by the
cabbages and spuds—
And all there is is won

What are black 4A Ms after all but black
4A Ms like anything else a tree,
a fork, a leaf, a pane of glass—?
And all there is is won

A relic of old decency, a very personal friend
And all there is is won

Figure 7.2 William Carlos Williams, 'Struggle of Wings', *Dial*, 81 (July 1926), 23.

24 STRUGGLE OF WINGS

[*Envoi*

Pic, your crows feed at your windowsill
asso, try and get near mine . . .
And all there is is won

[. . . . . . .

. . . . All
up and down the Rio Grande the sand is sand
on every hand (Grand chorus and finale)

[. . . . . . .

Out of such drab trash as this
by a metamorphosis
bright as wallpaper or crayon
or where the sun casts ray on ray on
flowers in a dish, weave, weave
for Poesy a gaudy sleeve
a scarf, a cap and find him gloves
white as the backs of turtledoves.
Make him magnificently bright
like the Little Man that's hight
Jesus Christ upon the altars
and oleochromes and sundry psalters
of his people. Cloath him
richly, those who loath him
will besmirch him fast enough.
A surcease to sombre stuff
black's black, black's one thing
but he's not a blackbird, bring
something else for him to wear.
See! he is young, he has black hair
all right then, a red vest . . .

So I say he shall be dressed

[*Incomplete*]

Figure 7.3 William Carlos Williams, 'Struggle of Wings', *Dial*, 81 (July 1926), 24.

Figure 7.4 J. J. Lanckes, *March Day in Georgetown*, *Dial*, 81 (July 1926), 25.

as 'rival', 'resting', 'round', as well as the clatter of clouds and occluding and then the pressing together of adjective and noun such as 'roundclouds' and 'slowspinning'. Here we are bombarded or, to borrow Williams's own term, 'beaten', by the skyscape, the patches of blue, the snow, the air, the steam. The use of the present participle in 'occluding', 'towering', 'spinning', 'resting', 'flashing', 'laughing' and 'burning' in the first two stanzas conveys the sense of constant motion, the restless and changing experience of seeing moving things. What then follows is the bizarre image of two pigeon heads or rather what look like two pigeon heads holding up something between them, which turns out to be a baby. This section culminates with the baby dropping its Socrates mask and the pigeons revealing themselves to be two women. The climax to this section concludes with the refrain: 'and/ . . . all there is is won'.[48]

There is then a sequence of ellipses bridging the gap between this mockingly elevated image of transcendence and the quotidian scene that follows. 'It is Poesy, born of a man and two women', the speaker suggests before turning to examine the ring attached to the cord of a window shade. We seem to now be with the insomniac poet contemplating the 'black 4 AMs' as he observes 'a tree/ a fork, a leaf, a pane of glass', surrounded by the everyday objects of modern suburban life. Here is the Williams who lingers on the seemingly mundane and familiar – the Williams who notices the parsley in a glass 'crisped green' ('Good Night'), 'the flat worsted flowers' on a doormat ('The Nightingales'), the 'gay pompoms' on his wife's new pink slippers ('The Thinker') the poet as the 'happy genius of [his] household' ('Danse Russe'). This middle section of the poem is pulled in perceptual terms by the cord of the window shade towards solid objects, what Douglas Mao refers to as the 'imperilled particular'.[49] Each of the four stanzas in this section concludes with the refrain 'and all there is is won' until the Envoi section of the poem, the mockingly titled, 'grand chorus and finale'.

The envoi continues to repeat the refrain of the poem but marks a distinct shift in form and tone away from the provisionality signalled by the use of ellipses, dashes and brackets in the previous two stanzas. This final stanza uses uncharacteristic heroic couplets. It offers an image of gaudy poesy personified as a young, black-haired man emerging out of the 'drab trash' of the preceding stanzas, a poesy 'magnificently bright', a personified youth who should be adorned in a red cloak. Though the young man has black hair, significantly he is not a blackbird. The more conventional line endings in the Envoi almost completely abandon enjambment but introduce playful, punning, textual extravagances such as 'crayon' rhyming with 'ray on', the deployment of language alien to the everyday American idiom such as 'oleochrome', 'psalter', 'surcease'. This is, I suggest, an imitation of Wallace Stevens's highly stylised poetics. The speaker's interlocution of the reader, his elegant archness echoes the speaker in a poem such as 'The Emperor of Ice Cream' (published in the

Dial in July 1922). Lines such as 'So I say he shall be dressed' and 'weave, weave/ for Poesy a gaudy sleeve' echo Stevens's: 'Let be be finale of seem' and his invocation to 'call the roller of big cigars', while the reference to the blackbird in Williams's poem: 'A surcease to sombre stuff/ but he's not a blackbird, bring/ something else for him to wear' alludes to 'Thirteen Ways of Looking at a Blackbird' first published in Alfred Kreymborg's *Others* magazine in 1917. The refrain to Williams's poem, 'and all there is is won' then seems to echo lines in stanza four of 'Thirteen Ways': 'A man and a woman and a blackbird/ Are one.' And once we have identified Stevens as a presence in the poem, the pigeons that hold the baby Poesy between them recall 'casual flocks of pigeons' sinking 'downward to darkness, on extended wings' in the concluding stanza of Stevens's 'Sunday Morning'.

Williams is also referencing his own discussion of the imagination in *Spring and All* where he compares birds with words: 'As birds' wings beat the solid air without which none could fly so words freed by the imagination affirm reality by their flight.'[50] In the prose passages interspersed between poems Williams describes the 'gap between the rigidities of vulgar experience and the imagination' and the 'sharp division [between] the energizing force of imagination on one side – and the acquisitive – PROGRESSIVE force of the lump on the other'.[51] Poetry occupies the space between these divisions, fills the gap between the 'simulations of present experience' and a form of reality that is 'actual'. The 'flight' of words releases an energy, a dynamic vitality capable of bridging the divide that separates experience from imagination.

Williams's punning refrain, on one/won signals simultaneously the 'struggle' that constitutes imaginative generation and what is won, what is gained through this struggle. Yet it also intimates a struggle for unity, for oneness that the poem itself cannot achieve, divided or split as it is between a surrealist image of procreation, a moment of close observation and a grand finale that returns us to gaudy 'Poesy', decked out in scarlet robes, who, like Jesus Christ, will soon be besmirched. As Douglas Mao reminds us, though Williams and Stevens agreed 'that the work of poetry was to lift sensible things to the imagination', they disagreed on how to do that.[52] In Williams's prologue to *Kora in Hell*, first published in the *Little Review* in April 1919, he writes:

> The true value is that peculiarity which gives an object a character by itself. The associational or sentimental value is the false. Its imposition is due to lack of imagination . . . The attention has been held too rigid . . . It is to loosen the attention, my attention since I occupy part of the field, that I write these improvisations. Here I clash with Wallace Stevens.[53]

By 1926 Stevens was publishing very little. As he explained to Moore when she asked him to submit some of his poetry, with a baby in the house he was unable to find time to write.[54] Williams has to conjure Stevens for himself in order to engage him in dialogue. And clearly at this point in Williams's poetry, 'sensible things' seem imperilled indeed. Squeezed between the surreal and the Stevensian, Williams's window shade ring, however, grips down, rather like the 'rooted' plants in 'Spring and All'. It is the centre of the poem, 'the circumference designedly in a design'. Here is an image of Williams's poetics – of the relation between reality and the imagination. In his attempt to loosen attention, to allow the thing itself its own integrity, its oneness, a struggle takes place between the 'antithesis of logic', the 'bestial', pre-linguistic, irrational sources of creativity on the one hand and the formal elegance of the Stevensian poet, an über poetic poetry that represents the 'rage for order'. Between these two 'wings' lies the 'real', the object born of creative energy and poetic precision.

Tantalisingly, Williams edits out the following lines from the version he prints in the *Collected Poems*:

> Make him magnificently bright
> like the Little Man that's hight
> Jesus Christ upon the altars
> and oleochromes and sundry psalters
> of his people.[55]

Williams's use of the archaic term 'hight', meaning named or called, suggests that the gaudy poet should be worshiped like Jesus, praised and studied. Crucially, however, he signals this omission in *Collected Poems* by leaving the space that the lines originally occupied and inserting another ellipsis; in this case, four dots. The less substantial omission of the final line is signalled by three dots at the end of the poem. Here are the last two stanzas of the version published in *The Collected Poems of William Carlos Williams*:

> Out of such drab trash as this
> by a metamorphosis
> bright as wallpaper or crayon
> or where the sun casts ray on ray on
> flowers in a dish, you shall weave
> for Poesy a gaudy sleeve
> a scarf, a cap and find him gloves
> whiter than the backs of doves
>
> . . . .
>
> Clothe him
> richly, those who loathe him
> will besmirch him fast enough.
> A surcease to sombre stuff –
> black's black, black's one thing
> but he's not a blackbird. Bring

> something else for him to wear.
> See! He's young he has black hair!
> Very well then, a red vest . . .[56]

Williams continues to reinforce the provisional nature of the poem with his strategic cuts making poetic struggle visible to his readers by signalling omission. As Anne Ferry has suggested in *By Design*, many modernists revised their work, noting as Sullivan does that there were more opportunities for them to revise their work as the publishing industry expanded. Yet Ferry observes that, unlike Pound, Eliot or Yeats, Williams was more interested in 'publicly exhibiting his revisions'.[57] In the case of 'Struggle of Wings' the proliferation of ellipses signal omissions that, in turn, signal other versions of the poem that either do exist or might have existed. The poem as it is published appears almost accidental, the result of processes, pressures and creative energies intersecting at one particular moment in time. When summarising the Objectivist turn in modernist poetry in his *Autobiography*, Williams suggested that 'the poem, like every other form of art, is an object, an object that in itself formally presents its case and its meaning by the very form it assumes'.[58] By the time Williams came to edit 'Struggle of Wings' in 1934, after Louis Zukofsky's 'Objectivist' issue of *Poetry* in 1931, he had more fully realised that this particular poem was working through the possibilities of a formal contingency capable of reflecting the mind moving between the imagination and reality. Williams had become more concerned with the poem as an object, shifting attention away from the things that the poem responded to and focusing more on the poem itself as the material effect of its circumstances. The reference to the gaudy poet as a modern-day Christ, may well have seemed in 1934 to focus too much on the creative energies of the poet rather than the energies of the poem.

'Struggle of Wings' appeared in the same issue as fellow *Others* poet, Maxwell Bodenheim. Bodenheim's poem 'Upon Her Face' shares page space with the end of an extract from Elizabeth Roberts's bestselling novel *The Time of Man*. As with Williams, Moore had agreed to publish the poem only with drastic cuts. The section published is part three of a much longer poem. Bodenheim had railed against the *Dial* in private correspondence to both Gregory and Moore and in public in the form of what Burke described as 'dark passes at the Dial' in the *Nation*.[59] He had been particularly incensed by Moore's review of his novels *Against This Age* and *Crazy Man*, published in the *Dial* in September 1924 and he wrote to her about what he described as her 'unfairnesses'.[60] She had taken a clear position against what she perceived to be Bodenheim's misogyny.[61] Bodenheim was not averse to coming into the office to 'interrogate' Moore on why, for instance, cummings was selected for The Dial prize rather than himself. It is to her credit that she dealt with Bodenheim's bullying with good humour and tact.[62]

It is surprising then that Bodenheim agreed to the changes to 'Upon Her Face', writing sarcastically, ''tis pleasant enough a miracle to see the Dial accepting anything of mine – even ten lines – and so I must not complain'. But complain he did in his final letter to Moore in January 1926 when she returned his poems:

> God, how I hate you and your mean, unfair, half-blind, apprehensively arbitrary, literary group. The Dial prints little, vaguely sneering reviews of my novels; selects a few, less rhythmical lines from my poetry, comparing them with much longer and fairly chosen passages from the work of Mr. Cummings; and rejects excellent work of mine, while lavishing acceptance and financial donations on other poets.[63]

It would be tempting to rename Bodenheim's poem 'In Her Face' for he seems to be replaying the misogynistic themes that Moore found so offensive. Bodenheim's free-verse poem is composed of two sentences in a single stanza; its use of enjambment, internal half rhymes and everyday idioms clearly signals its alignment with the free-verse revolution. It owes a debt to Pound's *Hugh Selwyn Mauberley* in terms of its content. While for Pound, culture is personified as 'an old bitch gone in the teeth', for Bodenheim 'she' is fickle, 'changing' and insincere.[64] The poem denigrates a fake, feminised culture, but it also points to the blind 'faith' of the enslaved artist who clings complacently to narrow conceptions of art. What might be perceived as sincerity, Bodenheim suggests, is simply the re-articulation of what is safe and 'snug'. The implication here is that the artist needs to relinquish this faith in a culture terminally 'unimpressed with life', in order to liberate himself and his art from convention. The figure of the tortured male writer, cruelly treated by an 'unrepentant' and 'shameless' mistress was, for Moore, a tired and sexist trope. Moore had complained about Bodenheim's 'grudging' view of women in her review of *Against This Age*.[65] She must have found it difficult to print Bodenheim's poem, albeit in truncated form:

UPON HER FACE
BY MAXWELL BODENHEIM

Ah yes, this word we call sincere
Is but the fervor of a slave
Turning his clink of chains to music
Snug within the smallness of his faith.
Her eyes are large with insincerity
Sometimes – shameless grimaces of light
Unimpressed by life
And changing from love to love
With unrepentant, searching cruelty.[66]

In the context of the *Dial*, however, Williams and Bodenheim were in a minority. This issue also features two poems by Thayer: 'False Light' and 'Jesus Again'. From a contemporary critical perspective, Thayer's poetry appears outmoded particularly when placed beside the free-verse forms of the *Others* poets. Moore was contractually obliged to accept his work and there is no doubt that if she hadn't been under this obligation, many if not all of his poems would never have been published. But they were published and as a result, they function within the pages of the *Dial*, as evidence of the persistence of a neo-aestheticism in modern American poetry.

Perhaps his most successful poem, the two-part 'Jesus Again', appearing in July 1926, is worth lingering over just to acquire a keener sense of the internal poetic dialogics of the magazine. The use of end-rhyme, the predominantly regular rhythms and the religious symbolism are in marked contrast to the quotidian themes and the everyday idioms of Williams and the biting satirical wit of Bodenheim. Yet both Williams and Thayer invoke the figure of Jesus Christ in their poems, the former in a mock-Stevensian flourish, the latter envisioning Christ as the 'twister of men's dreams'. For Thayer, as for his mentor Santayana, poetry and religion serve similar ends even as they adopt different strategies. Religion affords aesthetic pleasures; poetry offers spiritual sustenance. It is unsurprising then that 'Jesus Again' is Stevensian in tone, resonating with the meditative melancholy of 'Sunday Morning' (1915). The first section, entitled 'Rencontre Amoureuse', or 'romantic encounter', invokes the Stevensian idea of a new form of romanticism:

> I met beneath an olive-tree
> Lord Jesus Christ who died for me.
>
> He eyed me, and I smiled at him
> As girls, or flowers, or seraphim
>
> Do smile at heaven. He spoke not.
> But in my heart he straightly got
>
> And I was mighty like a tree
> Which roots in heaven gloriously.
>
> Its branches being firm in air
> Wrinkled about the sunlight there,
>
> And twisted into noble fault;
> There being in the sun more salt
>
> Than trees which should have grown from earth
> And kept to that mill-water birth

Can stomach without pain. He died for me.
And I was angry like a tree
That Jesus Christ should lonely be.

I do not know whereat he smiled
Or if indeed that heart beguiled

Gave any sign at all. He seemed.
And I awoke; and I had dreamed.[67]

The second section, subtitled 'proud blasphemy', is more 'knotted' and tightly textured indicating the shift away from the dream to a reflection on the dream. This is formally registered in the change from couplets to quatrains reinforcing the sense of a mind teasing out and working through the implications of the 'encounter'. The dominant image of weaving alludes not only to a literary tradition that relates writing to the silent signification of the weaver but also connects the poetic speaker to Thayer himself, the son of a wool merchant. Here Christ is the 'twister of men's dreams', a weaver of narratives, an artist. As the speaker passionately declares: 'You are the naked shuttle of my heart/ And weave more subtly than the mind can do'. The concluding rhyming couplet is an attempt to soar on Stevensian 'extended wings' as it weaves the materiality of the dusty earth into the transcendent realm of the spiritual: 'We are the dust wherein your shuttle plies; We are the stars, and you but light, and skies.' While James Dempsey interprets these last lines in terms of a 'resignation to the separation of the earthly and the spiritual', I would suggest that the 'tapestry of dreams' is the poem itself, which practises a 'proud blasphemy', capable of touching the divine: 'In dreams we have accosted your proud eyes/ And touched your feet, incredulous at our lips'.[68]

Thayer's poem reveals the extent to which a neo-aestheticism informed his approach to art and literature. While he does not have Stevens's lyrical dexterity, he does share his faith in poetry as the 'supreme fiction' capable of weaving dreams that can sustain the spirit. Thayer's investment in the *Dial* was not simply a financial one. He sought to bring what he described as 'the finer things in life' to the American reader in an effort to resist the pressures of 'modern industrialism'. In doing so, he not only offered an alternative poetics to Williams, Bodenheim and Moore herself but he provides further evidence of a strand of aestheticism at the heart of the modernist poetic project that found its full expression in the poetry of Wallace Stevens.

These poetic juxtapositions between modernism and aestheticism are further complicated by what Anne E. Carroll has referred to as the 'dynamic conjunctions of written and visual material' in magazines.[69] As previously argued, the *Dial* saw itself in competition with the magazines known as the qualities, yet at the same time, it set itself apart as distinct from those magazines, particularly as it presented poetry and visual images. In many magazines, poems were used to fill awkward empty spaces left by longer prose works. The *Dial* did use poems as fillers but it also led certain issues with poetry, as already discussed. In addition, unlike magazines such as the *Century*, it did not reproduce images to illustrate prose or poetry but rather presented images as art objects in their own right. For instance, the *Century* magazine published Robert Frost's poem 'Star Splitter' in September 1923. Here Frost's poem is accompanied by five specially commissioned woodcuts by J. J. Lanckes. Lanckes also provided illustrations for Frost's bestselling collection of poems, *New Hampshire* in 1923. Influenced by the Arts and Crafts movement, Lanckes did much to bring the art of woodcut into the modern art gallery. It is significant, therefore, that Moore selected a woodcut by Lanckes, 'March Day in Georgetown', to sit opposite the third and last page of Williams's poem with its gaudy 'Envoi'. The already established association between Lanckes and Frost may well have informed readers' reception of Williams's poem in the *Dial*.

Here, the first words of the last stanza, 'Out of such drab trash as this' are prominent, coming as they do after an ellipsis and occupying a fairly central space on the page. The bleakness of the wintry scene depicted by Lanckes with its protagonist bundled up against the weather; the delicate branches of the tree silhouetted against the clapboarding of the house might initially seem to point to economic rather than poetic struggles. The black-and-white image of Georgetown represents all that is drab about the metropolis with its insistent and repeated use of horizontal and vertical lines, hemming in the shadowy figure, cordoning off the solitary tree, the emblem of the natural world. The figure looks out at us from under her hat; a scarf wrapped around the bottom half of her face, assailed by the elements. The focal point of the design is the forlorn tree cut against the horizontal lines of the side of a house. One of its branches sits protectively over the bundled figure's head. At the top of the composition, smoke from a chimney rises vertically while the clouds stretch in long stringy threads repeating the lines of the pavement of the house and of the tops of the houses and chimneys. In Lancke's image, the struggle is between an industrialised landscape of manufactured structures, fences, houses, windows, doors, chimneys that circumscribe the subject's experience and the natural forms represented by the tree and the solitary figure. Lanckes's artistic method together with his themes, express a resistance to the 'age of mechanical reproduction'. His response, like Thayer's, is to adapt the archaic, to revive traditional forms to express a faith in the value of the natural world and individual subjective experience.

The alienating experience of modernity is graphically depicted in the high-quality production of 'March Day in Georgetown'. Juxtaposed with Williams's poem, it functions to downplay the representational restlessness of Williams's poem, its experimental 'struggle' with two creative forces, the surreal and the 'supreme' and its provisional yet ambitious complexity. The surreal elements of the poem, its fractured form and the built-in hesitancies recede, as does the seemingly triumphant conclusion, offering to dress the 'drab trash' of ordinary, everyday life, with the 'gaudy' colours of Poesy. The black 'surcease', the 'sombre stuff' of Williams's poem is privileged over the gaudy 'red vest' of the poet when read against Lancke's densely black figure. Perhaps more fundamentally, the juxtaposition between image and poem gives the impression of the poem as a reflection of external, economic and environmental struggles rather than the struggles of the poetic imagination.

Editorial Afterlives

In January 1929, Sibley Watson came to the *Dial* offices to speak privately with Moore about closing the magazine. Linda Leavell suggests that it was Watson who 'wanted out', while Thayer's biographer points out that Thayer's mother and his business manager, Herman Riccius, were increasingly uneasy about the cost of supporting such an expensive venture and so they were keen to relinquish what was a considerable financial burden.[70] Thayer was told of the closure in February of that year and it was agreed that the last issue of the *Dial* would be in July. Moore's expressions of gratitude to both Thayer and Watson point to the immense satisfaction she gained from working as editor of the magazine. Reflecting on the editorial experience in a letter to Thayer thanking him for bringing her into the *Dial* circle, she recognised how she had grown from her 'first timorous day in the office' and acknowledged that 'certain parts of [the job had] been the most rewarding of any [she] had ever had a part in'.[71]

When writing to her brother, Warner Moore, to reassure him that she was prepared for the consequences of the *Dial*'s closure, she pointed out that her own reputation had benefited from the association with the magazine: 'Any powers I have are not lessened by the discontinuing of the Dial. In fact I owe a prodigious amount to what its name has transferred to me of public confidence.'[72] Moore recognised that she had gained considerable cultural capital through her position at one of America's most prestigious highbrow magazines. Others recognised this as well. Morton Zabel, assistant editor at *Poetry* from 1928, had admired the reviews Moore published for the *Dial* and asked her to write something for the magazine he presided over. In 1931 Moore had been working on an introduction to a volume of essays on Pound's *A Draft of XXX Cantos* that Williams was assembling. When this project failed to materialise, she offered her essay on Pound to Zabel.[73] She would have been aware that the editors of *Poetry* held the essay in high esteem when they agreed to publish it without any cuts. It was the longest review *Poetry* had ever published.

When Harriet Monroe began to think about retiring in 1931, Pound recommended Moore as her successor. For Pound, 'Marianne has experience – quality dear to the cautious ploot. Kulchuh – more than enough. Conservatism but not absolute plantedness. At any rate I see no other successor who wd. do you honour and who is a practical proposition.' Pound also recognised that Moore would have a broader appeal than 'the wild and boisterous or cerebral younger males'.[74] Pound went so far as to ask Moore, in 1931, what terms she might accept if she were to take up the position of editor should she be offered the opportunity to do so.[75] Moore had proved herself capable of mediating between the 'wild and boisterous' and the more traditional and genteel tastes of the middle-class reader less inclined towards the experimental arts. She would also have brought with her a number of *Dial* connections; some inherited from Thayer and Watson and some she had cultivated herself, such as Gertrude Stein, I. A. Richards, George Saintsbury and Meridel Le Sueur. She had also proved capable of managing an office and maintaining cordial relations even with the most difficult contributors.

Moore was never offered the editorship of *Poetry* but she did provide editorial advice to Morton Zabel, particularly in the years immediately after Harriet Monroe's sudden death in 1936. It is ironic that the contributor causing Zabel the most concern is Pound himself, who submitted two Cantos on social credit for publication. Zabel eventually decided against publishing, but not before asking Moore for her opinion. She recognised his dilemma and made suggestions as to how to adapt the poems for publication. Her exchange with Zabel is instructive revealing as it does her editorial thought processes:

> Although The Dial's practice and my ideal of duty would lead me to counsel returning what would not be really useful to you, I naturally sympathize with an author's longing to have what he has written, appear whole. Also, I strongly wish that you might be delivered from gratuitous tribulations – the mere routine of an office is enough and too much.[76]

Moore went on to suggest that she herself pay for the printing of the two Cantos 'as a supplement in fine print perhaps'.[77] She is not entirely sure she can afford such a venture but notably, she writes that if Zabel thinks this a viable option; she need not see the material at all. In other words, for Moore it is not a question of whether Pound's work should be in print but whether it should be published in *Poetry* magazine. Acutely aware of the discursive style Monroe cultivated for her magazine, Moore recognises that Pound's poems are ill suited to publication in that venue.

Zabel clearly appreciated Moore's support. He wrote back informing her that Monroe had written to Pound two years earlier telling him that 'we could print no more of his political and vituperative cantos' and also that there were some troubling obscenities in the poems that were causing him concern.[78] Moore shifts her position after hearing further details from Zabel. Having been in a similar position as editor of the *Dial*, she helped Zabel to make the decision she thought Monroe would have made – to reject Pound, the poet who had done the most to break new ground, to promote poets like Moore herself and to support the little magazines that published modernism. After admiring 'some fine progressions' and rhythm in the submitted Cantos, Moore goes on to make a case against publishing these poems:

> Editorial obduracy is a good thing, not a bad thing and Miss Monroe's decision regarding material economies was for the good of the magazine and still remains in force. Subscribers to Poetry probably do not know about social credit, but they think they do, and unless the subject is presented in a way which they are accustomed, they will not pay attention. It is not for the good of a magazine to bombard the subscribers with what they do not know they have not read before.[79]

Here Moore puts to one side the obscenities, the quality of the poetry, the fact that she has been a 'beneficiary' of Pound's and that she has a certain loyalty to him. Instead, she considers the magazine and its regular subscribers, aware that the editor's decisions have to be 'for the good of [the] magazine'. She goes on to make a fundamental point, one that she was to make repeatedly throughout the 1930s: that poets do their best and most important work when writing poetry. A few years earlier, Moore had written to Zabel making it clear her admiration for Herbert Hoover and her lack of respect for many in the New York Democratic Party. She then concludes her political diatribe by saying, 'It would be more to the point if instead of this, I sent you a poem.'[80] Moore was undoubtedly a political animal and as an avid reader of the news, local, national and international, she was acutely aware of the dangers of indifference. At the same time, as she implies in her letter concerning Pound's Cantos on social credit, the danger of embedding the debate on social credit in the modernist poem was that the reader of poetry, unfamiliar with the complexities of that debate, might be led to think that she had a grasp of such things. The subtleties of Moore's argument are easily missed, particularly in the context of a decade where poets were required to take political sides. For Moore the danger is that Pound's cultural capital, coupled with the respectability of *Poetry* magazine, will bestow a legitimacy on Pound's ideas about social credit. To gloss Moore's rather cryptic last sentence in her letter to Zabel, readers may assume that this is the same Ezra Pound who so successfully introduced American audiences to the new poetry. In fact, as Moore is at pains to point out, this is a different Pound, one whose ideas might seem harmless in the context of *Poetry* magazine.

Moore's editorial influence, however, extended beyond Pound and *Poetry* magazine. As many critics have pointed out, she edited the work of Marsden Hartley and Elizabeth Bishop in the 1930s, offering lessons in textual compression. What remains hidden from accounts of the emergence of second-generation poetic modernism is a more pervasive sense of Moore's editorial agency as it reached beyond the pages of the *Dial* and beyond direct textual interventions. When Moore relocated to Brooklyn in 1929, she may have felt isolated as her biographer suggests, but her editorial role at the *Dial* reinforced Moore's 'distinction' as a charismatic, principled and 'pure' poet who mattered (to paraphrase Stevens on Moore), particularly in the context of economic crisis and political uncertainty.

In this context, it was all the more important when promoting the Objectivist poets that Moore's support was secured. This is why Pound repeatedly urged Moore to meet with Zukofsky, much to Moore's irritation. Writing to her brother in July 1932, she complains that even though Pound is 'very considerate and attentive' in his letter, this is the third time he has attempted to impose on Moore and her mother a social occasion they do not desire. As Moore's letters to Zabel reveal, she was not as enamoured of Zukofsky's poetry as Pound was. In a lengthy letter to Zabel in 1933, she admits Zukofsky has 'talent' but thinks that 'his term objectivism is forced'.[81] In response, Zabel gives his own low estimation of Zukofsky, of his 'wretched grammar, petulance and confused thinking'.[82] For Zabel, Zukofsky is only a poor imitation of Pound and does his 'master' a 'grave disservice' in being such an 'unabashed and conscienceless [. . .] imitator'.[83] Even though *Poetry* had dedicated a special issue to Zukofsky and objectivism in 1931, this had been largely the result of pressure that Pound put on Harriet Monroe to support the new generation of modernists emerging at the time. Moore's reluctance to host Zukofsky, however, is less important than Zukofsky's transferred allegiance from Pound to Moore.

It was Pound's continued support of Zukofsky in the 1920s and early 1930s that was to prove so important to the younger poet's career even if, as DuPlessis argues, Zukofsky came to resist a 'patriarchal structure of poetic practice'.[84] The filial attachments that DuPlessis traces in *Purple Passages* at least partly explain Moore's relative marginalisation in relation to objectivism. Where would she fit in the context of the homosocial bonds between 'spermatic poets'?[85] In 1930, suggests DuPlessis, Pound started to adopt a less paternal tone in his letters and Zukofsky resisted the role of disciple, resulting in a cooling off between the two poets. The first seven movements of '*A*' were produced as the two poets exchanged views in correspondence. By the mid-1930s Zukofsky was becoming increasingly impatient with his mentor's obsession with social credit and his anti-Semitism. It is interesting then that in 'A'-8, the poem Zukofsky writes that deals most explicitly with the themes of money, labour and the economy, he should turn from Pound to Moore, albeit in barely detectable ways.

Published in 1935, 'A'-8 is longer than all the previous movements of '*A*' combined. It is a sprawling, dialectical poem that engages directly with *Das Kapital*, as well drawing on historical accounts of conflicts between capital and labour. As Mark Scroggins notes, Zukofsky's poem has eight discrete themes: labour, Bach, economics, science, nominalism, personal history, literature and art, and the Adamses (Henry, Brooks and Charles Francis Jr).[86] All these themes are subsumed, however, under an overarching analysis of many varieties of labour. In a letter Zukofsky wrote to Moore many years later, he reveals that Moore herself makes an appearance in this poem as the figure of 'my Lady Greensleeves'.[87] He was delighted to learn that Moore was translating the fables of La Fontaine, not only because they had moved him, but also because he had anticipated her doing so in 'A'-8:

> Like and unlike whom –
> Who but my Lady Greensleeves
> Who lived so long
> And loved so long, so long ago,
> Whose sleep has no divisions
> Who played her role,
> Constant,
> Re-furbelowing La Fontaine's *Fables*.[88]

If Zukofsky's premonition of Moore's translations of La Fontaine is uncanny, so too is his image of her as 'my Lady Greensleeves'. It seems possible that Zukofsky may have been aware of the photograph taken of Moore at the Bryn Mawr May Day celebration in 1906, dressed as a Renaissance lady-in-waiting. Moore looks shyly at the camera, her hair is piled on top of her head and she is wearing an elaborate costume with a brocaded bodice, an Elizabethan ruff and the slashed sleeves that became fashionable in the sixteenth century. When H.D. wrote to Moore in 1915, she wondered whether Moore wore a green dress at the May Day celebrations (see Fig. 7.5).[89]

It seems quite a coincidence then that when Zukofsky wanted to write Moore into 'A'-8, he disguised her in the fashions of 'so long ago'. At first glance, the gendering of Moore's poetic labour as 're-furbelowing', a form of pleating or gathering of a skirt, seems to acknowledge Moore's 'constant' work but only in terms that limit its scope to the private, feminised sphere of domestic labour. Yet the poem also acknowledges that Moore 'played her role,/ constant'. Zukofsky's image of Moore as 'my Lady Greensleeves' at some level recognises the performative aspects of 'Miss Moore', the ways in which her work has been bound up with a fetishised image of poetic purity, one that effaces the labour of creative production. At the same time, Zukofsky gets himself caught up in the skirts of his own poetic image. While 'my Lady Greensleeves' represents the poet's work as a form of unalienated labour, it also transfers that labour to a fabled and timeless realm seemingly untouched by historical pressures.

A similar effect is evident in critical assessments of Moore's editorial role at the *Dial*. The institutional power Moore wielded at the *Dial*, the transgres-

Figure 7.5 *Marianne Moore on May Day, 1906.*

sive authority she practised as an editor has been effaced by the fetishised and feminised image of 'Miss Moore' as a 'beacon of literary value' or conversely, a 'hysterical virgin'. At the same time, as I have suggested in this book, as the editor of the most influential modernist magazine of the 1920s, one which successfully mediated between the avant-garde and quality magazine markets, 'Miss Moore' accrued considerable cultural authority. To adapt Moore's own words from the poem 'Marriage', as an editor she had institutional power and sometimes others were made to feel it.[90]

When Moore returned to writing poetry in the 1930s, she had acquired the textual imprimatur of the modernist author; her name had become inextricably linked to the highbrow magazine she edited. In 1920, in order to adapt to what she perceived to be the requirements of the *Dial*, Moore abandoned her syllabic stanzas in favour of the free-verse montage poems that at least looked a little more like the other poems being published in that venue. In 1932, with what she referred to as the 'public confidence' that came with editing the *Dial*, Moore returned to syllabics, publishing the triptych 'Part of a Novel, Part of a Poem, Part of a Play' in *Poetry* magazine and 'The Jerboa' in the *Hound and Horn*. Moore may have felt that appearing in smaller literary magazines required her to make fewer adjustments for readers who expected innovation. This is not to say, however, that Moore's post-*Dial* poems are somehow more authentic than the free-verse poems, but rather to assert the materiality of all poems. Moore's creative response to the constraints of the *Dial*, as both a poet and an editor, reveal the extent to which they might be viewed as part of the compositional process itself. Particularly in the context of modernism where compression is often the desired effect, such limitations proved to be expedient and for Moore, often pleasurable.

As we have seen, not all contributors shared Moore's predilection for contractility but those who did, such as Kenneth Burke, recognised the 'ingenuities' of her editorial method. It is worth leaving Burke with the last word on 'Miss Moore':

> You taught me much. When I was at The Dial during your editorship, you brought me to see things that I had never seen before and in all probability might never have seen otherwise. Whatever my coarseness (and we gotta live!) I can always pride myself on the fact that I was at least refined enough to be entranced by my glimpses of your refined ingenuities. And in this sense, to the best of my ability, you taught me.[91]

Notes

1. Moore, *Complete Prose*, p. 325; Moore, '"Things Others Never Notice"', *Poetry*, 44 (May 1934), 103–6 (p. 103).
2. Pierre Bourdieu, *The Rules of Art: Genesis and Structure of the Literary Field*, trans. Susan Emanuel (Cambridge: Polity Press, 1996, 2017), 70.
3. Charles Altieri, 'The Objectivist Tradition', in *The Objectivist Nexus: Essays in Cultural Poetics*, ed. Rachel Blau DuPlessis and Peter Quartermain (Tuscaloosa: University of Alabama Press, 1999), pp. 25–36 (p. 33).
4. Louis Zukofsky, 'Sincerity and Objectification with Special Reference to the Work of Charles Reznikoff', in *The Objectivist Nexus*, ed. DuPlessis and Quartermain, p. 26 (first publ. in *Poetry*, 37 (1931), 272–85).
5. Moore, *Complete Prose*, p. 325; Moore, '"Things"', p. 103.
6. Moore, *Complete Prose*, p. 326; Moore, '"Things"', p. 105.
7. DuPlessis and Quartermain, *The Objectivist Nexus*.
8. Louis Zukofsky, *'A'* (New York: New Directions, 2011), p. 65.
9. Jack Selzer, *Kenneth Burke in Greenwich Village: Conversing with the Moderns* (Madison: University of Wisconsin Press, 1996), pp. 135–6.
10. On 16 March 1926, Moore had asked Yeats to write a regular Dublin letter for the *Dial*. He declined but took the opportunity to ask Moore why she had refused his poems for publication. (W. B. Yeats to Marianne Moore, 23 April 1926, Beinecke,

ST/Dial Papers, Series I, Box 8, Fol. 300). Moore's response is rather contradictory. She finds that some of the poems submitted were more pleasing than others and not wanting to break up the group, Moore decided to refuse them all. (Marianne Moore to W. B. Yeats, 7 May 1926, Beinecke, ST/Dial Papers, Series I, Box 8, Fol. 300.)

11. For a fascinating discussion of Hillyer's involvement in the controversy surrounding the decision to award Pound the Bollingen prize in 1949 and Auslander blocking William Carlos Williams's appointment as poet laureate in 1952, see Karen Leick, 'Ezra Pound vs. The Saturday Review of Literature', *Journal of Modern Literature*, 25 (2001–2), 19–37.
12. Marianne Moore to Scofield Thayer, 29 June 1925. ST/Dial Papers, Beinecke, Series IV, Box 35, Fol. 978.
13. Joseph Auslander, 'The Death of Adonis', *Dial*, 84 (January 1928), 91–4 (p. 91).
14. Ibid. p. 94.
15. Ibid. pp. 91–2, 94.
16. Shelley, P. B., *Percy Bysshe Shelley: Poems and Prose*, ed. Timothy Webb (London: Everyman, 1995), pp. 281–96 (p. 281).
17. Auslander, 'Death of Adonis', p. 91.
18. Robert Hillyer, 'Manorbier', *Dial*, 84 (June 1928), 451–5 (p. 453).
19. Marianne Moore, *The Selected Letters of Marianne Moore*, ed. by Bonnie Costello, Celeste Goodridge and Cristanne Miller (London: Faber and Faber, 1998), p. 290.
20. Mark Scroggins, *The Poem of a Life: A Biography of Louis Zukofsky* (Berkeley: Shoemaker Hoard, 2007), p. 33.
21. Peter Quartermain, *Disjunctive Poetics: From Gertrude Stein and Louis Zukofsky to Susan Howe* (Oxford: Oxford University Press (1992).
22. Gilbert Seldes to William Carlos Williams, 17 November 1922, Beinecke/ST Dial Papers, Series I, Box 8 Fol. 280.
23. Cited from Eric White, 'In the American Grain: *Contact* (1920–3, 1932) and *Pagany: A Native Quarterly* (1930–3)', in *The Oxford Critical and Cultural History of Modernist Magazines, Vol. II: North America, 1894–1960*, ed. Peter Brooker and Andrew Thacker (Oxford: Oxford University Press, 2012), pp. 249–70 (p. 251).
24. William Carlos Williams to Marianne Moore, 20 December 1927, Beinecke, ST/ Dial Papers, Series I, Box 8, Fol. 285.
25. William Carlos Williams, *The Selected Letters of William Carlos Williams*, ed. John C. Thirlwall (New York: New Directions, 1957), p. 103.
26. Paul Mariani, *William Carlos Williams: A New World Naked* (New York: McGraw-Hill, 1981), p. 138.
27. Williams, *Selected Letters*, p. 103.
28. William Carlos Williams, *William Carlos Williams: Collected Poems I 1909–1939*, ed. A. Walton Litz and Christopher MacGowan (Manchester: Carcanet), p. 129.
29. William Carlos Williams, 'Marianne Moore', *Dial*, 78 (May 1925), 393–410 (p. 395).
30. Ibid. p. 397.
31. Ibid. pp. 395, 397.
32. Moore, *Selected Letters*, p. 235.
33. Moore, *Complete Prose*, p. 144; Moore, 'A Poet of the Quattrocento', *Dial*, 82 (March 1927), 213–15 (p. 213).
34. Moore, *Complete Prose*, p. 146; Moore, 'A Poet', p. 215.
35. William Carlos Williams to Marianne Moore, 20 December 1927, Beinecke, ST/ Dial Papers, Series I, Box 8, Fol. 284.
36. Marianne Moore to William Carlos Williams, 16 February 1926, Beinecke, ST/ Dial Papers, Series I, Box 8, Fol. 283.

37. William Carlos Williams to Marianne Moore, 18 February 1926, Beinecke, ST/Dial Papers, Series I, Box 8, Fol. 283.
38. William Carlos Williams to Marianne Moore, 24 February 1926, Beinecke, ST/Dial Papers, Series I, Box 8, Fol. 283.
39. Ann Ferry, *By Design: Intention in Poetry* (Stanford: Stanford University Press, 2008), p. 132.
40. Ezra Pound, 'Dr Williams's Position', *Dial*, 85 (November 1928), 395–404 (p. 402).
41. Jay Ladin, 'Breaking the Line: Emily Dickinson and William Carlos Williams', *Emily Dickinson Journal*, 3 (1994), 41–58 (p. 52).
42. William Carlos Williams to Marianne Moore, 9 April 1928, Beinecke, ST/Dial Papers, Series I, Box 8, Fol. 286.
43. Williams, *Collected Poems I*, p. 493.
44. I would like to thank colleagues at the University of York for their generous and helpful suggestions regarding this poem.
45. William Carlos Williams, 'Struggle of Wings', *Dial*, 81 (July 1926), 22–4 (p. 24).
46. Robert J. Cirasa, *The Lost Works of William Carlos Williams: The Volumes of Collected Poetry as Lyrical Sequences* (Madison, NJ: Fairleigh Dickinson University Press, 1995), p. 53.
47. Ibid. p. 22.
48. Ibid. p. 23.
49. Douglas Mao, *Solid Objects: Modernism and the Test of Production* (Princeton: Princeton University Press, 1998), p. 7.
50. Williams, *Collected Poems I*, p. 235.
51. Ibid. p. 220.
52. Mao, *Solid Objects*, p. 230.
53. William Carlos Williams, *Kora in Hell: Improvisations* (Boston, MA: Four Seas Company, 1920), p. 16. Available at: https://www.gutenberg.org/files/56681/56681-h/56681-h.htm (accessed 4 September 2018).
54. Wallace Stevens to Marianne Moore, 19 November 1925, Beinecke, ST/Dial Papers, Series I, Box 7, Fol. 237.
55. Williams, 'Struggle', p. 24.
56. Williams, *Collected Poems I*, p. 262.
57. Ferry, *By Design*, p. 132.
58. DuPlessis and Quartermain, *The Objectivist Nexus*, p. 3.
59. Kenneth Burke to Scofield Thayer, 23 June 1923, Beinecke, ST/Dial Papers, Series IV, Box 29, Fol. 765.
60. Maxwell Bodenheim to Marianne Moore, 29 June 1925, Beinecke, ST/Dial Papers, Series I, Box 1, Fol. 20.
61. For a discussion of this review, see Victoria Bazin, *Marianne Moore and the Cultures of Modernity* (Burlington, VT: Ashgate Publishing Company, 2010), pp. 58–59.
62. Marianne Moore to Monroe Wheeler, 3 January 1926. NYPL, Berg, MM Papers, Manuscript Box, Fol. 6.
63. Maxwell Bodenheim to Marianne Moore, 20 January 1926, Beinecke, ST/Dial Papers, Series I, Beinecke, Box 1, Fol. 20.
64. Maxwell Bodenheim, 'Upon Her Face', *Dial*, 81 (July 1926), 41.
65. Moore, *Complete Prose*, p. 104; Moore, 'Thistles Dipped in Frost', *Dial*, 77 (September 1924), 251–6 (p. 252).
66. Bodenheim, 'Upon Her Face', p. 41.
67. Scofield Thayer, 'Jesus Again', *Dial*, 81 (July 1926), 59–60 (p. 59).
68. James Dempsey, *The Tortured Life of Scofield Thayer* (Gainesville: University Press of Florida, 2014), p. 200.

69. Anne E. Carroll, 'Protest and Affirmation: Composite Texts in the *Crisis*', *American Literature*, 76 (2004), 89–116 (p. 89).
70. Linda Leavell, *Holding On Upside Down: The Life and Work of Marianne Moore* (New York: Farrar, Straus and Giroux, 2013), p. 246; Dempsey, *Tortured Life*, p. 177.
71. Dempsey, *Tortured Life*, p. 178.
72. Leavell, *Holding On*, p. 247.
73. Ibid. p. 258.
74. Ezra Pound, *The Letters of Ezra Pound, 1907–1941*, ed. D. D. Paige (London: Faber and Faber, 1950), p. 315.
75. Ezra Pound to Marianne Moore, 26 November 1931, RML Series V, Box 50, Fol. 6.
76. Marianne Moore to Morton Zabel, 27 October 1936, RML, Series V, Box 79, Fol. 29.
77. Ibid.
78. Morton Zabel to Marianne Moore, 30 October 1936, RML, Series V, Box 79, Fol. 29.
79. Marianne Moore to Morton Zabel, 18 November 1936, RML, Series V, Box 79, Fol. 29.
80. Marianne Moore to Morton Zabel, 22 February 1933, RML, Series V, Box 79, Fol. 29.
81. Marianne Moore to Morton Zabel, 14 March 1933, RML, Series V, Box 79, Fol. 29.
82. Morton Zabel to Marianne Moore, 19 March 1933, RML, Series V, Box 79, Fol. 29.
83. Ibid.
84. Rachel Blau DuPlessis, *Purple Passages: Pound, Eliot, Zukofsky, Olson, Creeley, and the Ends of Patriarchal Poetry* (Iowa City: University of Iowa Press, 2012), p. 72.
85. Ibid. p. 63.
86. Scroggins, *Poem of a Life*, pp. 176–7.
87. Louis Zukofsky to Marianne Moore, 7 October 1948, RML, Series V, Box 79, Fol. 36.
88. Zukofsky, '*A*', p. 65.
89. Patricia Willis, 'Marianne Moore on May Day, 1906', *Marianne Moore Newsletter*, 5 (1981), 21.
90. Marianne Moore, *Becoming Marianne Moore: The Early Poems, 1907–1924*, ed. Robin G. Schulze (Berkeley, Los Angeles, London: University of California Press, 2002), p. 301.
91. Kenneth Burke to Marianne Moore, 12 April 1957, RML, Series V, Box 08, Fol. 22.

BIBLIOGRAPHY

Aldington, Richard, 'Review of Observations', *Criterion*, 3 (1924), 588–94.

'Against the Faux Bon', *London Mercury*, July 1926, *Program Magazine*, 23 October 1926, 25 October 1926, the *Arts*, September 1926, the *Modern Quarterly,* May 1926, *Harpers Magazine*, December 1926, the *Arts*, March 1927, April 1927, February 1928, *Oriental Magazine*, February 1927, the *Arts*, August 1927, September 1928, *Virginia Quarterly Review*, October 1927, *Creative Art*, February 1928, April 1928, July 1928, Beinecke, ST/Dial Papers, Series II, Box 17, Fol. 345.

'Aloofness from Affairs of the Mart', *Minneapolis Tribune*, 7 June 1929, Beinecke, ST/Dial Papers, Series II, Box 9, Fol. 306.

Altieri, Charles, 'The Objectivist Tradition', in *The Objectivist Nexus: Essays in Cultural Poetics*, ed. Rachel Blau DuPlessis and Peter Quartermain (Tuscaloosa: University of Alabama Press, 1999), pp. 25–36.

Ardis, Ann, 'Staging the Public Sphere: Magazine Dialogism and the Prosthetics of Authorship at the Turn of the Twentieth Century', in *Transatlantic Print Culture, 1880–1940: Emerging Media, Emerging Modernisms*, ed. Ann Ardis and Patrick Collier (Basingstoke: Macmillan, 2008), pp. 30–47.

Ardis, Ann, 'Editor's Introduction Mediamorphosis: Print Culture and Transatlantic/Transnational Public Sphere(s)', *Modernism/Modernity*, 19 (2012), v–vii.

Ashton, Jennifer, 'Gertrude Stein for Anyone', *ELH*, 64 (1997), 289–311.

'The *Atlantic Monthly*', *Dial*, 7 (October 1924), Beinecke, ST/Dial Papers, Series II, Box 9, Fol. 308.

Auslander, Joseph, 'The Death of Adonis', *Dial*, 84 (January 1928), 91–4.

Barnes, Djuna, 'To the Dead Favourite of Liu Ch'e', *Dial*, 68 (April 1920), 444.

Bazin, Victoria, *Marianne Moore and the Cultures of Modernity* (Burlington, VT: Ashgate Publishing Company, 2010).

Berberova, Nina, *Moura: The Dangerous Life of Baroness Budberg*, trans. Marian Schwartz and Richard D. Sylvester (New York: New York Review of Books, 2004).

Berke, Nancy, '"Electric Currents of Life": Lola Ridge's Immigrant Flaneuserie', *American Studies*, 51 (2010), 27–47.

Berke, Nancy, *Women Poets on the Left: Lola Ridge, Genevieve Taggard, Margaret Walker* (Gainesville: University Press of Florida, 2001).

Binckes, Faith, *Modernism, Magazines, and the British Avant-Garde: Reading Rhythm, 1910–1914* (Oxford: Oxford University Press, 2010).

Bishop, Edward, 'Re-Covering Modernism: Format and Function in the Little Magazines', in *Modernist Writers and the Marketplace*, ed. Ian Willison, Warwick Gould and Warren Chernaik (London: Macmillan, 1996), pp. 287–319.

Blondel, Nathalie, *Mary Butts: Scenes from the Life: A Biography* (New York: McPherson & Co., 1998).

Bodenheim, Maxwell, 'Modern Poetry', *Dial*, 68 (January 1920), 95–8.

Bodenheim, Maxwell, 'Upon Her Face', *Dial*, 81 (July 1926), 41.

Bornstein, George, *Material Modernism: The Politics of the Page* (Cambridge: Cambridge University Press, 2006), p. 117.

Boroff, Marie, *Language and the Poet: Verbal Artistry in Frost, Stevens, and Moore* (Chicago: University of Chicago Press, 1979).

Bourdieu, Pierre, *Distinction: A Social Critique of the Judgement of Taste*, trans. Richard Nice (London: Routledge and Kegan Paul, 1979).

Bourdieu, Pierre, *Masculine Domination*, trans. Richard Nice (Oxford: Polity Press, 2001).

Bourdieu, Pierre, *Pierre Bourdieu, The Field of Cultural Production: Essays on Art and Literature*, ed. Randal Johnson (Oxford: Polity Press, 1993).

Bourdieu, Pierre, *The Rules of Art: Genesis and Structure of the Literary Field*, trans. Susan Emanuel (Cambridge: Polity Press, 1996, 2017).

Boyd, Ernest, 'Aesthete: Model 1924', *American Mercury*, January (1924), 51–6.

Briggs, Julia, *Reading Virginia Woolf* (Edinburgh: Edinburgh University Press, 2006).

Britzolakis, Christina, 'Making Modernism Safe for Democracy', in *The Oxford Critical and Cultural History of Modernist Magazines, Vol. II:*

North America, 1894–1960, ed. Peter Brooker and Andrew Thacker (Oxford: Oxford University Press, 2012), pp. 85–102.

Brodhead, Richard, *Culture of Letters Scenes of Reading and Writing in Nineteenth Century America* (Chicago: University of Chicago Press, 1993).

Brogger, Frederick, 'Grinding the Gears of Production and Consumption: Representational vs. Nonrepresentational Advertising for Automobiles in the Mid-1920s', *Prospects*, 15 (1990), 197–224.

Brooker, Peter and Andrew Thacker (eds), *The Oxford Critical and Cultural History of Modernist Magazines, Vol. II: North American 1894–1960* (Oxford: Oxford University Press, 2012).

Brooker, Peter and Andrew Thacker (eds), 'Editors and Programmes', in *The Oxford Critical and Cultural History of Modernist Magazines, Vol. I: Britain and Ireland, 1880–1955*, ed. Peter Brooker and Andrew Thacker (Oxford: Oxford University Press, 2013), pp. 339–45.

Brown, Richard, *A Companion to James Joyce*, ed. Richard Brown (Chichester: Wiley-Blackwell, 2008).

Budberg, Marie, 'Russian Letters', *Dial*, 82 (February 1927), 119–22.

Burke, Carolyn, 'Getting Spliced: Modernism and Sexual Difference', *American Quarterly*, 239 (1987), 98–121.

Butler, Judith, *Excitable Speech: A Politics of the Performative* (New York and London: Routledge, 1997).

Butts, Mary, 'Speed the Plough', *Dial*, 71 (October 1921), 399–406.

Carroll, Anne E., 'Protest and Affirmation: Composite Texts in the *Crisis*', *American Literature*, 76 (2004), 89–116.

Cecire, Natalia, 'Marianne Moore's Precision', *Arizona Quarterly: A Journal of American Literature, Culture and Theory*, 67 (2011), 83–110.

Cecire, Natalia, 'Ways of Not Reading Gertrude Stein', *ELH*, 82 (2015), 280–98.

Churchill, Suzanne and Ethan Jaffee, 'The New Poetry: *Glebe* (1913–14); *Others* (1915–19); *Poetry Review of America* (1916–17)', in *The Oxford Critical and Cultural History of Modernist Magazines, Vol. II: North American 1894–1960*, ed. Peter Brooker and Andrew Thacker (Oxford: Oxford University Press, 2012), pp. 299–319.

Churchill, Suzanne, *The Little Magazine Others and the Renovation of Modern American Poetry* (Burlington, VT: Ashgate, 2006).

Cirasa, Robert J. (ed.), *The Lost Works of William Carlos Williams: The Volumes of Collected Poetry as Lyrical Sequences* (Madison, NJ: Fairleigh Dickinson University Press, 1995).

Clark, Suzanne, *Sentimental Modernism: Women Writers and the Revolution of the Word* (Bloomington: Indiana University Press, 1991).

Coatsworth, Elizabeth J., 'Reflections', *Dial*, 71 (October 1921), 398.

Cohen, Debra Rae, '"Strange Collisions": Keywords Toward an Intermedial Periodical Studies', *English Studies in Canada*, 41 (2015), 93–104.

Collier, Patrick, 'Imperial/Modernist Forms in *The Illustrated London News*', *Modernism/Modernity*, 19 (2013), 487–514.

Costello, Bonnie, '"To a Snail": A Lesson in Compression', *Marianne Moore Newsletter*, 3 (1979), 11–15.

Costello, Bonnie, 'Marianne Moore and Elizabeth Bishop: Friendship and Influence', *Twentieth Century Literature*, 30 (1984), 130–49.

Crane, Hart, 'Again', *Dial*, 80 (May 1926), 370.

Crane, Hart, *The Letters of Hart Crane, 1916–1932*, ed. Brom Weber (Berkeley: University of California Press, 1965).

Crane, Hart, 'My Grandmother's Love Letters', *Dial*, 68 (April 1920).

cummings, e. e., *Selected Letters of e. e. cummings*, ed. F. W. Dupee and George Stade (London: Andre Deutsch, 1972).

Dempsey, James, *The Tortured Life of Scofield Thayer* (Gainesville: University Press of Florida, 2014).

Dettmar, J. H. and Stephen Watt (eds), *Marketing Modernisms: Self-Promotion, Canonization, and Rereading* (Ann Arbor: University of Michigan Press, 1997).

'Disappearance of the Dial', *Nation*, 19 June 1929, Beinecke, ST/Dial Papers, Series II, Box 17, Fol. 346.

Drohojowska, Philip Hunter, *Full Bloom: The Art and Life of Georgia O'Keeffe* (New York: Norton, 2004).

Drucker, Johanna, *Theorizing Modernity: Visual Art and the Critical Tradition* (New York: Columbia University Press, 1994).

Dudley, Dorothy, 'Brancusi', *Dial*, 82 (February 1927), 123–30.

DuPlessis, Rachel Blau, *Purple Passages: Pound, Eliot, Zukofsky, Olson, Creeley, and the Ends of Patriarchal Poetry* (Iowa City: University of Iowa Press, 2012).

DuPlessis, Rachel Blau and Peter Quartermain (eds), *The Objectivist Nexus: Essays in Cultural Poetics* (Tuscaloosa: Alabama University Press, 1999).

Earle, David M., *Re-Covering Modernism: Pulps, Paperbacks, and the Prejudice of Form* (Burlington, VT: Ashgate, 2009).

Edwards, Paul and Jane Beckett, *Blast: Vorticism, 1914–1918* (Burlington, VT: Ashgate, 2000).

Eldridge, Charles C., *Georgia O'Keeffe: American and Modern* (New Haven, CT and London: Yale University Press, 1993).

Eliot, T. S., 'Observations', *Egoist*, May (1918), 69–70.

Eliot, T. S. (ed.), *The Selected Poems of Marianne Moore* (London: Faber and Faber, 1935).

Erkilla, Betsy, 'Elizabeth Bishop and Marianne Moore: The Dynamics of Female Influence', in *Marianne Moore: Woman and Poet*, ed. Patricia C. Willis (Orono, ME: National Poetry Foundation, 1990), pp. 335–50.

Esdale, Logan, 'The Saintsbury Years of Marianne Moore', *Textual Cultures: Texts, Contexts, Interpretations*, 5 (2010), 46–75.

'An Exit from the Marketplace' (advertisement), *New Republic*, 12 August 1925, Beinecke, ST/Dial Papers, Series II, Box 17, Fol. 345.

Feldman, Jessica R., *Victorian Modernism: Pragmatism and the Varieties of Aesthetic Experience* (Cambridge: Cambridge University Press, 2002).

Ferry, Ann, *By Design: Intention in Poetry* (Stanford, CA: Stanford University Press, 2008).

Francis, Elizabeth, *The Secret Treachery of Words: Feminism and Modernism in America* (Minneapolis: University of Minnesota Press, 2002).

Freedman, Jonathan, *Professions of Taste: Henry James, British Aestheticism and Commodity Culture* (Stanford, CA: Stanford University Press, 1993).

Fryd, Vivien Green, 'Georgia O'Keeffe's "Radiator Building": Gender, Sexuality, Modernism and Urban Imagery', *Winterthur Portfolio*, 35 (2000), 269–89.

Gerogiannis, Nicholas (ed.), *The Complete Poems of Ernest Hemingway* (Lincoln: University of Nebraska Press, 1992).

Gilman, Benjamin Ives, *Museum Ideals of Purpose and Method* (Cambridge and Boston, MA: Boston Museum of Fine Arts, 1918).

Goldberg, David J., *Discontented America: The United States in the 1920s* (Baltimore, MD: Johns Hopkins University Press, 1999).

Golding, Alan, '*The Dial*, *The Little Review*, and the Dialogics of Modernism', *American Periodicals: A Journal of History, Critics and Bibliography*, 15 (2005), 42–55.

Golding, Alan, 'The *Little Review* (1914–29)' in *The Oxford Critical and Cultural History of Modernist Magazines, Vol. II: North America, 1894–1960*, ed. Peter Brooker andAndrew Thacker (Oxford: Oxford University Press, 2012), pp. 63–85.

Goldman, Jane, *The Feminist Aesthetics of Virginia Woolf: Modernism, Post-Impressionism and the Politics of the Visual* (Cambridge: Cambridge University Press, 1998).

Goodridge, Celeste, *Hints and Disguises: Marianne Moore and Her Contemporaries* (Iowa City: University of Iowa Press, 1989).

Goodridge, Celeste, 'Towards a Poetics of Disclosure: Marianne Moore and Henry James', *Sagetrieb*, 6 (1987), 31–43.

Graham, Vicki, '"The Power of the Visible": Marianne Moore and the "Mimetic Faculty"' *Sagetrieb*, 12 (1993), 33–50.

Graves, Robert and Laura Riding, *A Survey of Modernist Poetry* (London: William Heinemann, 1927).

'Great Merit', *New York Times*, 31 May 1929, Beinecke, ST/Dial Papers, Series II, Box 17, Fol. 34.

Green, Barbara, 'Complaints of Everyday Life: Feminist Periodical Culture and Correspondence Columns in *The Woman Worker*, *Women Folk* and *The Freewoman*', *Modernism/Modernity*, 19 (2012), 461–85.

Green, Fiona, '"The Magnitude of Their Root Systems": "An Octopus" and National Character', in *Critics and Poets on Marianne Moore: 'A Right Good Salvo Of Barks'*, ed. Linda Leavell, Cristanne Miller and Robin G. Schulze (Lewisburg, PA: Bucknell University Press, 2005), pp. 137–49.

Greenough, Sarah (ed.), 'Georgia O'Keeffe: A Flight to the Spirit', in *Modern Art in America: Alfred Stieglitz and His New York Galleries* (Boston, MA: Bulfinch Press, 2000).

Gregory, Alyse, 'A Modern Yellow Book', *Century Magazine*, September 1924, Beinecke, ST/Dial Papers, Series II, Box 14, Fol. 340.

Gregory, Elizabeth, 'Combat Cultural: Marianne Moore and the Mixed Brow', in *Critics and Poets on Marianne Moore: 'A Right Good Salvo Of Barks'*, ed. Linda Leavell, Cristanne Miller and Robin G. Schulze (Lewisburg, PA: Bucknell University Press, 2005), pp. 208–21.

Gregory, Elizabeth, 'Flaring Moore: The Revisionist Reviewed', in *The Critical Response to Marianne Moore*, ed. Elizabeth Gregory (Westport, CT: Praeger, 2003), pp. 1–17.

Gregory, Elizabeth and Stacy Carson Hubbard (eds), *Twenty-First Century Marianne Moore: Essays from a Critical Renaissance* (New York: Palgrave Macmillan, 2017).

H.D., *End to Torment: A Memoir of Ezra Pound*, ed. Norman Holmes Pearson and Michael King (New York: New Directions, 1979).

H.D., 'Marianne Moore', *Egoist*, August (1916), 3–4.

Harding, Jason, *The Criterion: Cultural Politics and Periodical Networks in Inter-War Britain* (Oxford: Oxford University Press, 2002).

Harding, Jason, 'The Idea of a Literary Review: T. S. Eliot and The Criterion', in *The Oxford Critical and Cultural History of Modernist Magazines, Vol. I: Britain and Ireland, 1880–1955*, ed. Peter Brooker and Andrew Thacker (Oxford: Oxford University Press, 2013), pp. 346–63.

Harding, Jason (ed.), *Ford Madox Ford: Modernist Magazines and Editing* (Amsterdam and New York: Rodopi, 2010).

Hartley, Marsden, 'In the Frail Wood', *Poetry*, 12 (1918), 195–6.

Hartley, Marsden, *Marsden Hartley: Selected Poems*, ed. Henry W. Wells (New York: Viking, 1945).

Hemingway, Ernest, *A Moveable Feast* (London: Jonathan Cape, 1964).

Hillyer, Robert, 'Manorbier', *Dial*, 84 (June 1928), 451–5.

Honey, Maureen, 'Feminist New Woman Fiction in Periodicals of the 1920s', in *Middlebrow Moderns: Popular American Women Writers of the 1920s*, ed. Lisa Botshon and Meredith Goldsmith (Boston, MA: Northeastern University Press, 2003), pp. 87–109.

Honigsblum, Bonnie, 'Marianne Moore's Revisions of "Poetry"', in *Marianne Moore: Woman and Poet*, ed. Patricia C. Willis (Orono, ME: National Poetry Foundation, 1990), pp. 185–222.

Hubbard, Stacy Carson, 'Mannerist Moore: Poetry, Painting, Photography', in *Critics and Poets on Marianne Moore: 'A Right Good Salvo of Barks'*, ed. Linda Leavell, Cristanne Miller and Robin G. Schulze (Lewisburg, PA: Bucknell University Press, 2005), pp. 113–36.

Humm, Maggie (ed.), *The Edinburgh Companion to Virginia Woolf and the Arts* (Edinburgh: Edinburgh University Press, 2010).

Jaffe, Aaron, *Modernism and the Culture of Celebrity* (Cambridge: Cambridge University Press, 2005).

Joost, Nicholas, *Scofield Thayer and The Dial: An Illustrated History* (Carbondale: Southern Illinois University Press, 1964).

Joost, Nicholas and Alvin Sullivan, *D. H. Lawrence and The Dial* (Carbondale and Edwardsville: Southern Illinois University Press, 1970).

Josephson, Matthew, *Life Among the Surrealists* (New York: Holt, Rinehart and Winston, 1962).

Josephson, Matthew, 'Poems: Marianne Moore', *Broom*, 4 (1923), 138–9.

Kahan, Benjamin, '"The Viper's Traffic-Knot": Celibacy and Queerness in the "Late" Moore', *GLQ*, 14 (2008), 510–33.

Kammen, Michael, *The Lively Arts: Gilbert Seldes and the Transformation of Cultural Criticism in the United States* (New York and Oxford: Oxford University Press, 1996).

Kindley, Evan, 'Picking and Choosing: Marianne Moore Among the Agonists', *English Literary History*, 79 (2012), 685–713.

Kingham, Victoria, '"Audacious Modernity": *The Seven Arts* (1916–17); *The Soil* (1916–17) and *The Trend* (1911–1915)', in *The Oxford Critical and Cultural History of Modernist Magazines, Vol. II: North American 1894–1960*, ed. Peter Brooker and Andrew Thacker (Oxford: Oxford University Press, 2012), pp. 400–19.

Kinnahan, Linda A., 'Marianne Moore and Modern Labor', in *Twenty-First Century Marianne Moore: Essays from a Critical Renaissance*, ed. Elizabeth Gregory and Stacy Carson Hubbard (New York: Palgrave Macmillan, 2017), pp. 149–66.

Kreymborg, Alfred, *Troubadour* (New York: Boni and Liveright, 1925).

Ladin, Jay, 'Breaking the Line: Emily Dickinson and William Carlos Williams', *Emily Dickinson Journal*, 3 (1994), 41–58.

Latham, Sean, 'Affordance as Emergence: Magazine as New Media', *MLA* (2013). Available at: https://seeeps.princeton.edu/wp-content/uploads/sites/243/2015/03/mla2013_latham.pdf (accessed 31 August 2018).

Latham, Sean, 'The Mess and Muddle of Modernism: The Modernist Projects Journal and Modern Periodical Studies', *Tulsa Studies in Women's Literature,* 30 (2011), 407–28.

Lawrence, D. H., *The Collected Letters of D. H. Lawrence: Volume II*, ed. Harry T. Moore (London: Heinemann, 1962).

Lawrence, D. H., *The Complete Poems of D. H. Lawrence*, ed. Vivian De Sola Pinto and Warren Roberts (London: Penguin, 1964).

Lawrence, D. H., 'Introduction', *Dial*, 86 (July 1929), 543.

Leavell, Linda, *Holding On Upside Down: The Life and Work of Marianne Moore* (New York: Farrar, Straus and Giroux, 2013).

Leavell, Linda, 'Marianne Moore, the James Family, and the Politics of Celibacy', *Twentieth Century Literature*, 49 (2003), 219–56.

Leavell, Linda, *Marianne Moore and the Visual Arts: Prismatic Color* (Baton Rouge: Louisiana State University Press, 1995).

Leavell, Linda, Cristanne Miller and Robin G. Schulze (eds), *Critics and Poets on Marianne Moore: 'A Right Good Salvo of Barks'* (Lewisburg, PA: Bucknell University Press, 2005).

Lee, Judith Yaross, 'From the Field: The Future of American Periodicals and American Periodicals Research', *American Periodicals: A Journal of History, Criticism and Bibliography*, 15 (2005), 196–201.

Leick, Karen, 'Ezra Pound vs. The Saturday Review of Literature', *Journal of Modern Literature*, 25 (2001–2), 19–37.

Leick, Karen, 'Popular Modernism: Little Magazines and the American Daily Press', *PMLA,* 123 (2008), 125–39.

Levenson, Michael, *Genealogy of Modernism: A Study of English Literary Doctrine, 1908–1922* (Cambridge: Cambridge University Press).

Levine, Caroline, *Forms: Whole, Rhythm, Hierarchy, Network* (Princeton, NJ and Oxford: Princeton University Press, 2015).

Levy, Ellen, 'Borrowing Paints from a Girl: Greenberg, Eliot, Moore and the Struggle Between the Arts', *Modernism/Modernity*, 17 (2010), 1–20.

Lovell, Terry, 'Resisting with Authority: Historical Specificity, Agency and the Performative Self', *Theory, Culture and Society*, 20 (2003), 1–17.

Lovell, Terry, 'Thinking Feminism with and against Bourdieu', *The Sociological Review*, 1 (2000), 27–47.

Loy, Mina, 'Brancusi's Golden Bird', *Dial*, 73 (November 1922), 507–8.

Loy, Mina, 'Modern Poetry', in *Modernism: An Anthology*, ed. Lawrence Rainey (Oxford: Blackwell, 2005).

Loy, Mina, 'Poe', *Dial*, 71 (October 1921), 406.

Lunday, Elizabeth, *Modern Art Invasion: Picasso, Duchamp, and the 1913 Armory Show That Scandalized America* (Guilford, CT: Lyons Press, 2013).

Lynes, Barbara Bubler, *O'Keeffe, Stieglitz, and the Critics, 1916–1928* (Ann Arbor: University of Michigan Press, 1989).

Mao, Douglas, *Solid Objects: Modernism and the Test of Production* (Princeton: Princeton University Press, 1998).

Marek, Jayne, *Women Editing Modernism: 'Little' Magazines and Literary History* (Lexington: University Press of Kentucky, 1995).

Mariani, Paul, *William Carlos Williams: A New World Naked* (New York: McGraw-Hill, 1981).

Martin, Taffy, 'Comment as Aesthetic Equivalent', *Missouri Review*, 7 (1983), 213–22.

Martin, Taffy, 'Portrait of a Writing Master: Beyond the Myth of Marianne Moore', *Twentieth Century Literature*, 30 (1984), 192–209.

Materer, Timothy, 'Make it Sell! Ezra Pound Advertizes Modernism', in *Marketing Modernisms: Self-Promotion, Canonization, and Rereading*, ed. J. H. Dettmar and Stephen Watt (Ann Arbor: University of Michigan Press, 1997), pp. 17–36.

McBride, Henry, 'Modern Art', *Dial*, 82 (February 1927), 172–4.

McBride, Henry, 'O'Keeffe at the Museum', *New York Sun*, 18 May 1946, p. 9.

McCabe, Susan, *Cinematic Modernism: Modernist Poetry and Film* (Cambridge: Cambridge University Press, 2005).

McCabe, Susan, '"Let's Be Alone Together": Bryher's and Marianne Moore's Aesthetic–Erotic Collaboration', *Modernism/Modernity*, 17 (2010), 607–37.

McGann, Jerome, 'The Socialization of Texts', in *The Book History Reader*, ed. David Finkelstein and Alistair McCleery (London: Routledge, 2006), pp. 66–73.

McKible, Adam, *The Space and Place of Modernism: The Russian Revolution, Little Magazines, and New York* (New York and London: Routledge, 2002).

'Men of Genius', *Yale Daily News*, 25 November 1922, Beinecke, ST/Dial Papers, Box 14, Fol. 340.

Miller, Cristanne, *The Cultures of Modernism: Marianne Moore, Mina Loy, and Else Lasker-Schuler: Gender and Literary Community in New York and Berlin* (Ann Arbor: University of Michigan Press, 2005).

Miller, Cristanne, *Marianne Moore: Questions of Authority* (Cambridge, MA: Harvard University Press, 1995).

Miller, Cristanne, 'Tongues "loosened in the melting pot": The Poets of Others and the Lower East Side', *Modernism/Modernity*, 14.3 (2007), 455–76.

Mitchell, W. J. T., *Picture Theory: Essays on Verbal and Visual Representation* (Chicago: University of Chicago Press, 1994).

Moi, Toril, 'Appropriating Bourdieu: Feminist Theory and Pierre Bourdieu's Sociology of Culture', *New Literary History*, 22 (1991), 1017–49.

Monroe, Harriet, 'A Symposium on Marianne Moore', in *Critical Essays on Edna St. Vincent Millay*, ed. William B. Thesing (New York: G. K. Hall, 1993).
Moore, Marianne, *Becoming Marianne Moore: The Early Poems, 1907–1924*, ed. Robin G. Schulze (Berkeley, Los Angeles and London: University of California Press, 2002).
Moore, Marianne, 'Comment', *Dial*, 79 (July 1925), 87–8.
Moore, Marianne, 'Comment', *Dial*, 79 (August 1925), 177–8.
Moore, Marianne, 'Comment', *Dial*, 79 (September 1925), 264–6.
Moore, Marianne, 'Comment', *Dial*, 79 (November 1925), 443–4.
Moore, Marianne, 'Comment', *Dial*, 80 (May 1926), 444–8.
Moore, Marianne, 'Comment', *Dial*, 82 (March 1927), 449–50.
Moore, Marianne, 'Comment', *Dial*, 86 (February 1929), 179–80.
Moore, Marianne, 'Compactness Compacted', *Nation*, 15 November 1941, 486.
Moore, Marianne, *The Complete Poems of Marianne Moore*, ed. Clive E. Driver (London and Boston, MA: Faber and Faber, 1981).
Moore, Marianne, *The Complete Prose of Marianne Moore*, ed. Patricia C. Willis (London: Faber and Faber, 1987).
Moore, Marianne, 'England', *Dial*, 68 (April 1920), 422–3
Moore, Marianne, 'Feeling and Precision', *Sewanee Review*, 52 (Autumn 1944), 499–507.
Moore, Marianne, 'Henry James as a Characteristic American', *Hound and Horn*, 7 (April–May 1934), 363–72.
Moore, Marianne, 'Humility, Concentration, and Gusto', *Grolier Club Gazette*, 2 (May 1949), 289–300. Available in New York Heritage Digital Archives at: https://cdm16694.contentdm.oclc.org/digital/collection/Grolier01/id/650 (accessed 6 September 2018).
Moore, Marianne, 'Hymen', *Broom*, 4 (January 1923), 133–5.
Moore, Marianne, 'Is the Real Actual?' *Dial*, 73 (December 1922), 620–2.
Moore, Marianne, 'Kora in Hell by William Carlos Williams', *Contact*, 4 (January–March 1921), 5–8.
Moore, Marianne, *New Collected Poems: Marianne Moore*, ed. Heather Cass White (London: Faber and Faber, 2017).
Moore, Marianne, 'A Note on T.S. Eliot's Book', *Poetry*, 12 (April 1918), 36–9.
Moore, 'A Poet of the Quattrocento', *Dial*, 82 (March 1927), 213–15.
Moore, Marianne, *A-Quiver with Significance: Marianne Moore, 1932–1936*, ed. Heather Cass White (Victoria, BC: ELS Editions, 2008).
Moore, Marianne, 'The Sacred Wood', *Dial*, 70 (March 1921), 336–9.
Moore, Marianne, *The Selected Letters of Marianne Moore* ed. Bonnie Costello, Celeste Goodridge and Cristanne Miller (London: Faber and Faber, 1998).

Moore, Marianne, 'Serious Pleasure', Beinecke, ST/Dial Papers, Series II, Box 13, Fol. 337.

Moore, Marianne, 'Sir Francis Bacon', *Dial*, 76 (April 1924), 343–6.

Moore, Marianne, 'The Spare American Emotion', *Dial*, 80 (February 1926), 153–6.

Moore, Marianne, '"Things Others Never Notice"', *Poetry*, 44 (May 1934), 103–6.

Moore, Marianne, 'Thistles Dipped in Frost', *Dial*, 77 (September 1924), 251–6.

Moore, Marianne, 'Without Respect of Persons', *Creative Art*, August 1928, *Drawing and Design* in December 1928, *The Arts* in January 1928 and *World Unity* in February 1929. Beinecke, ST/Dial Papers, Series II, Box 17, Fol. 345.

Morrisson, Mark, *The Public Face of Modernism: Little Magazines, Audiences and Reception, 1905–1920* (Madison: University of Wisconsin Press, 2001).

Mullin, Katherine, 'Joyce Through the Little Magazines', in *A Companion to James Joyce*, ed. Richard Brown (Chichester: Wiley-Blackwell, 2008), pp. 374–89.

Mumford, Lewis, 'On The Dial', *New York Review of Books*, 20 February 1964. Available at: https://www.nybooks.com/articles/1964/02/20/on-the-dial (accessed 4 September 2018).

Munson, Gorham, *The Awakening Twenties: A Memoir-History of a Literary Period* (Baton Rouge and London: Louisiana State University Press, 1985).

Mussell, James, 'Repetition: "In Our Last"' *Victorian Periodicals Review*, 48 (2015), 343–58.

Newcomb, John Timberman, 'Poetry's Opening Door: Harriet Monroe and American Modernism', *American Periodicals: A Journal of History, Criticism, and Bibliography*, 15 (2005), 6–22.

O'Keeffe, Georgia, *Georgia O'Keeffe* (New York: Viking Press, 1976).

Oliver, Elizabeth, 'Aestheticism's Afterlife: Wallace Stevens as Interior Decorator and Disruptor', *Modernism/Modernity*, 15 (2008), 527–45.

Oliver, Elizabeth, 'Redecorating Vorticism: Marianne Moore's "Ezra Pound" and the Geometric Style', *Journal of Modern Literature*, 34 (2011), 84–113.

Ozieblo, Barbara, 'Alyse Gregory, Scofield Thayer, and the "Dial"', *Twentieth Century Literature*, 48 (2002), 487–507.

Paul, Catherine, *Poetry in the Museums of Modernism: Yeats, Pound, Moore, Stein* (Ann Arbor: University of Michigan Press, 2002).

Philpotts, Matthew, 'The Role of the Periodical Editor: Literary Journals and Editorial Habitus', *Modern Language Review*, 107 (2012), 39–64.

Pizer, Donald, 'Dorothy Dudley's Forgotten Frontiers: Dreiser and the Land of the Free', *Studies in American Naturalism*, 7 (2012), 193–206.

Pollnitz, Christopher, 'The Censorship and Transmission of D. H. Lawrence's *Pansies*: The Home Office and the "foul-mouthed fellow"', *Journal of Modern Literature*, 28 (2005), 44–71.

Pound, Ezra, 'Dr Williams's Position', *Dial*, 85 (November 1928), 395–404.

Pound, Ezra, *Gaudier-Brzeska* (New York: John Lane, 1916), p. 108. Available at: https://archive.org/details/gaudierbrzeska00pounrich (accessed 15 October 2017).

Pound, Ezra, *The Letters of Ezra Pound, 1907–1941*, ed. D. D. Paige (London: Faber and Faber, 1950).

Pound, Ezra, *The Literary Essays of Ezra Pound*, ed. T. S. Eliot (London: Faber, 1954).

Pound, Ezra, 'Marianne Moore and Mina Loy', *Little Review*, 10 (1918), 57–8.

Powys, John Cowper, 'An American Tragedy', *Dial*, 80 (April 1926), 331–8.

'Publication of the Dial Discontinued', *Saturday Review of Literature*, 8 June 1929, Beinecke, ST/Dial Papers, Series II, Box 17, Fol. 346.

'The Quality Group', *New York Times*, 5 February 1922, p. 48.

Quartermain, Peter, *Disjunctive Poetics: From Gertrude Stein and Louis Zukofsky to Susan Howe* (Oxford: Oxford University Press, 1992).

Rainey, Lawrence, *Institutions of Modernism: Literary Elites and Public Culture* (New Haven, CT: Yale University Press, 1998).

Rainey, Lawrence, *The Annotated Waste Land with Eliot's Contemporary Prose* (New Haven, CT: Yale University Press, 2005).

Raitt, Suzanne, 'The Rhetoric of Efficiency in Early Modernism', *Modernism/Modernity*, 13 (2006), 835–851.

Reed, Brian, *Hart Crane: After His Lights* (Tuscaloosa: University of Alabama Press, 2006).

Reynolds, Guy, *Willa Cather in Context: Progress, Race, Empire* (Basingstoke: Palgrave, Macmillan, 1996).

Richie, Eugene (ed.), *John Ashbery: Selected Prose* (Ann Arbor: The University of Michigan Press, 2004).

Ridge, Lola, 'Ray', *Dial*, 82 (February 1927), 118.

Rosenfeld Paul, 'American Painting', *Dial*, 71 (December 1921), 649–70.

Rosenfeld Paul, 'El Greco's Portrait of Himself', in *By Way of Art: Criticisms of Music, Literature, Painting, Sculpture, and the Dance* (New York: Books for Libraries Press Inc., 1967), pp. 99–110.

Rosenfeld Paul, 'El Greco's Portrait of Himself', *Dial*, 79 (December 1925), 485–90.

Rosenfeld Paul, 'Sherwood Anderson', *Dial*, 72 (January 1922), 29–42.

Rosenfeld Paul, 'Stieglitz', *Dial*, 70 (April 1921), 397–409.

Rosner, Victoria, *Modernism and the Architecture of Private Life* (New York: Columbia University Press, 2005).

Ross, Shawna, 'Hashtags, Algorithmic Compression and Henry James's Late Style', *The Henry James Review*, 36 (2015), 24–44.

Rubin, Joan Shelley, *The Making of Middle/Brow Culture* (Chapel Hill: University of North Carolina Press, 1992).

Russell, Bertrand, 'Things That Have Moulded Me', *Dial*, 83 (1927), 181–6.

Santayana, George, *The Degenerate Muse: American Nature, Modernist Poetry, and the Problem of Cultural Hygiene* (Oxford: Oxford University Press, 2013).

Santayana, George, 'The Genteel Tradition in American Philosophy'. Available at: http://monadnock.net/santayana/genteel.html (accessed 14 September 2017).

Scott, Evelyn, 'Nine Poems', *Dial*, 68 (January 1920), 71–6.

Scott, Evelyn, 'The Old Lady', *Dial*, 78 (May 1925), 369–97.

Scroggins, Mark, *The Poem of a Life: A Biography of Louis Zukofsky* (Berkeley: Shoemaker Hoard, 2007).

Seaver, Edwin, 'A Literalist of the Imagination', *Nation*, 18 (1925), 297–8.

Seaver, Edwin, 'The Road To Calvary', *Dial*, 82 (April 1927), 341–3.

Seldes, Gilbert, *The 7 Lively Arts* (New York: Harpers and Brothers 1924; repr. New York: Dover, 2001).

Seldes, Gilbert, 'Toujours Jazz', *Dial*, 75 (August 1923), 151–66.

Selzer Jack, *Kenneth Burke in Greenwich Village: Conversing with the Moderns* (Madison: University of Wisconsin Press, 1996).

Setina, Emily, '"Mountains Being a Language with Me": Marianne Moore, Marsden Hartley, and Modernist Revision', *Modernism/Modernity*, 22 (2015), 153–82.

Shelley, P. B., *Percy Bysshe Shelley: Poems and Prose*, ed. Timothy Webb (London: Everyman, 1995), pp. 281–96.

Sigler, Amanda, 'Expanding Woolf's Gift Economy: Consumer Activity Meets Artistic Production in The Dial', *Tulsa Studies in Women's Literature*, 30 (2011), 317–42.

Simon, Marc (ed.), *The Complete Poems of Hart Crane* (New York: Liveright, 1986).

Slatin, John, *The Savage's Romance: The Poetry of Marianne Moore* (University Park: Pennsylvania State University Press, 1986).

'Steadily the Gap', *New York Times*, April 1927, Beinecke, ST/Dial Papers, Series II, Box 17, Fol. 345.

Stein, Gertrude, *The Autobiography of Alice B. Toklas* (London: Penguin, 1966).

Stein, Gertrude, *A Stein Reader*, ed. Ulla Dydo (Evanston, IL: Northeastern University Press, 1993).

Sullivan, Hannah, *The Work of Revision* (Cambridge, MA: Harvard University Press, 2013).

Sutton, Walter (ed.), *Pound, Thayer, Watson and The Dial: A Story in Letters* (Gainesville: University Press of Florida, 1994).

Taggard, Genevieve, 'Letter in Solitude', *Dial*, 83 (September 1927), 237–8.

Taylor, Julie, 'On Holding and Being Held: Hart Crane's Queer Intimacy', *Twentieth Century Literature*, 60 (2014), 305–335.

Tebbel, John and Mary Ellen Zuckerman, *The Magazine in America, 1741–1990* (Oxford: Oxford University Press, 1991).

Thayer, Scofield, 'Announcement', *Dial*, 78 (January 1925), 89–90.

Thayer, Scofield, 'Comment', *Dial*, 68 (March 1920), 408–10.

Thayer, Scofield, 'Comment', *Dial*, 69 (July 1920), 106–8.

Thayer, Scofield, 'Comment', *Dial*, 69 (August 1920), 216–18.

Thayer, Scofield, 'Comment', *Dial*, 69 (November 1920), 557–8.

Thayer, Scofield, 'Comment', *Dial*, 73 (August 1922), 239–40.

Thayer, Scofield, 'Comment', *Dial*, 73 (December 1922), 685–7.

Thayer, Scofield, 'Comment', *Dial*, 74 (February 1923), 213–14.

Thayer, Scofield, 'Comment', *Dial*, 74 (April 1923), 417–19.

Thayer, Scofield, 'Comment', *Dial*, 76 (January 1924), 96–7.

Thayer, Scofield, 'Comment', *Dial*, 76 (March 1924), 291–2.

Thayer, Scofield, 'Comment', *Dial*, 76 (May 1924), 469–73.

Thayer, Scofield, 'Comment', *Dial*, 78 (February 1925), 174–80.

Thayer, Scofield, 'Comment', *Dial*, 78 (March 1925), 265–8.

Thayer, Scofield, 'Comment', *Dial*, 78 (April 1925), 354–6.

Thayer, Scofield, 'Jesus Again', *Dial*, 81 (July 1926), 59–60.

Thesing, William B. (ed.), *Critical Essays on Edna St. Vincent Millay*, ed. William B. Thesing (New York: G. K. Hall, 1993).

Trueblood, Charles, 'The Poetry of Thomas Hardy', *Dial*, 82 (June 1927), 522–5.

Turner, Elizabeth Hutton, 'O'Keeffe and Abstraction', in *Georgia O'Keeffe: Abstraction*, ed. Barbara Haskell (New Haven, CT: Yale University Press, 2009), pp. 65–74.

Unterecker John, *Voyager: A Life of Hart Crane* (New York: Farrar, Straus and Giroux, 1969).

Vincent, John Emil, *Queer Lyrics: (Difficulty and Closure in American Poetry)* (New York: Palgrave 2002).

Wasserman, Rosanne, '"A Tutelary Muse": Moore's Influence on Bishop', in *Marianne Moore: Woman and Poet*, ed. Patricia C. Willis (Orono, ME: National Poetry Foundation, 1990), pp. 351–70.

Wasserstrom, William, 'Marianne Moore, The *Dial*, and Kenneth Burke', *The Western Humanities Review*, 17 (1963), 249–62.

Watson, Hildegarde Lasell, *The Edge of the Woods: A Memoir* (South Lunenburg, VT: Stinehour Press, 1979).

Watson, Sibley, 'Comment', *Dial*, 83 (September 1927), 269–70.

Watson, Sibley (as W. C. Blum), 'Some Remarks on Rimbaud as Magician', *Dial*, 68 (June 1920), 719–32.

White, Eric, *Transatlantic Avant-Gardes: Little Magazines and Localist Modernism* (Edinburgh: Edinburgh University Press, 2013).

White, Heather Cass, 'Relentless Accuracy and a Capacity for Fact: Authorship in Marianne Moore and Gertrude Stein', in *Critics and Poets on Marianne Moore: 'A Right Good Salvo of Barks'*, ed. Linda Leavell, Cristanne Miller and Robin G. Schulze (Lewisburg, PA: Bucknell University Press, 2005), pp. 98–112.

Williams, William Carlos, *The Autobiography of William Carlos Williams* (New York: MacGibbon and Kee, 1968), p. 146.

Williams, William Carlos, *Kora in Hell: Improvisations* (Boston, MA: Four Seas Company, 1920). Available at: https://www.gutenberg.org/files/56681/56681-h/56681-h.htm (accessed 4 September 2018).

Williams, William Carlos, 'Marianne Moore', *Dial*, 78 (May 1925), 393–410.

Williams, William Carlos, *The Selected Letters of William Carlos Williams*, ed. John C. Thirlwall (New York: New Directions, 1957).

Williams, William Carlos, 'Struggle of Wings', *Dial*, 81 (July 1926), 22–4.

Williams, William Carlos, *William Carlos Williams: Collected Poems I 1909–1939*, ed. A. Walton Litz and Christopher MacGowan (Manchester: Carcanet, 2000).

Williams, William Carlos, 'Marianne Moore on May Day, 1906', *Marianne Moore Newsletter*, 5 (1981), 21.

Williams, William Carlos, 'The Road to Paradise: First Notes on Marianne Moore's "An Octopus"', *Twentieth Century Literature*, 30 (1984), 242–66.

Wilson, Edmund, *Axel's Castle: A Study in the Imaginative Literature of 1870–1930* (New York: Scribner's Sons, 1931).

Wilson, Edmund, 'The Stieglitz Exhibition', *New Republic*, 18 March 1925. Available as 'Georgia O'Keefe [*sic*] Outblazed Other Female Painters of Her Time' at: https://newrepublic.com/article/115597/georgia-okeefe-paintings-outblazed-contemporaries (accessed 7 August 2015) (para. 2 of 4).

Wilson, Frances I., 'The Shack', *Dial*, 82 (February 1927), 130.

Winters, Yvor, 'Holiday in the Day of Wrath', *Poetry*, 26 (1925), 39–44.

Woods, Gregory, *Articulate Flesh: Male Homo-Eroticism and Modern Poetry* (New Haven, CT: Yale University Press, 1987).

Wordsworth, William, *Wordsworth's Poetry and Prose*, ed. Nicholas Halmi (New York: W. W. Norton and Co., 2014).

Zukofsky, Louis, *'A'* (New York: New Directions, 2011).

Zukofsky, Louis, 'Sincerity and Objectification with Special Reference to the Work of Charles Reznikoff', in *The Objectivist Nexus: Essays in Cultural Poetics*, ed. Rachel Blau DuPlessis and Peter Quartermain (Tuscaloosa: Alabama University Press, 1999), p. 26 (first publ. in *Poetry*, 37 (1931), 272–85).

INDEX

CPSIA information can be obtained
at www.ICGtesting.com
Printed in the USA
JSHW030346041120
9291JS00002B/47

9 781474 463904